BEST PRACTICES IN LITERACY INSTRUCTION

BEST PRACTICES IN
LITERACY INSTRUCTION

Linda B. Gambrell
Lesley Mandel Morrow
Susan B. Neuman
Michael Pressley

Editors

Susan Anders Mazzoni, *Assistant to the Editors*

Series Foreword by Louise Cherry Wilkinson
Foreword by Dorothy S. Strickland

THE GUILFORD PRESS
New York   London

© 1999 The Guilford Press
A Division of Guilford Publications, Inc.
72 Spring Street, New York, NY 10012
http://www.guilford.com

Printed in the United States of America

This book is printed on acid-free paper.

Last digit is print number: 9 8 7 6 5 4 3

Library of Congress Cataloging-in-Publication Data

Best practices in literacy instruction / Linda B. Gambrell . . . [et
    al.], editors.
        p.   cm.
    Includes bibliographical references and index.
    ISBN 1-57230-442-1 (hardcover : alk. paper). — ISBN 1-57230-443-X
(paperback : alk. paper)
    1. Language arts—United States.   2. Reading comprehension—United
States.   3. Literacy—United States.   I. Gambrell, Linda B.
LB1576.B486   1999
428.4'07—DC21   99-12553
                                                                      CIP

ABOUT THE EDITORS

Linda B. Gambrell is Professor in the College of Education at the University of Maryland, where she teaches graduate and undergraduate courses and conducts research. Prior to coming to the University of Maryland, she was an elementary classroom teacher and reading specialist in Prince George's County, Maryland. She has coauthored books on reading instruction and written numerous articles published in journals such as *Reading Research Quarterly, The Reading Teacher, Educational Psychologist,* and *Journal of Educational Research.* She recently coauthored "Literature Based Reading Instruction" for the *Handbook of Reading Research,* Volume 3. From 1992 to 1997, she was a principal investigator at the National Reading Research Center where she directed the Literacy Motivation Project, and has served on the Board of Directors of the International Reading Association and the National Reading Conference. From 1993 to 1996, she served as coeditor of *The Journal of Reading Behavior,* a publication of the National Reading Conference. In 1998, she was the recipient of the International Reading Association's Outstanding Teacher Educator in Reading Award. She was recently elected to serve as President of the National Reading Conference in 1999. Her current interests are in the areas of reading comprehension strategy instruction, literacy motivation, and the role of discussion in teaching and learning.

Lesley Mandel Morrow is Professor at Rutgers University's Graduate School of Education. She is coordinator of the Early Childhood/Elementary Cluster and a member of the Literacy Cluster. She began her career as a classroom teacher and later became a reading specialist. Her area of research deals with early literacy development with an emphasis on physical and social contexts to motivate reading. In addition, Dr. Morrow has more than 150 publications. Her articles have appeared in journals such as *Reading Research Quarterly, Journal of Educational Psychology,* and *The*

Reading Teacher. Her most recent books are *Literacy Development in the Early Years: Helping Children Read and Write* and *The Literacy Center: Contexts for Reading and Writing.* She received the Rutgers University awards for research and teaching, the International Reading Association's Outstanding Teacher Educator of Reading Award, and Fordham University's Alumni Award for Outstanding Achievement. She is also a member of the Board of Directors of the International Reading Association.

Susan B. Neuman is an Associate Professor in Curriculum, Instruction, and Technology in Education at Temple University and a Coordinator of the Reading and Language Arts Graduate Program. Her chief interests focus on early literacy. She has written over 50 articles for such journals as *American Education Research Journal, Reading Research Quarterly, The Reading Teacher,* and *Early Childhood Research Quarterly.* In addition, she has written *Literacy in the Television Age;* coedited a book with Sandra McCormick, *Single-Subject Experimental Research: Applications for Literacy;* and coauthored a book with Kathy Roskos, *Language and Literacy Learning in the Early Years: An Integrated Approach.* She is currently Chair of the Reading and Early Childhood Committee of the International Reading Association, and of the Literacy Development for Young Children Special Interest Group.

Michael Pressley is the Notre Dame Professor of Catholic Education and Professor of Psychology at Notre Dame. He has studied student cognition, especially students' use of strategies, for more than 20 years, including programs of research on children's imagery, mnemonics, cognitive monitoring, reading comprehension, and the nature of excellent beginning reading instruction. He is the author or coauthor of more than 200 scientific publications and is considered an expert in the areas of children's memory, educational psychology, and reading education. In recent years, he has been honored by the American Educational Research Association (Outstanding Contributions to Research on Learning) and the International Reading Association (Outstanding Contributions to Research on Children at Risk for Reading and Writing Failure). Professor Pressley has distinguished himself as an outstanding doctoral-level advisor, teacher educator, and undergraduate professor.

CONTRIBUTORS

Richard L. Allington is Professor of Education and Chair of the Department of Reading at the University at Albany, State University of New York. He is a Research Scientist with the National Research Center on English Learning and Achievement and codirects two large-scale projects, one studying educational policymaking in four states and another studying exemplary integrated classroom literacy instruction in schools serving large numbers of poor children. He was corecipient of the Albert J. Harris Award from the International Reading Association in recognition of his work contributing to the understanding of reading and learning disabilities, and has been named to the International Reading Association Reading Hall of Fame. He currently serves on numerous editorial boards and is the author of over 100 research articles and several books, including *Classrooms That Work* and *Schools That Work,* both coauthored with Pat Cunningham; *No Quick Fix: Rethinking Reading Programs in American Elementary Schools,* with Sean Walmsley; and *Teaching Struggling Readers,* a collection of articles from *The Reading Teacher.*

Harriette Johns Arrington is currently Assistant Professor of Curriculum and Instruction in the College of Education at the University of Kentucky, Lexington, Kentucky. In addition to teaching undergraduate- and graduate-level elementary and middle school courses, she coordinates the elementary student teaching program. Prior to this position, she supervised Reading/Language Arts in Newport News, Virginia. Her first children's book was *The Heart of Friendship.* Dr. Arrington is an active member of several professional organizations, including the National Middle School Association, the International Reading Association, the Kentucky Reading Association, and the National Council of Teachers of English. She also serves on the storytelling committee for the National Council of Teachers of English and frequently makes national, state, and local presentations in the areas of storytelling, African-American literacy issues, and literacy instruction and assessment.

Elizabeth Asbury has a broad range of teaching experience from preschool through university. She taught music in kindergarten through eighth grades prior to becoming a classroom teacher. In addition to teaching preschool and kindergarten classes, her early childhood teaching experiences include designing the curriculum and physical environment for a new preschool and teaching a multiage kindergarten–first grade. Currently, she is a doctoral student at Rutgers University, where she teaches two courses in the teacher education program, Learning and Teaching in the Early Childhood Classroom and Literacy Development in the Early Years. Her research studies focus on guided reading instruction for beginning readers.

Kim Baker is Assistant Professor in Reading and Special Education in the Department of Education at The Sage Colleges in Troy, New York. She teaches undergraduate and graduate courses in language arts methods, diagnosis, and remediation. She also supervises student teachers in elementary and special education and in a reading practicum. For both the International Reading Association and the New York State Reading Association, she is on the Teacher as Researcher Committee, where she encourages teachers to be active participants as they research and reflect on their classroom instruction. She is presently working on a Federal Project that focuses on at-risk elementary students with exemplary teachers, their practice, and literature-based instruction. Interested in the educational opportunities provided for at-risk students, she directs an after-school literacy program in the inner city.

Thomas W. Bean is Professor of Reading/Literacy and currently coordinates the doctoral program in the Department of Curriculum and Instruction at the University of Nevada, Las Vegas. His numerous research articles and book reviews have been published in the *Journal of Educational Research, Reading Research Quarterly, Journal of Adolescent and Adult Literacy,* and other journals in literacy. He recently authored a chapter entitled "Reading in the Content Areas: Social Constructivist Dimensions" in *Handbook of Reading Research: Volume III,* and is coauthor of *Content Area Literacy: An Integrated Approach,* now in its sixth edition. He teaches graduate seminars in literacy research, literacy issues for a diverse society, and content in area literacy. His most recent research has focused on reader response to multicultural literature in secondary English classrooms.

Cathy Collins Block is Professor in the Department of Curriculum and Instruction at Texas Christian University, where she teaches graduate and undergraduate courses. She has been an elementary classroom teacher in Wisconsin, Oklahoma, and Texas, and the Director of Reading for a Texas Teacher Center. She is the author or coauthor/coeditor of 13 books on language arts instruction and coauthor of the Stanford Early School Achievement Test (SESAT) and Yale Assessment of Thinking Abilities. She has written numerous articles in journals such as *Journal of Reading, The Reading Teacher, Journal of Educational Research*, and *Elementary School Journal*. Her primary research interests are in the areas of comprehension, cognitive strategies, curriculum development, and teacher education. She is the Educational Advisor for the PBS television series *Wishbone*, and has served as a consultant for numerous school districts and educational agencies in the United States, Finland, Mexico, Canada, Russia, and Hungary.

Karen Bromley is Professor in the School of Education and Human Development at Binghamton University, State University of New York, where she teaches graduate courses in literacy, language arts, and children's literature. She has been a third-grade teacher and reading specialist in New York and Maryland schools and is the author of four books for teachers—*Language Arts: Exploring Connections*, third edition; *Webbing with Literature*, second edition; *Journaling: Engagements in Reading, Writing, and Thinking*; and *Graphic Organizers*—and many articles in professional journals such as *The Reading Teacher*. She recently received the Reader Educator Award from the New York State Reading Association.

James W. Cunningham is Professor of Literacy Education at the University of North Carolina–Chapel Hill. During summers, he has taught by invitation at seven different universities around the country. He is also Research Associate on Reading ABC, an alternative assessment grant from the U.S. Office of Education. He is coauthor of four published textbooks, two of which are in their third editions. One of these books was a Main Selection of the NEA Professional Library Book Club. In addition he has numerous other publications in professional books and journals, and has presented research and theoretical papers at many national conferences. He is on the editorial advisory board of *Reading Research Quarterly*, has been elected Fellow by the National Conference on Research in Language and Literacy, and is an elected member of the Board of Directors of the National Reading Conference. He also has taught at the elementary and secondary levels in the public schools of Tennessee, Georgia, and North Carolina.

Patricia M. Cunningham is Professor at Wake Forest University in Winston Salem, North Carolina. In addition to university teaching, she worked for ten years in public school positions that included first-grade teacher, fourth-grade teacher, remedial reading teacher, curriculum coordinator, and director of reading. Dr. Cunningham has published numerous research and applied articles. For four years, she wrote "The Clip Sheet," a materials review column in *The Reading Teacher*. She also wrote a "Trends in Reading" column for *Educational Leadership* and a column for the intermediate teacher in *Reading Today*. Dr. Cunningham has coauthored several reading textbooks as well as *Phonics They Use: Words for Reading and Writing*. She and Richard Allington have recently coauthored two books, *Classrooms That Work* and *Schools That Work*. Dr. Cunningham's major interest is in finding alternative teaching strategies for students struggling with literacy.

Judith Diamondstone is Assistant Professor in the Literacy Cluster of Rutgers University's Graduate School of Education, where she teaches at both the graduate and undergraduate levels. In her research, she examines classroom discourse, both spoken and written, in order to understand complex interactions that have consequences for students. She is currently interested in helping students to become more critically aware of how language works; to that end, she is investigating linguistically informed curricula and pedagogies in the United States and other English-speaking areas of the world. She also oversees an Internet-supported project of teacher research that focuses on the teaching and learning of expository writing, a project funded by the Spencer Foundation. Her work has appeared in journals such as *Written Communication* and *Linguistics and Education*, and she has presented at a number of national and international conferences. She serves on the editorial board of the *Journal of Adult and Adolescent Literacy*.

Douglas Fisher is Assistant Professor in the College of Education, Department of Teacher Education, at San Diego State University, where he teaches classes in English language development and literacy. His background includes adolescent literacy and instructional strategies for diverse student needs. He often presents at local, state, and national conferences and has published a number of articles on reading/literacy, differentiated instruction, accommodations, and curriculum.

James Flood, Professor of Reading and Language Development at San Diego State University, (SDSU), has taught in preschool, elementary, and secondary schools and has been a language arts supervisor and vice-principal. He was a Fulbright scholar at the University of Lisbon in Portugal and has been President of the National Reading Conference. He is currently involved in teacher preparation and research in language arts/reading. Dr. Flood has chaired and cochaired many IRA, NCTE, NCRE and NRC committees. Currently Dr. Flood teaches preservice and graduate courses at SDSU. He has coauthored and edited many articles, columns, texts, handbooks, and children's materials on reading and language arts issues and has served on the review boards of a number of journals. His many educational awards include being named as the Outstanding Teacher Educator in the Department of Teacher Education at SDSU, the Distinguished Research Lecturer from SDSU's Graduate Division of Research, and a member of the California Hall of Fame.

Linda B. Gambrell (*see* About the Editors).

James V. Hoffman is Professor of Language and Literacy Studies at the University of Texas at Austin and directs the undergraduate specialization program in reading for elementary education students. A former classroom teacher and reading specialist, he currently teaches graduate courses in history of reading, assessment, and program development. He is past president of the National Reading Conference, former editor of *The Reading Research Quarterly*, and currently serves on the board of directors of the International Reading Association. Dr. Hoffman is the author of more than 100 scholarly articles, chapters, monographs, and books. His current research interests are in the areas of reading teacher education and beginning reading.

Linda D. Labbo is Associate Professor of Education at the University of Georgia in the Department of Reading Education. She has served as a principal investigator with the National Reading Research Center and has published in scholarly journals such as *Journal of Literacy Research*, *Reading Research Quarterly*, *The Reading Teacher*, and *Language Arts*. She is the current editor of the reviews section of *Reading on Line*, the International Reading Association's on-line journal, and the Chair of the Microcomputers in Reading International Reading Association Special Interest Group. Her research interests focus on the role of computers in young children's literacy development, issues of diversity and literacy, and young children's content area literacy acquisition and development.

Diane Lapp is Professor of Reading and Language Development in the College of Education at San Diego State University (SDSU) and has taught in elementary and middle schools. Dr. Lapp, who codirects and teaches field-based preservice and graduate courses, is currently on sabbatical and team teaching in a public school first-grade classroom. Dr. Lapp has coauthored and edited many articles, columns, texts, handbooks, and children's materials on reading and language arts issues. She has also chaired and cochaired several IRA and NRC committees. Her many educational awards include being named as the Outstanding Teacher Educator and Faculty Member in the Department of Teacher Education at SDSU, the

Distinguished Research Lecturer from SDSU's Graduate Division of Research, a member of the California Hall of Fame, and IRA's 1996 Outstanding Teacher Educator of the Year.

Susan Anders Mazzoni is a doctoral fellow in the Department of Curriculum and Instruction at the University of Maryland, College Park (UMCP), where she is studying reading education. She also teaches reading methods at UMCP and has worked as a research assistant at the National Reading Research Center. Her work has been published in *The Reading Teacher, Educational Psychology Review,* and in a number of edited books. Ms. Mazzoni has teaching experience in Baltimore County and Baltimore City public schools and has been teaching adults to read at the Learning Bank of Baltimore since 1988. She is a member of the International Reading Association and Phi Delta Kappa, and her research interests are in the area of comprehension strategy instruction and motivation.

Michael C. McKenna is Professor of Education at Georgia Southern University in Savannah, where he teaches graduate courses in reading education. He presently serves on the editorial boards of *Reading Research Quarterly, Journal of Literacy Research, Reading and Writing Quarterly, Scientific Studies in Reading,* and *The Reading Teacher.* He has published articles in each of these journals and also in *Educational Researcher, Educational Psychologist, Journal of Educational Psychology, Journal of Adolescent and Adult Reading,* and *Language Arts.* He has conducted research through the National Reading Research Center and is presently Publications Chair of the College Reading Association. His four major research interests include reading attitudes, technological applications in literacy education, content literacy, and approaches to beginning reading. He has coauthored four textbooks, coedited three scholarly books, and has written about 60 articles and book chapters, nearly all of which have focused on these four areas.

Lesley Mandel Morrow (*see* About the Editors).

Susan B. Neuman (*see* About the Editors).

P. David Pearson is the John A. Hannah Distinguished Professor of Education in the College of Education at Michigan State University, where he holds appointments in the Department of Teacher Education and the Department of Counseling, Educational Psychology, and Special Education. He serves as a principal investigator and codirector of the Center for the Improvement of Early Reading Achievement (CIERA). Within CIERA, he continues to pursue a line of research related to reading instruction and reading assessment policies and practices at all levels—local, state, and national. He has been active in the International Reading Association, the National Council of Teachers of English, the National Reading Conference, the National Conference of Research in English, and the American Association of Colleges of Teacher Education. He has written and edited several books about research and practice, most notable being the *Handbook of Reading Research,* now in its second volume. He has also published materials for teachers and children in his role as an author for the *World of Reading.* He has served on the boards of many educational research journals, including two terms as coeditor of *Reading Research Quarterly.*

Michael Pressley (*see* About the Editors).

Taffy E. Raphael is Professor in the Department of Reading and Language Arts at Oakland University, Rochester, Michigan, and teaches courses at the master's and doctoral levels. Dr. Raphael's work in teacher education earned her the Outstanding Teacher Educator in Reading Award from the International Reading Association in May, 1997. Dr. Raphael's research has focused on question–answer relationships, strategy instruction in writing, and Book Club, a literature-based reading program. She has published in journals such as *Reading Research Quarterly, Research in the Teaching of English, The Reading Teacher,* and *Language Arts.* She has co-authored and edited several books on literacy instruction, including *The Book Club Connection: Literacy Learning and Classroom Talk* and *Literature-Based Instruction: Reshaping the Curriculum.* She is active in the National Reading Conference, the International Reading Association, and the American Educational Research Association.

David Reinking is Professor of Education and Head of the Department of Reading Education at the University of Georgia. Before his involvement in higher education, he was an elementary and middle-grade teacher. Currently, he is the editor of the *Journal of Literacy Research,* a highly regarded peer-reviewed research journal published by the National Reading Conference. From 1992 to 1997, he was a principal investigator of the National Reading Research Center, funded by the Office of Educational Research and Improvement, U.S. Office of Education. Professor Reinking's publications have appeared in all of the field's major outlets, including *Reading Research Quarterly, Journal of Reading Behavior* (now *Journal of Literacy Research*), *The Reading Teacher,* and *Journal of Reading* (now *Journal of Adolescent and Adult Literacy*). He was also lead editor for *Handbook of Literacy and Technology.* He is widely recognized in the field for his work investigating how digital forms of reading and writing affect literacy.

D. Ray Reutzel is Provost at Southern Utah University in Cedar City, Utah. He has been a past Karl G. Maeser Distinguished Research Professor and

Associate Dean of Teacher Education in the David O. McKay School of Education at Brigham Young University. He took a leave from his university faculty position to return to full-time, first-grade classroom teaching in Sage Creek Elementary School several years ago, where he piloted Balanced Reading practices. Dr. Reutzel is the author of more than 100 articles, books, book chapters, and monographs. He has published in *Reading Research Quarterly, Journal of Reading Behavior, Journal of Literacy Research, Journal of Educational Research, Reading Psychology, Reading Research and Instruction, Language Arts, Journal of Reading, Reading World,* and *The Reading Teacher,* among others. He is currently the editor of *Reading Research and Instruction* and a coauthor of *Teaching Children to Read,* second edition, and *Balanced Reading Strategies.* He is a program author and consultant for Scholastic Incorporated's Literacy Place school reading program.

Nancy L. Roser is Professor of Language and Literacy Studies and the Flawn Professor of Early Childhood in the College of Education at the University of Texas at Austin. She is a former elementary teacher, and now teaches preservice and graduate classes in elementary reading and language arts. In addition, she is coeditor of *Book Talk and Beyond,* with Miriam Martinez, and *Adventuring with Books,* with Julie Jensen, as well as author of over 100 chapters and articles related to the teaching of reading and the language arts. She has served on the editorial team producing the Summary of Investigations Related to Reading, an annual compilation of research sponsored by the International Reading Association, and is a member of the International Reading Association's Research Committee and the Committee Against Censorship for the National Council of Teachers of English. She serves on the advisory boards of *The Reading Teacher, Sesame Street,* and *Teaching, K–8.* She has also served as an advisor to *Journal of Reading Behavior, Reading Research Quarterly,* and *Language Arts.* Most recently, she has served as codirector of the QuEST project, which helped to produce the standards for English Language Arts in Texas, and as director of the Texas Center for Reading/Language Arts.

Michael W. Smith teaches English education in the Literacy Cluster of Rutgers University's Graduate School of Education. In his research, he works to understand both how experienced readers read and talk about literacy texts and how teachers can use that understanding to help prepare students to have more meaningful transactions when they read. His thinking about reading and teaching literature is most clearly seen in *Authorizing Readers: Resistance and Respect in the Teaching of Literature,* written with Peter Rabinowitz. In addition, he has published three monographs with the National Council of Teachers of English, articles in such journals as *English Education, English Journal, Journal of Adolescent and Adult Literacy, Journal of Educational Research, Linguistics and Education, Research* *in the Teaching of English,* and *Review of Educational Research,* as well as a number of chapters in edited collections. He has been Chair of the Literature Special Interest Group of the American Educational Research Association and Cochair of NCTE's Assembly for Research. He is currently coeditor of *Research in the Teaching of English.*

Dixie Lee Spiegel is Professor of Literacy Studies at the University of North Carolina at Chapel Hill, where she is also Associate Dean for Students in the School of Education, codirector of the Total Literacy Professional Development Schools project, and a member of the advisory council and trainer for the UNC AmericaReads project. Dr. Spiegel teaches literacy courses to graduate and undergraduate students. Previously, she taught third grade for five years in Maryland and was a reading teacher for elementary grades in Wisconsin for five years. She is the author of numerous articles in a variety of professional journals, including *The Reading Teacher, Language Arts,* and the *Journal of Reading Behavior.* Her current interests focus on balanced literacy programs and literature response groups.

Lisa Stevens is the Learning Strategist at Lied Middle School in Las Vegas, Nevada, where she works with other teachers in creating and implementing lessons that foster strategic reading in all content areas. She works with students in "pull out" and "push in" programs to increase reading comprehension and has taught reading, French, and English as a second language in the Las Vegas and San Diego metropolitan areas. She is also a doctoral student at the University of Nevada, Las Vegas. Her primary research interests are in the areas of content area reading, authentic assessment, and the integration of the reading and writing processes across the curriculum.

Paul Cantú Valerio is a doctoral student in Literacy Education at the University of Las Vegas, Nevada. His research interests center on the ecological adaptations of language in linguistic and ethnic minority cultures.

Peter Winograd is Professor and Director of the Center for Teacher Education at the University of New Mexico. Dr. Winograd's research focuses on the implementation and effects of education reform, performance assessment in the areas of reading and writing, helping children become strategic readers, and the cognitive and motivational factors involved in the reading difficulties of children at risk. His articles have been published in a variety of journals, including *Reading Research Quarterly, Journal of Educational Psychology, Journal of Reading Behavior, American Educational Research Journal, Educational Psychologist, Educational Leadership, Remedial and Special Education, Written Communication,* and *The Reading Teacher.* He has also served on the Board of Directors of the National Reading Conference.

SERIES FOREWORD

The profession of education was shaken nearly two decades ago when national attention focused critically on education and on educators. Both critics and friends raised some basic questions about our profession, including whether education professionals have met the challenges that the students and the schools present and, even more fundamentally, if they are *able* to meet those challenges in the future. Beginning with the highly publicized *A Nation at Risk*, seemingly endless and often contradictory criticisms, analyses, and recommendations have appeared from virtually every segment of contemporary American society.

In this explosion of concern and ideas for educational reform, we saw a need for a general and national forum in which the problems of education could be examined in the light of research from a range of relevant disciplines. Too often, in the academy, analyses of complex issues and problems occur solely within a single discipline. Aspects of a problem that are unfamiliar to members of the discipline are largely ignored, and the resulting analysis is limited in scope and unsatisfactory. Furthermore, when educational issues are investigated only by members of one discipline, there is seldom an attempt to examine related issues from other fields or to apply methods developed in other fields that might enhance understanding.

The national debate on educational reform has suffered from this myopia, with problems and issues identified, and analyses and solutions proposed, only within the narrow confines of a single disciplinary boundary. In the past, national discussions have been ill informed or uninformed by current research, in part because there are too few mechanisms for interdisciplinary analyses of significant issues.

The series of symposia, the *Rutgers Invitational Symposia Education*, addresses this gap. Each symposium focuses on timely issues and problems in education by taking a critical and interdisciplinary perspective. The symposia papers are published in separate volumes, eleven thus far. Each volume focuses on a particular problem, such as the critical contributions of early childhood education to learning, how to assess literacy skills, the structure of effective schools, the role of cognitive psychology on how to teach mathematics, and optimizing peer tutoring in schools. The series presents a cumulative corpus of high-quality education research on topics of interest to practitioners and policy makers. Each volume provides an interdisciplinary forum through which scholars disseminate their original research and extend their work to potential applications for practice, including guides for teaching, learning, assessment, intervention, and policy formulation. These contributions increase the potential for significant analysis and positive impact on the problems that challenge educators.

This volume is based on original papers to be presented by the authors at a conference in March 1999 in New Brunswick, New Jersey, at the Rutgers Graduate School of Education. The topic, best practices in literacy, could not be more timely. At the national level, we will soon have the first national test in U.S. history—*The Fourth Grade Voluntary Reading Test*—and we have just implemented the national voluntary reading tutor program, *America Reads*. It is with great pleasure that we contribute this volume to the series, the *Rutgers Invitational Symposia on Education*.

LOUISE CHERRY WILKINSON
Dean and Professor of Educational Psychology
Rutgers Graduate School of Education

FOREWORD

Learning to read and write is arguably the most complex task humans face. Becoming literate requires experiences that help make the meaning and importance of print transparent. It requires active involvement and engagement to ensure that the joys of being literate as well as the value of what literacy can do in a very practical sense is appreciated. Although it is undoubtedly true that becoming literate still involves the development of some basic skills and strategies, today low-level basic skills that merely involve surface level decoding and the recall of information are hardly enough. Critical thinking and the ability to personalize meanings to individual experience and apply what is read or written in the real world, under many different circumstances and with many different types of texts, may now be termed the "new basics."

Not only has what we are required to do with texts changed—the texts themselves have changed. Today, texts are presented to us and generated by us in endless variety: books, magazines, and pamphlets of every conceivable design; letters and memoranda arriving via fax, e-mail, and snail mail; television screens, computer screens, and numerous other electronic screens and displays in our kitchens as well as our offices; and the indecipherable array of documentation for everything we buy that must be assembled, cared for, or operated. The list goes on and on. It serves as a constant reminder that the definition of what it means to be literate has evolved with the increasing demands of all aspects of our lives—personal, social, and economic. It is also a reminder of the critical role schooling plays in making literacy accessible to every child.

Best Practices in Literacy Instruction could not have been conceived at a better time. Its content takes on special meaning in a time when national, state, and local school reform efforts in the United States have raised expectations for what readers and writers should know and be able to do. The public awareness of the critical need for proficient readers and writers has never been greater—nor, I might add, has its criticism of the job the schools are doing. An unprecedented amount of open dissension and debate about the content of literacy instruction has led to state directives and legislative mandates that dictate specific curriculum content.

Fortunately, the knowledge base for improving literacy has never been richer. The scholars contributing to *Best Practices in Literacy Instruction* are representative of many of those whose work has contributed to that knowledge. In addition to being highly respected researchers in the field of literacy, the contributors to this volume represent a wide range of perspectives and specialization within literacy education. *Best Practices in Literacy Instruction* offers both practical suggestions and a research base for educators, policy makers, and others as they consider how they might help children meet today's higher literacy standards.

Becoming literate in the modern world is indeed an increasingly complex task. Reading and writing abilities don't just happen. They are acquired, nurtured, and refined through the acts of those who provide appropriate instructional contexts and support. The best of these practices is what this book is about. All who read *Best Practices in Literacy Instruction* will be indebted to the editors for their superb efforts in bringing clarity to where so much confusion and dissent often exists.

DOROTHY S. STRICKLAND
Rutgers University

CONTENTS

INTRODUCTION

Linda B. Gambrell
Lesley Mandel Morrow
Susan B. Neuman
Michael Pressley

For several years we thought, talked, and dreamed about bringing together in one volume recent insights from the research that have direct implications for classroom practice. This volume is the fulfillment of that dream. We designed this book with one goal in mind—to help beginning and experienced classroom teachers become more effective literacy teachers. We hope that it will provide teachers at all levels with fresh ideas and insights about literacy instruction. With that in mind, this volume was designed to focus on research-based best practices in literacy instruction and provide practical suggestions for enhancing the literacy development of all students. While this book is designed for preservice and in-service teachers, it is also appropriate for use in reading and language arts courses and staff development workshops that focus on literacy development. It should also be useful in introductory graduate courses and of value to reading specialists and administrators of school literacy programs.

In recent years, literacy research has begun to address specific questions about the efficacy of instructional techniques and procedures. Researchers now take into account various influences such as classroom context, motivation, teaching methods, social interaction, and teacher–student interactions. In this volume we want to emphasize that both the *what* and the *how* of literacy research are important. *What* research reveals about literacy instruction should inform *how* we go about the very important job of providing literacy experiences and instruction for our students. The contributors to this volume have been active in conducting classroom-based research and program innovations that focus on literacy development. They believe in empowering teachers to become informed decision makers and provide thorough and consistent information that integrates new, research-based information with valid traditional ideas about literacy instruction. Thus, the chapters in this book provide practical, classroom-based strategies and techniques as well as principles to assist in instructional decision making.

This book is organized into three parts: Perspectives on Exemplary Practices in Literacy, Strategies for Learning and Teaching, and Special Issues. In Part I, the authors explore core beliefs and philosophies of classroom literacy instruction and acknowledge the collaborative and change-oriented nature of the field of literacy. We believe that this multiplicity of perspectives can only increase awareness of the theoretical bases for best practices in literacy instruction. Readers of this volume should consider the merits of each position as they interpret and translate these ideas to practice. We believe that the discussion about best practices in literacy is enriched as we listen to multiple voices and engage in conversations. Part II presents current, research-based information about classroom literacy practices. Topics include balanced early literacy programs, phonics, self-regulated comprehension, crafting understanding, the role of literature in literacy programs, the role of basal readers in literacy programs, writing instruction, content area literacy instruction, and assessment. Part III provides an overview of many of the current issues in the field of literacy instruction. The issues covered in this part include, meeting the individual needs of each child, continuity across home and school contexts, organizing for literacy instruction, teaching children with special needs, and the use of technology in literacy programs.

PART I: PERSPECTIVES ON EXEMPLARY PRACTICES IN LITERACY

In Chapter 1, Linda Gambrell and Susan Mazzoni contend that it is time for literacy researchers and educators to move beyond terms, labels, and factions and move toward "common ground." In order to help accomplish this goal, they describe a number of research-based best practices as well as principles of best practice. However, Gambrell and Mazzoni warn that although best practices can be described, they cannot be *pre*scribed. They assert that best practices can only be achieved when knowledgeable, dedicated, and reflective teachers adapt instruction to fit the strengths and needs of children in their classrooms.

In Chapter 2, P. David Pearson and Taffy Raphael describe how narrow, oversimplified views of literacy and instruction mask critical areas that educators must balance to promote lifelong learning. They begin their chapter with a summary of historical and current debates in literacy education and then describe how "narrow" views of balanced instruction are detrimental to best practices. They then offer a broader, restructured view of balanced instruction using the metaphor of multiple balance beams—each possessing its own set of dimensions. They specifically describe content and contextual aspects of literacy instruction that need balance, such as curricular-/student-centered instruction, reader response/text-driven understandings, and narrative/expository texts and argue that it is crucial for teachers to be afforded the opportunity to balance literacy instruction along each continuum.

In Chapter 3, James Cunningham raises a number of current, critical issues regarding conditions that prohibit best practices in classrooms. More specifically, Cunningham argues that fadism and holding teachers accountable for students' literacy learning are particularly prohibitive conditions. He also explains why he believes that these conditions are unlikely to change in the near future. Cunningham then offers suggestions for promoting effective instruction. He recommends professional consensus, school-by-school/team approach to reform, school-based assessments, and balanced literacy programs as keys to promoting best practices in America's schools.

PART II: STRATEGIES FOR LEARNING AND TEACHING

In order to create a model of effective early literacy instruction, Lesley Morrow and Elizabeth Asbury visited the classrooms of six first grade teachers who were identified as exemplary by their administrators. In Chapter 4, the authors present a case study of one exemplary first grade teacher who possessed all of the characteristics that were associated with best practices in literacy instruction. They then present overarching characteristics of exemplary early literacy instruction, including knowledge of effective instructional strategies and efficient, effective classroom management practices. Readers will glean general guiding principles as well as specific ideas and activities for implementing best practices for a balanced early literacy program.

After summarizing "what we know" about phonics, reading, and writing, Patricia Cunningham, in Chapter 5, describes a balanced approach for primary reading and writing instruction called "The Four Blocks." She provides a detailed, vivid description of "The Words Block," where students learn high-frequency words and strategies for decoding and spelling. Cunningham offers clear explanations of activities that practitioners can use in their classrooms and illustrates her points with many practical examples. She also provides a rationale for employing an analogic approach to teaching phonics in the literacy program.

While Michael Pressley, in Chapter 6, acknowledges the importance of word recognition skills, he concludes that comprehension strategy instruction is also critical for the development of self-regulated readers who actively construct meaning from text. Pressley first describes strategies that are used by skilled readers. He then reports the instructional processes that facilitate children's use of these strategies and result in improved reading comprehension. Despite the evidence of the effectiveness of comprehension strategies instruction, Pressley reports that little strategy instruction is taking place in classrooms today and offers an explanation for these findings. Pressley also describes issues for future research in the field of reading comprehension.

Cathy Collins Block, in Chapter 7, views meaning making as a crafting process that occurs on multiple levels within shared learning experiences. She presents a three-part approach for enriching students' interactions with texts. Each lesson type focuses on particular aspects of reading comprehension, such as promoting unique interpretations of texts, facilitating comprehension strategy use, and engaging in discovery discussions about texts and the reading process in one-to-one conferences. Block provides practical examples of how to create each type of lesson in the classroom and grounds her three-part approach in both theory and research.

Douglas Fisher, James Flood, and Diane Lapp shed insight into the value of a literature-based literacy curriculum in Chapter 8. Readers visit a third-grade teacher's multicultural classroom where literature is used as the cornerstone for instruction. The authors also describe research to support the contribution of literature to children's literacy growth. Practical, instructional strategies that can be incorporated into a literature-based classroom are also provided, as well as suggestions for literature selection, grouping, and assessment.

Nancy Roser and James Hoffman offer an in-depth look at basal readers in Chapter 9. The authors begin by tracing the history of basals, "born" approximately 150 years ago. They discuss the development of basals and point out criticisms that have been levied against them. They then examine changes that have occurred in basals and teachers' guides over the past decade and describe the struggles that today's publishers face developing texts for a diverse community. The teaching philosophy and language arts instruction of three teachers are also presented— each teacher eliciting instruction in different ways, yet all teachers resisting the practice of strictly adhering to teachers' guides and the sole use of basal readers. Roser and Hoffman conclude with a concern about how the notion of balanced instruction will materialize in new basal series.

In Chapter 10, Karen Bromley asserts that sound writing instruction must balance process and product approaches, and she describes many effective methods for addressing both in K through 8 classrooms. Bromley provides numerous concrete ideas that teachers can use for writing instruction. Her chapter includes a discussion on topics that range from standards and assessment, direct instruction, the value of literature and peer interaction in children's writing development, graphic organizers, and writing across the curriculum, to how to integrate electronic literacy in the language arts curriculum. Bromley embeds many examples of effective writing instruction within descriptions of real-life classrooms.

Thomas Bean, Paul Cantú Valerio, and Lisa Stevens offer, in Chapter 11, an insiders' look at best practices in content area instruction that is student-centered and thematically integrated across content domains. The authors begin the chapter with a portrait of *teacher*-centered instruction and then present current research that suggests the need for greater *student*-centered learning that promotes higher order thinking skills. Bean, Valerio, and Stevens illustrate their views of best practices in content area literacy assessment and instruction by placing the reader in the role of a seventh-grader who experiences an integrated unit on slavery across history, reading, English, and mathematics, which was designed to foster students' comprehension and independent learning. Many practical methods are presented for implementing teaching and learning strategies across content domains.

In Chapter 12, Judith Diamondstone and Michael Smith assert that current controversy in the teaching of literature and composition in secondary schools revolves around what educators want students to learn as a result of instruction. They contrast three stances for reading narrative texts: (1) "What does this text mean?", (2) "What does this text mean to me?", and (3) "What attitudes, knowledge, reading behaviors, and values is the author counting on and how do I feel about that?" (authorial stance). Diamondstone and Smith contend that teaching secondary students to read authorially is the best way to foster democratic, meaningful learning and help students experience the power of literature. The authors then describe what it means to write authorially: to write for real purposes; to consider the situational, sociocultural, and rhetorical context of a piece of writing; and to know the tools of written language needed to complete different tasks. They illustrate their points with "thought experiments" and instructional vignettes and offer recommendations for helping students become adept, authoritative language users.

Peter Winograd and Harriette Arrington assert in Chapter 13 that best practices in literacy assessment include a variety of indicators that address the needs of multiple audiences, improve teaching and learning, and help to ensure that schools are thriving. However, they contend that in order to improve the lives of students in our nation's schools, we must understand broad as well as particular issues related to education, such as national statistics; the need for an adequate supply of well-prepared teachers and teacher-supportive schools; the tension that exists between assessment for accountability and instruction; valid, fair, and wise use of assessments; the limited role of assessment in improving the lives of children; and the influence of sociopolitical and economic contexts on education. Although Winograd and Arrington hesitate to identify which literacy practices are "best" (because effectiveness depends primarily on how wisely assessments are used), they explicitly describe authentic assessment strategies that can be beneficial for students, teachers, and parents: performance tasks and rubrics, portfolios, observation/anecdotal records/developmental checklists, and student–teacher conferences. They conclude with a presentation of questions that provide insight into issues concerning effective assessment reform.

PART III: SPECIAL ISSUES

In Chapter 14, Dixie Lee Spiegel explores issues related to the importance of addressing the diversity of students' strengths and needs in classrooms. While she notes the plethora of decisions that teachers must make every day, she focuses on two issues within the context of meeting individual needs: teacher-directed instruction/learner-directed discovery and isolated strategy emphases/use of whole texts. Spiegel offers guidelines for helping teachers decide what is best practice for each child at a given point of time and applies the guidelines to three students who differ by grade as well as by strengths and needs. She also suggests methods for managing the task of meeting individual needs within whole classrooms.

Susan Neuman asserts in Chapter 15 that children's learning is improved when classroom instruction fuses elements of home learning into instructional activities and cites research to support her claim. Neuman describes a culturally responsive approach to instruction that aims at "building bridges" between home and school. Four elements of culturally responsive instruction are presented, though she focuses on the fourth element—continuity between home and school. She highlights three activities, a family album, literacy-related prop boxes, and parent–

child book clubs, as ways to promote home–school connections and literacy learning.

As Ray Reutzel points out in Chapter 16, teachers often group students in order to meet individual needs. However, he cites extensive research suggesting that persistent, static ability grouping is detrimental in many ways. So what is the alternative? Reutzel recommends that educators incorporate a variety of grouping patterns in their classrooms, including flexible groups, basal reader selection groups, literature circles, cooperative learning groups, needs grouping, and guided reading groups. He provides a description of each type of grouping pattern and illustrates his points with examples. Reutzel then presents an instructional framework that incorporates a variety of grouping patterns in K through 2 classrooms called "language routines." His plan consists of six routines, "Tune-In," "Old Favorites," "Learning about Language," "New Story," "Independent Reading/Writing," and "Closing Sharing Time."

In Chapter 17, Richard Allington and Kim Baker contend that, first and foremost, struggling readers and writers must have access to high-quality literacy instruction if they are to succeed. They point out that exemplary classroom teachers have a positive impact on the literacy achievement of their lowest achieving children, yet there is some evidence to suggest that paraprofessionals—who are often poorly trained—do not. Allington and Baker assert that some children do need extra support but that specialists must both foster and enhance classroom instruction. They provide two case studies that illustrate high-quality instruction. The first is a description of a day in the life of an exemplary first-grade teacher; the other describes the practices of an exemplary reading resource teacher. The authors conclude by summarizing practices that characterize exemplary early intervention efforts.

In Chapter 18, Linda Labbo, David Reinking, and Michael McKenna call upon educators to "transcend perfunctory use" of computers in literacy programs and, instead, to weave technology into "the fabric of daily classroom routines" in order to facilitate both conventional and electronic literacy learning. They offer suggestions for integrating technology into planned instruction through teacher interactive demonstrations, thematic integration and innovation, and collaborative opportunities. Ideas are presented for children as young as the kindergarten grade level. The authors also describe ways that technology can be used to support special needs students' literacy learning, including struggling readers and writers, nonfluent, reluctant, and ESOL readers. Many practical activities as well as principles for integrating technology into literacy teaching are provided.

It is our hope that this volume will enrich the lives of literacy learners and inspire the use of best practices in literacy instruction so that all our students become proficient readers and writers. We want to extend our sincere and heartfelt appreciation to the authors who contributed to this volume and to our literacy colleagues at the University of Maryland, Rutgers University, Temple University, and the University of Notre Dame.

Part I

PERSPECTIVES ON EXEMPLARY PRACTICES IN LITERACY

Chapter 1

PRINCIPLES OF BEST PRACTICE: FINDING THE COMMON GROUND

Linda B. Gambrell
Susan Anders Mazzoni

While we have learned a great deal about literacy and instruction over the past decades, there remains significant controversy over what constitutes "best practices" in literacy education. Interestingly, our increased understanding of the literacy process appears to have contributed to current debate. We have become increasingly aware of the complexity of reading and instruction; consequently, many researchers have adopted broadened perspectives regarding the nature of literacy and how learning occurs. For example, since the 1970s, researchers have moved from performing laboratory controlled experiments, where one aspect of learning was studied independent of context, to naturalistic classrooms settings where contextual variables, such as affective environment, authenticity of tasks, social interaction, parental involvement, or types of materials could be evaluated. Research has shown that, indeed, many contextual variables make a difference in literacy learning. Furthermore, as our need for higher levels of literacy grew as a result of changes in workplace demands, we have redefined what is basic to becoming literate. Simply being able to decode and answer low-level literal questions about a piece of text is no longer sufficient. Becoming fully literate means, among many things, being able to independently use strategies to construct meaning from text, draw upon texts to build conceptual understanding, effectively communicate ideas orally and in writing, as well as possess an intrinsic desire to read and write. Literacy and instruction have, indeed, become complex, multifaceted tasks.

While many literacy researchers have adopted multiple perspectives to help interpret and account for this complexity, tacitly or explicitly adopting a single lens has caused rifts and divides among members of the education community. With "pendulumlike persistence" (Allington, 1994), we have swung from teacher-directed to child-centered teaching and learning and back, from phonics to comprehension and back, and from decoding to whole language and back; the list goes on. While the reading debates roar on in the media, many researchers are calling for mutual respect, conversation, and courtesy among members of the reading community (Allington, 1997; J. Cunningham, Chapter 3, this volume; Kamil, 1995; Stanovich, 1997). It is becoming increasingly clear that in order to fully achieve the goal of literacy for all, we must move beyond the terms and labels that are driving us apart. We must move from dealing with trivial matters and move toward what Vail (1991) has called the "common ground." But the questions remain: Is there a common ground for best practice? If so, what best practices can we agree upon?

We believe that there is a common ground, and in this chapter we will present a number of generally accepted research-based best practices. We will also present principles of best practice that are derived from constructivist theory and transverse the chapters in this book. However, before doing so, we must interject this important caveat: We believe there is no simple, narrow solution to the "best practices" debate. While simple solutions are appealing by their very nature, applying simple solutions to complex enterprises, such as teaching children to become literate in the fullest sense, cannot result in best practice. For example, employing a method that research has shown to be effective for improving a particular aspect of literacy learning will not be a "best practice" if instruction is not adapted to fit the strengths and needs of a particular group of learners, or if classroom management is an issue, or if a "risk-taking" environment has not been fostered, or if other aspects of literacy instruction are not included in the total program. Also, it is important to remember that teachers work with children who come to school with unique personalities and understandings; therefore, different children will often respond differently to the same instruction. This means that best practices involve a "custom fit"—not a simple "one size fits all"—approach. This also means that effective teachers not only bring research into practice; they understand their students' strengths and needs as well as their cultural community and adapt instruction to promote optimal learning in the fullest sense of what it means to become literate. Effective teachers constantly self-question, reflect, teach, and reevaluate in order to inform instruction.

We are reminded of an elementary school teacher who read about the practice of using "Author's Chair" (Graves, 1994) and "PQP" (Praising/Questioning/Polishing) where student writers share their works with other children who then comment on the author's work by "Praising" (positive comments only), "Questioning" (ask the author questions about their work), and "Polishing" (constructive comments). Although Author's Chair may be considered a "best practice" by many educators, this teacher noticed that the children in her class tended to make the same low-level comments to the student authors, like "That was really good" or "I liked your story." Consequently, she determined that her students would benefit from instruction on how to critique an author's work. Thus, the generally accepted practice of Author's Chair was improved as a result of her ongoing reflection and deliberation. We believe that this vignette illustrates a very important point: No matter how well a particular practice is shown to be effective by research, *optimal assessment and instruction can only be achieved when skillful, knowledgeable, and dedicated teachers are given the freedom and latitude to use their professional judgment to make instructional decisions that enable each child to achieve their literacy potential.* Teachers are ultimately the instructional designers who develop practice in relevant, meaningful ways for their particular community of learners. In other words, best practices can be *de*scribed—but not *pre*scribed.

RESEARCH-BASED BEST PRACTICES

With the notion of the teacher as ultimate instructional designer in mind, we will now present 10 research-based best practices that are generally accepted by experts in the field and are worthy of consideration (see Table 1.1). You will notice that these practices are based on a rich model of the reading process, one that incorporates the full range of experiences that children need in order to reach their literacy potential. We believe that best practices are characterized by meaningful literacy activities that provide children with both the *skill* and the *will* they need to become proficient and motivated literacy learners. You will find that the authors in this book have addressed and expanded upon these best practices.

COMMON-GROUND PRINCIPLES OF BEST PRACTICE

In this section we highlight eight *principles* of best practice that we believe represent "common ground." We believe that since each teacher is ultimately in the best position to bring principles into practice in a meaningful way for his/her particular community of learners, the notion of principled instruction is particularly supportive of teacher empowerment and professionalization. The following eight principles are grounded in

TABLE 1.1. Research-Based Best Practices

1. Teach reading for authentic meaning-making literacy experiences: for pleasure, to be informed, and to perform a task.

2. Use high-quality literature.

3. Integrate a comprehensive word study/phonics program into reading/ writing instruction.

4. Use multiple texts that link and expand concepts.

5. Balance teacher- and student-led discussions.

6. Build a whole class community that emphasizes important concepts and builds background knowledge.

7. Work with students in small groups while other students read and write about what they have read.

8. Give students plenty of time to read in class.

9. Give students direct instruction in decoding and comprehension strategies that promote independent reading. Balance direct instruction, guided instruction, and independent learning.

10. Use a variety of assessment techniques to inform instruction.

constructivist learning theory, which suggests that the goal of schools is to help students learn new meanings in response to new experiences rather than to simply learn the meanings others have created (Poplin, 1988). This view of learning emphasizes the personal, intellectual, and social nature of literacy learning.

As we read each of the chapters presented in this book we noticed that although the authors addressed a wide variety of topics, there were a number of similarities among themes. You will find that the following eight principles also reflect "common ground" themes related to best practices that are presented in this book.

1. Learning Is Meaning Making

Learning is the "natural, continuous construction and reconstruction of new, richer, and more complex and connected meanings by the learner" (Poplin, 1988, p. 404). Proficient readers and writers actively search for and construct new meanings. When students are involved in literacy tasks and activities that are purposeful and authentic, they are more motivated to learn and come to view reading and writing as relevant, dynamic, interactive processes that involve decision making and problem solving (see Allington & Baker, Chapter 17; Bean, Valerio, &

Stevens, Chapter 11; Block, Chapter 7; Bromley, Chapter 10; P. Cunningham, Chapter 5; Diamondstone & Smith, Chapter 12; Fisher, Flood, & Lapp, Chapter 8; Labbo, Reinking, & McKenna, Chapter 18; Morrow & Asbury, Chapter 4; and Neuman, Chapter 15, this volume). Basic to this principle is the notion that learning most often proceeds from whole (meaning/context) to part (skills/strategy instruction) to whole (meaning). It is *wholeness* and *context* that give meaning to our experiences and to our learning. Children learn new words more easily when they occur in a personally meaningful context. Workbooks that "teach" isolated skills are seen by most children as having little relevancy to what they really are interested in and what they want to know about. Instruction in skills and strategies (such as decoding and comprehension strategies, spelling, punctuation, and grammar) is most effectively addressed in the context of each student's own personal need for meaning making. Moreover, a whole–part–whole approach provides an opportunity for children to apply the skills and strategies they have learned to authentic, meaningful tasks.

2. Prior Knowledge Guides Learning

The best predictor of what students will learn is what they already know. Prior knowledge is the foundation upon which new meaning (or learning) is built (Pressley, Chapter 6, this volume). Effective teachers assess students' conceptual understanding, beliefs, and values, and *link* new ideas, skills, and competencies to prior understandings (Bean et al., Chapter 11; Block, Chapter 7; Bromley, Chapter 10; Diamondstone & Smith, Chapter 12; Fisher et al., Chapter 8; Morrow & Asbury, Chapter 4; Neuman, Chapter 15; Spiegel, Chapter 14; Winograd & Arrington, Chapter 13, this volume). They also provide experiences that equip each child with sufficient background knowledge to succeed with literacy tasks (Bean et al., Chapter 11, this volume). This principle is also consistent with Vygotsky's (1978) notion of "zone of proximal development," which suggests that optimal learning occurs when teachers determine children's current level of understanding and teach new ideas, skills, and strategies that are at an appropriate level of challenge.

3. The Gradual Release of Responsibility Model and Scaffolded Instruction Facilitate Learning

Children often need concentrated instructional support when they need to learn important skills and strategies that they would have difficulty discovering on their own. The gradual release of responsibility model offers such support. In general, the model describes a process where students gradually assume a greater degree of responsibility for a particular aspect of learning. During the first stage, the teacher assumes most of the responsibility by modeling and describing a particular skill or strategy. During the second stage, the teacher and students assume joint responsibility; children practice applying a particular skill or strategy and teachers offer assistance and feedback as needed. Once students are ready, instruction moves into the third stage where students assume all, or almost all, of the responsibility by working in situations where they independently apply newly learned skills and strategies. This gradual withdrawal of instructional support is also known as scaffolded instruction because "supports" or "scaffolds" are gradually removed as students demonstrate greater degrees of proficiency.

We view the gradual release of responsibility and scaffolded instruction as consistent with constructivist principles when they are used within meaningful, authentic contexts (Graham & Harris, 1996; Harris & Graham, 1994). Indeed, many authors in this volume have provided examples of how to integrate these models within meaningful reading and writing programs that include use of literature, technology, authentic writing experiences, choice, and collaborative learning (Allington & Baker, Chapter 17; P. Cunningham, Chapter 5; Labbo et al., Chapter 18; Morrow & Asbury, Chapter 4; Pressley, Chapter 6; Reutzel, Chapter 16; Spiegel, Chapter 14).

4. Social Collaboration Enhances Learning

From a social-constructivist perspective, literacy is a social act. Readers and writers develop meanings as a result of co-constructed understandings within particular sociocultural contexts. This means, among many things, that text interpretation and level of participation are influenced by the size and social makeup of a group, the cultural conventions of literacy (e.g., "What are reading and writing *for*? What are the literacy *goals* of the community?), as well as the different perspectives others convey about text.

Specifically, collaborative learning refers to individuals who actively and substantively engage in an exchange of ideas that result in co-constructed understanding. Collaborative learning and the social perspective have brought to the fore the importance of peer talk as well as small group learning (Allington & Baker, Chapter 17; Bean et al., Chapter 11; Block, Chapter 7; Bromley, Chapter 10; Diamondstone & Smith, Chapter 12; Fisher et al., Chapter 8; Labbo et al., Chapter 18; Morrow & Asbury, Chapter 4; Neuman, Chapter 15; Reutzel, Chapter 16, this volume). Interest in the positive benefits of these contexts has resulted in new classroom participation structures, such as book talk discussion groups, literacy clubs, and small group investigations of specific topics related to a content area and communication of findings to others.

We know, however, that collaborative learning doesn't just "happen." Children need assistance in developing interpersonal skills. They also need a degree of teacher assistance and influence in order to stimulate new learning. However, research has shown that the rewards are great. Collaborative learning contexts have been found to result in greater student achievement and more positive social, motivational, and attitudinal outcomes for all age levels, genders, ethnicities, and social classes than are achieved by individualized or competitive learning structures (Johnson & Johnson, 1983; Johnson, Johnson, & Maruyama, 1983; Johnson, Maruyama, Johnson, Nelson, & Skon, 1981; Sharan, 1980; Slavin, 1983, 1990).

5. Learners Learn Best When They Are Interested and Involved

Motivation exerts a tremendous force on what is learned and how and when it will be learned. Motivation often makes the difference between learning that is superficial and shallow and learning that is deep and internalized. Clearly, students need both the skill and the will to become competent and motivated readers (Paris, Lipson, & Wixson, 1983). Best practices include ways to support students in their reading development by creating classroom cultures that foster reading motivation. Several key factors include a book-rich classroom environment, opportunities for choice, opportunities to socially interact with others, and a teacher who values reading and is enthusiastic about sharing a love of reading with students (Allington & Baker, Chapter 17; Bean et al., Chapter 11; Block, Chapter 7; Bromley, Chapter 10; P. Cunningham, Chapter 5; Fisher et al., Chapter 8; Labbo et al., Chapter 18; Morrow & Asbury, Chapter 4; Neuman, Chapter 15; Reutzel, Chapter 16; Roser & Hoffman, Chapter 9, this volume). The goal of a successful instruction program should be the development of readers who can read and who *choose* to read.

6. The Goal of Best Practice Is to Develop High-Level Strategic Readers and Writers

The authors in this volume have moved well beyond traditional low-level conceptions of literacy. Clearly, each author describes best practices as those that promote high-level thinking and strategic, versatile reading and writing. For example, ideas are presented for how to help children (1) become independent users of comprehension strategies to help them gain meaning from text relative to their goal (Pressley, Chapter 6); (2) comprehend texts at multiple levels (Bean et al., Chapter 11; Block, Chapter 7; Diamondstone & Smith, Chapter 12); (3) acquire word recognition skills and strategies so that students will have "thinking power" left for meaning (P. Cunningham, Chapter 5); (4) use literature to examine the multicultural world as well as genres, styles, and perspectives (Fisher et al., Chapter 8); (5) write in different genres and for a variety of purposes and audiences (Bromley, Chapter 10); and (6) use computers in high-level literacy activities such as searching for information and making intertextual links (Labbo et al., Chapter 18). Chapter 13 on assessment, by Winograd and Arrington, also signals the trend toward higher-level literacy skills and tasks as reflected in their description of performance and portfolio assessments.

We are clearly in the process of redefining what it means to be "literate" in today's world. Print, in various forms, is playing an ever-important role in our society, and jobs are requiring a level of literacy that is unsurpassed in history. Best practices, then, must include instruction that will help meet these demands.

7. Best Practices Are Grounded in the Principle of Balanced Instruction

Although there has been considerable controversy over which practices are best for teaching children to read and write, there is evidence that effective instruction provides a balanced program in which a skillful, committed teacher adapts and integrates a multitude of components to enable each student to achieve his/her literacy potential (Slavin & Madden, 1989). You will notice that many of the authors in this volume have also argued for balanced instruction. For example, the authors have recommended that teachers need to balance (1) curricular- and student-centered instruction, reader response and text-driven understandings, and use of narrative and expository texts (Pearson & Raphael, Chapter 2); (2) the use of multiple assessment measures in a variety of meaningful contexts (Winograd & Arrington, Chapter 13); (3) phonics and comprehension instruction (P. Cunningham, Chapter 5); (4) meaning making at multiple levels (Block, Chapter 7); (5) the use of basal texts with meaningful instruction (Roser & Hoffman, Chapter 9); and (6) process and product approaches to writing (Bromley, Chapter 10). It is clear that best practice encompasses both the elegance and complexity of the reading and language arts processes. Such a model recognizes and acknowledges the importance of both form (i.e., phonics, mechanics, etc.) and function (i.e., comprehension, purpose, meaning) of the literacy processes as well as the notion that learning occurs most often and most effectively in a whole–part–whole context.

8. Best Practices Are a Result of Informed Decision Making

One of the most striking similarities among the ideas presented in this volume is the view that the teacher *is* the necessary foundation, the architectural support, for building a successful literacy program. None of the authors herein advocate a prescriptive, programmed approach to literacy instruction. Instead, many of them address the issue of best practices by specifically offering *principles* of instruction. For example, Neuman (Chapter 15) points out that learning is enhanced when classroom instruction fuses elements of home learning into instructional activities; Reutzel (Chapter 16) recommends that educators incorporate a variety of grouping patterns in their classrooms; Bean et al. (Chapter 11) maintain that an integrated curriculum across content area instruction helps to foster meaningful learning; and Spiegel (Chapter 14) argues that teachers need to modify instruction, tasks, and materials to meet each child's literacy needs. While the authors suggest concrete ways of bringing principles into practice, none have presented a step-by-step, programmed approach for literacy instruction (see also Morrow & Asbury, Chapter 4).

On the contrary, effective teachers guard against the tendency to teach reading and language arts processes as solely a series of subskills or components to be taught in a prescribed, linear fashion, yet effective teachers recognize the important contribution that each component plays in the literacy development of their students. You may have seen a performer juggle several objects of different sizes and shapes, a task that seems incredibly difficult. But by knowing how to handle each object while keeping several objects in constant motion, the juggler achieves the rhythm and flow necessary for a successful performance. Exemplary teachers must also perform a challenging juggling act. Many literacy components of varying importance must be included or juggled and given just the right amount of emphasis by the teacher to keep his/her particular community of learners moving toward the desired instructional goal. To further complicate this task, adjustments must continually be made to adapt to the changing particular needs of each child. As the juggler, the teacher remains the key to a successful reading program by guiding students, modeling strategic literacy behaviors and processes, providing support when the going gets rough, and—most importantly—introducing children to books, stories, and informational text that are worth reading (Winograd & Greenlee, 1986).

FINDING THE COMMON GROUND

As literacy educators, it is critical that we avoid labels and acknowledge our "common ground." One common challenge that we face is that as we increase our understanding of literacy and instruction, our conception of best practices broadens and deepens and we are less able to offer simple, narrow solutions. As suggested by Strickland (1994/1995), our students need and deserve instruction that is well informed and based on a *rich* model of the reading process. Her vision of best practices embraces the richness and complexity of literacy and instruction: "A literacy curriculum that emphasizes what is basic values and builds on the knowledge that students bring to school, emphasizes the construction of meaning through activities that require higher order thinking, and offers extensive opportunities for learners to apply literacy strategies and their underlying skills in the context of meaningful tasks" (pp. 296–297). Unquestionably this is no easy task. It requires commitment, time, and knowledge. It must begin with an enlightened teacher who looks at the particular strengths and needs of each child and plans instruction that is based on those strengths and needs. The rewards, however, are great as we help children become lifelong, engaged readers.

REFERENCES

Allington, R. (1994). The schools we have. The schools we need. *The Reading Teacher, 48,* 14–29.

Allington, R. (1997). Why does literacy research so often ignore what really matters? In C. K. Kinzer, K. A. Hinchman, & D. J. Leu (Eds.), *Inquiries in literacy theory and practice: Forty-sixth yearbook of the National Reading Conference.* Chicago: National Reading Conference.

Graham, S., & Harris, K. R. (1996). *Making the writing process work: Strategies for composition and self regulation.* Cambridge, MA: Brookline Books.

Graves, D. (1994). *A fresh look at writing.* Portsmouth, NH: Heinemann.

Harris, K. R., & Graham, S. (1994). Constructivism: Principles, paradigms, and integration. *Journal of Special Education, 28*(3), 233–247.

Johnson, D. W., & Johnson, R. T. (1983). The socialization and achievement crisis: Are cooperative learning experiences the solution? In L. Bickman (Ed.), *Applied social psychology* (Annual 4). Beverly Hills, CA: Sage.

Johnson, D. W., Johnson, R. T., & Maruyama, G. (1983). Interdependence and interpersonal attraction among heterogeneous and homogeneous individuals: A theoretical formulation and a meta-analysis of the research. *Review of Educational Research, 533,* 5–54.

Johnson, D. W., Maruyama, G., Johnson, R. T., Nelson, D., & Skon, L. (1981). Effects of cooperative, competitive, and individualistic goal structures on achievement: A meta-analysis. *Psychological Bulletin, 89,* 47–62.

Kamil, M. L. (1995). Critical issues: Some alternatives to paradigm wars in literacy research. *Journal of Reading Behavior, 27,* 243–261.

Paris, S., Lipson, M., & Wixson, K. (1983). Becoming a strategic reader. *Contemporary Educational Psychology, 8,* 293–316.

Poplin, M. (1988). Holistic/constructivist principles of the teaching/learning process: Implications for the field of learning disabilities. *Journal of Learning Disabilities, 21,* 401–416.

Sharan, S. (1980). Cooperative learning in small groups: Recent methods and effects on achievement, attitudes, and ethnic relations. *Review of Educational Research, 50,* 241–271.

Slavin, R. E. (1983). *Cooperative learning.* New York: Longman.

Slavin, R. E. (1990). *Cooperative learning: Theory, research, and practice.* Englewood Cliffs, NJ: Prentice-Hall.

Slavin, R. E., & Madden, N. (1989). *Effective programs for students at risk.* Boston: Allyn & Bacon.

Stanovich, K. E. (1997). *Twenty-five years of research on the reading process: The grand synthesis and what it means for our field.* Oscar S. Causey Research Award address, National Reading Conference, Scottsdale, AZ.

Strickland, D. (1994/1995). Reinventing our literacy programs: Books, basic, balance. *The Reading Teacher, 48,* 294–302.

Vail, P. (1991). *Common ground: Whole language and phonics working together.* Rosemont, NJ: Modern Learning Press.

Vygotsky, L. S. (1978). *Mind in society.* Cambridge, MA: Harvard University Press.

Winograd, P., & Greenlee, M. (1986). Students need a balanced reading program. *Educational Leadership, 43,* 16–21.

Chapter 2

TOWARD AN ECOLOGICALLY BALANCED LITERACY CURRICULUM

P. David Pearson
Taffy E. Raphael

Our chapter represents a work in progress, a treatise on reading policy and practice with particular emphasis on today's debates around the elusive concept called "balanced reading instruction." "Balance," a key term of the late 1990s, has advocates from both sides of the aisle—those who wish to infuse balance into whole language programs (e.g., McIntyre & Pressley, 1996) and those who argue that an early code emphasis is the cornerstone of a balanced framework (e.g., Lyon, 1997). Each side claims they are the balanced parties in this debate.

In this chapter, we try to wrest this term, balance, from the semantic turf of both extremes: (1) those who publicly assert balance while they champion direct instruction and systematic, synthetic phonics, and (2) those who insinuate balance while pushing for a curriculum shrouded in the developmental discourse—the authentic, genuine, natural reading and writing activities of everyday (i.e., not school) communication contexts. We share our professional vision of the concept of balance, guided by three overarching questions: (1) What is this debate all about? (2) What are the dangers in "balance gone astray"? (3) What is to be done?

WHAT IS THE DEBATE ALL ABOUT?

We can think of this debate as a single debate or a family of narrower debates about issues such as curricular content, nature of texts, forms and focus of teacher preparation and professional development, and control over decisions related to all of these areas. In either case, these are not new issues. Debate(s) about the issues have been going on for decades, perhaps centuries. Right after World War II, it was "look–say" (as exemplified by the classic Dick and Jane readers) versus phonics (see Chall, 1967; Mathews, 1966). And 100 years ago, it was the ABCs (synthetic phonics) versus the analytic phonics (words first, then the letters) (Mathews, 1966). In one form or another, the debate has always been the *emphasis* during earliest stages of formal reading instruction—*breaking the code* or *understanding what we read* (see Chall, 1967, 1997, for a historical treatment of the debate), or what Chall described as *code emphasis* versus *meaning emphasis.*

One side takes a simple view of reading (Gough & Hillinger, 1980): reading comprehension = decoding + listening comprehension. Those who advocate the simple view argue that since the code (the cipher that maps letters onto sounds) is what students do not know, the sooner they learn it the better. Get it out of the way early so that students can begin to engage in regular reading—by translating letters into the sounds of oral language and then using the same cognitive processes that enable listening comprehension to understand what they read.

The other side argues that since making meaning is the ultimate goal of reading, it is best to start students off with that very expectation; if teachers offer lots of "scaffolding" to help students determine textual meaning(s), they will, as a natural by-product, acquire the cipher for mapping sounds onto letters. One side says teach them what they do not directly know; the other, bootstrap what they do not know by relying on what they do know (see Pearson, 1976, for a full treatment of these issues).

In addition to debating early emphases, the debate has also been about *instructional focus*—whether the growth of each *child* or the sanctity of the *curriculum* dominates the decision-making processes of the teacher. One side wants to make sure that each child experiences the optimal curriculum for his/her development; Harste, Woodward, and Burke (1984), for example, talk about approaches that ensure that the child is the primary curriculum informant. This position requires as many curricula as there are children in a classroom. The other side, while certainly acknowledging the individuality of each reader, emphasizes the importance of making sure that each and every child goes through particular stages and acquires certain requisite bodies of knowledge on the way to skilled reading. Put differently, one side argues that there are many paths to reading acquisition, whereas the other argues that there are many variations in the way the single path is traversed.

There are also certain "overlays" that complicate the debate by introducing peripheral issues (see Bergeron, 1990). Whole language rhetoric is often shrouded in romanticism—sometimes incorporating aspects of radical individualism, usually couched as a right to academic freedom (Bialostock, 1997; Goodman, 1992); other times revealing a commitment to communitarianism (see Goodman, 1992); and occasionally hinting at a fundamental distrust of the institutions of power and authority, such as governmental agencies and commercial enterprises (Bialostock, 1997, p. 627; Goodman, Shannon, Freeman, & Murphy, 1988). The rhetoric of those who want to return to more skills and phonics has its own set of "shrouds," many moralistic in character. The argument for a "return" to systematic phonics is sometimes characterized as a return to our national roots (Sweet, 1997) or as a struggle to return the power of literacy to individual children and their families (Honig, 1996).

WHAT ARE THE DANGERS IN BALANCE GONE ASTRAY?

As each side of the aisle has attempted to appropriate the term "balance," our field has seen a conflating of all sorts of issues and constructs that are not necessarily the property of one side or the other. Thus, on one side of the balance beam, we pile up, along with phonics, other sometimes related constructs like direct instruction, skills emphasis, ability grouping, formal treatment of genre, and curriculum-centered curricula. These constructs are pitted against everything that gets piled up on the other side of the balance beam—literary response, genre study, student-centered curricula, and whole language philosophies (see Figure 2.1). Oversimplification actually masks crucial areas literacy educators must balance to effectively teach literacy as a lifelong process.

We believe that this oversimplification isn't simply inaccurate—it can actually contribute to a dangerous situation for the field of literacy education, given our current professional context. Specifically, legislative mandates appear to be replacing the marketplace of ideas as the norm in our approach to curriculum change. Enacted (e.g., California Assembly 1086) and proposed (e.g., HR 2614) bills provide strong evidence for this trend. Many states have mandated phonics courses for all teachers (e.g., Ohio, California, Arizona), required phonics for teacher educators (California), and prior approval of the content of inservice programs (California).

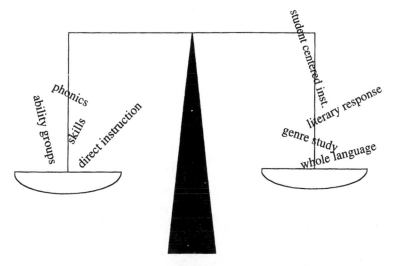

FIGURE 2.1. "Balance" out of control.

It is not as though the education profession has been immune from legislative mandates in the past. In fact, colleges and universities have long lobbied for particular patterns of coursework as requisite elements of teacher education programs and done so in the name of quality and rigor. What is different this time around is the specificity of the mandate. It is one thing to have a legislative mandate or an executive order for 6 or 9 hours of coursework in language arts methods; it is quite another to mandate the particular philosophical content of the course. While teachers have a long history of responding to mandates from every level of policy making, in the past it did not mean they might be violating a highly specific law.

If highly specific legislative mandates become the rule, then most (perhaps all) of our values regarding the professionalism of teachers and schooling will be eroded or irretrievably lost. Concepts such as empowerment, professional prerogative, inquiry and reflective practice, agency and intellectual freedom, and local curricular control make sense only under the assumption that what is available to teachers and school communities is a marketplace of research-based ideas from which to make judicious choices about the particular nature of curriculum in our corner of the world. The classic enlightenment ideal of disseminating knowledge so that enlightened citizens (i.e., those informed by our best knowledge and practice) can exercise freedom of choice is a mockery if there are no choices left to make. Notice that in the bargain we also compromise the values and practices we have extolled in the recent reform movements (local decision making, community involvement in schools, ownership). These are high prices to pay for one particular model of research-based practice.

WHAT IS TO BE DONE?

We think that by unpacking and then reassembling this phenomenon we call "balance," we can build a case for the rich knowledge bases teachers will need so they can implement a truly balanced curriculum. In so doing, we will recomplexify balance, arguing that there are many independent elements that must be simultaneously balanced. As we unpack this construct, we find it useful to think of a series of continua that reflect the *context* and the *content* of literacy instruction.

Contextual Continua

There are at least four contextual aspects that literacy educators balance in their daily teaching activities (see Figure 2.2).

First, the notion of *authenticity* has been identified as crucial to students' literacy learning. The argument underlying promoting authenticity is that too many school tasks are unauthentic, unrealistic, and—by implication—not useful for engaging in real-world literacy activities; that is, instead of teaching kids how to "do school," we should be teaching them how to "do life." Writing, reading, and talk about text must be grounded in authentic tasks and goals. These include writing for a real audience and purpose (Bruce & Rubin, 1993) or reading to engage in book club or literacy circle discussions with teachers and peers (e.g., Daniels, 1994; McMahon & Raphael with Goatley & Pardo, 1997), rather than writing to demonstrate knowledge of conventions or reading to successfully answer a set of comprehension questions. It may be difficult to find controversy in an emphasis on authenticity. However, if this notion is pursued too literally, some useful skills might never be acquired. There may be no occasion, if all instruction is subjected to the authenticity criterion, for dealing with formal features of language, such as phonics, grammar, and punctuation, as objects of study. For example, children arguably need to understand the "code"—how sounds are captured in written language, conventions for conveying stress and intonation—for engaging in lifelong literacy; yet the practice activities associated with becoming fluent in such areas may be limited to school practice tasks or reading practice readers. Clearly, balance is important across "doing school" and "doing life."

A second contextual aspect is the type of *classroom discourse* students experience. Sociolinguists such as Cazden (1988) and Philips (1972) note

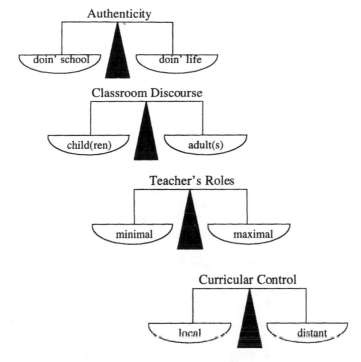

FIGURE 2.2. Balancing contextual factors.

the importance of control, specifically over topics and turn taking. Teachers may control topics and turns, topics but not turns, turns but not topics, or neither topics nor turns. Similar control can be exerted by students. Depending on the goal of the literacy event, activity or lesson, different patterns of classroom talk are appropriate.

Third, the *teachers' roles* within a classroom are closely related to the type of classroom discourse. Au and Raphael (1998) characterize variations in teachers' roles in terms of the amount of teacher control and student activity. They define five teacher roles: (1) explicit instructing; (2) modeling; (3) scaffolding; (4) facilitating; and (5) participating. Roles 2–5 reflect decreasing control by the teacher and increased activity on the part of the student. Au and Raphael's description implies that it is just as mistaken to assume literacy learning is limited to situations in which the teacher is engaged in explicit instruction as it is to assume that learning is meaningful only when the teacher is out of the picture.

A fourth aspect is that of *curricular control*. At one extreme, control is most distant from the classroom (e.g., at the national or state levels) where curriculum is controlled by those least familiar with the specific students studying the curriculum. Such control may be exerted by mandating text-books to be used, specifying of specific standards or benchmarks of performance, and so forth. At the other extreme, control is in the hands of those most intimately involved with the students, specifically classroom teachers or grade-level teams. Balancing across these two extremes is crucial. On the one hand, educators must make clear those standards to which we would hold our students accountable as they move through the curriculum. Fourth-grade teachers have the right to be able to assume that certain curriculum content was covered and mastered prior to students entering grade 4. Similarly, the fourth-grade teacher has a right to know what information his/her students will be held accountable for when they matriculate to their next grade level. To dictate specific instructional methods and even specific curriculum materials for reaching benchmarks and standards is to deny students the right to have those decisions made by the individuals who know them best—their teachers.

Content Continua

Balancing the contextual aspects of literacy instruction sets the stage for balance within the content of what is taught. We next highlight three aspects of the curricular content that have been central to debates about literacy instruction: (1) skill contextualization; (2) text genres; and (3) response to literature (see Figure 2.3).

Skill contextualization reflects the degree to which skills related to our language system, comprehension strategies, composition strategies, and literary analysis are taught within the context of specific texts—either in response to these texts or as invited by them. At one extreme, teachers may rely on a predetermined curriculum of skill instruction, often tied to a curricular scope and sequence that operates within and across grade levels. At the other extreme, the texts and tasks are the determining force behind what is taught: The curriculum is unveiled as teachable moments occur, with the text and tasks functioning as springboards to skill or strategy instruction.

We suggest the need for teachers to operate flexibly between these two extremes. It makes a great deal of sense, for example, to teach about *point of view* as students read historical fiction related to the American Civil War, even if the subject of point of view happens to be scheduled somewhere else in the academic year's guide to curriculum. Conversely, it makes little sense, in the context of reading Bunting's (1994) *Smoky Night* to a group of second graders, to highlight the /fl/ blend in the word *flames* simply because it appeared in the text at the same time that the /fl/ blend popped up in an instructional scope and sequence plan. Yet, strict reliance on emerging questions, issues, or teachable moments

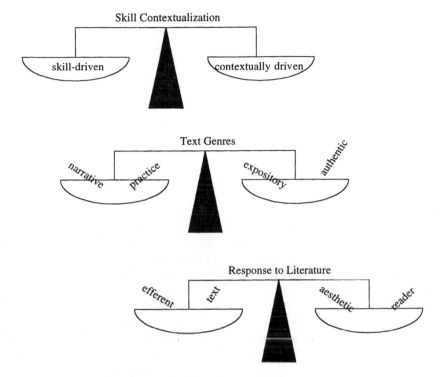

FIGURE 2.3. Balancing curricular content.

as the standard by which teachers determine the content of the literacy curriculum creates problems or uncertainties since, at some point, aspects of the literacy curriculum really do have to be covered.

A second area of content balance is *genre* (see Hicks, 1998; Pappas & Pettegrew, 1998). Genre refers to the types of texts that form the basis of the literacy curriculum—stories, personal narratives, poems, essays, descriptions, and a whole range of specific expository structures. Results of state tests such as the Michigan Educational Assessment Program, as well as the National Assessment of Educational Progress demonstrate the difficulties students have reading and understanding expository text, especially when contrasted with narrative. While there are different explanations of the source of these disparate scores, there is agreement that young children find informational texts challenging to both read and write (Englert, Hiebert, & Stewart, 1988). In our efforts to balance the curriculum, we must ensure that students have the opportunity and the instructional support necessary to make meaning across the range of genres that exist.

The genre debate also involves authentic versus instructional texts. Some literacy educators argue that young readers learn best when reading and responding to authentic literature, which reflects purposeful use of language, complex natural language, and compelling story lines. Others have argued that such literary criteria make little sense for selecting books that young readers need so as to become fluent readers (e.g., Hiebert, 1998). Teachers need the flexibility to travel the full range of positions on this axis as well. Even our youngest students must be able to handle, read (even if it's "pretend read"), and respond to high-quality literary texts—texts written by authors to inform, persuade, entertain, and inspire. However, when it comes to acquiring the skills that enable authentic reading, relying on literature to promote skill development may serve neither the literature nor the skills well. Factors from word placement on a page to relationships between words and pictures may actually make wonderful literary texts poor materials for practicing and fine-tuning skills. Also, the sheer amount of practice reading that early readers need to engage in calls for a host of easy-to-read books that students can read at their independent level. As engaging as these books may be to young and enthusiastic readers, many, perhaps most, may never qualify as quality literature. Neither high-quality trade books nor practice books can serve as the sole diet of books for young readers if they are to become proficient in literate activities.

The third dimension of content balance is *response to literature*. The debate here stems from complex issues related to readers' individual interpretations of text and the tensions concerning social and cultural values that almost inevitably arise in literature discussions. This debate has been traveled along two axes—reader-driven versus text-driven understandings, and conventional (i.e., culturally sanctioned) versus personal interpretations. As our field has moved toward authentic literature as the basis for our reading programs, teachers find themselves face to face with students' response to the content of literature: the enduring themes of the human experience (love, hate, prejudice, friendship, religious values, human rights, and so forth). In reading and discussing Taylor's (1990) *Mississippi Bridge,* students will undoubtedly initiate conversations about how the African Americans were treated by southern whites in the 1930s, which can lead to conversations about racial relations today. When students read and respond to Babbitt's (1975) *Tuck Everlasting,* they often get into issues related to conceptions of life after death, heaven and hell, and the advantages or disadvantages of eternal life.

Debates about response are deeply rooted in beliefs about the functions of schooling, the separation of church and state, and the role of parents and teachers. Further, they are rooted in beliefs about the development of students' interpretive dispositions—whether we privilege the readers' interpretation of the story's meaning, or author's message, or whether there is a "correct" (official or conventional) meaning that teachers are obligated to help students learn for later demonstration that they have acquired that conventional meaning. Balancing response to literature actually involves balancing the tension between the two goals of schooling—connecting to the past and preparing to meet an uncertain future. On the one hand, schools are obligated to teach students the cultural lore of our society, our history, our cultural and linguistic tools, our norms for interaction, and so forth. On the other, schools must build our future citizenry, helping students become adults who can live in a world that will undoubtedly differ significantly from the world we live in today. This tension, between convention and invention, must be addressed through a curriculum that balances the individual with the culture.

CONCLUDING COMMENT: RETHINKING BALANCE

Unpacking the cluster of dimensions in our balance beam metaphor, focusing on the specifics of content and contextual facets that constitute reading instruction, demonstrates some of the complexities in that debate. If we allow teachers the prerogative, for situations and particular students, of positioning themselves on each of these scales independently of the others, then we go a long way toward avoiding the oversimplifications that can so easily overwhelm us in this debate. Teachers are not simply either whole language or skills teachers. At times, for some children, they look like the one; at other times, for other children, they look like the other. This is because they make conscious, intentional decisions about individual students based upon each of these important dimensions. Thus, we believe, there is merit in the metaphor of not one but multiple balance beams, each with at least one axis, sometimes two, that must be traversed thoughtfully and independently. It makes balance a more elusive construct, but also a more powerful one—one that we hope we can all strive to achieve in our teaching.

REFERENCES

Au, K. H., & Raphael, T. E. (1998). Curriculum and teaching in literature-based programs. In T. E. Raphael & K. H. Au (Eds.), *Literature-based instruction: Reshaping the curriculum* (pp. 123–148). Norwood, MA: Christopher-Gordon.
Babbitt, N. (1975). *Tuck everlasting.* New York: Farrar, Straus & Giroux.

Bergeron, B. S. (1990). "What does the term *whole language* mean?: Constructing a definition from the literature." *Journal of Reading Behavior, 22*(4), 301–329.

Bialostock, S. (1997). Offering the olive branch: The rhetoric of insincerity. *Language Arts, 74*(8), 618–629.

Bruce, B. C., & Rubin, A. D. (1993). *Electronic quills: A situated evaluation of using computers for writing in classrooms.* Hillsdale, NJ: Erlbaum.

Bunting, E. (1994). *Smoky night.* San Diego, CA: Harcourt.

Cazden, C. (1988). *Classroom discourse: The language of teaching and learning.* Portsmouth, NH: Heinemann.

Chall, J. S. (1967). *Learning to read: The great debate.* New York: McGraw-Hill.

Chall, J. S. (1997). *Learning to read: The great debate* (3rd ed.). New York: McGraw-Hill.

Daniels, H. (1994). *Literature circles: Voice and choice in the student-centered classroom.* York, ME: Stenhouse.

Englert, C. S., Hiebert, E. H., & Stewart, S. R. (1988). Detection and correction of inconsistencies in the monitoring of expository prose. *Journal of Educational Research, 81,* 221–227.

Goodman, K. (1992). Whole language research: Foundations and development. In S. J. Samuels & Alan E. Farstrup (Eds.), *What research has to say about reading instruction* (2nd ed., pp. 46–69). Newark, DE: International Reading Association.

Goodman, K. S., Shannon, P., Freeman, Y., & Murphy, S. (1988). *Report card on basal readers.* Katonah, NY: Owen.

Gough, P. B., & Hillinger, M. L. (1980). Learning to read: An unnatural act. *Bulletin of the Orton Society, 30,* 171–176.

Harste, J. C., Woodward, V. A., & Burke, C. L. (1984). *Language stories and literacy lessons.* Portsmouth, NH: Heinemann.

Hicks, D. (1998). Narrative discourses as inner and outer world. *Language Arts, 75,* 28–34.

Hiebert, E. H. (1998). Selecting texts for beginning reading instruction. In T. E. Raphael & K. H. Au (Eds.), *Literature-based instruction: Reshaping the curriculum* (pp. 195–218). Norwood, MA: Christopher-Gordon.

Honig, B. (1996). The role of skills in a comprehensive reading program. *California English, 1,* 16–20.

Lyon, G. R. (1997, July 10). *Statement before the Committee on Education and the Workforce.* Washington, DC: U.S. House of Representatives.

Mathews, M. M. (1966). *Teaching to read: Historically considered.* Chicago: University of Chicago Press.

McIntyre, E., & Pressley, M. (1996). *Balanced instruction: Strategies and skills in whole language.* Boston: Christopher-Gordon.

McMahon, S. I., & Raphael, T. E., with Goatley, V. J., & Pardo, L. S. (Eds.). (1997). *The book club connection: Literacy learning and classroom talk.* New York: Teachers College Press.

Pappas, C., & Pettegrew, B. S. (1998). The role of genre in the psycholinguistic guessing game of reading. *Language Arts, 75,* 36–44.

Pearson, P. D. (1976). A psycholinguistic model of reading. *Language Arts, 53,* 309–314.

Philips, S. U. (1972). Participant structures and communicative competence: Warm Springs children in community and classroom. In C. Cazden, V. P. John, & D. Hymes (Eds.), *Functions of language in the classroom.* New York: Teachers College Press.

Sweet, R. W. (1997, May/June). Don't read, don't tell. *Policy Review,* pp. 38–42.

Taylor, M. D. (1990). *Mississippi bridge.* New York: Bantam, Doubleday, Dell.

Chapter 3

HOW WE CAN ACHIEVE BEST PRACTICES IN LITERACY INSTRUCTION

James W. Cunningham

Be aware up front that this chapter is a mix of hopeful optimism and cynical pessimism. I believe that we can achieve best practices in literacy instruction and that eventually we will. On the other hand, I believe that it is highly unlikely we will achieve those practices in the near future and that the situation may well get worse before it gets better. Why do I hold these seemingly contradictory beliefs? Because 28 years of experience working in one or another area of public education have led me to conclude that there are certain unlikely conditions that must prevail before literacy instruction can become widely based on best practices. The first part of this chapter will discuss those conditions and their relationship to the achievement of a best practices approach to teaching reading and writing. The second and last part of this chapter will discuss what we can do as individuals to work for the day when best practices will determine the literacy instruction U.S. public school students receive.

ESSENTIAL CONDITIONS FOR THE ESTABLISHMENT OF BEST PRACTICES IN AMERICAN LITERACY INSTRUCTION

There are at least two essential conditions for the establishment of best practices in literacy instruction in pre-K to grade 12 public schooling: (1) we must stop holding teachers accountable for student literacy learning, and (2) faddism in literacy instruction must give way to a continuing professional consensus.

We Must Stop Holding Teachers Accountable for Student Literacy Learning

Whether in literacy, mathematics, history, or any other school subject, it is antiprofessional to hold teachers accountable for student learning. Think about it. You cannot successfully sue your doctor just because you did not get well. You cannot successfully sue your dentist just because your teeth still hurt. You cannot successfully sue your lawyer just because you were convicted or lost a civil case. You cannot successfully sue your clinical psychologist because you are still anxiety ridden. But you can successfully sue your doctor, dentist, lawyer, or clinical psychologist. The basis for any successful suit, however, must be proof that the professional failed to conform to best practices when treating or defending you. The label for such suits, "malpractice," says it all; they are not called "maloutcome" suits! Why can these professionals and others like them be successfully sued but teachers cannot? Because teachers are being held accountable for student learning outcomes. If we held doctors and clinical psychologists accountable for healing people, dentists accountable for ending tooth pain, and lawyers accountable for winning their cases, then none of those professionals could be successfully sued for malpractice either.

While the ability to be sued successfully is an unfortunate negative indicator of whether one's profession has established best practices, the more-than-compensating positive side is that the members of such professions are free to practice what they know is best without fear of an outcome they cannot control. Again, think about it. There are lawyers who spend their careers defending the poor or the victims of various kinds of discrimination. While they seldom get rich and their percentage of legal victories is often relatively low, they do not live under the constant fear that their state or local government may come in and take over their jobs because they are not "getting results." They are free to practice their profession without fear where it is needed most.

Similarly, there are physicians who spend their careers treating the victims of diseases for which there is currently no known cure or where the success rate is very low. These physicians do not fear that they will be fired or put on probation because they are unable to completely cure their patients. They, too, are free to practice their profession without fear where it is needed most.

Contrast the teaching of literacy. As the push for teacher accountability to reading and writing test scores increases, fewer and fewer teachers want to teach literacy in schools or classrooms with large numbers of struggling readers and writers. And who can blame them? Those who do choose to teach in such places do so at the peril of their careers and reputations. The teachers who are rewarded with merit pay and the praise of their "superiors" are usually those who teach in schools and classrooms with large percentages of middle-class children from highly literate and academically supportive homes.

As long as we hold teachers accountable for student learning, we will not and cannot have best practices. To establish best professional practices in literacy instruction, it must be the practices, not the professional, that are held responsible for teaching students to read and write better.

Why We Won't Soon Stop Holding Teachers Accountable for Student Literacy Learning

There are at least two reasons why it will probably be a long time before we have a best practices model of literacy education in place of holding teachers accountable for students' literacy learning: (1) the nature of our current education elites, and (2) the current politics of public education.

Education Elites

Too many professors of education, employees of state departments of public instruction, employees of central offices in school districts, and public school principals insist on maintaining the current accountability system in some form. Why? Because they do not have to know anything except how to threaten and cajole teachers into "increasing achievement." In a best practices mode, they would actually have to know what those best practices were and how to support and guide teachers' implementation of those best practices in classrooms. It is much easier to use, or advocate the use of, carrots and sticks to get teachers to try harder to do what you could not do yourself.

The Politics of Public Education

Democracy is a very good thing, but it has its limits. Why do we not just let people vote on what the best treatments are for, say, lung cancer? Why do we not allow ads in the media for lung cancer treatments? Would that not be the democratic way? Of course, Laetrile, vitamin C, and the laying on of hands might well become the treatments of choice while chemotherapy, radiation therapy, and surgery might become far less frequently used!

Politics should play no role whatsoever in determining specific professional practices. Think about it. From professional encounters, you ordinarily cannot tell whether your doctor, dentist, lawyer, or clinical psychologist is a democrat or a republican, a conservative or a liberal. Yet, currently we have representatives and senators in Washington, DC, governors and legislators in many states, and local school board members across the country making curricular and instructional decisions in literacy—prescribing this practice, proscribing that practice, and micromanaging school and classroom instructional activities. The vast majority of those politicians could not teach successfully even one day in a public school classroom.

Why is literacy instruction so political? Because it is so important, because such a large portion of local and state budgets go toward the support of public education, and because everyone has experienced or witnessed some of its failures. Health and medical issues have recently become more political for the same reasons. Why aren't politicians legislating medical treatments the way they are legislating literacy instructional materials and methods? Because medicine has a professional consensus and we literacy educators do not.

Faddism in Literacy Instruction Must Give Way to a Continuing Professional Consensus

Instead of holding teachers accountable for student literacy learning, our society must hold them accountable for conforming to best practices in their teaching of literacy. Any literacy teacher who conformed to best practice in his/her teaching would then be protected from responsibility for any lack of student literacy learning. To improve student literacy learning in schools or classes where best practices had been used, the definition of what constitutes best practice in that type of setting would have to be changed. In other words, teachers of literacy would be held accountable for employing best practices and those practices would be held accountable for student literacy learning. The direct link between literacy teachers and student learning outcomes would be severed and replaced by the indirect link all true professions have. Only then will those of us who teach literacy have a profession like dentistry, medicine, clinical psychology, and the law have. Once we had a true profession and its best practices in place, those practices could gradually improve toward the goal of helping all America's children read and write well. Unfortunately, the faddism that has long marked literacy instruction in the United States prevents the establishment of best practices. Before best practices can be established, faddism must give way to a professional consensus about what constitutes the finest reading and writing instruction.

The Various Lores of Literacy Instruction Must Be Reconciled

There are identifiable methods of teaching reading or writing, including methods for teaching particular aspects of the reading or writing process at particular developmental levels. For the most part, each of these methods has a lore—a tradition and a set of beliefs—governing it. While we would be far worse off without the accumulated wisdom of teachers and other literacy educators, the competition of these lores in the arenas of public and professional opinion prevents us from increasing our overall success very much, if at all—especially for struggling readers and writers.

The problem with lore is that it resists change. Because it depends on tradition and beliefs for its power, it must never allow those traditions and beliefs to change more than most adherents are comfortable with. Quantum leaps of progress in lore are just not possible. For example, when medicine was governed by lore, bleeding with leeches and the lack of hand washing before surgery continued for centuries in spite of no successes and numerous failures. Since medicine became a profession with established best practices, the rate of change in how different diseases are treated is almost constant.

Best Practices Must Be Defined and Modified by
Professional Institutions and Procedures

Best practices are not established in a field because the practitioners can generally agree on what the best practices are. Best practices are established because the practitioners can generally agree on how they will decide which practices are best. It is the commitment to a process of evaluating practice, rather than a set of practices, that constitutes the beginning of the establishment of best practices. In most professions with established best practices, the process to which practitioners are generally committed involves funded research on professional practices and boards of professionals empowered to modify best practice, given new research findings. Literacy education will not have best practices until the majority of us agree on how to settle our controversies. Almost certainly, the means for achieving a continuing professional consensus in literacy education will include funded research on literacy professional practices and boards of literacy professionals empowered to apply that research in defining and modifying best literacy instructional practices.

Why Faddism Won't Soon Give Way to Professional Consensus

Faddism results from the competition between lores and coalitions of lores. As soon as the lore that is currently in fashion for teaching literacy is widely shown to be less than satisfactory, it is quickly displaced by a competing lore. Every few years, the same process will be repeated.

A Star Trek Pendulum?

That education, especially literacy education, is a swinging pendulum is an old metaphor. Any of us who have been around long enough to experience a pendulum swing, like the most recent one from whole language to intensive phonics, knows that there is certainly truth to the metaphor. After we have experienced several such pendulum swings, we are no longer inclined to question the metaphor. There is, however, a serious problem with the pendulum metaphor. Watch a clock that has a pendulum. A real pendulum spends as much time at any one point in the arc as it does in another. That is demonstrably not the case with the literacy education pendulum. Our pendulum spends almost all of its time more or less at rest against one extreme limit of the arc. When it does swing, it goes through the middle points so swiftly that some may well question whether it doesn't really enter a *Star Trek*-style warp and instantaneously move to the opposite extreme without ever going through the middle! Our pendulum swings may each be more like a Kuhnian paradigm shift: a revolution followed by an extended period of "normal" practice defined by that revolution.

If the swinging pendulum, albeit with long periods of rest at each extreme, is a metaphor with much truth to commend it, one must wonder why it works that way. My answer is simple: The literacy education pendulum is swung or held in place by passion. Consider the eras that American reading instruction has experienced over the past four or five decades:

- A phonics era (1956–1964)
- A language, literature, and discovery-learning era (1965–1974)
- An individualized specific-skill instruction era (1975–1986)
- A language, literature, and discovery-learning era (1987–1995)
- A phonics era (1996–????)

Of course, different schools and school systems enter or leave an era at various times and implement the new fad to varying degrees, but it is a rare school or system whose reading program remains totally uninfluenced throughout an era.

I believe the case can be made that each of these recent eras in reading education was brought into currency by the zeal of true believers and the tireless efforts of national leaders whom, if this were a history, we could name. As the passion of one set of zealots waned and that of another set of zealots waxed, the pendulum was finally wrested from its extreme position and quickly swung over to the other extreme, where it was again held in position by passion for another 9–12 years.

Interestingly, and sadly, my passion hypothesis also explains why we have never had a "balanced" or "eclectic" era in spite of the fact that most teachers of reading are and have long been balanced/eclectic in their instructional orientation. The downside of balance/eclecticism is precisely its reasoned moderation, its lack of emotion, its innate wishy-washiness. Yet at present, only balance/eclecticism allows us a means to reconcile competing lores. We do not have the funded research on professional practices and boards of professionals empowered to modify best practice, given new research findings, that are the necessary procedures and institutions to establish best practices.

The Politicization of Educational Research

If research on professional practices is essential for the establishment and maintenance of best practices in literacy education, the recent politicization of educational research in general and literacy educational research in particular is a cause for additional concern. Quantitative and qualitative research have recently been taken captive by conservatives and liberals to do their bidding rather than to serve as avenues to new knowledge. For example, today we hear calls for beginning literacy instruction to be based on (and only on) "scientific, replicable research." Of course, those who use this political slogan are demonstrably disingenuous or, at least, woefully ignorant. If they really believed that, they would be as zealously opposed to retention and grammar instruction in the primary grades as they are in favor of synthetic phonics instruction. Moreover, their zeal for synthetic phonics would be mitigated by the fact that scientific, replicable research has so far found no difference by fourth grade on the comprehension or reading habits of children taught to read by synthetic phonics. They would stop concluding that synthetic phonics is best from studies that compared synthetic phonics with no phonics. They would stop concluding that synthetic phonics is best from studies that only found an advantage for synthetic phonics on a test of nonsense words in isolation. Yet, sadly, the research conducted or cited by those who question the research supporting synthetic phonics is often aimed only at audiences who already agree with the authors; they do not present evidence that could persuade fair-minded moderates. Until literacy educational research becomes depoliticized, faddism in literacy instruction will continue to reign.

The Extremism of the Present Is Always Justified
by the Extremism of the Past

The mark of an extremist is that he/she takes the attitude that "those who are not with us are against us." Extremists divide everyone into "them" and "us" (true believers), glossing over differences between moderates and the opposite extreme. The wonderful example today of this kind of extremist thinking is how all those who question intensive, synthetic phonics as the only way to teach beginning reading are labeled by some phonics-firsters as "whole language advocates," even if they questioned whole language in the past as strongly as they now question intensive, synthetic phonics. Of course, it was not many years ago when some in the whole language camp labeled everyone else as "behaviorists" in a parallel manner.

If this glossing over of all but extreme differences were restricted to merely labeling moderates as members of the opposite extreme, it would be relatively harmless ("Sticks and stones may break my bones . . ."). However, this attitude (on the part of whichever group of extremists the most recent pendulum swing has put in position of influence over literacy instruction) causes them to adopt extreme measures to rid classrooms of the vestiges of the now discredited recent era. Without this attitude, the extremists now in the saddle would have to recognize that in fact they share with the moderates a disenchantment with the excesses of the recent era and would work with them to improve matters. Because they would be working together with moderates, the new era would be less extreme, more likely to work, and more likely to last beyond the 9–12 year period we can now expect literacy instructional eras to last. The extreme measures of the current group in power or fashion eliminate that which was good about the last era while eliminating the bad and thereby alienate the moderates who also had concerns about the last era. If we are ever to move from competing lores to best practices in American literacy instruction, we will have to replace the principle that the extremism of the past always justifies the extremism of the present with the principle that two wrongs don't make a right.

TAKING PROFESSIONAL ACTION
IN AN ANTIPROFESSIONAL ERA

As long as we continue to hold teachers accountable for student literacy learning and as long as faddism continues to reign in literacy instruction, I believe we will not, indeed cannot, establish best practices in teaching reading and writing. The question then arises: What should we do in the meantime? To me, the answer to this question is straight-forward: We should focus our efforts on improving literacy instruction school by school.

As a group, teachers are the strongest link in the educational chain, stronger than principals, school board members, supervisors, or college professors. Yet, an individual teacher trying to improve literacy instruc-tion is often powerless against the educational bureaucracy or even against the consensus of the other teachers in his/her school. Moreover, all chil-dren deserve, and many require, a good literacy instructional program every year. One year of good literacy instruction, no matter how effec-tive, is not enough if all our children are to realize their potential in read-ing and writing. Our efforts to improve American literacy instruction therefore cannot focus on just improving teacher education, providing literacy teachers with more money to purchase computers or other in-structional materials, or having good system-wide inservices.

On the other hand, much evidence and common professional ex-perience suggest that top-down mandates from Washington, DC, the state capital, or the central office are unevenly implemented at best. It is par-ticular schools in almost every school district, with their particular prin-cipals, teachers, and communities, that excel or fail in teaching literacy. Our efforts to improve American literacy instruction therefore cannot focus on adopting the right commercial or other literacy program and mandating it across the board.

It seems that the school is neither too big nor too small but just right as the unit of change in literacy education, at least in the current educa-tional environment. How then can one go about working for improved reading and writing instruction at the building level?

Help the School Achieve a Balance in Literacy Instruction

A balanced literacy program is a program that has elements and compo-nents from competing lores of the past and present combined into an efficient and practical composite. While having a balanced program will not ensure best practices in literacy instruction, it is the closest we can ever come to achieving best practices in the current educational environ-ment. Working for balance at the building level means that, in the ab-sence of a national or international professional consensus, individual schools can each construct their own version of what that consensus would be likely to look like.

In my experience, most teachers are balanced/eclectic in disposi-tion, knowing that different emphases from different eras and schools of thought can make a real contribution to some children's literacy learn-ing. The fact that it is so difficult to implement and maintain balanced literacy instruction in schools as a whole indicates how little say teachers have in the way they are expected to teach.

Help the School Achieve a School-Wide Literacy Program

Without the support of the principal, and the teachers as a whole, at least at targeted grade levels, there cannot be a true school-wide literacy program. Change can begin in one or a few classrooms as a pilot program, but there still has to be leadership and consensus building among teachers if children are going to have consistent, high-quality literacy instruction year after year. Teaching all children to read and write well in a school requires a team approach. All regular education, Reading Recovery, Title 1, and Special Education teachers have a role to play in helping children move through the grades and toward their maximum literacy ability. The team approach does not mean that there will be no professional discretion or individual differences across teachers, but it does mean that teachers have to be willing to listen, compromise, grow, and work well together with those who disagree with them. In the absence of established best practices, two (three, four, etc.) heads are better than one.

Help Teachers Execute the Fundamentals of Each Component in Their School's Balanced Program

It is in the nature of top-down mandates in education that those making the mandates believe it is the big things that matter (e.g., what single method of beginning reading you use, what standardized test you administer, what basal reading series you adopt, how many computers each classroom has). Actually, anyone familiar with any professional ability from cabinetmaking to golf can tell you that the little things, the fundamentals, are what really make the difference. In teaching literacy, it is the minute-to-minute, second-to-second execution of discipline and instruction, with all the affective dimensions of both, that determines whether children are learning in that classroom. That, I believe, is the lesson of the classic "First-Grade Studies" and of other more recent research on effective schools. Every method can succeed with most children if taught well by a good teacher. That does not mean that some methods are not better or easier to teach well than others or that one method is better than several done in balance, but it does mean that no method or set of methods will work in the absence of good execution of fundamentals. If we live long enough to see the establishment of best practices in literacy instruction, those best practices will emphasize the execution of fundamentals within whatever broad dimensions of instruction there are.

Help Teachers and Principals Broaden Their Evaluation of Their School's Literacy Program

As long as we continue to hold teachers accountable for student literacy learning, there will be mandated high-stakes assessments of one type or another. We cannot eliminate or ignore them. The main problem with these assessments for a school is that they tend to reduce what the school is trying to teach to that which the high-stakes test assesses. And, the more a school is under the gun because of low scores, the more that school is likely to reduce the breadth and scope of its literacy instruction. Yet, because test scores are never as high as someone would like, even schools with good test scores feel some pressure to reduce their instructional goals to match the content or tasks on the high-stakes assessment. In spite of protests to the contrary, I have yet to see a literacy assessment of any type that does not narrow the curriculum when it is given high-stakes status in a state or district.

There is only one current solution to this problem: Have school-based assessments of the other important goals of literacy instruction not being directly tested for accountability. Because they are school-based assessments only, they can be informal or observational in nature, inexpensive in terms of time and money costs, and do not have to be shared with anyone outside the school. Their value, however, is considerable. They can help keep teacher morale up when the school is improving its instruction in ways that will not significantly impact the high-stakes test for several years. They can be shared with parents to elicit support for the new instructional program of a school that is still being criticized in the media and at school board meetings for relatively low test scores. Most importantly, they serve as an incentive not to narrow instruction to the high-stakes test to the detriment of children's long-term literacy development.

Schools should take action when their high-stakes test scores are low. The problem is that all worthwhile solutions, all solutions that are good for children in the long run, require gradual improvements in all areas of literacy instruction. Broadening the evaluation of literacy instruction in the school is the only way to buy time for the school to put good instruction in place as opposed to instruction designed only to raise students' test scores without actually teaching them to read and write much better.

A FINAL WORD

We can achieve best practices in American literacy instruction, and one day we will. To do so, however, we will have to stop holding teachers accountable for student literacy learning, and faddism in literacy instruction will have to give way to a continuing professional consensus. Of course, we should all work hard for that day to come.

In the meantime, those of us who work in classrooms, schools, central offices, state departments of public instruction, colleges and universities, or other agencies can focus our attention on doing things to help individual schools within our purview develop and execute balanced literacy instruction. Such efforts may well coalesce over time into best literacy instructional practices that will command national or even international consensus. If not, the improved literacy of the children in the schools we were able to affect will still have been worth all our labors.

Part II

STRATEGIES FOR LEARNING AND TEACHING

Chapter 4

BEST PRACTICES FOR A BALANCED EARLY LITERACY PROGRAM

Lesley Mandel Morrow
Elizabeth Asbury

Many theories have been proposed to describe the nature of effective primary literacy instruction. Each theory has emphasized the usefulness of distinctive processes and instruction. Advocates of a particular model hypothesize that children will acquire literacy skills more effectively if they experience one form of literacy instruction rather than another (Chall, 1967; Goodman & Goodman, 1979). Each hypothesis has led to many tests of early literacy programs (Barr, 1984).

The "First-Grade Studies" investigated many approaches to reading instruction and were among the first to research best practices (Bond & Dykstra, 1967). Yet, there wasn't one clear strategy that surpassed another in this work. Investigations continued studying the effectiveness of whole language approaches, decoding systems, and cognitive science-inspired instruction (Adams, 1990; Chall, 1967; King & Goodman, 1990; Pressley et al., 1992).

Studies of the past that compared types of early reading instruction have not provided a complete answer to the question, "What is the nature of effective primary reading instruction?" What we have learned is that effective early literacy instruction is multifaceted rather than based upon one approach or another (Pressley, 1994; Stahl, McKenna, & Pagnucco, 1994). Still, existing data give us few details to add to the generalization that effective instruction often integrates whole language strategies, letter- and word-level teaching, and comprehension processes.

In this chapter, we will describe a study where we observed exemplary practice that created a model for effective literacy instruction. The information from this investigation should provide a window into the details of a balanced early literacy program. In this study it was hypothesized that observations of effective teachers would reveal exemplary practice based upon the teachers' decisions and rationales about what does and does not work in their classrooms.

We observed two first-grade teachers from each of three different school districts. Teachers from these districts were identified as exemplary by their administrators. The designation of exemplary was based upon the evaluation of supervisors concerning the strategies teachers used and ways in which the classrooms were managed. Children's literacy achievement entered into the decision-making process as well.

We visited each classroom eight times during the language arts block and remained twice for a full day. The researchers did 25 hours of observation in each classroom. During our visits we recorded information about literacy instruction that included the schedule of the language arts block, word analysis instruction, comprehension development, language development, assessment strategies, social interaction during literacy instruction, and the physical environment. The data were coded into categories that emerged such as types of reading and writing, teaching skills, use of teachable moments, content area connections, literacy-rich environments, and classroom management.

After the data were coded we began to create a model of exemplary first-grade literacy instruction by integrating data collected on all six teachers. The following description is a case study of one of the teachers involved who had all the characteristics we found to create the model. We believe the model provided by this individual is an example of best practices for first-grade literacy instruction.

A CASE STUDY OF LYDIA KELLY, A TEACHER DISPLAYING EXEMPLARY PRACTICES

Lydia Kelly has been teaching for 9 years in the Hills Park Public Schools. Prior to teaching first grade, she was a kindergarten teacher. Lydia earned her BA degree with a teaching certification and later returned to the university and earned a Master's degree in Education.

The administration of the Hills Park Public Schools placed a high priority on providing staff development for their teachers. The staff development was usually conducted by a person from within the district who received the training necessary to provide the in-service work. In Sterling School, where Lydia Kelly taught, teachers were given a great deal of responsibility in decision making about instruction and development, though the principal assumed a major role. He visited classrooms regularly, frequently interacted with the teachers, and earned their respect. The climate in the school was professional and friendly, the collaboration between the administrators, teachers, and parents creating a positive and productive atmosphere.

Sterling School is a kindergarten through second grade building located in an older but well-maintained suburban community on the outskirts of a major urban city in the Northeast. The school services families of middle to lower-middle incomes. The population in the school is diverse, with 50% of the children white, 20% African American, 10% Hispanic, and 10% from various other backgrounds.

Lydia's students were diverse in ability. The policy in the school supported mixed-ability grouping from the highest to the lowest in all classrooms. Lydia had 23 children in her class. She reported that at the beginning of the school year a few of her first graders were reading, and several read at the second- or third-grade level. Others were still emergent readers who did not yet know the names of letters of the alphabet.

Lydia had a daily 40-minute preparation period. Once a week the prep period was scheduled during the school day. On the other 4 days it was scheduled after the children left school to go home. All of the first-grade teachers met together during their prep time at least twice a week to collaborate with one another about the first-grade curriculum.

A DAY IN THE LIFE OF LYDIA KELLY'S CLASSROOM

As soon as the children entered Lydia Kelly's class, they began to engage in literacy activities. Each child located his/her name and photograph on the attendance chart and turned the picture face up to indicate that he/she was in attendance. Children who were buying lunch signed their names under their choices on the lunch chart. The children then focused their attention onto the daily jobs chart. Lydia changed the children's names on the job chart every day after school. This caused the children to read the chart as soon as they entered the classroom each morning. Those with morning jobs quickly got busy. Damien watered the plants, while Angel fed the rabbit. Patty and Ashley worked together to write the date on the calendar and complete the days of the week charts. Kelly was responsible for completing the weather graph and asked Dalton to help her. Stephanie and Justin were the reporters whose job it was to write one or two sentences of daily news. The news could be something they wanted

to share with the class, or they could talk to Lydia about what was going to happen during the school day and write about it.

The children who were not assigned morning jobs were given a choice of three activities in which they could engage: journal writing, independent or buddy reading, or solving the daily word problem. Angelica wrote about her upcoming sleepover. Darius finished his journal entry and began reading a book about winter, which was the content area theme being studied. As they solved the day's theme-based word problem, David and Joel chorused, "Yes!" At 8:55 Ms. Kelly clapped a rhythm that indicated to the students they had 5 minutes to clean up and come join her on the rug for their morning meeting.

During that meeting, math and language concepts were woven throughout a discussion around the calendar and the weather. The children counted how many days had passed and how many days remained in January. They wrote the date in tallies and represented it in popsicle sticks grouped in tens and ones. Discussion around the calendar was rich with new winter words learned in the winter thematic unit. The two daily reporters read their news aloud.

Lydia then began to write a theme-related morning message that contained news about an upcoming trip to the ice-skating rink. Lydia modeled conventions of print and good penmanship and punctuated her writing with explanations about how print works. Because she was working on punctuation with her students, she included a question and an exclamatory sentence in her message. This enabled her to discuss and explain the question mark and the exclamation point and their appropriate use.

After the message was written and read, Lydia focused the children's attention onto the print by asking them if there was anything in the message they noticed and wanted to point out to the class. The "sh" digraph was a "chunk" they had discussed. David said he noticed the "sh" in "shivers" and circled it in the message. Shanaya noticed the word "ink" in the word "rink." Lydia took the opportunity to reinforce looking for a little word you know inside of an unknown word as being an excellent strategy to use when reading. Lydia asked the children to see if "rink" was written on their Word Wall under the "ink" chunk. Since it was not, Shanaya offered to write it onto the chart along with an illustration.

Next, two children had the opportunity to share things with the class that were brought from home. In the biweekly newsletter, Lydia explained to the parents that the children were learning about winter. She asked them to help the children choose something related to winter to bring to school and to write three clues about what they chose. The item and the clues were carried to school in special lunch boxes marked with question marks, "secret," and "keep out." Each child carefully removed the clues from his/her lunch box, being careful not to expose the item he/she brought. As the child read aloud each clue, he/she called on a classmate to guess what the secret item was. Justin brought an ice hockey puck. No one guessed George had brought a nosewarmer.

Lydia then read a theme-related piece of children's literature, *The Wild Toboggan Ride* (Reid & Fernandes, 1992). The story was about the last toboggan ride of the day, which becomes a zany adventure for a little boy, his grandpa, and some surprised toboggan riders. Lydia chose this text because of its sequenced plot episodes and repeated language patterns. Prior to reading the story, Lydia initiated a discussion about riding down a snow-covered hill. The children brainstormed ways to go down a snowy hill as Lydia listed their ideas. Using the cover illustration, she then explained that a toboggan was a type of sled. The word "toboggan" was added to the posted Winter Words list.

Next, Lydia set a purpose for reading by asking the children to listen while she read in order to learn who rides on the toboggan and why the ride is "wild." While reading aloud, she encouraged the children to join in by reading the repeated words and phrases.

After the story was read, the class talked about who rode on the toboggan and how they got involved in the ride down the hill. As each character in the story was mentioned, Lydia wrote what the children said about his/her role in the story onto sentence strips. She asked the children to read the strips and put them in the correct order in which they happened in the story. Then she introduced the words "first," "next," and "last" as a means to express sequence in a story. She explained that the children would be writing about a time they went sledding or played in the snow. She showed the children a graphic organizer they could use to help them sequence their own stories. The graphic organizer followed the model of the sentence strip activity. Copies of the organizer were placed in the Writing Center for the children's use when writing their own story response.

After engaging in shared reading and writing experiences, Lydia began what she called her Reading Workshop. Lydia explained, and if necessary modeled, center activities for the children to participate in while she met with small groups for guided reading instruction. The following activities were available to the children during the Reading Workshop:

1. *Reading alone or buddy reading books from your book basket.* Each child had a small basket containing books that were on the child's independent reading level. Books read during guided reading groups were placed in the basket along with self-selected texts from the classroom library. Because theme-related books were featured in the class library and in classroom activities, many children were reading books about winter.

2. *Art Center.* Materials for making puppets were available to the children in this area. Lydia had chosen three winter stories with well-defined, sequenced plot episodes for use during shared reading: *The Wild Toboggan Ride* (Reid & Fernandes, 1992), *Do Like Kyla* (Johnson, 1990), and *The Mitten* (Brett, 1989). The children selected characters from the stories to make as puppets that could be used in retellings of the stories. The class was going to work on the puppet shows and perform them for the kindergarten classes at the end of their winter unit.

3. *Writing Center.* In the Writing Center, children wrote their responses to the shared book reading of *The Wild Toboggan Ride* (Reid & Fernandes, 1992). The graphic organizers that were previously modeled were in the center to help the children sequence their stories. Each child collaborated with a partner while writing. After completing the organizer, the children conferred with Lydia and each other to check if their stories were clearly sequenced and if their use of sequencing words was appropriate.

4. *Listening Center.* In this center, the children listened on headsets to tape-recorded stories. Lydia had placed several theme-based books of assorted genres in this area. Some titles were *The Hat* (Brett, 1997), *Rabbit's Wish For Snow: A Native American Legend* (Tchin, 1997), *When Winter Comes* (Maass, 1993), and *Manatee Winter* (Zoehfeld, 1994). Lydia had also made available two tape recorders for the students to record and listen to their own reading of favorite stories and poems. She found this to be a motivating way for the children to develop fluency and expression.

5. *Word Work.* A copy of the Winter Words list was kept in this area. Lydia asked the children to choose a word from the list and, using letter tiles, see how many new words they could make from the letters of the selected word. They were to write their new words on a recording sheet in the center. Completed recording sheets were placed in a marked folder. Recording sheets "still in progress" were placed in another folder for later use.

6. *Computer Center.* Two computers were used throughout the day. During this morning, two children were copying winter poems that had been learned earlier that week. Lydia frequently used poems along with children's books in her themed literacy instruction. She found poetry to be a rich context for teaching word chunks, high-frequency words, phonics, and rhyming. She also highly valued the joy of poetry. Many of the children had started their own "Favorite Poems" books. They often used the computers to write and illustrate the poems they wanted to include in their collections.

7. *Science Center.* Lydia was planning on conducting an experiment with the class later in the day. The children would be timing how long it took for different frozen items to melt. She wanted the children to think

about, write, and explain their estimations prior to carrying out the experiment. A recording sheet was provided. Their predictions would be tallied and graphed prior to the experiment and confirmed and discussed after the experiment was carried out.

The children were reminded that they were required to do two of the activities, read alone or with a buddy and the writing response. They had to spend at least 20 minutes on each. They then could choose which center area they wanted to work in for the remainder of the Reading Workshop. Because the science experiment was to be done that afternoon, Lydia reminded those who had not yet made their predictions to do so today.

While the children engaged in these self-directed activities, Lydia met with small groups of students for guided reading instruction. Lydia had organized her class into five groups of four to five children who had similar reading behaviors, had control of like reading strategies, and were reading on the same level. It was common for the children to frequently move from group to group based upon Lydia's ongoing assessment of their progress. She met with each group three or four times a week for 20–30 minutes. After each group, she assessed the reading development of one or two children by taking running records and listening to the children's story retellings.

This morning's first guided reading group began with a minilesson about attending to print. Lydia had observed that these children were attending only to the first letter of an unknown word, rather than gleaning all the information found in the print. She also wanted these children to learn to cross-check printed information by checking to see if the word they used made sense in the sentence. She wrote a sentence on a small white board leaving one word blank. She asked the children to predict what word might make sense in the blank. She then asked them to predict what the word would look like by writing it onto their small white boards. They then worked together to correctly fill in the missing word of the sentence. After doing three sentences this way, the children discussed how this might help them when they were reading.

Then a new book was introduced to the group. Each child had his/her own copy of the story, *The Crazy Quilt* (Avery & McPhail, 1993). Lydia used a set of leveled books for most of her guided reading instruction. She also used a rubric to level some of her easier-to-read classroom books about winter. She used the books she leveled for guided reading instruction whenever appropriate.

Lydia did a page-by-page "book walk" with the children in which necessary background information and vocabulary was discussed so that the children could read and comprehend the book independently. Following the book walk, the children were directed to begin reading. Each child began to independently read the book. They all read at the same time. Because these were beginning readers, they read aloud in quiet voices. Lydia "listened in" as they read, guiding children who needed it.

After reading the story through twice, the children participated in a brief discussion wherein Lydia praised the use of good reading strategies she had observed in the children's reading. She particularly reinforced cross-checking behaviors and attending fully to print. The children then composed a sentence that modeled the repetitive pattern of the story. The sentence was cut apart and reassembled word by word. Lydia then selected two words from the sentence to be cut apart and reassembled, again emphasizing the need to attend to all the graphophonemic information in a word. As the group was dismissed, each child placed the book he/she had read into his/her book basket to be read later during independent or buddy reading time. Lydia kept records regarding the children's performance during guided reading group on a clipboard. She wrote brief anecdotal notes during and after the group meeting.

Reading Workshop ended at 11:15. Lunch and recess followed from 11:30 to 12:20. When the children returned from recess, Lydia read aloud from *Little Polar Bear, Take Me Home!* (de Beer, 1996). The afternoon's instruction began with the Writing Workshop. Lydia started the workshop with a 10-minute minilesson about the use of capital letters and punctuation. She noticed during her writing conferences with the students that they needed review as to when to use capitals. Though most students were regularly using periods and quotation marks, she wanted to move her students toward consistent use of question marks and exclamation points.

Lydia had written a paragraph from *Little Polar Bear, Take Me Home!* (de Beer, 1996) onto an overhead transparency. She omitted capitals and punctuation from the paragraph. As a class, the children discussed where and why capitals and punctuation needed to be inserted as they edited the paragraph. The children were then dismissed to get their writing folders and went to work for the remaining 35 minutes. Many chose to write books related to the winter theme.

Because the children worked independently, they were at different stages in their writing. Some were drafting new stories; others were editing or working on final drafts at the computer. Throughout the workshop period, Lydia conferred with students individually to discuss their progress and to help them plan on the next step in their writing process. Because Lydia's minilessons often focused on how to peer tutor, the children productively and actively engaged with one another.

After the Writing Workshop, Lydia conducted the whole-group science lesson on melting. The science lesson was followed by a 45-minute Math Workshop period. The day concluded with a 10-minute whole-class meeting where two students' accomplishments were applauded: Paul and Linda had completed publishing their books that day and would share them with the class tomorrow. Lydia then gave last-minute reminders about homework and returning permission slips.

A MODEL OF EXEMPLARY PRACTICE

Lydia's classroom was indeed exemplary. From our observations of Lydia "in action," we see two overarching characteristics of exemplary instruction. First, an exemplary teacher such as Lydia demonstrates intimate knowledge of effective instructional strategies and can masterfully implement them as meaningful learning activities for students. Second, an exemplary teacher has efficient, effective classroom management practices. Lydia's masterful application of instructional theory and practice was observed in three areas of the literacy curriculum—reading, writing, and skills development. We will next look at each of these in detail.

Exemplary Reading Instruction

In Lydia's classroom, the children were engaged in a wide variety of reading contexts and experiences on a daily basis. Reading was done to, with, and by the children (Mooney, 1990). During the morning gathering on the rug, Lydia read a story aloud to the whole class. She always carefully selected a high-quality piece of children's literature that related to the theme under study. The story was read as Lydia sat on a comfortable chair with the children seated on the rug in front of her.

Lydia often formatted this whole-group instruction time as a directed listening–thinking activity. She set a purpose for the reading which was reinforced with discussion before, during, and after the story. The purpose was directly related to a particular reading skill she was working on with the children. The discussions focused the children's attention onto the desired skill.

One day the skill of character development was being emphasized. Lydia wanted her students to add more depth and detail to the characters of their written stories. Lydia drew the children's attention to the characters within the story through discussion. The class then made character webs as Lydia led the children in discovering the details that added to the richness and realness of the characters in the story. Other comprehension skills were emphasized as well in the whole-class reading, as were opportunities for reinforcing word analysis skills. Whole-group reading often entailed reading from large poetry and language experience charts that were later placed around the room.

Children engaged in partner reading independent of the teacher on a daily basis. Each child selected a book of his/her choice from the well-organized and well-stocked classroom library. Lydia taught the children how to self-select books. She taught them strategies to self-select books at their reading level. She also taught the children to determine if they were readers who enjoyed reading books with a lot of illustrations and a little text on a page or readers who preferred a lesser amount of illustrations with a majority of text. The partners helped each other if they needed it and were very engaged in social interactions during the reading. The children kept records of the books they read in their reading logs.

Reading also occurred during the daily meeting of guided reading groups. Lydia used this context to teach the greatest percentage of skills instruction and to individually assess each student's progress on a regular basis. There was a 5-day plan for the meetings, with a different instructional emphasis each day. The basic format for the lessons was, however, an adaptation of the Reading Recovery Model. The lesson most often began by rereading a story previously read and carrying out word analysis activities based upon the vocabulary in the story. Then a new story was introduced to the children by a "book walk" appropriate to the needs of the children in the group. Each child then read his/her own copy of the story.

Lydia listened in as the children read and made anecdotal records to remember their special needs. The discussion that ensued was based upon the observations of the children's reading that Lydia had noted. Throughout the discussion, emphasis was placed on comprehension. Sound symbol relationships and phonemic awareness were discussed as needed. The children then arranged cut-up words from the story into sentences and had sentence strips to sequence and read. They mixed up their words and sentence strips and had to reorganize them to make sense.

Each day in guided reading group lessons Lydia focused attention on a particular child in order to assess his/her strengths and weaknesses. The child was asked to participate in more tasks than the other students had on that given day. Other children participated, but the focus child was especially closely monitored. In this way, not only was the child participating in a small-group setting, but once a week he/she was the target child in an approximation of a one-on-one setting as well. The focus child usually met with Lydia for a few minutes after the group was dismissed so that Lydia could take a running record and listen to a retelling. This was later analyzed and put into the child's reading folder.

Lydia then discussed homework, which often included reading a familiar book to a family member, practicing word cards associated with that book, and reading the new book. A personal note was written to each child's family briefly stating what reading strategies the child had used that day and explaining the homework. Parents were asked to sign the homework card nightly and were encouraged to add notes of their own.

Exemplary Writing Instruction

Children had many opportunities throughout the school day to engage in meaningful writing activities. Lydia valued the symbiotic relationship between reading and writing development. Therefore, she provided her students with many opportunities to write within a variety of meaningful contexts. Writing occurred throughout the day and was integrated into all content areas.

Lydia made use of several journals in her classroom. Each child had a personal journal in which he/she wrote entries on a regular basis, as well as a journal for math and a science journal. Writing in the journals gave the children the opportunity to clarify their thinking, express opinions and feelings, or ask questions about what they were learning in content areas. Lydia found the journals to be useful assessment tools which informed her classroom instruction.

Lydia's students participated in the Writing Workshop on a daily basis. The children generated their own topics as they worked through the writing process. Lydia began the sessions with a whole-group minilesson concerning some element of writing such as using adjectives. The topics for the lessons were selected based upon needs Lydia observed when she met with the children in one-on-one writing conferences. As the children wrote their stories, they engaged in peer conferencing to help them edit and clarify their ideas. The children were guided in how to offer feedback during the whole-class meeting that took place at the end of the Writing Workshop. Lydia carefully taught the children how to offer helpful suggestions to a writer through modeling and through guided practice. Often students who published works shared them with the class at this time. The children's masterpieces, which had often taken 1 or 2 weeks to write, were celebrated by all and placed in the classroom library.

Lydia's students had many opportunities to engage in collaborative writing. The children often worked together as a class to compose messages and stories while Lydia acted as scribe. She used the children's dictation as an opportunity to model concepts about print and meaning making. Often classmates chose to write stories and plays together in the Writing Center. The children frequently collaborated when writing responses to a story that was read during morning group time or during guided reading. The children were encouraged to talk about what they would write with a partner. They would then draft their story and read it to a partner, who offered suggestions for revisions.

Exemplary Skills Instruction

Skill development was evident throughout the day. It was planned and purposeful as well as spontaneous. Lydia had a very systematic method for teaching skills. Her comprehension skill development was embedded in her whole-class storybook reading and small-group guided reading instruction. Many comprehension strategies were taught to the students. These included story retellings, repeated readings of stories to instill the notions of revisiting a text, prediction, drawing conclusions, and knowledge of story structure.

Lydia also had a very strong word analysis program. She worked with vowels, consonants, word chunks, and patterns. She was observed to include some work in word analysis during each visit. It was taught within a whole-group minilesson and reinforced in small-group guided reading and independent work. Poems were used to emphasize specific word analysis skills. Word lists were posted around the room and were added to on a regular basis. Among these were lists of high-frequency words and familiar word families. Rhyming games and the like were available to the children during the language arts block.

Lydia's knowledge about the teaching of skills was impressive. She supported the idea of a strong emphasis upon the learning of skills, but the manner in which they were taught was tantamount. Skills were taught within the context of literature and themes and without the use of commercially prepared worksheets. Any worksheets Lydia used for skill development were self-made and supported her personal philosophy of learning that they must be framed within the context of authentic reading and writing experiences.

Though Lydia had well-planned programs for reading, writing, and skills development, she also consistently took advantage of spontaneous "teachable moments" when they arose. For example, during one of our visits a parent unexpectedly showed up with her daughter's pet rabbit and asked if it could be shown to the children in the class. Lydia graciously accepted the offer and, rather than perceive the visit as an interruption, saw it as a rich learning opportunity.

Lydia quickly planned a system where all of the children could see the rabbit in an organized manner. As the children took turns signing up for visiting times, two children were sent to the library to bring back three books about rabbits, two informational and one picture story book. Lydia was working on stimulating interest in informational books, especially now that her students were stronger readers. She was teaching the children how to use the genre to gather information and saw this as an opportunity to integrate informational literature. The children were then directed to take out their journals. Because Lydia was working on writing questions using appropriate language and punctuation, she directed the children to write two questions they would like to ask about the rabbit.

As the children worked at literacy learning centers, they followed the schedule for visiting with the rabbit. After their visit, they wrote the answers to the questions they had in their journals. They then worked with partners to write and illustrate two facts about rabbits based upon the answers they had written in their journals. The pages were assembled into a class book, which was read at the end of the day.

Lydia masterfully seized this teachable moment. Though this represented a major change in plans, most instances of her taking advantage of teachable moments occurred during brief interactions with students where she would help them to make connections between what they knew and what they were learning. These happened frequently throughout the school day in a variety of teaching contexts.

Another characteristic of exemplary practice as seen in Lydia's classroom was her ability to integrate content area teaching. Lydia's teaching was filled with cross-curricular connections. Her instruction was always based upon a theme. These included author studies, holidays, special events, and natural science or social studies topics. Stories read aloud, books for sustained silent reading, partner reading, and even guided reading were often theme related. Topics for writing were connected, as were center activities for independent work.

Integration across content areas was one of the outstanding characteristics of her classroom. Language arts were woven throughout the fabric of the school day. It is difficult to pull together so many ideas and materials on a daily basis in order to connect reading, writing, math, social studies, science, art, and music by a particular theme. Lydia, however, was able to do this on a daily basis. We were so impressed that we asked her about it. She said it was something she learned about in college and believed in strongly. She said she had worked on this over her years of teaching. "It isn't easy," she stated, "but I believe it's very important to make learning meaningful. Every year I teach, I add to my repertoire of stories, songs, poems, art activities, math, science, social studies, and vocabulary for units of study, holidays, and other special days, and now it isn't difficult to accomplish. I have the materials and ideas."

The second overarching characteristic of exemplary instruction is evidenced in Lydia's classroom management practices. The exemplary teacher has effective and efficient management techniques. Lydia demonstrated these in three areas of classroom life, the first being in the role of rules, routines, and procedures. Secondly, the exemplary teacher recognizes the role played by the physical environment as it affects learning and teaching. Lastly, and perhaps most importantly, the exemplary teacher recognizes the critical role of the affective environment.

THE ROLE OF RULES, ROUTINES, AND PROCEDURES

From the first day of school Lydia worked on teaching her students to be self-directed learners. She believed students should be taught to be responsible for their own learning and progress and to think for themselves. Additionally, it was the only way she could manage her guided reading groups. Therefore, the first few weeks of school were used to master the rules, routines, and procedures for the language arts block which included whole-class minilessons, buddy reading, guided reading, and independent literacy center activities.

An established routine was followed daily. Therefore, children knew what to do in specific settings with or without the teacher. There were routines for morning meetings, for how to find a seat on the rug, for how to handle attendance, and for sharing things brought from home. The management of the day was so well coordinated that when it was snack time, the child who was in charge put on a tape of classical music that signaled everyone to set aside what he/she was doing, take out his/her snack, and enjoy eating and socializing. After approximately 15 minutes, the child in charge turned the tape off and the class went back to work.

There were a set of rules to manage the centers and a set of classroom rules that the children helped to create. Because the rules were created by the class, the children felt a sense of ownership and responsibility to carry them out. Lydia was consistent in making sure she and the children followed the rules that had been formulated. For example, there were three rules for when the children played rhythm instruments together. One rule stated that the instruments were to be silent when the teacher or another student was talking. If a child broke the rule, he/she had to put their instrument away. During one of our visits, Lydia was teaching syllabication using the instruments. When Jennifer played her drum while Lydia was giving directions, Lydia looked over at her and said, "I'm sorry. You'll have to put your drum away, Jennifer." Although she was not happy about having to put away her instrument, Jennifer appeared to understand the reason behind it. Lydia never raised her voice and kept her tone free of antagonism. She almost sounded as if she was giving positive reinforcement.

Because Lydia was consistent in her management techniques, the children knew what was expected of them and acted accordingly. The day flowed seamlessly from one activity to another. Rather than restrict the children, the routines, rules, and procedures provided the structure that ultimately led to children's independence, choice, and intrinsic motivation.

THE ROLE OF THE CLASSROOM PHYSICAL ENVIRONMENT

Lydia recognized the role played by the physical setup of the classroom in classroom management. Lydia designed her classroom space to be "student friendly." Materials were housed so that children had easy access to them. The room was rich with materials that supported instruction. Indeed, Lydia's classroom could be described as a literacy-rich environment.

The room was average in size and rectangular in shape. The children's desks were arranged in groups of four so social interaction was encouraged and space was economized. Provision was made for whole-group, small-group, and one-on-one instruction. The perimeter of the room housed learning centers. The front of the room had a rug for group meetings and minilessons. On the walls by the whole-group area were a calendar, weather charts, a helper chart, rules for the classroom, and other charts with functional information to help the class run smoothly. In this area was a special chair in which Lydia read to the children and where the children could tell about interesting experiences and read stories they had written. An experience chart on an easel was also located in this area.

The table for guided reading was shaped like a half-moon. The teacher sat on one side and the children sat on the other. In this area, the teacher had a pocket chart for sentence strips, individual white boards for word analysis work, leveled reading materials, record-keeping folders, and a flip chart stand for writing charts. There was a spot where the children stored their guided reading books in individual book boxes labeled with their names. Each child also had a small plastic basket that held crayons, scissors, and other materials necessary to carry out his/her work during the day. Lots of charts containing print, including children's work, were hung around the room.

In the literacy center Lydia had a large collection of children's literature that was sorted into separate baskets labeled according to topics, genres, and levels of reading, which made for easy selection for independent reading. A large, colorful rug, soft pillows, and stuffed animal story characters helped to attract students to this area. Children were encouraged to read and to borrow these books. An easy-to-follow borrowing procedure facilitated independent reading of these materials at home. Storytelling materials to accompany certain pieces of literature were also available for the students' use and enjoyment.

Other center areas included art, math, science, and social studies. Each of these areas had materials about content area and special materials linked to current thematic topics. Whatever was being studied was quite evident by the written work, artifacts, charts, posters, and student work on display. There was also an area for manipulative and more playful activities such as blocks, building toys, and puzzle-type materials.

In preparation for independent work, Lydia carefully modeled each of the new tasks at each of the center areas. Students confidently knew how to work productively at each center. Children had to accomplish all tasks described for their self-directed learning, but not in any particular order. The children were free to work at any center in which there was space. Most of the centers comfortably housed four students. Lydia had devised a system for her students to check in and out of the center areas and a means for the students to keep track of what they had done while working in each area. Lydia provided choice within boundaries for her students. She recognized that choice positively affects a student's motivation toward involvement in reading and writing activities.

Lydia was aware of what was happening in her class at all times. Kounin (1970) describes this desirable teacher trait as "withitness." She was always in a position where she could see everyone in the room. If she was involved in a guided reading lesson, she was in a corner of the room where she could simultaneously glance at all the children.

Lydia realized that good planning of interesting activities, movement from one area of the room to the next, and different settings for whole-group, small-group, and one-to-one meetings helped children stay engaged and acted as preventive measures for misbehavior. According to Lydia, if children were actively involved in interesting experiences that were challenging yet could bring success, they were likely to remain engaged in their work.

THE ROLE OF A MOTIVATING AFFECTIVE ENVIRONMENT

Lydia consistently spoke in a soft, warm, and pleasant voice. When she needed to speak to a child about being on task, it was in the same tone of voice that she used when she was teaching a lesson or giving positive feedback. At all times students appeared to respect her and the rules of the classroom. This nurturing and sensitive atmosphere very effectively aided in maintaining discipline and ongoing task involvement. If she saw children off task, she went over to them and helped them redirect their energies. In general, the children were rarely in need of disciplinary action since rules, routines, procedures, and a respectful atmosphere created by the teacher provided a productive, self-correcting atmosphere.

Lydia had a large vocabulary filled with encouraging, positive, and reinforcing phrases such as "I'll bet you'll get that right if you try" and "You really do understand that." The positive reinforcement she offered was for real accomplishment. She offered constructive criticism when necessary, but, once again, it was done with respect and concern for the children's self-esteem.

She said in her interview, "I treat the children as if they are adults. I never talk down to them. I address them in a manner that demonstrates respect since I think they appreciate this. In turn, I have found they treat me and each other in the same way."

Lydia's expectations for her students were high but not unrealistic. Students experienced success often. She made sure of it. She was constantly encouraging them to go forward—but not in a way to cause anxiety.

SUMMARY

Lydia Kelly's classroom was a happy, productive, and wonderful place for any first-grade child. She built a community of learners in her classroom filled with cooperation and respect that was grounded upon high expectation for hard work and achievement.

The children in Lydia's room had the benefit of experiencing literacy in many forms. There was extensive exposure to literature through the use of shared read alouds, independent reading, buddy reading with a peer, and guided reading for skill development. Writing experiences were similar, with journal writing, Writing Workshop, and language experience activities. Both the reading and writing activities were done with authentic purpose. Whatever the literacy theme or the content area unit, it was integrated into the literacy experiences to bring meaning to skill development.

Lydia's classroom was rich with materials for children to experience choice, challenging activities, social interaction, and success. The school day was structured to include varied experiences that were developmentally appropriate yet still retained an emphasis on the acquisition of skills. Children were taught rules, routines, and procedures for using the classroom materials when in self-directed roles. Lydia was consistent in her management techniques. Therefore, the children knew what was expected of them and consequently carried out the work that needed to be done. Consistent routine allowed the day to flow smoothly from one activity to another.

The affective quality in the room was indeed exemplary. Part of this came naturally to Lydia; she was a warm, relaxed, and gentle person. However, a great deal of it was conscious and purposeful. She spoke to the children with respect and in an adult manner. She did not raise her voice, nor did she use punitive remarks, facial expressions, or intonation. Yet, the children learned to understand appropriate classroom behavior.

Several factors contributed to the creation of this very fine classroom. Lydia was a person with a natural talent for teaching who brought a rich wealth of experiential knowledge to her class. Moreover, she was willing to put forth great effort, dedication, and hard work to ensure her students' success. Additionally, Lydia's school supported and expected exemplary practice. The atmosphere in the building was professional and collaborative, one with commitment to excellence.

As a result, what we observed was a very balanced approach to literacy development with strategies that utilized an integrated language arts approach. The children learned through explicit instruction and by collaborative problem-solving situations. Lydia Kelly had developed her own sound philosophy for literacy instruction that was the basis for her classroom instruction. What we saw in her classroom was the result of careful thought, planning, experience, and expertise.

REFERENCES

Adams. M. J. (1990). *Beginning to read.* Cambridge, MA: Harvard University Press.

Avery, K., & McPhail, D. (1993). *The crazy quilt.* Glenview, IL: Scott Foresman.

Barr, R. (1984). Beginning reading instruction: From debate to reformation. In P. D. Pearson (Ed.), *Handbook of reading research* (pp. 545–581). New York: Longman.

Bond, G. L., & Dykstra, R. (1967). The cooperative research program in the first-grade reading instruction. *Reading Research Quarterly, 2,* 5–142.

Brett, J. (1989). *The mitten.* New York: Putnam & Grosset.

Brett, J. (1997). *The hat.* New York: Putnam & Grosset.

Chall, J. S. (1967). *Learning to read: The great debate.* New York: McGraw-Hill.

de Beer, H. (1996). *Little polar bear, take me home!* New York: North-South Books.

Goodman, K. S., & Goodman, Y. M. (1979). Learning to read is natural. In L. B. Resnick & P. A. Weaver (Eds.), *Theory and practice of early reading* (Vol. 1, pp. 137–154). Hillsdale, NJ: Erlbaum.

Johnson, A. (1990). *Do like Kyla.* New York: Scholastic.

King, D. F., & Goodman, K. S. (1990). Whole language: Cherishing learners and their language. *Language, Speech, and Hearing Services in Schools, 21,* 221–227.

Kounin, J. (1970). *Discipline and group management in classrooms.* New York: Holt, Rinehart & Winston.

Maass, R. (1993). *When winter comes.* New York: Scholastic.

Mooney, M. (1990). *Reading to, with, and by children.* Katonah, NY: Owen.

Pressley, M. (1994). Commentary on the ERIC whole language debate. In C. B. Smith (Moderator), *Whole language: The debate* (pp. 155–178). Bloomington, IN: ERIC/REC.

Pressley, M., El-Dinary, P. B., Gaskins, I., Schuder, T., Bergman, J., Almasi, L., & Brown, R. (1992). Beyond direct explanation: Transactional instruction of reading comprehension strategies. *Elementary School Journal, 92,* 511–554.

Reid, S., & Fernandes, E. (1992). *The wild toboggan ride.* New York: Scholastic.

Stahl, S. A., McKenna, M. C., & Pagnucco, J. R. (1994). The effects of whole language instruction: An update and reappraisal. *Educational Psychologist, 9,* 175–186.

Tchin. (1997). *Rabbit's wish for snow: A Native American legend.* New York: Scholastic.

Zoehfeld, K. W. (1994). *Manatee winter.* Norwalk, CT: Trudy.

Chapter 5

WHAT SHOULD WE DO ABOUT PHONICS?

Patricia M. Cunningham

In the mid-1960s when I began my "postcollege" life, the Beatles' "All You Need Is Love" was a hit song and, being young, newly married, and eager to enter the adult world, I wanted it to be true. I wanted to believe that life was simple and that love was "the answer." Before too long, however, I concluded that while you did indeed need love, love was not all you needed.

For the past 50 years, every decade or so, voices start calling out for a simple solution to the "reading problem." In the media, at school board meetings, and in legislatures, you hear the refrain, "All you need is phonics!" While there is a large body of research to support the notion that children do indeed need phonics instruction, the research also suggests that phonics is not all they need. In the first part of this chapter, I will summarize what we know about phonics, reading, and writing. The remainder of this chapter will describe activities that teach phonics in ways that promote its use in real reading and writing.

WHAT WE KNOW ABOUT PHONICS, READING, AND WRITING

Good Readers Can Decode Words— Most Struggling Readers Can't!

The inability of struggling readers to "figure out" words is a fact—obvious to reading specialists and novice parents. The obvious difficulty struggling readers have with decoding is, I believe, the major reason that so many people accept "more phonics" as the obvious solution. But there are many other differences, not nearly so obvious, between good and struggling readers. Good readers are much more apt to have been read to before coming to school. Children who have been read to want to learn to read and pay better attention to beginning reading instruction. They have already learned some words and have developed print concepts that allow them to experience success in their first reading attempts. They have developed phonemic awareness, probably from experiences with nursery rhymes and other rhyming books. They have lots more words in their "listening" vocabularies and thus can decode words more quickly because they get feedback when they recognize them as words. These are just a few of the other not so obvious differences between good readers and struggling ones. A program that will help struggling readers become good readers should include phonics, but it will have limited success if it is limited to phonics.

Phonemic Awareness Is Essential for Children to Learn Phonics

Phonemic awareness is the ability to manipulate the sounds of oral speech. Children who have phonemic awareness can tell you that the first sound in *dog* is "ddd." If you separate the sounds of a word, "hhh—a—ttt," they can tell you that the word you are saying is *hat!* Phonemic awareness is not "beginning phonics." Phonics is knowing relationships between the written form—letters and words—and sounds. Phonemic awareness is strictly an oral ability and does not involve recognizing or naming letters or knowing which letters make which sounds.

Children who enter school with phonemic awareness have a very high likelihood of learning to read successfully. Children who lack phonemic awareness have a great deal of difficulty learning to read. Obviously, children who come without phonemic awareness need to develop it! The question is not *if* but *how.* There have been some elaborate programs developed in which kindergarten and first graders are given 45 minutes to an hour of "pure" phonemic awareness training every day. While these children do indeed develop phonemic awareness, they develop it in a very different way from the children who developed it through home literacy experiences. Phonemic awareness is indeed an understanding about oral language, but many of the home experiences that develop it involve print—rhyming books and early attempts at writing. As they are read to and join in on the reading of books and as they write, children develop phonemic awareness, but that's not all! They also take those important initial steps—desire to read and write, concepts of print, etc.—described in the previous subsection.

Phonemic awareness, an oral understanding of how sounds make up words, is essential to learning phonics, the relationships between letters and sounds. If children lack phonemic awareness when they come to school, it is the responsibility of the school to see to it that they have every opportunity to develop it. The caveat here is to consider how the ones who come with it got it and try to "simulate" the same experiences so that children develop phonemic awareness along with other essential and less obvious understandings (for a thorough discussion of phonemic awareness, see Cunningham, Cunningham, Hoffman, & Yopp, 1998).

Good Readers Develop a Store of Immediately Recognized "Sight" Words

The first time you encounter an unfamiliar-in-print word, you don't recognize it immediately. You have to figure out what it is. You might decode it, or you might hear someone pronounce it. The next time you see that word, you might remember having seen it but you might not remember what it is. Again, you could figure it out or you could ask someone, "What's that word?" Depending on how many repetitions you need to learn words (and that varies greatly from child to child) and on how important and distinctive the word is (most children learn *pizza* and *dinosaur* with few repetitions!), you will eventually get to the point where you "just know it." A sight word, like a good friend, is recognized instantly anywhere. Recognizing most words instantly—and only having to stop and figure out the occasional word—is what allows us to read quickly and fluently.

Children do need to learn to decode—figure out words—but there is a danger in having them figure out all, or almost all, the words as they are beginning to learn to read. The danger is that they will get in the habit of "sounding out" every word, and that is not how good readers read. During the last "phonics era," it was not uncommon to hear children who read like this: "I-t w-i-ll b-e a g—oo—d d—ay." Many of these children had read these common words—*it, will, be, good,* and *day*—many times and should have recognized them as sight words. But they had gotten into the habit of sounding out every word, and habits are hard to break.

Some phonics advocates want to restrict materials that beginners read to include only words they can decode and the absolutely necessary sight words. They argue that this will give children lots of practice decoding and require them to use their decoding skills as they read. In the past, the overuse of "decodable text" has resulted in some children not developing the sight vocabulary necessary for fluent reading.

When You Read, Your Mind Uses the Words to Create Meaning

Again, this is so obvious, it shouldn't be an issue, but if too great an emphasis is placed on figuring out every word, some children will devote all their attention to decoding and will have little "thinking power" left for meaning. This too was evident during the last phonics era when the phenomena of "word callers" was not uncommon. Word callers were wonderful oral readers. Their parents, and sometimes their teachers, were dazzled by what wonderful expressive readers they were! But word callers often couldn't tell you what they'd read immediately after reading it. To them, reading was saying all the words exactly right with great expression, and that is what their brains did when they read.

Making meaning from the words you read does not happen automatically. You have to expect meaning, and you have to develop a self-monitoring system that stops you when "it doesn't make sense." This brings us to another concern about highly decodable text. It is very hard to make much meaning if the text you are reading can only contain words you can decode and if you have only learned a few elements. Many of us remember the linguistic era of the 1960s when children's first texts read: "Dan is in the van. Jan is in the van. The van is tan. Dan ran the van. Jan fans Dan." Children learned to read this and did apply their decoding, but what did it mean? In those days, almost no one had a van and a tan was what you got at the beach, not a common color. If you were telling who was driving, you would say, "Dan *drove* the van," not "Dan *ran* the van." And why does Jan fan Dan? Again, we must think about the habits beginning readers form. If a child is just learning to read and the text being read makes no sense but is just there to practice decoding, some children will get in the habit of turning the meaning-making part of their brains off when they read. This is more apt to be true for children who have not have had lots of experiences of being read to before coming to school—the very children most at risk for reading failure.

The call for decodable text is to a great extent a response to the irresponsible beginning reading texts of the last era in which the demand for real literature and real authors resulted in reading books that even average readers couldn't read! Teachers and publishers are now realizing that beginning readers need meaningful text that they are able to read. In thinking about "only real literature" or "highly decodable text," I am reminded that "Two wrongs don't make a right!"

There is No "Research-Proven" Best Way to Teach Phonics

Bonita Grossen (1997) summarized NICHD (National Institute for Child Health and Development) studies and claimed that these studies supported a *synthetic phonics* approach in which children are explicitly taught the individual sounds and then practice making these sounds and blending (or "synthesizing") them together into words. In a review of these NICHD studies, Allington and Woodside-Jiron (1997) find, however, that their own data do not support the conclusion that synthetic phonics is best: "Thus, the NICHD-supported researchers seem to acknowledge that an early emphasis on code-oriented activities enhances performance on both phonological awareness and pseudo-word pronunciation tasks but that such an emphasis [does] not produce reliable achievement gains on word reading or text comprehension" (p. 8).

Another review of one of these studies (Torgenson, Wagner, & Rashotte, 1997) supports Allington's conclusion: "A second concern is that the gains in phonetic reading skill shown by these children in the group that received direct instruction in these skills did not translate into differential improvement in real-word reading ability" (p. 220). The evidence for synthetic phonics suggests that the children given this type of phonics instruction become better at reading "nonsense words" but not at reading real words or at comprehension.

The question of how best to teach phonics is an important one and should not be too difficult to answer. In reality, it is quite difficult. Basically, there are three kinds of approaches to phonics—synthetic, analytic, and analogic.

Synthetic phonics programs teach sounds first, and then children read words that contain those sounds. When children have learned the short sound for *a* and the sound for *m, t,* and *b,* they read the words *am, at, mat, bat, tab, tam,* and *bam.* As more sounds are added, more "decodable" words are read. The first "stories" the children read contain only words with the sounds they have been taught and a few necessary high-frequency words such as *the, is,* and *on.* "Real" stories are read aloud to the children, but the stories they read are intended primarily to practice decoding. Children also write, but their writing is limited to the words that contain the sounds they have been taught.

Analytic programs begin by teaching children some words and then helping children to "analyze" those words and learn phonics rules and generalizations based on those words. The phonics in most basal readers is analytic, and children read stories using sight words, context, and prediction as they are learning the phonics rules. Phonics is taught gradually over a longer period of time, and children are encouraged to read all kinds of text and write about all kinds of topics. Their reading and writing is not controlled by or limited to the sounds they have been taught.

Analogic phonics is also based on words children have learned to read, but rather than teach them phonics rules, children are taught to notice patterns in words and to use the words they know to figure out other words. In an analogic approach to phonics, children would be taught that if you know how to read and spell *cat,* you can also read and spell *bat, rat, hat, sat,* and other rhyming words. Analogic phonics, like analytic phonics, is taught gradually, and children's reading and writing are not restricted just to the patterns that have been taught.

Determining which phonics approach is best is difficult because at different times children taught in one approach will have a particular though limited advantage over children taught in another approach. Children learning in analytic and analogic approaches will know more sight words in the very early stages of reading, but they won't be as good at decoding isolated words and particularly isolated nonsense words as will children being taught in a synthetic approach. If you look at the early results of these different types of phonics instruction, you will get different results depending on what you measure. By the end of third grade, the differences based on how phonics was taught seem to disappear. When all the other variables are kept equal, none of the three approaches to phonics has been shown to be consistently better.

SO, HOW SHOULD PHONICS BE TAUGHT?

So, what should you do? How should phonics be taught? In the remainder of this chapter, I will describe the approach we take to phonics as part of our balanced literacy framework—the Four Blocks. I will begin by briefly describing the Four Blocks and then describe in more detail what happens during our Words Block, where the phonics instruction takes place. Finally, I will explain why, lacking a clear direction from research, we feel our approach, which is primarily an analogic one, is the best approach in the long run for the wide range of children we teach.

The Four Blocks Framework

The Four Blocks is a framework for primary reading instruction that has two goals. The first is to avoid the pendulum swing and, instead, find a way to combine the major approaches to reading instruction. The second is to meet the needs of children with a wide range of entering literacy levels without putting them into ability groups. In order to meet the goal of providing children with a variety of avenues to becoming literate, instructional time is divided fairly evenly between the four major historical approaches to reading instruction. Each block—Guided Reading, Self-Selected Reading, Writing, and Working with Words—gets 30–40 minutes each day. To meet our second goal of providing for a wide range of literacy levels without ability grouping, we make the instruction within each block as multilevel as possible. Results from a number of different primary classrooms indicate that implementing the Four-Blocks framework resulted in superior reading achievement for a wide range of children (Cunningham, Hall, & Defee, 1998; Cunningham & Allington, 1999).

The Guided Reading Block

Depending on the time of year, the needs of the class, and the personality of the teacher, guided reading lessons are carried out with the currently adopted basal reader, basal readers from previously adopted series, multiple copies of trade books, articles from *My Weekly Reader* or similar magazines, big books, and combinations of these. The purposes of this block are to expose children to a wide range of literature, teach comprehension, and teach children how to read materials that become increasingly harder. The block usually begins with a discussion led by the teacher to build or review any background knowledge necessary to read the selection. Comprehension strategies are taught and practiced during this block. The reading is done in a variety of small-group, partner, and individual formats. After the reading is completed, the whole class is called together to discuss the selection and practice strategies. This block sometimes includes writing in response to reading.

While we don't put children in fixed ability groups for the Guided Reading Block, we use a variety of structures to meet the needs of children who read on a variety of levels. Guided reading time in not spent in grade-level material all week. Rather, teachers choose one grade-level selection and one easier-to-read selection each week. Each selection is read several times, each time for a different purpose in a different format. Rereading enables children who couldn't read the text fluently the first time to achieve fluency by the last reading. Children who need help are not left to read by themselves but are supported in a variety of ways. We do a lot of partner reading and teach children how to help their partners rather than do their reading for them. While some children read the selection by themselves and others read with partners, teachers usually meet with small groups of children. These teacher-supported small groups change on a daily basis and do not include only the low readers. In addition to the daily Guided Reading Block in which all children are included, many teachers schedule a 10-minute easy-reading support group. One way or another, we try to ensure that every child has some guided reading instruction in material at instructional level or easier several days each week.

The Self-Selected Reading Block

During self-selected reading, children choose what they want to read and what parts of their reading they want to respond to. Opportunities are provided for children to share and respond to what is read. Teachers hold individual conferences with children about their books. The Self-Selected Reading Block includes a read-aloud period by the teacher, who reads to the children from a wide range of literature. Next, children read "on their own level" from a variety of books. Every effort is made to have the widest possible range of genre and level available. While the children read, the teacher has conferences with several children each day. The block usually ends with one or two children sharing their book in a "reader's chair" format.

Self-selected reading is multilevel because children choose their own books from a wide range of materials. During the weekly conferences, teachers encourage children to read books on their level and steer them toward books they want to and are able to read.

The Writing Block

The Writing Block is carried out in "Writing Workshop" fashion. It begins with a minilesson during which the teacher writes and models all the things writers do. The teacher thinks aloud—deciding what to write about and then writes. While writing, the teacher models looking at the Word Wall for the spelling of a word as well as inventing the spelling of a few big words. The teacher also makes a few mistakes relating to the items currently on the editor's checklist. When the piece is finished or during the following day's minilesson, the children help the teacher edit the piece for the items on the checklist.

Next the children go to their own writing. They are at all different stages of the writing process—finishing a story, starting a new story, editing, illustrating, etc. While the children write, the teacher has conferences with individuals who are getting ready to publish. The piece they have chosen to publish is revised and edited. This block ends with "author's chair" in which several students each day share work in progress or their published piece.

Because it is not limited by the availability or acceptability of appropriate books, writing is the most multilevel block. When teachers allow children to choose their own topics, accept whatever level of first-draft writing each child can accomplish, and allow them to work on their pieces as many days as needed, all children write on their level. Another opportunity for meeting the various needs and levels of children comes in the publishing conference. As teachers help children publish the piece they have chosen, they have the opportunity to truly "individualize" their teaching. Looking at the writing of the child usually reveals both what the child needs to move forward and what the child is ready to understand. The publishing conference provides the "teachable moment" in which both advanced and struggling writers can be nudged forward.

There is another way in which writing is multilevel. For some children, writing is their best avenue to becoming readers. When children who are struggling with reading write about their own experiences and then read it back (even if no one else can read it!), they are using their own language and experiences to become readers. Often these children who struggle with even the simplest material during the Guided Reading Block can read everything in their writing notebook or folder.

The Words Block

During the daily Words Block, we help children learn to read and spell high-frequency words and teach them strategies for decoding and spelling. The first 10 minutes of this block each day are given to the Word Wall. In the remaining 20–25 minutes, we do a variety of decoding and spelling activities, including Making Words, Using Words You Know, Guess the Covered Word, and others that space does not permit me to describe here (for detailed descriptions of Words Block activities, see Cunningham & Hall, 1997, 1998; Hall & Cunningham, 1998).

Doing the Word Wall. "Doing the Word Wall" is not the same thing as just *having* a Word Wall. Having a Word Wall might mean putting all these words up somewhere in the room and telling students to use them. In our experience, struggling readers can't use them because they don't know them and don't know which is which! "Doing a Word Wall" means (1) being selective and limiting the words to those really common words that children need a lot in writing; (2) adding words gradually—five a week; (3) making words accessible by putting them where everyone can see them, writing them in big black letters and using a variety of colors so that the constantly confused words (*for, from; that, them, they, this,* etc.) are on different colors; (4) practicing the words by chanting and writing them because struggling readers are not usually good visual learners and can't just look at and remember words; (5) doing a variety of review activities to provide enough practice so that the words are read and spelled instantly and automatically; and (6) making sure that Word Wall words are spelled correctly in any writing students do. Teachers who thus "*do* Word Walls" (rather than just *have* Word Walls) report that *all* their children can learn these critical words!

Most teachers add five new words each week and do at least one daily activity in which the children find, write, and chant the spelling of the words. The activity takes longer on the day that words are added because we take time to make sure that students associate meanings with the words and we point out how the words are different from words that they are often confused with.

To begin the Word Wall practice, students number a sheet of paper from 1 to 5 (Figure 5.1). The teacher calls out five words, putting each word in a sentence. As the teacher calls out each word, a child finds and points to that word on the wall and all the children clap and chant its spelling before writing it. When all five words have been written, the teacher writes the words as students check/fix their own papers. On the day that new words are added, the new words are called out, clapped, chanted, and written. These new words are often reviewed on the second day. During the rest of the week, however, any five words from the wall can be called out. Words with which children need much practice are called out almost every day.

Making Words. We spend 10 minutes working on reading and spelling high-frequency words through our Word Wall activity each day. We do a variety of activities during the second part of the Words Block. In

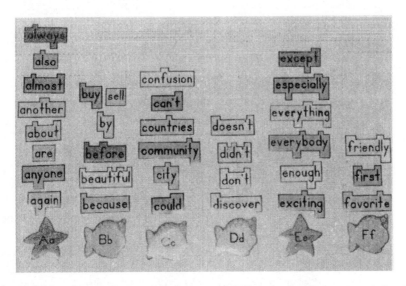

FIGURE 5.1. A partial Word Wall from a third-grade classroom, containing frequently misspelled words, homophones (with clues—buy–sell), and examples for common prefixes, suffixes, and spelling changes (confusion, community, friendly, exciting, countries).

most classrooms, Making Words is done once or twice a week. Making Words is a "hands on" activity in which children learn how changing/adding letters changes words. Each Making Words lesson has three parts. First, children manipulate letters to make 10–15 words, including a "secret" word made from all the letters. Next, they sort the words into patterns. Finally, they learn how to transfer their phonics knowledge by using rhyming words they have made to decode and spell some other rhyming words.

To plan a Making Words lesson, we begin with the "secret" word. We choose the secret word because it fits in with something we are studying and or it has letter patterns we want to work with. The word for this lesson is *Martin*. The children have been learning about famous African Americans, including Martin Luther King, Jr. The words we make from the letters in *Martin* allows us to sort for the *t-r* blend and lots of rhymes. *Using* the letters in Martin, we choose 10–15 words that will give us some easy and harder words and several sets of rhymes. We then decide on the order in which words will be made, beginning with short words and building to larger words. We write these words on index cards to use in the sorting/transferring parts of the lesson.

As the children make the words in their holders, we choose one child who has made the word correctly to come and make it in the pocket chart. As the lesson begins, the letters *a i m n r t* are in the pocket chart. The children have the same letters and a holder. The teacher leads them to make words by saying:

> "Take two letters and make *am*. I *am* your teacher."
> "Now, change just one letter and you can spell *at*. We are *at* school."
> "Add a letter to make the three-letter word *rat*."
> "Now change just one letter and *rat* can become *mat*. In kindergarten you slept on your *mat*. Everyone say *mat*."
> "Change a letter again and turn your *mat* into a *man*."
> "Now change just one letter and *man* can become *tan*."
> "Change *tan* into *ran*."
> "Now change one letter and change *ran* into *ram*. Our high school's mascot is a *ram*. Everyone say *ram*."
> "Let's make one more three letter word *rim*. The top of something like a glass is called a *rim*. Everyone say *rim*."
> "Now, we are going to make some four letter words. Add one letter to *rim* and you will have *trim*. *Trim* is another word for decorate. At Christmas, we *trim* the tree. Stretch out the word *trim* and listen to the sounds you hear yourself saying."
> "Change *trim* to *tram*. You can ride in a *tram*. Everyone say *tram*."

"Take all your letters out and start over and make another four letter word—*main.* You can only hear three sounds in *main* but it takes
four letters to spell it. Think about what letter you can't hear and
where to put it."

"Now change just one letter and *main* can become *rain.*"

"Now, let's make a five-letter word. Add just one letter to *rain* and
you will have a *train.*"

"Has anyone figured out the secret word? I will come around to see
if anyone has the secret word."

Children often have trouble figuring out the secret word when it is a
name—even though all their letters have a capital letter on one side. For
this lesson, no one has yet figured out the secret word and the teacher
gives them a hint:

"It's the name of one of the African Americans we have been studying."

Now several children quickly figure out that their letters can spell *Martin*
and a child who has spelled it correctly—with a capital M in her holder—
goes up and makes it with the pocket chart letters. Then everyone makes
Martin in their holders to finish the first part of the lesson (Figure 5.2).

For the sorting part of the lesson, we put the words on index cards
in the pocket chart. The first sort in this lesson is for beginning sounds.
The teacher tells the children to sort out all the words that don't begin
with a vowel and put them together in columns with all the same letters
up to the vowel. The children are used to sorting for all beginning letters and quickly arrange the pocket chart index cards so that these words
are grouped together:

rat	mat	tan	trim
ran	man		tram
ram	main		train
rim	Martin		
rain			

The teacher and children pronounce all the words, paying special attention to the three *t-r* words. They stretch out *trim, tram,* and *train* and agree
that you can hear both the *t* and the *r* "blended together."

Next we help them sort the words into rhymes:

am	at	man	main	rim
ram	rat	tan	rain	trim
tram	mat	ran	train	

FIGURE 5.2. The "making" part of a Making Words lesson ends when the secret word *Martin* is made with the pocket chart letters and the children all have
Martin made in their holders.

Once the words are sorted into rhymes, we remind the children that rhyming words can help them read and spell words. We then write two new
rhyming words on cards and have them place these words under the
rhyming words and use the rhymes to decode them:

    swim   Spain

Finally, we say two rhyming words and help them use the rhyming words
to figure out how to spell them (Figure 5.3):

    clan   Spam

Making Words is a versatile format for learning about how words
work. We can make the lessons easier by using fewer letters and harder
by including more letters. Our first Making Words lessons contain only
five letters and one vowel. From the letters *a, d, h, n,* and *s,* we can make
the words *an, ad, had, sad, Dan, and, sand, hand,* and *hands.* We can then

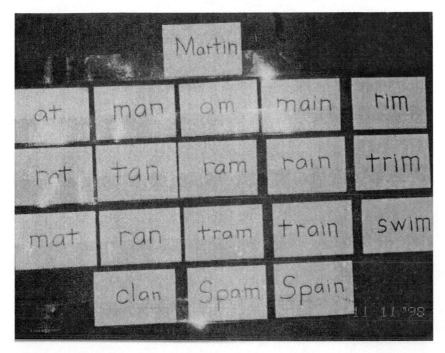

FIGURE 5.3. Here are the rhyming words along with the four transfer words: swim, clan, Spam, and Spain.

sort them by beginning letters and notice that the words that begin with the same letters begin with the same sounds. The final sort is always for rhyming words. Once we have the rhyming words sorted, we can use them to read a few new words—*bad* and *stand*—and spell a few new words— *land* and *plan*. From the letters *a a e b b l l s* we can make *all lab slab blab ball bell sell seal sale bale able sable baseball*. After sorting the words into rhymes, we can use these rhyming words to read *cable* and *swell* and spell *crab* and *whale*.

Using Words You Know. Another activity used in the Words Block to help children learn patterns and how patterns help you read and write is called Using Words You Know. To plan a Using Words You Know lesson, we pick three or four words that our children can read and spell and that have many rhyming words spelled the same way. While about half the Word Wall words are irregular words such as *they, was,* and *have,* other words follow the expected pattern. Many teachers put a star on those Word Wall words such as *big, play, not, make, ride,* and *thing* that help you spell lots of other words and use these in a Using Words You Know activity. Recently we have begun using some well-known brand names that have lots of rhyming words. We bring in packagings with the product names and then use those names as the known words. Children are highly motivated by these products and are fascinated to see how many other words these products can help them read and spell. Here is a sample lesson using ice cream and Cool Whip.

We begin the lesson by displaying the products and letting children talk a little about them. Next we draw their attention to the names and tell them that these names will help them spell and read a lot of other words. Using the board, chart, or overhead, we make columns and head each with one of the key words, underlining the spelling pattern. The students do the same on a sheet of paper. At the beginning of the lesson, their papers look like this:

<u>ice</u>   cr<u>eam</u>   c<u>ool</u>   wh<u>ip</u>

We then show them words that rhyme with *ice, cream, cool,* or *whip.* We do not say these words and do not allow them to say the words but rather have them write them in the column with the same spelling pattern. We send one child to write the word on the chart, board, or overhead. When everyone has the word written under the word that will help them read it, we have them say the known word and the rhyming word. We help them to verbalize the strategy they are using by saying something like "If c-r-e-a-m is *cream,* g-l-e-a-m must be *gleam*" or "If c-o-o-l is *cool,* d-r-o-o-l is *drool.*"

After showing them 8–10 words and having them use the known word to decode them, we help them practice using known words to spell unknown words. To help them spell, we can't show them a word. Rather, we say a word, such as "twice," and have them say the word and write it under the word that it rhymes with. Again, we help them verbalize their strategy by leading them to explain, "If *ice* is spelled i-c-e, *twice* is probably spelled t-w-i-c-e; if *whip* is spelled w-h-i-p, *strip* is probably spelled s-t-r-i-p." Here are what the children's sheets might look like when all the rhyming words have been added:

<u>ice</u>	cr<u>eam</u>	c<u>ool</u>	wh<u>ip</u>
nice	gleam	drool	tip
mice	stream	pool	skip
slice	scream	fool	trip
twice	dream	spool	strip
dice	beam	stool	clip

It is very important for Using Words You Know lessons (and the transfer step of Making Words lessons) that you choose the rhyming words for them to read and spell rather than ask them for rhyming words. In English, there are often two spelling patterns for the same rhyme. If you ask them what rhymes with *cream* or *cool,* they may come up with words with the *e-e-m* pattern such as *seem* and words with the *u-l-e* pattern such as *rule.* The fact that there are two common patterns for many rhymes does not hinder us while reading. When we see the word *drool,* our brain thinks of other *o-o-l* words such as *cool* and *school.* We make this new word *drool* rhyme with *cool* and *school* and then check out this pronunciation with the meaning of whatever we are reading. If we were going to write the word *drool* for the first time, we wouldn't know for sure which spelling pattern to use and we might think of the rhyming word *rule* and use that pattern. Spelling requires both a sense of word patterns and a visual checking sense. When you write a word and think, "That doesn't look right!" and then write it using a different pattern, you are demonstrating that you have developed a visual checking sense. Once children become good at spelling by pattern rather than by putting down one letter for each sound, we help them develop their visual checking sense through a Words Block activity we call "What Looks Right?" (Cunningham, 1995). During Using Words You Know lessons, we are trying to get them to spell based on pattern, and we "finesse" the problem of two patterns by choosing the words we present to them.

Using Words You Know lessons are easy to plan if you use a good rhyming dictionary. We use the *Scholastic Rhyming Dictionary* (Young, 1994). Children enjoy Using Words You Know, especially if the words used are popular products such as *Coke, Crest, Tang,* and *Cat Chow.*

Guess the Covered Word. Many words can be figured out by thinking about what would make sense in a sentence and seeing if the consonants in the word match what you are thinking of. Guess the Covered Word lessons help students learn to cross-check—to simultaneously think about what would make sense and about letters and sounds. To prepare for a Guess the Covered Word activity, we write four to six sentences on the board and cover one word in each sentence. We use sticky notes to cover the words and cover them in such a way that after three or four guesses are made with no letters showing, we can uncover all the letters up to the first vowel. For our first lessons, the sentences follow a similar word pattern, we cover the final word, and we include in our covered words only words that begin with a single initial consonant:

Kevin likes to play <u>soccer</u>.
Sarah likes to play <u>softball</u>.
Devon likes to play <u>basketball</u>.
Juan likes to play <u>hockey</u>.

We begin the activity by reading the first sentence and asking students to guess the covered word. We write three or four guesses next to the sentence. Pointing out to the children that "It sure can be a lot of words when you can't see any letters," we uncover all the letters up to the first vowel (which in these first lessons leaves only one letter covered). We erase guesses that don't begin with that letter and have students suggest possible words that make sense and begin with the correct letter and write these responses. When all the guesses that begin correctly and make sense are written, we uncover the whole word and go on to the next sentence.

We use Guess the Covered Word activities to teach and review all the beginning sounds. As the children begin to understand the strategy they need to use, we don't limit the covered word to the final position. Now they read the whole sentence, skipping the covered word and then coming back to it to make their guesses. We follow the same procedure of getting three or four guesses with no letters showing and then uncovering all the letters up to the first vowel. Here are some sentences we might use when we are focusing on the digraphs *sh, ch, th,* and *wh*:

> Dottie likes to eat <u>cherries</u>.
> <u>Watermelon</u> is Chad's favorite fruit.
> Sean likes <u>cookies</u> with raisins.
> Bob likes strawberry <u>shortcake</u>.
> Chris bakes pies for <u>Thanksgiving</u>.
> David can't decide <u>which</u> pie he likes best.

We teach and practice all the blends with Guess the Covered Word activities:

> Justin goes to camp in the <u>summer</u>.
> Curtis plays baseball in the <u>spring</u>.
> <u>Skiing</u> is Jennifer's favorite sport in the winter.
> Ebony likes to <u>skate</u>.
> <u>Swimming</u> is what Erica is best at.
> Val likes to play all kinds of <u>sports</u>.

Like the other activities, Guess the Covered Word is a versatile strategy. We sometimes use big books and cover a word or two on each page. We also write paragraphs summarizing what we have learned during a science or social studies unit and cover words in it. Through Guess the Covered Word activities, children learn how just guessing words is not a good decoding strategy but when they guess something that makes sense in the sentence, has all the right letters up to the vowel (not just the first one!), and is the right length, they can figure out many new words.

Why We Teach Phonics in the Way We Do

Earlier in this chapter, I contended that their is no "research-proven" best way to teach phonics and that after describing the role our Words Block plays in our balanced reading framework and what we do in our Words Block, I would explain why we do it the way we do.

The Words Block Gets No More—and No Less— than One-Quarter of Our Time

In Four Blocks classrooms, children spend the majority of their time reading and writing. While they read and write, they use the strategies taught during the Words Block. Because they spend so much time reading and writing, they come to enjoy reading and writing and want to get better at them. They attend better to our Word Wall instruction and strategy instruction about how to decode and spell words because they know that very soon they will need to use these words and strategies.

In Our Words Block, We Stress Transfer to Reading and Writing; In the Other Blocks, We Coach Students to Use the Strategies Learned during Words Block

We practice Word Wall words daily, but the real test of the Word Wall is whether or not our students spell Word Wall words correctly in their first-draft writing. As we do the transfer step of Making Words, we emphasize how the words we made and sorted can help students when they come to a word they don't immediately recognize in their reading or need to spell a word while writing. Using Words You Know works directly, enabling children to employ words they already know to decode and spell other words. In Guess the Covered Word, children practice the critical strategy of cross-checking in which they use context and letter-sound knowledge simultaneously to figure out words.

As children are reading and writing, we coach them to apply what we have practiced during the Words Block. When they come to an unknown word in their reading, we encourage them to think of a word with the same spelling pattern or use all the letters up to the vowel just as we do in Guess the Covered Word. While helping children edit their writing, we congratulate them on all the correctly spelled Word Wall words and "fuss a little" at them if they have misspelled a Word Wall word. When we see a word such as *hike* spelled letter-by-letter *hik,* we ask them if they know a word that rhymes with *hike* that might help them figure out how to spell it. In a variety of ways, we constantly remind the children—and ourselves—that what we learn during Words Block is only useful if we apply it while reading and writing.

In Our Words Block, We "Cover All the Bases"

When we are reading, we recognize many words instantly because we have read them before. We figure out other words—sometimes using phonics, other times using the letter sounds we know in that context. When we are writing, we spell most words automatically because we have written them many times before. We have to figure out how to spell other words, and sometimes the pattern we used to spell it doesn't look right and we try another pattern or look it up or hope our computer has the word in its spell check. As people read and write, they know some words and use a variety of strategies to figure out others. Some people are quicker at learning words after just seeing them one or two times, and others rely more on decoding words and figuring out spellings. Some readers rely more on context than phonics to figure out words. Sight word, letter-sound knowledge, and context are all important to decoding and spelling. In our Words Block, we provide abundant practice with all three.

Our "Phonics" Instruction Follows an Analogic Model

Earlier, I suggested that there were three approaches to phonics—synthetic, analytic, and analogic. We use an analogic model because we believe that research on how the brain works is most supportive of that model. Psychologists talk about our brain as a pattern detector. When we see something new, our brain goes looking for other things like that—with the same pattern. For short words, the patterns are beginning letters—all the letters up to the vowel (sometimes called onsets and spelling patterns) and then the vowel and what follows (sometimes called rimes, phonograms, or word families). While there is no research showing that analogic phonics is better than analytic phonics or synthetic phonics, there is abundant evidence that children can decode and spell based on analogy and that analogic instruction improves decoding and spelling (Moustafa, 1997).

Words Block Activities Are Multilevel

If you watched children doing the daily Word Wall practice, you would assume that they were all learning the same thing—how to spell words.

But what they are doing externally may not reveal what they are processing internally. Most of the children can read the Word Wall words. During the daily Word Wall practice, those children who have learned to read the words are learning to spell them. Other children, however, who require lots of practice with words, have not yet learned to read them; through the daily Word Wall practice, they first learn to read them, can spell them correctly when they write because they can find them, and eventually learn to spell them.

Making Words lessons are multilevel in a number of ways. Each lesson begins with short easy words and progresses to some bigger words. Every Making Words lesson ends by the teacher asking, "Has anyone figured out the word we can make if we use all our letters?" Figuring out the secret word in the limited time available is a challenge to even our most advanced readers. Making Words includes children with very limited literacy who enjoy manipulating the letters and making the words even if they don't get them completely made until the word is made with the big pocket chart letters. By ending each lesson by sorting the words into patterns and then using those patterns to read and spell new words, we help children of all levels see how they can use the patterns to read and spell other words.

Using Words You Know lessons provides children who still need it with lots of practice with rhyming words and with the idea that spelling pattern and rhyme are connected. Depending on what they already know, some children realize how words they know can help them decode while other children realize how these words help them spell.

Guess the Covered Word lessons provide review for beginning letter sounds for those who still need it. The most sophisticated readers are consolidating the important strategy of using meaning, all the beginning letters, and word length as cues to the identification of an unknown word.

The Activities Are Fun!

We take the morphemic relationship between the words *activities* and *active* very much to heart and try hard to have our activities be hands on, minds on, manipulative activities. The children cheer for and write the Word Wall words. They manipulate letters as they make words and move words around as they sort them. They write the words in the right columns during Using Words You Know. In addition to engaging our children physically in the activities, we try to include a "puzzle-solving" quality. Every Making Words lesson has a secret word. Can you figure it out? Which of the words you know will help you spell *Spam*? What long word that begins with *s-k* could fit in the following sentence:

He broke his leg when he fell off his _____.

We try to make all our Words Block activities include some active involvement and puzzle solving. Most of our children would tell you, "Words Block is fun!"

Data Support the Four Blocks Framework

Finally, while we don't have data to prove or refute our particular approach to phonics, we do have data that support the Four Blocks framework that includes our approach to phonics. For many years now we have administered Informal Reading Inventories to children in our Four Blocks classrooms, and we are amazed at how well all the children read. Most astonishing are the reading levels of the top and the bottom children in each classroom. We also have standardized test data from a number of different schools around the country that support the use of the Four Blocks framework in many different types of school settings. Our data (Cunningham, Hall, & Defee, 1998) along with our daily observations in Four Blocks classrooms support both the notion of a balanced literacy framework and our answer to the question, "How should we teach phonics?"

REFERENCES

Allington, R. L., & Woodside-Jiron, H. (1997). *Adequacy of a program of research and of a "research synthesis" in shaping educational policy* (No. 1.15). Albany, NY: National Research Center on English Learning and Achievement, University at Albany.

Cunningham, J. W., Cunningham, P. M., Hoffman, J., & Yopp, H. (1998). *Phonemic awareness and the teaching of reading.* Newark, DE: International Reading Association.

Cunningham, P. M. (1995). *Phonics they use: Words for reading and writing.* New York: HarperCollins.

Cunningham, P. M., & Allington, R. L. (1999). *Classrooms that work: They can all read and write* (2nd ed.). New York: HarperCollins.

Cunningham, P. M., & Hall, D. (1997). *Month-by-month phonics for first grade.* Greensboro, NC: Carson-Dellosa.

Cunningham, P. M., & Hall, D. (1998). *Month-by-month phonics for third grade.* Greensboro, NC: Carson-Dellosa.

Cunningham, P. M., Hall, D., & Defee, M. (1998). Nonability grouped multilevel instruction: Eight years later. *The Reading Teacher, 51,* 652–664.

Grossen, B. (1997). *Thirty years of research: What we now know about how children learn to read: A synthesis of research on reading from the National Institute of Child*

Health and Development (www.cftl.org). Santa Cruz, CA: The Center for the Future of Teaching and Learning.

Hall, D., & Cunningham, P. M. (1998). *Month-by-month phonics for second grade.* Greensboro, NC: Carson-Dellosa.

Moustafa, M. (1997). *Beyond traditional phonics.* Portsmouth, NH: Heinemann.

Torgenson, J. K., Wagner, R. K., & Rashotte, C. A. (1997). Prevention and remediation of severe reading disabilities: Keeping the ear in mind. *Scientific Studies of Reading, 1,* 217–234.

Young, S. (1994). *The Scholastic rhyming dictionary.* New York: Scholastic.

Chapter 6

SELF-REGULATED COMPREHENSION PROCESSING AND ITS DEVELOPMENT THROUGH INSTRUCTION

Michael Pressley

For me, best practices are those that stimulate students to read as excellent, mature readers do. I envision a mature reader as a fully self-regulated comprehender. Thus, I begin this chapter with an overview of fully self-regulated comprehension.

Given the recent debates in beginning reading instruction, a word of warning is warranted: Nothing in this chapter is about word recognition or how to teach word recognition skills. Fully self-regulated readers can recognize words fluidly, but so can many readers who are not fully self-regulated. Being able to recognize words and comprehend individual words with facility is a necessary but not sufficient condition for fully self-regulated reading. Fully self-regulated reading is much more about getting the meaning from whole texts than about processing of individual words: hence, such comprehension is emphasized in this chapter. It then follows that instruction which stimulates fully self-regulated reading emphasizes meaning getting above the word level much more than do word-level processes.

THE COMPREHENSION STRATEGIES THAT FULLY SELF-REGULATED COMPREHENDERS USE

Fully self-regulated comprehenders consciously attempt to get the most out of reading, particularly doing what they can to abstract information that serves their goal in reading a text (e.g., to find information for something they are writing, to develop a fuller understanding of the topic of the text, or to figure out the hidden agendas of the author of a text). The most telling studies about conscious processing during skilled reading have employed an approach known as *verbal protocol analysis* (Pressley & Afflerbach, 1995). With this method, skilled comprehenders think aloud as they read a text.

The following strategies and processes are regularly highlighted in such verbal protocols:

- Good comprehenders generally read from first page to last, although they also jump around some, sometimes looking for information they thought might be in the text, sometimes looking back for additional clarification about a point that was confusing at first.
- When good comprehenders encounter information relevant to their current reading goal, they read more slowly than when processing less relevant parts of the text.
- Based on their prior knowledge, good comprehenders anticipate the content of the text being read. As they read, they monitor whether their predictions are accurate.
- Indeed, good comprehenders monitor a great deal as they read. They are aware of the difficulty of the text, the familiarity of the ideas in it, and the quality of the writing.
- Good comprehenders are passionate as they read, reacting to the text based on prior knowledge, accepting some ideas and rejecting others.
- Good comprehenders reflect on the ideas in the text, constructing summaries and reasoning about whether the ideas in the text are sensible.
- Good comprehenders are interpretive, with prior knowledge driving interpretations.
- Good comprehenders often continue to process a text after a first reading, sometimes rereading or reskimming portions that seem especially important. Good readers sometimes explicitly attempt to restate important ideas or summarize the text to make certain that important points can be recalled later.

In summary, good comprehenders are very *strategic* as they read. Their strategies include the following: overviewing, selectively reading, summarizing, and rehearsing information they want to remember for later. Good readers are highly *metacognitive*, which is particularly evident in their monitoring of their comprehension as they read. They consciously use their prior knowledge as they read, for instance, to make predictions about what might be reported in the text. Self-regulated comprehenders unambiguously articulate a variety of comprehension strategies as they read. It is for that reason that teaching students to articulate comprehension strategies is essential in reading programs based on best practices.

One motivation for teaching students to articulate active comprehension processes (i.e., strategies) follows from a disturbing conclusion emanating from analyses of adult comprehension processes: Many adults are not nearly as active as they could be and probably should be in order to read selectively and abstract important information from the text. That is, although some excellent adult readers are active in reading in the ways documented by Pressley and Afflerbach (1995), many adults do not predict before reading, nor do they respond to what they read by generating images and asking questions, nor attempt to summarize and reflect on what they have read. More positively, when researchers have evaluated the hypothesis that children can be taught to self-regulate their reading comprehension processing, often such instruction has proven successful.

INSTRUCTION OF SELF-REGULATED READING

In this section, I will review how self-regulated comprehension processing can be increased by teaching students to use comprehension strategies. Much progress has been made in recent years in understanding the effects of comprehension strategy instruction.

Roehler and Duffy's Conception of Reading Strategies Instruction

Roehler and Duffy (1984) hypothesized that reading strategies instruction should begin with teacher explanations of the various strategies that students can use to read text, followed by mental modeling of the use of the strategies (i.e., showing students how to apply reading strategies by thinking aloud; Duffy & Roehler, 1989). Then students are provided opportunities to practice the strategies in the context of real reading, with the students thinking aloud about how they are using strategies as they read. Such practice is monitored by the teacher, who provides additional explanations and modeling as needed. Teacher feedback and instruction is reduced as students become more and more independent (i.e., instruction is scaffolded). Teachers encourage transfer of strategies by going over when and where the strategies being learned might be used. Throughout the day and across days, weeks, and months, teachers can cue use of strategies when students encounter situations where they might be applied profitably. Cuing and prompting continues until students autonomously apply the strategies they were taught.

Roehler and Duffy's analysis particularly stimulated a number of educators to teach repertoires of comprehension strategies directly (Pressley et al., 1992). My associates and I dubbed such instruction as "transactional strategies instruction" (Pressley et al., 1992), because it emphasized reader transactions with texts (Rosenblatt, 1978)—that is, interpretations constructed by readers thinking about text together (i.e., transacting; e.g., Hutchins, 1991), and teacher's and students' reactions to text affecting each other's individual thinking about text (i.e., interactions were transactional; e.g., Bell, 1968).

Transactional Strategies Instruction

Transactional strategies instruction involves direct explanations and teacher modeling of comprehension strategies, followed by guided practice of strategies. Teacher assistance is provided on an as-needed basis (i.e., strategy instruction is "scaffolded"; Wood, Bruner, & Ross, 1976). There are lively discussions of texts, with students encouraged to interpret and respond to text as they are exposed to diverse reactions to it by their classmates. Student discussions are flexible, with no restrictions on the order of strategies execution or when the particular members of the group can participate (see Gaskins, Anderson, Pressley, Cunicelli, & Satlow, 1993). The transactional strategies instructional approach succeeds in stimulating interpretive dialogues in which strategic processes are used as interpretive vehicles, with consistently high engagement by all group members. One of the most striking aspects of transactional strategies instruction is that it takes a while, with instruction occurring over semesters and years. This contrasts substantially with the very brief comprehension strategies instruction that was evaluated in the early 1980s (e.g., Palincsar & Brown, 1984).

There have been three published experimental evaluations of long-term transactional strategies instruction: Brown, Pressley, Van Meter, and Schuder (1996) with grade 2 students; Collins (1991) with grades 5 and 6 students; and Anderson (1992) with middle school and high school students (see also Anderson & Roit, 1993). Transactional strategies instruction produced better comprehension test scores and more interpretive readers in these studies, with the effects quite striking in all three of the evaluations.

In summary, in the past quarter century there has been a great deal of evidence produced consistent with the general conclusion that comprehension strategies instruction improves understanding of text, especially when children are taught to use such strategies. Although the early studies were extremely limited in scope (i.e., single or a few strategies evaluated in short-term experiments), the more recent work reviewed briefly in this section has evaluated credible instructional packages delivered over a semester to a year of instruction, consistent with the practices of many educators who are committed to developing strategic comprehension processing in their students through instruction followed by strategies practice.

Success in teaching comprehension strategies at the grade 2 level in Brown et al. (1996) made clear that such instruction is possible during the primary years. In contrast, when my colleagues and I have observed the teaching of individual comprehension strategies at the grade 1 level (Pressley et al., 1992), prediction is the one strategy we frequently observed in first grade. I have never observed grade 1 teachers who succeeded in getting their students to coordinate the use of two or more comprehension strategies, however.

Because this chapter is brief, I could not possibly begin to do justice to describing how transactional strategies instruction unfolds in a classroom. The paper by Pressley et al. (1992) does so, as does the chapter on comprehension instruction in Pressley, Woloshyn, and associates (1995).

CONCLUDING REFLECTIONS

At any age/grade level, there are students who can pretty much read on their own those texts that are intended for their age and grade, with good comprehension. The instructional work reviewed in this chapter makes clear that those other students at the same age/grade level who are experiencing difficulties in reading comprehension can improve their reading through instruction of reading comprehension strategies.

Much of the instructional research was informed by researcher understanding of the nature of skilled reading. Successful strategy instructional researchers typically have tested a particular version of the hypothesis that teaching weaker readers to do what better readers do will improve the reading of the weaker readers. That said, I emphasize that there really has been very little long-term research aimed at development of self-regulated reading in students. Moreover, the really telling experiment in which students would receive instruction promoting self-regulation throughout their schooling remains to be performed. In short, I reflect with regret that no one has yet evaluated the hypothesis that a schooling career immersed in high-quality instruction aimed at promoting self-regulated comprehension would, in fact, produce much better comprehenders than typical elementary-grades instruction.

Virtually all of the instructional work considered in this chapter was carried out with weaker readers. An interesting possibility is that weaker readers are not the only ones who might benefit from instruction to promote self-regulation, especially with respect to the more advanced reading skills, such as comprehension strategies. There is a very great need for serious study of the effects of instruction for self-regulation on the reading of good and average readers. Until such work is carried out, my thinking is that it makes sense to teach comprehension strategies to all readers, for the bottom line is that when verbal protocols of children's and high school students' reading are studied, there is little evidence of fully self-regulated comprehension strategy use (Pressley & Afflerbach, 1995).

Despite the prominent work validating comprehension strategies instruction in the elementary grades, there is good reason to believe that little such instruction is occurring. Recently, Pressley, Wharton-McDonald, Mistretta, and Echevarria (1998) observed grade 4 and grade 5 classrooms in upstate New York, watching literacy instruction in them over the course of the school year. One of the most striking observations was that very little comprehension strategies instruction was occurring. Rather, most teachers seemed to operate by the theory that students can learn how to comprehend simply by doing massive reading. Virtually every classroom included a poster saying, "Read, Read, Read, Read." Of course, that is good advice but not enough. Thus, despite the fact that much more is now known than when Durkin (1978/1979) observed little comprehension instruction in the later elementary grades, things have not changed much with respect to comprehension instruction in the elementary grades.

Is there an explanation? The current enthusiasm for the "Read, Read, Read, Read" philosophy of literacy development is the whole language perspective. Whole language is a decided anti-instructionalist position. Although the potential negative impact of the whole language perspective on the primary-level curriculum has been the focus of much discussion in recent years, whole language has also had great effects on upper-grades language arts instruction—in fact, slanting it toward an immersion in literature approach to the exclusion of other approaches.

There are certainly many in the great debates who seem to feel that if primary-level word recognition skills are mastered, the reading development problem is solved. In fact, based on the perspective developed in this chapter, the conclusion is quite the contrary—that word recognition skills are an important beginning, but that skilled reading requires the development of many skills that permit operation on text above the word level. The evidence is growing that elementary children can be taught to use the comprehension strategies used by excellent, mature comprehenders. Moreover, when they learn such strategies, their comprehension improves (Pressley & Afflerbach, 1995). It is my hope that the lessons from the research covered in this chapter go far toward changing the way reading instruction occurs in the upper elementary grades and beyond. There is plenty of reason to believe that student comprehension can be improved by consistent instruction that encourages students to relate their prior knowledge to the text being read, predict ideas that might be in the text, interpret the text, construct images and summaries capturing the ideas expressed there, and raise questions and seek clarification when confused. In best practices classrooms in the upper elementary grades and beyond, students should be taught to use such strategies along with much encouragement to apply the above comprehension processes during reading.

REFERENCES

Anderson, V. (1992). A teacher development project in transactional strategy instruction for teachers of severely reading-disabled adolescents. *Teaching and Teacher Education, 8,* 391–403.

Anderson, V., & Roit, M. (1993). Planning and implementing collaborative strategy instruction for delayed readers in grades 6–10. *Elementary School Journal, 94,* 121–137.

Bell, R. Q. (1968). A reinterpretation of the direction of effects in studies of socialization. *Psychological Review, 75,* 81–95.

Brown, R., Pressley, M., Van Meter, P., & Schuder, T. (1996). A quasi-experimental validation of transactional strategies instruction with low-achieving second grade readers. *Journal of Educational Psychology, 88,* 18–37.

Collins, C. (1991). Reading instruction that increases thinking abilities. *Journal of Reading, 34,* 510–516.

Duffy, G. G., & Roehler, L. R. (1989). Why strategy instruction is so difficult and what we need to do about it. In C. B. McCormick, G. Miller, & M. Pressley (Eds.), *Cognitive strategy research: From basic research to educational applications* (pp. 133–154). New York: Springer-Verlag.

Durkin, D. (1978/1979). What classroom observations reveal about reading comprehension instruction. *Reading Research Quarterly, 15,* 481–533.

Gaskins, I. W., Anderson, R. C., Pressley, M., Cunicelli, E. A., & Satlow, E. (1993). Six teachers' dialogue during cognitive process instruction. *Elementary School Journal, 93,* 277–304.

Hutchins, E. (1991). The social organization of distributed cognition. In L. Resnick, J. M. Levine, & S. D. Teasley (Eds.), *Perspectives on socially shared cognition* (pp. 283–307). Washington, DC: American Psychological Association.

Palincsar, A. S., & Brown, A. L. (1984). Reciprocal teaching of comprehension-fostering and monitoring activities. *Cognition and Instruction, 1,* 117–175.

Pressley, M., & Afflerbach, P. (1995). *Verbal protocols of reading: The nature of constructively responsive reading.* Hillsdale, NJ: Erlbaum.

Pressley, M., El-Dinary, P. B., Gaskins, I., Schuder, T., Bergman, J., Almasi, L., & Brown, R. (1992). Beyond direct explanation: Transactional instruction of reading comprehension strategies. *Elementary School Journal, 92,* 511–554.

Pressley, M., Wharton-McDonald, R., Mistretta, J., & Echevarria, M. (1998). The nature of literacy instruction in ten grade-4/5 classrooms in upstate New York. *Scientific Studies of Reading, 2,* 159–194.

Pressley, M., Woloshyn, V. E., & associates. (1995). *Cognitive strategy instruction that really improves academic performance* (2nd ed.). Cambridge, MA: Brookline Books.

Roehler, L. R., & Duffy, G. G. (1984). Direct explanation of comprehension processes. In G. G. Duffy, L. R. Roehler, & J. Mason (Eds.), *Comprehension instruction: Perspectives and suggestions* (pp. 265–280). New York: Longman.

Rosenblatt, L. M. (1978). *The reader, the text, the poem: The transactional theory of the literary work.* Carbondale: Southern Illinois University Press.

Wood, S. S., Bruner, J. S., & Ross, G. (1976). The role of tutoring in problem solving. *Journal of Child Psychology and Psychiatry, 17,* 89–100.

Chapter 7

COMPREHENSION: CRAFTING UNDERSTANDING

Cathy Collins Block

Something happened today. I took out our class tape recorder because Tiana wanted to hear herself read. No matter how hard I jiggled the wires, pushed buttons, and checked batteries, the recorder wouldn't work. I apologized and explained that I had tested it the night before so that it would be ready for her. Feeling my distress, Tiana leaned across the table, touched my arm, and gently whispered, "I understand how you feel. Until today, I felt the same way when I read. Things never worked out for me either. I had no idea why. I did everything I was supposed to." To make me feel better, she picked up *The Velveteen Rabbit,* read the first page perfectly, and then continued, "Yesterday, during our Meaning-Makers Group, you asked me what I wished I could do to comprehend better. For the first time I realized that I wanted to cling to meanings more. What everyone suggested worked! Today, I'm reading the words more rapidly and the thoughts more slowly. I don't combine every word that the author says so quickly that I can't know each idea. Today, ideas just jump off the page. I must rush down the lines to capture them as they leap into the pictures in my mind." Prior to this moment, Tiana had never read voluntarily and she had talked only after someone else had done the reading. Today Tiana truly began to comprehend.

*   *   *

The purpose of this chapter is to describe the recent history and effective methods of teaching comprehension. A basic tenet of this discussion is that understanding occurs on several levels simultaneously and that in order to help students comprehend more completely, reading programs must differentiate the types of instruction that they provide. Just as students employ a variety of strategies to decode new words, they must also be taught to use a variety of comprehension strategies before making meaning can come more directly under their control.

This new instructional approach presents comprehension as a crafting process—one in which understanding is constructed by students, authors, and teachers working artistically together to create knowledge. This process also enables readers to initiate their own thinking and discover authors' intentions as they simultaneously learn content. In addition, from this perspective, comprehension is viewed as more than a type of imprinting, whereby authors and educators impart ideas and universally accepted truths. Students are more than tabulae rasae to be scripted, or as molds to be filled. They are sculptors.

The approach is also influenced by sociopsycholinguistics. A reader's purpose, state of mind, experiences with the English language, and background knowledge are as important in making meaning, as are the printed words and the social/historical/political context in which every text is interpreted (Bakhtin, 1993; Bloome, 1986; Rosenblatt, 1978). Thus, if students are to craft a more enriched understanding they must be taught how to experience a broad continuum of thoughts, bordered on one side by authors' intended meanings and on the other by their personal applications of text to their lives. Through such lessons, books can also more frequently become the windows through which students look at the world anew, see who they are, and increase their own personal insights (Galda, 1997; Pressley, Harris, & Guthrie, 1995; Gaskins, Gaskins, & Gaskins, 1991; Mangieri & Block, 1996).

Before students can reach these levels of crafting ability, schools must overcome the limitations in present forms of instruction. First, new comprehension lessons should demonstrate how students can use authorial clues and comprehension strategies interactively. Second, teachers must model how it is useful to stop reading from time to time so as to craft meaning. In addition, as debates intensify as to the prominence that direct instruction should hold in teaching comprehension, lessons which promote a middle-ground philosophy have become fashionable but ill defined. Proponents sympathetic to the position that students can learn to read by reading are acknowledging the need for more direct instruction. At the same time, those who champion structured instruction are realizing the benefits of encouraging affective responses to literature (Gambrell, 1997; Hillerich, 1991; Morrow, 1997).

Further, new comprehension lessons must be neither too prescriptive, stifling, and depersonalized, on the one hand, nor too free flowing and unmonitored, on the other. When these conditions exist, students do not learn how to craft meaning unless a specific genre is very familiar to them (Block, 1993, 1997). Similarly, when free reading and unlimited choices of reading materials overdominate direct instruction, many pupils will not develop adequate comprehension skills and will continuously struggle to attain only a semblance of meaning. In these instances, the intense concentration necessary to make meaning gives way to the less effort-filled goal of reading merely to confirm their own ill-formed opinions and unsubstantiated positions. Alternatively, no matter how well students engage in comprehension strategies, if they do not have the opportunity to read what they want, they may never fall under the spell of wonderful texts.

A fifth limitation with some of our past comprehension lessons is that while beginning and struggling readers spend time listening to high-quality literature, they often do not master enough comprehension strategies so that they can read silently unaided. Likewise, without adequate instruction older readers are "making compromises with the demands of text." In other words, rather than pausing to investigate a detail, many students merely "come up with a make-do interpretation that will enable them to keep reading" (Mackey, 1997, p. 454). They do not craft their own understanding, but instead engage in "good enough reading." At this level of comprehension, students simply (1) accept that some ideas will remain vague to them, (2) skip too many words, (3) resist ferreting meaning from long sentences and paragraphs, (4) fail to capture enough of the authors' details to accurately interpret upcoming events, and (5) fill gaps in literal comprehension by inserting personal experiences rather than textual information. Moreover, when such students realize that their limited understanding is not sufficient to create a complete comprehension, they merely press on, reading word by word, and hope that clarity will somehow magically emerge.

To overcome these limitations, three new types of comprehension lessons should be used to (1) build eustress and positive values toward literacy (Type 1 lessons); (2) increase risk taking through interactive use of strategic thinking processes so that a more complete comprehension can occur during silent reading (Type 2 lessons); and (3) strengthen students' desires to learn more about the reading process and about their own efficacy as valid crafters of comprehension (Type 3 lessons). Through such lessons, students can learn how to integrate their literal/interpretive/applied/metacognitive thoughts with past experiences, story grammar, and the author's writing style to concurrently realize his/her purposes and their own reading goals. These lessons do not cast comprehension as dichotomous processes, such as individual reader responses versus literal comprehension gains, fictional rather than nonfictional reading, self-selection of books as opposed to direct instruction, or stimulating efferent responses devoid of aesthetic responses to reading. Instead, these lessons capitalize upon the interactive qualities that all of these components contribute to comprehension. To teach students to craft meaning, these lessons demonstrate how understanding demands patience, skill, continuous revision, accurate interpretation of the information at hand, and strategic thinking that generates new insights through individual and collective metacognition, discussions of printed text, and personal reflection.

Each of these new comprehension lessons have a unique goal. When successful, Type 1 lessons culminate with students using reading to grow as human beings; Type 2s increase students' repertoire of comprehension strategies; and Type 3s enable students to learn more about themselves as readers and how they can continue to advance to higher levels of comprehension ability.

TYPE 1 LESSONS: SUSTAINING FLUSTRESS

The purpose of Type 1 lessons is to provide enough time for students to not merely read but to live within a book. In these lessons, students are provided the supports and choices necessary to transport themselves into narrative and expository texts so they can make their own meanings and expand or enhance their lives. Such crafting emphasizes the personal value of reading, which is facilitated—but not controlled—by the teacher. To craft comprehension at this level, Type 1 lessons teach transformational thinking. Students are guided to create personal meanings, deduced from texts. These individualized interpretations become broader and deeper (and often only tangentially related to the text's original intent) than in Type 2 or Type 3 lessons. Often students will move texts in ways that the authors never imagined. They will also learn that every text is communicating an incomplete message. Books are a restrained reflection of reality because authors must be selective and as a result leave gaps in the stories that they pen. Students are taught that printed stories are only glimpses of the messages and lives that writers have to give. Moreover, if students had been present to experience an author's story, they would not have selected the exact words to describe the journey, emphasized the same meanings, nor deduced the same lessons as the author. Students will experience why a complete comprehension can not occur if they merely accept authors' messages without reflection. For all of these reasons, Type 1 lessons are designed to teach students how to develop their personal reflection, to free their creativity, to value their own worth as valid comprehension crafters, to respond to print uniquely, to care deeply about authors' messages, and to interpret new ideas into the broader contexts in their own lives.

To reach these goals, Type 1 lessons must be incorporated into instruction each week. Students need privacy, and larger blocks of uninterrupted time than are presently allotted in many classrooms. Students need to learn what to read, for how long, and where they will read so as to most enjoy the crafting of comprehension. Moreover, Type 1 lessons don't begin with instruction, brainstorming, semantic webs, picture walks, student discovery, or KWLs (*K*now; *W*ant to Learn; *L*earned), nor do they end with asking students to perform a task about what they comprehended. Instead, students select their own books and reading goals and are taught to self-initiate processes that expert readers use to surmise and reengage their motivation when it wanes. Books selected for these lessons keep students thinking about what they discovered in them days after they are finished; other books will seem lacking in comparison.

To review, in Type 1 lessons, students have time to read without having to perform a task about what they comprehended; they craft for their own purposes, which they establish just before they begin. For example, in Mr. Gonzales's fifth-grade classroom in Grapevine–Colleyville Elementary School, right before a Type 1 lesson begins, he reviews the qualities of avid readers that he wants his pupils to emulate and that are posted on a chart in the room: "TAKE RISKS to infer so your reading becomes informative and enjoyable simultaneously; REREAD when you become confused or your mind wanders; STAY ENGAGED by adding to your purposes and making a deeper commitment to use this time to improve your knowledge and your lives." He also displays sentence starters to help students set a goal before reading: "I want to become a better reader by _____; I want to learn more about _____; I don't know _____; I'm curious about _____; To make better grades, I'll _____; I have ideas about _____; or, I have these questions that I want to answer by reading this book: _____."

Type 1 lessons are different from past basal homogeneous group instruction and guided reading experiences in that high-quality literature is not used to teach skilis. When literature is used solely for this purpose, it fuels students' misconceptions that there are only a few acceptable interpretations and that reading is to be done only for someone else's good (e.g., they must read so that their teachers can measure how much they have learned or to determine how good they are at recalling words and remembering facts). In our past, some schools attempted Type 1 lessons through the use of Sustained Silent Reading (SSR). SSR was ineffective in moving students into a relaxed and receptive state of mind ("eustress") because the experience was not preceded by teaching them how to engage their own purposes, how to craft their understandings on several levels simultaneously, and how to use expert crafting abilities throughout each SSR experience. Such lessons also inadvertently decreased students' volition and pleasure in reading because, when left to their own devices, they often limited the breadth and depth of literature which they selected to read. Contrastingly, the primary purpose of Type 1 lessons is to provide time at school for students to attain these goals unaided and to learn that reading can become a highly personal and meaningful activity.

Type 1 lessons can result in other educational benefits as well. They can increase reading comprehension, writing complexity, self-esteem, and attitude toward school (Block & Cavanaugh, 1998; Elley, 1992; Krashen, 1993). For example, if students read silently for 20 minutes a day, they can increase their speaking, listening, and reading vocabularies by 2,000 words annually (Baker & Brown, 1984) and significantly increase their reading achievement (Allington, 1996; Fielding, Wilson, & Anderson, 1984). Moreover, all children, including second language learners (Weber, 1991), emergent readers (Purcell-Gates, 1996), and less able readers (Block, 1997), can acquire more control over language through Type 1 lessons.

What Do Type 1 Lessons Look Like in the Classroom? There are two kinds of Type 1 lessons. The first are silent reading experiences for the whole class, small groups, or individuals. At these times, teachers become master craftsmen roaming the room as students raise their hands when text becomes confusing. Students are seated in places of choice, as shown in Figure 7.1. At these moments, teachers tell individual students the meaning of specific words rather than teach them a decoding lesson so as not to interrupt eustress, an engrossed reading experience. Similarly, in Type 1 lessons, teachers address individual comprehension needs within a text *as single pupils encounter a point of confusion while crafting alone.*

The second kind of Type 1 lesson involves orally reading books to a whole class or small group. Through teachers' oral readings students can enjoy the pleasure of quality literature and shared reading experiences. These lessons differ from traditional shared reading experiences, however, in that teachers may pause from these Type 1 lessons' read alouds only for two purposes: (1) for children to report *how they are making the author's story their own,* or (2) to answer students' questions about how to make meaning. Moreover, the teacher does not say the first words after a reading; students do. This is necessary because whoever performs most of the dialogue during a book discussion controls the crafting. Discus-

FIGURE 7.1. Ms. Dormier Collier's first graders selected which books they wanted to read, why they wanted to read them, whom they would read it with, and where they would read. After 20 minutes, these students were still engrossed in their readings, unaware that it was time to go to recess.

sions are student-initiated conversations that focus upon how this oral reading enriched students' knowledge or life (Raphael & Au, 1997), and/ or how students are making this author's story their own. Such conversations will be more powerful if the books selected to be read aloud contain (1) a surprise that reversed the plot; (2) an action-filled segment; (3) a character who repeatedly attempts to resolve a problem and/or says and does something insightful; or (4) an event that triggers a change in the usual order of things happening in students' lives.

To illustrate, contrast the way books were read aloud by Ms. Martin in her Type 1 lesson to traditional shared reading experiences. In this second-grade class, students selected the book that would be read orally to the class and decided whether they wanted classmates to stop the reading to make comments or whether this reading was to be completed without students inserting their comments. Because the latter was chosen, during Ms. Martin's reading students raised their hands when they had something to share but no one spoke. An adult volunteer (or, in other classrooms, an older schoolmate) listed students' names in order and recorded the page numbers that triggered each thought. This list determined who would begin the book conversation when the oral reading was complete. Questions at the close of this (and all Type 1 lessons) were transformational, about growth in students themselves or humanity, as discovered through issues examined in the text. This activity was brought to an end by students suggesting a strategy that they wanted to learn to deepen their crafting competencies. This strategy became the objective of the Type 2 lesson that Ms. Martin taught the next day.

In summary, Type 1 lessons replicate real-world reading as closely as possible. They enhance the former practices of going to the library to appreciate good literature, comprehension skill-building activities, SSR periods, and Rosenblatt's (1978) methods of setting a stage for aesthetic reading. How? First, Type 1 lessons help students to become self-seeking lifetime readers because they build time at school for students to develop the habit of curling up with good books. Second, they increase the time students spend at school in an uninterrupted sustained reading of quality literature. Third, because Type 1 lessons are prefaced by instruction in how to set their own goals, students learn to turn to reading to discover more about topics that they value.

TYPE 2 LESSONS: LEARNING HOW TO CRAFT MEANING

The purpose of Type 2 lessons is to teach students how to make meanings by integrating several comprehension strategies simultaneously. Teachers achieve this goal by telling stories about themselves as readers and about what they do to craft meaning at specific points in a text. They demonstrate how they craft by sharing expanded explanations, preparing examples in advance, and teaching in the cognitively and affectively rich context of quality literacy so that students want to read. Through Type 2 lessons, students learn how to (1) build intertextuality; (2) comprehend on literal/inferential/applied levels simultaneously; (3) add depth and breadth to their knowledge base; (4) link efferent/aesthetic thinking processes as they craft meaning; (5) make connections between words, facts, and concepts and the historical/political context in which they were written (Turner & Paris, 1995; Block & Mangieri, 1996); (6) fill the gaps in narrative and expository trajectories (Golden & Rumelhart, 1993); (7) craft meaning by relating two books; and (8) "till a text." A description of these strategies is provided in Table 7.1.

"Tilling" strategies prepare students to more fully comprehend the unique features of an individual text that they are about to read. These tilling strategies are modeled after the agricultural model. Students must learn how to prepare their minds (as farmers first prepare the soil) before authors' ideas can blossom and bear the fruits of meaning, reflection, and productive translations into students' lives. Tilling the text

TABLE 7.1. How to Create Type 2 Lessons

In the past, comprehension instruction included:	In instructing students how to *craft* comprehension, we:
Preteaching vocabulary in isolation	Teach that most new long words will be content specific
	Model how to derive meaning from approximately five new concept words in key paragraphs from the text while tilling the text.
"Picture walking"	Demonstrate skimming and scanning of subtitles, length of paragraphs, and tilling the text to discern author's intentions. Be aware that a considerable level of energy will need to be invested to reach goals before students begin to read.
KWL (Know; Want to know; Learned), mapping, story grammar	Assist readers to understand the connections between events in a story (story maps or story frames) and the types of paragraph structures that author's use. By doing so, we will increase their abilities to predict while reading (Loxterman, Beck, & McKeown, 1994). When connections between writing formats are made clear, students also begin to think ahead more frequently and gain a greater sense of control over reading. In turn, when story grammar is contemplated while reading, literary works can come to be viewed more as "friends" because they possess the quality of dependability.
Setting purposes for students	Try to avoid establishing readers' purposes too often so that they may instead learn to do so themselves. It often takes repeated trials before readers trust themselves that they *can* assume ownership before they read. To teach them to do so, ask them to scan the text to discern which part captured their mind and attention.

(*continued*)

TABLE 7.1. (*continued*)

In the past, comprehension instruction included:	In instructing students how to *craft* comprehension, we:
Building background knowledge	Help readers to recognize when their prior knowledge contains naive or incorrect information. In the process, they must learn how to successfully reconcile new and conflicting information. Without this instruction, students will either ignore new vocabulary because they believe that they already have the needed information or, when a conflict in information occurs, they are "pushed out" of crafting (Sipe, 1997). To help students discern naive background knowledge (1) demonstrate how they can probe their beliefs prior to reading; (2) model how they can know when their background experiences are inadequate to "read between the lines" in a book; (3) encourage students to place themselves in the story; and (4) teach students to identify the questions they want to ask when they read.
Encouraging reader response	Seek to build motivation out of children's natural curiosity, social inclinations, and yearnings for self-determination. Such motivation comes in the act of setting and reaching a goal about something important.
Teaching skills	Promote strategies that (1) emphasize deeper reflection; (2) help students interpret new information for themselves; (3) afford opportunities to form opinions by learning to collect evidence and take a reasoned stand; (4) develop language cuing systems, such as the graphophonic system (spelling, sound, and phonic relationships), the syntactic system (grammar or structure of the language), and the semantic/pragmatic system (personal and social meaning in a specific situational context).

(*continued*)

TABLE 7.1. *(continued)*

In the past, comprehension instruction included:	In instructing students how to *craft* comprehension, we:
Telling names of authors/illustrators	Help readers focus their attention on authorial writing styles. Among the first steps in text tilling is to understand how and why an author divides his/her topic into chapters or subtopics. In performing this analysis, readers become alert to dense concepts and writing styles, apply more intense concentration, and use comprehension and metacognitive processes. They also become aware that each text was composed by an author who had a specific purpose in mind, and they consider what that is.
Asking literal questions	Teach paragraph functions while building reflectivity. Read a story orally to the class that is displayed on an overhead transparency. Pause to talk about the story along the way, and model the thought processes you used. Then, ask students to talk about subsequent paragraphs as they read the story with you. Provide an overview for the entire text; explain to readers the various roles of paragraphs, such as the introductory, explanatory/descriptive cause–effect, time/spatial/sequential, and summarizing/concluding functions. Build reflectivity by teaching students how to (1) generate alternate hypotheses; (2) describe how characters evolve through the story and how images are created; (3) ask questions that link background knowledge to the story; and (4) stop and reflect by giving them a comprehension strategy and asking under what circumstances they think they will be called upon to use similar strategies in the future.

expands students' use of content, authorial, and textual clues as they appear in individual and representative texts. Through Type 2 lessons, students learn how to (1) attend to author's writing style as they read; (2) scan a text to integrate subheadings and print features (such as the length of paragraphs and amount of white space) to set their own purposes for reading as well as to judge its conceptual density; (3) apply their own background knowledge so it does not interfere with but expands meaning making; and (4) deduce the meanings of new, content-specific vocabulary (Block, 1997).

In Type 2 lessons, crafting strategies are taught *before point of need*. Teachers plan Type 2 lessons by identifying literary strategies students need and points in a book that will call upon those types of strategies to craft a specific meaning. Teaching how to craft at these specific, difficult points in a text, before students begin to read, results in fewer students misinterpreting literal meanings. By doing so, pupils can glean more ideas from the author's literal/inferential meanings, taking more risks to posit their own possibilities and predictions with higher levels of thought and accuracy. By tilling a text before they read, students also discover subdivisions of subject matter and story grammar that will support continuous, uninterrupted strategic thinking throughout a reading. In Type 2 lessons, teachers also explain textual features, subtleties in the author's choice of words, and how to use the *teacher within* (students' metacognitions, prior experiences, and personal goals) and *teachers without* (peers, teachers, and other print/visual/oral media) when comprehension difficulties emerge. These Type 2 strategies assist students to overcome comprehension deficits created by their lack of knowledge about the subject matter (Cain-Thoreson, Lippman, & McClendon-Magnuson, 1997; Pressley & Afflerbach, 1995).

For example, teachers say, "Here's a difficult point that you will experience in this and other texts. Whenever you come to a paragraph like this I suggest that you do something like this . . . [perform a think aloud]." To teach an author's intent, instead of allowing students to just read a selection and then asking, "What was your favorite part?" teachers say, "This is a study about . . . [the author's intent in a work]. What do you believe will be important to do in reading this piece?" In like manner, instead of asking, "Who was your favorite character and why?" teachers integrate interpretative/applicative strategies with instruction in how characters develop. They say, "This character was my favorite because _____. Am I correct, in your judgment? Why or why not?" Similarly, to teach young readers how to find main ideas, teachers ask students to hold up a finger for the first sentence in the paragraph and to hold up a second finger when the subject changes. Then, at the end of the paragraph, if only one finger is held up, the first sentence is the main idea. Also, they describe what it is about a selection that students can love (e.g., "This piece gives us the opportunity to reach for ideas about _____.") The best books for Type 2 Lessons are quality fictional and nonfictional works that present big themes, reflect real issues about life and the world, and describe common human conditions that are written on students' instructional level (Galda, 1997; Pardo, 1997; Raphael & Au, 1997).

Type 2 lessons eliminate isolated skill and strategy instruction because strategies are taught within the context of reading individual texts and a specific authorial style. Without such lessons, when some teachers become overwhelmed at how limited their students' comprehension is, they reduce the breadth of their objectives, overly prescribe repetitive worksheet drills, and merely monitor their pupils' decoding performances. In the process, a step-by-step, word-by-word language emerges that shapes the way reading is perceived by students. Teaching Type 2 lessons limits the possibility that such a segmented conception of reading will be created by teachers and passed on to students.

What Do Type 2 Lessons Look Like in the Classroom? Type 2 lessons begin with teachers surveying a text that provides something students need. For example, if students are experiencing difficulty comprehending author's intent, teachers select a book that has ample opportunities to apply that set of strategies and crafting process to address that particular need as students read. Then, they model how to integrate these strategies with those previously taught to craft greater understanding and to uncover more inferential meanings. Teachers demonstrate how to make such meanings by stopping at key points in the text to apply strategies interactively, and they describe what they are thinking as they do. Next, students practice such interactive reading with that text until they can self-initiate these strategies unaided. For example, Ms. Canteras showed her fourth graders how to till the text, simultaneously using predicting and context clues strategies to tie new words and ideas together (see Figure 7.2). Then, in a postreading discussion readers regrouped to report new connotations they created and how these new crafting tools enhanced their comprehension abilities. Thus, in Type 2 conversations, students do not repeat something they heard their teachers' say or have memorized; they report what they thought as they are creating meaning and how they crafted their comprehension.

In summary, Type 2 lessons increase the power of reader response discussions because they scaffold a text at critical points so students can continue to craft meaning. Through these lessons, teachers strengthen pupils' volition and reflection; they do not allow students to struggle alone without a master craftsmen to guide them, nor do they go to the opposite extreme and teach skills only after a reading has stumped and frus-

FIGURE 7.2. Ms. Dana Perez has introduced the predictive thinking cycle and is asking students to use this process while they deduce the meanings of new vocabulary terms in the shared reading of a book.

trated their students. They are present when students read silently and when they are in small groups. They talk students through their first applications of integrating comprehension strategies through suggestions and feedback. As pupils attempt to apply crafting strategies interactively, teachers model how knowledge-transforming thinking can permeate their minds as they read; so students can come to more automatically connect text to their background knowledge, engage in inferencing, and integrate information across paragraphs. Such metacognition is highly correlated to strong comprehension scores. On the other hand, without Type 2 lessons, at best many students simply store literal information in incomplete, often inaccurate paraphrases. This practice is negatively correlated with comprehension achievement (Pressley, 1998; Block, 1997).

TYPE 3 LESSONS: CHOOSING WHAT THEY WANT TO LEARN ABOUT READING

The goal of Type 3 lessons is to create time in the reading curriculum for students to discuss new methods of improving their reading abilities. These lessons allow students to apply both the cognitive and affective powers of choice and challenge (Turner & Paris, 1995) to solve problems in their reading abilities that they diagnose. Type 3 lessons enable pupils to become their own guides as master craftsmen. Alternatively, if comprehension instruction disregards students' ideas about how to become better readers, it neglects an essential glue that activates the depth of self-knowledge necessary for them to select reading as a lifelong, essential, and pleasure-filled endeavor. Moreover, because structures in the brain link emotion, memory, and perception, reaching deeper levels of comprehension rests upon students' abilities to unite reason, feelings, knowledge of self, and authors' goals simultaneously when reading. Thus, as students become more aware of and expand their capabilities as crafters, they will experience more enriched feelings and gains in knowledge (Caine & Caine, 1997). Thus, when Type 3 lessons are successful, students craft more memorable understandings, enhance their own comprehension strengths, and eliminate their reading weaknesses. Such elicitation of this self-concept involvement is essential, as at all times students are the people who are most aware of the level of effort (and are sensitive to the level of drive) that they can and are willing to expend to become more powerful crafters. Increasing their levels of effort and drive is the purpose of Type 3 lessons.

Because optimal motivation emerges when individuals operate at their highest capability, Type 3 lessons strengthen intrinsic motivation. In the ideal situation, as new insights about the reading process are discovered, students improve their reading skills because they want to employ these new insights to meet more difficult comprehension challenges. Similarly, in order to avoid boredom, they will self-initiate more effort and drive to learn new comprehension strategies so that they can craft understandings of more advanced authors' thoughts. The goal is for students to choose to use their full cognitive capacities as they read and to recognize that unleashing their intuition can play an important role in all levels of comprehension, even in grasping literal facts (Greene, 1998).

These lessons provide time for teachers to listen to students' stories about their lives as readers, their reading abilities, and their literacy goals so that they can incorporate these valuable insights into their comprehension instructional program. In Type 3 lessons, students tell their teachers what they depend on to read, as well as what they need to comprehend more completely. Much like days of old when knowledge grew through fireside family conversations and time spent in by-the-bench mentoring discussions, these lessons enable teachers to ask more questions of students, such as "What are you thinking?" or "What are you learning?" or "What is bothering you about your reading abilities?" Teachers can then use these oral story-like answers to guide literacy instruction. Without this time, many students would not report this information.

Type 3 activities extend the benefits of book clubs, literature circles, and reading responses groups because they allow students to choose what they want to learn *about the reading process* and not just what they want to read. Books selected for Type 3 lessons are rich in opportunities for students to practice reading strategies selected by students as their greatest areas of need. Both expository and narrative texts are used.

What Do Type 3 Lessons Look Like in the Classroom? There are two kinds of Type 3 lessons. The first, discovery discussions, are one-to-one conferences where teachers and students form a partnership. In discovery discussions, either students or teachers can initiate a discussion about insights they have had about a pupil's reading ability. These discovery discussions enable single students to tell very specific stories about their reading abilities, learn intensely in their zone of proximal development, and communicate with their teachers about the very next step they want to take to become a better reader. Discovery discussions are not top-down interrogations as is the case with many one-to-one teacher–student conferences. Instead, when they have something they want to discuss, students can sign up for a time to meet with their teacher as a regular segment of the reading instructional schedule. Simultaneously, teachers can request a discovery discussion by signing up for time in a student's schedule to discuss something that they just observed about that student's reading abilities. To become trusted mentors, teachers do not rush from one student to another. During discovery discussions segments of the day, teachers must provide individual pupils with undivided attention, as the most important part of discovery discussions often occurs at the end of the session. It is at these latter times that many students gain the confidence and comfort level to risk asking a very important question or sharing a very personal insight about their reading weaknesses.

The second kind of Type 3 lesson is student-initiated literacy process learning groups. These small group meetings begin by asking students, "What strategy do you need to read better?" Students select a group where that aspect of the reading process will be taught and discussed in a more focused way than in other types of lessons. During these group meetings, students discuss what they do to accomplish this aspect of the reading process. Students and teachers also offer suggestions for overcoming specific reading problems within this domain of the comprehension process, as Tiana illustrated in the vignette that opened this chapter. These meetings are held no more frequently that twice a week; between meeting times, students practice the suggestions they have learned. During the second student-initiated literacy learning meeting each week, students teach peers what they have learned about that aspect of crafting meaning. For example, Figure 7.3 describes the student-selected

MEANING MAKERS	We want to learn how to understand better, make more in-depth responses to material read, and learn new strategies to craft understanding.
TRANSFORMER TITANS	We want to learn how we can more rapidly apply what we read to our lives.
BREADTH BUILDERS	We want to find more genres that we want to read so we can enjoy more types of books.
WORD WANTERS	We want to learn more decoding strategies. We will bring a book we are reading to group meetings to model how we decoded a difficult word. We will ask classmates to find similar words using these methods in their books and try out their strategies in our books.
SPEED MONGRELS	We want to increase our speed of oral and silent reading.
MEMORY MENDERS	We want to find ways to retain more of what we read.
CRITICAL ANALYZERS	We want to learn how better to connect what we read to other readings and aspects of the world. We also want to learn how to reflect on what we read more.
AUTHOR ASKERS	We want to confront the author with such questions as "What does he/she mean here? Does this make sense with what he/she told us before?" (Beck, McKeown, Hamilton, & Jucan, 1997, p. 332). We also want to learn how to consider the author's ideas and fallibility, grappling with his/her text to dig for deeper meanings; to write to authors about fictional writing decisions they have made; and to call on experts in fields related to our nonfictional quests.

FIGURE 7.3. Student-initiated literacy learning groups.

groups as created by Ms. Edward's fourth graders at Bell Manor Elementary School (in Bedford, Texas). As the closing question for all Type 3 lessons, we ask, "What is your plan when this obstacle arises today and in the future when you read?"

Type 3 lessons are based on the premise that often best teaching occurs through active listening. To change control in the classroom, teachers must permit students to have choice over what they want to learn about themselves as readers (Figure 7.4). Such lessons create a learning community where inside jokes, shared personal insights, and laughter assist students and their teacher to bond together as a group and to enhance the enjoyment of reading. Type 3 lessons also increase the number of questions students ask about reading, which in turn expands their comprehension ability, as students who pose questions score higher on standardized comprehension tests than do students who simply discuss the material they have read (Block, 1993; Graham & Block, 1994; King, 1994). This occurs because the act of generating questions requires reconceptualization, which in turn enhances learning and reinforces retention (King,

FIGURE 7.4. Ms. Dormier Collier, first-grade teacher at Waverly Park Elementary, is holding a Word-Wanters Student-Initiated Literacy Process Group meeting. While she was doing this, Figure 7.1 (p. 104) depicts what other students were doing, as they were engaged in a Type 1 comprehension lesson.

1994; Collins, 1992; Block & Cavanaugh, 1998; Block, 1993). Hence, the thinking process taught during Type 3 lessons, knowledge construction, is a powerful tool to expand children's comprehension.

In summary, when the teaching of comprehension is viewed as a crafting process, students' understanding about reading is advanced and reading classes become more like literacy in the adult world. Ms. Evelyn Eddington, a teacher in our study stated:

> Lessons that teach students to craft their comprehension set pupils up for success. In the past, we focused too much on what students' could not do and tried to go from there. Now, through Types 1, 2, and 3 crafting comprehension lessons we communicate that no matter what level of ability students have now, instruction can lift them up until they fall magically under the spell of, and become emersed in, their own understanding and appreciation of a captivating text. Because no one is belittled, students feel safe. They learn in an environment that cultivates taking risks to move to higher levels of comprehension, and to participate in discussions which revolve around issues of timeless importance.

Through the differentiated lessons described in this chapter, students can learn more about the power of (1) reading quality literature; (2) knowing how to craft meaning continuously as they read; and (3) gaining more information about themselves as readers. Through these means, students have the opportunity to select the type of clay they will use to create new knowledge. These choices of molding material enable them to access specific authors who can contribute to their knowledge gain. Students also have the opportunity to ask for assistance in learning how to craft more masterfully. Passing on various "tricks of the crafting trade" enables teachers to contribute to students' abilities to sculpt their new knowledge. Students contribute their own goals, meanings, procedures, and values to their sculptures. As a result, students attain higher levels of comprehension because the making of meaning has come more directly under their control.

REFERENCES

Allington, R. (1996, December). *What we need instructionally.* Presidential address at the National Reading Conference, Charleston, SC.

Baker, L., & Brown, A. L. (1984). Metacognitive skills and reading. In P. D. Pearson (Ed.), *Handbook of reading research* (pp. 491–572). New York: Longman.

Bakhtin, M. M. (1993). *Toward a philosophy of the act* (V. Liapunov & M. Holquist, Eds.; V. Liapunov, Trans.). Austin: University of Texas Press.

Beck, I. L., McKeown, M. G., Hamilton, R. L., & Jucan, L. (1997). *Questioning the author: An approach for enhancing student engagement with text.* Newark, DE: International Reading Association.

Block, C. C. (1993). Strategy instruction in a literature-based reading program. *Elementary School Journal, 72,* 139–149.

Block, C. C. (1997). *Literacy difficulties: Diagnosis and instruction.* Fort Worth, TX: Harcourt Brace.

Block, C. C., & Cavanaugh, C. (1998). Teaching thinking: How can we and why should we? In R. Bernhardt, C. N. Hedley, G. Cattaro, & V. Svolopoulous (Eds.), *Curriculum leadership: Rethinking schools for the 21st century* (pp. 301–320). Alexandria, VA: Association for Supervision and Curriculum Development.

Block, C. C., & Mangieri, J. N. (1996). *Reason to read: Thinking strategies for life through literature* (Vol. 1). Palo Alto, CA: Addison Wesley.

Bloome, D. (1986). Building literacy and the classroom community. *Theory into Practice, 15,* 71–76.

Cain-Thoreson, C., Lippman, M. Z., & McClendon-Magnuson, D. (1997). Windows on comprehension: Reading comprehension processes as revealed by two think-aloud procedures. *Journal of Educational Psychology, 89*(4), 579–591.

Caine, R. N., & Caine, G. (1997). *Education on the edge of possibility.* Alexandria, VA: Association for Supervision and Curriculum Development.

Collins, C. (1992). Improving reading and thinking: From teaching or not teaching skills to interactive interventions. In M. Pressley, K. Harris, & I. Guthrie (Eds.), *Promoting academic competence and literacy in schools* (pp. 149–167). San Diego, CA: Academic Press.

Elley, W. (1992). Acquiring literacy in a second language: The effect of book-based programs. *Language Learning, 41*(3), 375–411.

Fielding, R., Wilson, P., & Anderson, R. (1984). A focus on free reading: The role of tradebooks in reading instruction. In T. E. Raphael (Ed.), *The contexts of school-based literacy* (pp. 149–160). New York: Random House.

Galda, L. (1997). Mirrors and windows: Reading as transformation. In T. E. Raphael & K. H. Au (Eds.), *Literature-based instruction: Reshaping the curriculum.* Norwood, MA: Christopher-Gordon.

Gambrell, L. (1997, December). *Effects of discussion before and after writing on peer-led reading response groups.* Paper presented at the annual meeting of the National Reading Conference, Scottsdale, AZ.

Gaskins, R. W., Gaskins, J. C., & Gaskins, I. W. (1991). A decoding program for poor readers—and the rest of the class, too! *Language Arts, 68,* 213–225.

Golden, R., & Rumelhart, D. (1993). A parallel distributed processing model of story comprehension and recall. *Discourse Processes, 16*(3), 203–237.

Graham, M., & Block, C. C. (1994). Elementary students as co-teachers and co-researchers. *Greater Washington Journal of Literacy, 12,* 34–48.

Greene, M. (1998, April). *Imagination, passion, and intelligence.* Paper presented at the annual meeting of the Teaching for Intelligence Conference, New York.

Hillerich, R. L. (1991). *Teaching children to write, K–8: A complete guide to developing writing skills.* Englewood Cliffs, NJ: Prentice Hall.

King, A. (1994). Guiding knowledge construction in the classroom: Effects of teaching children how to question and how to explain. *American Educational Research Journal, 31*(2), 338–368.

Krashen, S. (1993). *The power of reading.* Englewood, CO: Libraries Unlimited.

Loxterman, J. A., Beck, I. L., & McKeown, M. (1994). The effects of thinking aloud during reading on students' comprehension of more or less coherent text. *Reading Research Quarterly, 29*(4), 353–366.

Mackey, M. (1997). Good-enough reading: Momentum and accuracy in the reading of complex fiction. *Research in the Teaching of English, 31*(4), 428–458.

Mangieri, J. N., & Block, C. C. (1996). *Power thinking for success.* Cambridge, MA: Brookline Books.

Morrow, L. (1997, December). *Case study of exemplary first grade teachers: Characteristics present in their teaching that are not present in typical teachers' repertoires.* Paper presented at the annual meeting of the National Reading Conference, Scottsdale, AZ.

Pardo, L. S. (1997). Criteria for selecting literature in upper elementary grades. In T. E. Raphael & K. H. Au (Eds.), *Literature-based instruction: Reshaping the curriculum.* Norwood, MA: Christopher-Gordon.

Pressley, M. (1998). *Balanced reading instruction.* New York: Guilford Press.

Pressley, M., & Afflerbach, P. (1995). *Verbal protocols of reading: The nature of constructively responsive reading.* Hillsdale, NJ: Erlbaum.

Pressley, M., Harris, K., & Guthrie, J. (1995). Mapping the cutting edge in primary level literacy instruction for weak and at-risk readers. In D. Scrubles & M. Mastropileri (Eds.), *Advances in learning and behavioral disabilities.* Greenwich, CT: JAI Press.

Purcell-Gates, V. (1996). Stories, coupons and the *TV Guide:* Relationships between home literacy experiences and emergent literacy knowledge. *Reading Research Quarterly, 31*(4), 406–430.

Raphael, T. E., & Au, K. H. (Eds.). (1997). *Literature-based instruction: Reshaping the curriculum.* Norwood, MA: Christopher-Gordon.

Rosenblatt, L. (1978). *The reader, the text, the poem: The transactional theory of the literary work.* Carbondale: Southern Illinois University Press.

Sipe, L. R. (1997). First- and second-grade literary critics: Understanding children's rich responses to literature. In T. E. Raphael & K. H. Au (Eds.), *Literature-based instruction: Reshaping the curriculum* (pp. 39–46). Norwood, MA: Christopher-Gordon.

Turner, J., & Paris, S. (1995). How literacy tasks influence children's motivation for literacy. *The Reading Teacher, 48*(8), 662–673.

Weber, R. (1991). Linguistic diversity and reading in American society. In R. Barr, M. L. Kamil, P. B. Mosenthal, & P. D. Pearson (Eds.), *Handbook of reading research* (Vol. 2, pp. 97–119). New York: Longman.

Chapter 8

THE ROLE OF LITERATURE IN LITERACY DEVELOPMENT

Douglas Fisher
James Flood
Diane Lapp

In *Literature and the Child,* Cullinan (1989) notes that literature is both a window to the world and a mirror of it. It is through literature that students learn about people they might never meet and places they may never visit in their lifetimes. As teacher-educators who are field based in many schools, we know many classroom teachers who believe that children must see themselves in books to affirm themselves and must see others to expand their conception of the world. Ms. Jesse Katz, a third-grade teacher in an urban school in San Diego County, believes so strongly in the efficacy of literature that she has designed her entire program to promote literacy development through literature.

Let's look into Ms. Katz's classroom. As she interacts with her students, it is easy to see the important role of literature in her classroom. Jessica, a student in Ms. Katz's class, tells us: "Everyone in my class reads a lot every day. Sometimes we all read different books about the same topic, and sometimes we read a book with Ms. Katz. She likes to ask us questions about what we have read. We also keep reflections in our journals, make our own books, and work on projects!"

Ms. Katz's 27 students come from a variety of backgrounds. Three students receive support from the resource specialist, and two students who speak Spanish receive services from a bilingual educator in Spanish. Five other students are receiving bilingual services in Vietnamese. Ms.

Katz's print-rich classroom is filled with Spanish, English, and Vietnamese words, phrases, books, and pieces of literature.

During the morning discussion, Ms. Katz encourages her children to share experiences about their families. As they do, Ms. Katz records their talk on a language chart that the children read and reread together, individually and in pairs. When the children return to their tables, Ms. Katz encourages them to write, illustrate, and share a story about a tradition that is a part of their family. Throughout this activity, her children are grouped heterogeneously, actively interacting with one another, sharing their family's rituals and routines.

After they work for a while on their stories, she calls them to the rug to read *The Patchwork Quilt* (Flournoy, 1995), the target text in her unit on family. The previous day she had introduced several new vocabulary words in semantic maps that she knew the students would encounter, including *costume, recognized, realized, material, examined,* and *several.* Now, students are given time to respond to the text and to write questions about their responses in their journals (see Figure 8.1). After writing, students talk with a partner about their responses to the book. After several minutes of partner talk, Ms. Katz asks her students to share with the whole class. Justin excitedly tells the whole group that Cheyenne has a great idea. Before Cheyenne has a chance to speak, Justin tells the group that Cheyenne thought that the class should look on the Internet for quilts around the world. As we smile at their excitement, we glance at the classroom library and note that several theme extension books are available: *Uncle Max's Secret* (Whitney, 1997), *Sandra Bustles Along* (Cohen, 1997), and *Talking Turkey* (Cowell, 1997). After the children read and discuss *The Patchwork Quilt,* Ms. Katz invites them to go to their learning centers.

Response	Question

FIGURE 8.1. Student journal page.

At one center, Kaila is working on her family quilt. She decorates the pieces of her quilt with a variety of family traditions that she had discussed with her mother. Ms. Katz had sent home a note to families about the upcoming theme and assigned "homework"—a discussion with relatives about family traditions, customs, and routines. Kaila's family is from the island of Samoa, and her quilt highlights island life and her move to the mainland. During this time, Ms. Katz also meets with small homogeneous groups of children who need explicit instruction in the vocabulary included in the story. She asks the children to create semantic maps so that the literal meanings of words can be extended. For example, Allen tells her that a costume was a mask worn on Halloween. Through his semantic map and their discussion, he realizes that a costume can be clothes or other personal effects, such as makeup, used to hide a person's identity and can be worn at any time.

Jessica is part of the Famous People center, which invites children to look at the customs and traditions of their families. Jessica chose to write about Jackie Robinson. She loved the book *In the Year of the Boar and Jackie Robinson* (Lord, 1984), which they finished last month. Muhammed decided to write about Helen Keller because she was identified as a person who had a disability during the class discussion on the book *Welcome Home, Jellybean* (Shyer, 1988). Dominique decided to write about Ryan White, the teenager who died of AIDS. Dominique's uncle had died the year before and his mother had given the class a copy of *Losing Uncle Tim* (Jordan, 1989).

After the centers are completed, Ms. Katz gives her students time for free reading. Some children choose to read selections related to their morning centers, some read about the experiences shared from the opening conversation, while others choose new themes. Ms. Katz encourages students to select books from the classroom library for this Sustained Silent Reading (SSR) time because her classroom library contains some of the best books, magazines, and newspapers available. She shares library books with other classroom teachers to provide variety for her students and to accommodate the wide range of reading fluency of her students. The bilingual resource teacher also adds many materials to the classroom library. All of the children love bilingual books where English is on one side of the page and the target language is on the other.

Later in the week, Ms. Katz explains to the class that they will be creating class books about their families. She tells them that the beauty of class books is that they contain the students' own words and that they can read them over and over again.

Monique's group moves quickly to the floor near the classroom library where they begin to look through previous class books to select one they would like to reread. After reviewing several, Erica has an idea for their book. She suggests that they write a book called *A Good Friend* and give the book to Ms. Katz because the students consider her their friend. Each of the students in the group takes turns writing ideas about good friends. Erica writes, "A good friend is someone you can walk on the beach and talk with." Jessica writes, "A good friend is someone you care about and love." When each of the groups have finished writing, illustrating, binding, and sharing their books, they are added to the classroom library for everyone to read.

As Ms. Katz teaches, assesses, groups and regroups her students, we are constantly delighted with the importance she places on each child's literacy level and development. We know that she has carefully considered many questions in designing her reading/language arts program. The next section will focus on her questions about literature instruction. We will use these questions to organize our discussion:

- Why teach literature?
- What types of literature are important to use in the program?
- How does oral language development relate to literature instruction?
- How does written language development relate to literature instruction?
- How can literature affirm students' views of themselves and broaden their conceptions of the world?

LITERATURE AND CURRICULUM

Why Teach Literature?

Researchers (e.g., Huck, Hepler, & Hickman, 1993; Rosenblatt, 1990; Roser & Martinez, 1995) indicate that teachers use literature as a significant part of the reading/language arts program for at least three reasons: modeling of language structures, connecting lessons to students' prior knowledge, and motivating readers. We believe that each of these reasons for using literature is important and worthwhile. We now turn to some of the research that has informed these three generalizations.

Modeling Language Structure

When children are read to, they hear the sounds of the author. Over time these exposures to the language structure of texts enable them to understand how stories work (e.g., Power & Hubbard, 1996): "Stories told or read to children give them opportunities to hear words in use and, in the process, to support, expand, and stimulate their own experiments with language" (Cullinan, 1989, p. 15). Reading good literature encourages students to imitate language patterns and to create their own stories. Literature also provides students with an appreciation of different genres, styles, and perspectives (Lapp & Flood, 1992). When students in Ms. Katz's class were asked to create classroom books, Charise's group wrote about their grandparents. They used several words in their book that they encountered while reading *The Patchwork Quilt,* such as *maternal* and *paternal, immigration,* and *generations.* The books from the classroom library on this topic included *Grandma's Latkes* (Druker, 1992), *Grandfather's Journey* (Say, 1993), and *How My Family Lives in America* (Kuklin, 1992). Some children even brought in books from home. Lewis told the class how much he loved *Walk Two Moons* (Cheech, 1994).

Accessing Prior Knowledge

Marshall (1996) maintains that all new knowledge is based on existing knowledge and that the previous experiences of students are central to completing the cycle. Children's literature can activate prior knowledge as an information source. Ms. Katz's activated her children's prior knowledge when she asked them to talk about their family traditions before introducing them to *The Patchwork Quilt.* The family quilt was one way that Ms. Katz encouraged her students to use information that they already knew so that they can make connections between what they know and what they are learning in the literature unit.

Motivating through Literature

Literature motivates readers, especially when readers see themselves "living through the literary character" (Ruddell & Ruddell, 1995, p. 259). When children want to read, their attitude toward reading improves (Gambrell, 1996). A positive attitude toward reading usually results in more reading, and this in turn helps students develop fluency. The students in Ms. Katz's class gained a new understanding of their family's traditions by exploring the issues in *The Patchwork Quilt* (Flournoy, 1995).

What Types of Literature Are Important to Use in the Program?

Books chosen for children should cover a wide variety of genres, including folk tales, tall tales, fables, myths, legends, poems, fantasy, realistic and historical fiction, science fiction, and nonfiction. Books selected for use in classrooms must also be well written and include well-developed characters, interesting language, and engaging plots. We must also be aware of gender, racial, and ability stereotypes that might exist within the text. Like Ms. Katz, teachers should select books that depict a variety of family structures and perspectives on the world. We suggest that teachers should choose texts with (1) literary quality that has been demonstrated by reviews, awards, and trusted word of mouth recommendations; (2) aesthetic qualities that cover a wide array of genre that will elicit thoughtful responses from children; (3) concepts and ideas that children can grasp with guidance; and (4) opportunities to lead children to unique discoveries.

In choosing appropriate literature for the class, we may want to examine several book awards that are presented annually to newly published books worthy of distinction (see Table 8.1 for a list of such award winners). Books that are selected for your classroom should depend on goals,

TABLE 8.1. Children's Literature Award Winners

Year	Title	Author
	Newbery Medal winners (1987–1997)	
1997	*The View From Saturday*	E. L. Konigsburg
1996	*The Midwife's Apprentice*	Karen Cushman
1995	*Walk Two Moons*	Sharon Creech
1994	*The Giver*	Lois Lowry
1993	*Missing May*	Cynthia Rylant
1992	*Shiloh*	Phyllis Reynolds Naylor
1991	*Maniac Magee*	Jerry Spinelli
1990	*Number the Stars*	Lois Lowry
1989	*Joyful Noise: Poems for Two Voices*	Paul Fleischman
1988	*Lincoln: A Photobiography*	Russell Freedman
1987	*The Whipping Boy*	Sid Fleischman
	Caldecott Medal winners (1987–1997)	
1997	*Golem*	David Wisniewski
1996	*Officer Buckle and Gloria*	Peggy Rathmann
1995	*Smokey Night*	Eve Bunting
1994	*Grandfather's Journey*	Allen Say
1993	*Mirette on the High Wire*	Emily Arnold McCully
1992	*Tuesday*	David Wiesner
1991	*Black and White*	David Mccaulay
1990	*Lon Po Po: A Red-Riding Hood Story From China*	Ed Young
1989	*Song and Dance Man*	Karen Ackerman
1988	*Owl Moon*	Jane Yolen
1987	*Hey, Al!*	Arthur Yorinks

themes, the languages spoken in the classroom, and the fluency of the students. In Ms. Katz's classroom and in many other classrooms throughout the United States, basal reading programs with anthologies of the very best children's literature are used along with individual titles that make up the classroom library.

How Does Oral Language Development Relate to Literature Instruction?

Literacy involves viewing, reading, writing, listening, and speaking. Among these, speaking is often forgotten or neglected in the literacy curriculum. Discussions about literature have been shown to positively affect literacy development (e.g., Roser & Hoffman, 1992). One way to promote the development of oral language skills in the classroom is the implementation of literature circles in which students have the opportunity to talk and share their ideas. Teachers use book clubs or literature circles in a variety of ways (Roser & Martinez, 1995).

In Ms. Katz's classroom, students are required to read a variety of works that provide an opening for discussion and examination of the multicultural world in which they live. Seated in a large circle, students read, write, speak, and listen based on a process that is established during the first week of school (see Table 8.2). As a class, children agree on several general guidelines for operating a book club discussion (see Table 8.3).

TABLE 8.2. Guidelines for Moderators (Teachers or Students)

1. Have students write a journal response to the text being read (2–4 minutes; individually).

2. Share responses with a partner (2–4 minutes; pairs).

3. Lead discussion with the group (1–15 minutes; group).

   Begin by asking students to share thoughts based upon their reading/writing and discussion of text with their partner.

   Have content-specific questions ready to focus the discussion if it strays too far afield or becomes bogged down on a point that seems to be unresolvable.

4. Postdiscussion writing (4 minutes; individually).

5. Share responses with a partner (4 minutes; pairs).

6. Return to discussion with whole group (10 minutes; group).

   Invite responses based on the previous writing.

7. Write a journal entry (2–4 minutes; individually).

   Ask students to write about their response to the text as a result of reading, writing, and discussing with their peers.

TABLE 8.3. Classroom Guidelines for Literature Discussion

- Be prepared to discuss your thoughts about the text by completing your reading and writing before the literature discussion begins.
- Be courteous by listening to everyone's comments.
- Be sensitive to people's feelings as you make contributions to the discussion.
- Wait until the speaker is finished before beginning your comments.
- Make your comments positive and constructive.
- Feel free to question and agree/disagree by clearly and calmly stating your opinion.
- Assume responsibility for your own growth.

Students are accustomed to the Read, Write, Pair, and Share strategy in Ms. Katz's class. They expect to write in their journals after reading. By talking with their partners about their readings and writings, they have the opportunity to speak first with one person before they are expected to share their ideas in a large group. This often makes them feel more comfortable and builds trust in the classroom. Children tend to see themselves and their partner as a team. For example, in one conversation Justin said that Cheyenne had a great idea about the book. He not only shared her idea with the class, he also credited Cheyenne with accolades that made her feel that her ideas were worth offering. Using the Read, Write, Pair, and Share procedures, Ms. Katz provides herself with opportunities to listen to students' ideas as well as opportunities for students to listen to one another. Ms. Katz also uses Choral Reading and Reader's Theater as vehicles for enhancing her children's oral language skills through literature.

How Does Written Language Development Relate to Literature Instruction?

Children need to hear, see, and use language so that they can notice the connections between their thoughts, words, letters in printed words, and the way the words sound. Children need to be exposed to a print-rich environment to become aware of sound–symbol associations. This print-rich environment should reflect the range of languages represented in the class. As children interact with written and spoken languages, they begin to improve their vocabulary, decoding and encoding, and develop their reading comprehension and writing strategies.

Ms. Katz uses shared reading, guided reading, and partner reading in her class to help children choose their topics. She selects vocabulary words from these readings and makes these words her spelling words for the class. In this way, students have already encountered the word in context and can return to the text to find out more about the use of the word. In addition, Ms. Katz teaches her students "word attack" strategies for situations in which they encounter unfamiliar words. Her students become quite familiar with use of the Word Wall to identify word families and to spell words correctly. In addition, Ms. Katz integrates other elements of phonics when a need is indicated.

Students also need explicit writing instruction from Ms. Katz. Most of the writing assignments in Ms. Katz's class extend over several days. Children in the class understand the writing curriculum for the class. Generally, this writing curriculum takes the following form:

1. *Creating the writing assignment.* Students develop their topics as Ms. Katz guides and supports them. Students often talk with partners about their ideas and answer questions about their topics.
2. *Planning the writing.* Students inform Ms. Katz of their role as the writer, their intended audience, and the format.
3. *Writing.* Students write at their desks, at centers, or in the media center based on the plan they have developed.
4. *Receiving feedback on written work.* Students meet with writing partners and Ms. Katz at a teacher editing table to share and respond to questions about their writing.
5. *Revising and editing.* With feedback in hand, students return to their desks, centers, or the media center to create a new draft of their text. Students in Ms. Katz's class know that this step may be repeated several times to produce a quality work.
6. *Finalizing the writing.* When all the feedback has been considered and incorporated, students produce a display copy of their work. Some students use computers while others handwrite. Everyone knows that illustrations are an important part of the writing process. All students also know that they may choose to edit their work in the future as they learn more about a topic, but for now it can be displayed for others to read.

During the unit on families, Ms. Katz provides students specific feedback about their writing, spelling, editing, and grammar at the teacher editing table. Ms. Katz meets with small groups of students while they discuss their papers with each other and the teacher. Children also make decisions about which pieces to publish on the Writing Wall and which pieces will be added to their writing portfolios. Students also create visual representations of their writing as Kaila did when she worked on her quilt.

How Can Literature Affirm Students' Views of Themselves and Broaden Their Conceptions of the World?

Students arrive in our classes with a number of assumptions about people. Often these assumptions are stereotypes born of lack of adequate information. Multiple literacy experiences in literature about children and adults from a variety of backgrounds enhances children's overall literacy development as it expands their worldview. Providing students with opportunities to discuss individual differences based on literacy experiences offers them new insights about people who are different from themselves (Katz, Sax, & Fisher, 1998). Discussing literature enables all children to look inward to examine their values, beliefs, and behaviors.

As teachers, choosing books may be our most important task. We suggest the selection of literature that is representative of the full range of human experiences found in our world. In Ms. Katz's classroom, students read about Maizon (Woodson, 1995), a girl who decides to leave a boarding school because she is unwilling to conform to the expectations of various cliques. Students also read about Chinese children's lives, studies, habits, and hobbies in *City Kids in China* (Thomson, 1991). *Mother Jones and the March of the Mill Children* (Colman, 1994) provides students with opportunities to think about child labor, workers' rights, and the Chicago fire of 1871. As teachers we must broaden our own perspectives so that our students are prepared for the diverse world in which we all live.

In Ms. Katz's class, students meet people from all over the world in their exploration of the family. In Jessica's group, the children study famous people and their families. She and her classmates learn about the families of Jackie Robinson, Helen Keller, and Ryan White. The impact that Ms. Katz's library of books has had on these students is inestimable.

The remainder of this chapter is devoted to instructional strategies that are useful in a literature curriculum. We will use these questions to organize our discussion:

- What is a balanced approach to literacy?
- What is the role of literature in beginning reading instruction?
- How should students be grouped for effective literature instruction?
- How do we assess students in a literature curriculum?

INSTRUCTIONAL STRATEGIES

What Is a Balanced Approach to Literacy?

We believe that literature is essential in an effective, well-balanced program. We also think that explicit instruction is critical to a balanced approach. Every student is someplace on a nonhierarchial literacy continuum; as Farnan, Flood, and Lapp (1994) note, "There is no point on the continuum that denotes too much literacy or, for that matter, not enough. There are no good or bad places to be, only places informed by children's previous knowledge and construction of literacy concepts" (p. 136). This perspective suggests that we should focus on what students know and are able to do and then build our literacy approach from there. The basis of this child-centered approach is the use of literature to access prior knowledge and provide students information about the structure of their language.

Phonemic awareness, the awareness that words and parts of words are composed of sounds, has gained increased attention in recent years. We believe that one of the best ways to address phonemic awareness is through children's books that play with the sounds of language (Griffith & Olson, 1992). *Miss Spider's Tea Party* (Kirk, 1997) contains several word rhymes. For example,

> Some ants strode in, they numbered six,
> But ants with spiders will not mix.
> She brewed them tea from hips of roses;
> The proud platoon turned up their noses. (p. 12)

Books that encourage playing with sounds through the use of rhyme, rhythm, and repetition are especially good in a balanced literacy approach. Children see and hear words in context and also receive explicit instruction on the structure of language.

What Is the Role of Literature in Beginning Reading Instruction?

Unarguably, emerging readers, like their middle- and upper-grade schoolmates, deserve a rich supply of the very best literature as the core to literacy learning. Children need literature because good stories help them make sense of the world, challenge their intellect, enlighten their imagination, nurture their desire to read, and heighten their awareness of self and others. Fortunately, by helping children develop all of their language skills—reading, writing, speaking, listening, and viewing—good literature also supports literacy achievement (e.g., Tunnell & Jacobs, 1989).

Hickman (1983) maintains that books must be unavoidable. Ms. Katz has her books propped against the fish tank, on the window ledges, and displayed prominently in her science, social studies, and math centers. She believes that books should boldly announce their invitations to be read, talked about, laughed about, reread, inspected, referred to, again read, written about, enacted, and read yet again. When books permeate the classroom, literacy gains its surest foothold.

But especially for emerging and newly fluent readers, the supply of literature in the classroom must include another kind of text: decodable books that children can read themselves. These books should include all types of patterns, from rhyming to rhythmic. While these books may not prove to elicit the deepest classroom discussion, they certainly entreat students to learn to read.

One effective way to teach literacy through literature is the use of Big Books, which provide each student with the intimacy of an individual storytime while allowing everyone visual access to the print and illustrations. Some teachers create their own Big Books and tape in the children's drawings so they can be removed and returned to the artist. Using enlarged texts, young readers follow along as the teacher reads, using a pointer to indicate each word. Young readers may predict events or story language. Almost immediately the children chime in, read along, and beg to "read it again." Reading repeatedly ensures familiarity and supports the children's own emergent reading of the stories. Through Big Books and shared reading, teachers help emerging readers work on the development of concepts of print—how books work, how print records and preserves language, how words travel on a page, and the significance of spaces marking them. Big Books, along with the children's opportunities to write, support emergent reading and the developing of understanding of the written language system (Roser, 1994).

However, all books are not created equally. Children need books that are inherently satisfying or meaningful as a story that can be "lived" through, such as *The Very Hungry Caterpillar* (Carle, 1979), or as rhythmical as *Engine, Engine, Number Nine* (Calmenson, 1997), or as instantly mastered as *It Looked Like Spilt Milk* (Shaw, 1947). Beginning reading is a very complex task that is best accomplished when children have opportunities to read fascinating great works while also learning and practicing the skills that they are in the process of mastering.

How Should Students Be Grouped for Effective Literature Instruction?

Traditionally, students have been grouped by their teachers' perception of their ability. This traditional grouping strategy has sometimes been a permanent assignment for each child. For much of their instructional day, students are grouped with others who teachers' believe have similar abilities. However, research over the past 25 years indicates that this type of grouping creates serious social problems for students that may well have lasting effects on their academic development (e.g., Flood & Lapp, 1997; Indrisano & Parratore, 1991). Students in the "low-ability" groups are often required to complete more drill work in skill materials, are exposed to less literature, do far less silent reading than their peers in higher-ability groups, and are frequently asked comprehension questions that do not require critical thinking skills (Flood, Lapp, Flood, & Nagel, 1992).

How then should teachers' group students for effective instruction? Ms. Katz uses flexible grouping to meet the array of student needs within the class. Flexible grouping allows teachers to use a variety of grouping patterns to enhance student learning. These patterns include individual assignments, partners or pairs activities, cooperative groups with defined roles, one-to-one time with the teacher, cross-age groups that focus on themes, whole-class lessons, and learning centers.

In Ms. Katz's class, students are grouped and regrouped several times during the day. Some of the activities, such as the Famous People learning centers are completed in small heterogeneous groups. Other times, such as when Ms. Katz read *The Patchwork Quilt* aloud (Flournoy, 1995), she provides instruction to the entire class. Still other times her students work individually and in pairs. You'll recall that sometimes Ms. Katz meets with a small group of students who need specific skill instruction in one area. For instance, a group needs skill instruction in vocabulary, which Ms. Katz is able to provide during learning centers time. Ms. Katz uses the Center-Activity Rotation System (CARS) as her primary strategy for grouping students (Flood & Lapp, in press). This system is based on three core beliefs:

1. Teachers use flexible groups that alternate membership efficiently.
2. Teachers work with individual students and small groups of students.
3. Teachers require students to participate in all activities, lessons, and units that have been designed.

When teachers use CARS, students are grouped heterogeneously for center activities. During the course of a week long lesson, students participate in one center per day. Throughout the week, each student meets several times with the teacher in a smaller group or individually. During this time, the teacher provides skill instruction, feedback on reading and writing strategies, and assessment information for her students. Flood and Lapp (in press), provide detailed information about the implementation of the Center-Activity Rotation System in *Theoretical Models of Writing*, edited by R. Indrisano and J. Squire.

How Do We Assess Students in a Literature Curriculum?

We believe that children need to have instruction in all the processes of literacy—reading, writing, speaking, listening, and viewing—and that this instruction should be based on assessments of student performance

(Lapp, Flood, Fisher, & Cabello, in press). However, assessments of literature knowledge have been restricted in the past to evaluations of student's knowledge of plot and characterization. While such knowledge is critical, it is only a small piece of what needs to be assessed in literature (Purves, 1994). New forms of assessment, including performance and portfolio assessment, need to be developed that will enable students and teachers to understand the ways in which students develop insights and interpretations. More specifically, new assessments that are compatible with response-based literature must be developed and used. To accomplish this, at least five different dimensions of literacy development must be considered as we design assessment instruments that will adequately measures our students' growth in literature. These include the following:

- *Application of various kinds of knowledge.* Students should be able to use their knowledge from literature and apply it to their personal experiences, background, and culture. They should also be able to apply knowledge to different genres and generalize terminology and theories.
- *Selection of material.* Students should not only select reading materials that develop their habit of reading but also those that vary in format and complexity.
- *Articulation of a reasoned understanding of the text.* Reading literature is not done in isolation. Rather, students should display their understanding of the text in group discussions, during interactions with the teacher, and in their writing.
- *Reflection upon the readings.* Students should develop an understanding of the distinctions between personal and public implications and be able to place the text in the larger context of literature and culture.
- *Consideration of the role of literature in society.* Students should be able to distinguish between personal and public criteria for judging texts and recognize levels and types of taste and quality.

Using these five dimensions, it should be possible to collect a variety of assessment materials, including reading logs, interviews, performances, writing samples, speaking checklists, and other pieces that inform us about students' skills and knowledge of literature.

The Complete Picture

Many researchers believe that literature is the foundation for literacy development (e.g., Flood & Langer, 1994; Huck, Hepler, & Hickman,

1993). Ms. Katz holds fast to this belief. Her classroom reflects her strong belief that literature is the cornerstone of her literacy curriculum:

- She reads aloud pieces of great literature.
- She provides experiences in listening comprehension of important literary works.
- She encourages oral language development through discussion as a vehicle for understanding and appreciating literature.
- She models guided reading using literature.
- She uses literature that is socially sensitive and culturally specific.
- She provides a wide range of literary experiences, including the reading of many genres, topics, and difficulty levels.
- She models, encourages, and guides writing about each child's literary experiences.
- She provides time for students to choose books that they want to read.

REFERENCES

Calmenson, S. (1997). *Engine, engine, number nine.* New York: Hyperion Press.

Carle, E. (1979) *The very hungry caterpillar.* New York: Collins.

Cheech, S. (1994). *Walk two moons.* New York: HarperCollins.

Cohen, D. (1997). *Sandra bustles along.* New York: Macmillan McGraw-Hill.

Colman, P. (1994). *Mother Jones and the march of the mill children.* New York: Millbrook.

Cowell, E. (1997). *Talking turkey.* New York: Macmillan McGraw-Hill.

Cullinan, B. E. (1989). *Literature and the child* (2nd ed.). San Diego, CA: Harcourt Brace Jovanovich.

Druker, M. (1992). *Grandma's latkes.* New York: Harcourt Brace.

Farnan, N., Flood, J., & Lapp, D. (1994). Comprehending through reading and writing: Six research-based instructional strategies. In K. Spangenberg-Urbschat & R. Pritchard (Eds.), *Kids come in all languages: Reading instruction for ESL students* (pp. 135–157). Newark, DE: International Reading Association.

Flood, J., & Langer, J. (Eds.). (1994). *Literature instruction: Practice and policy.* New York: Scholastic.

Flood, J., & Lapp, D. (1997). Grouping: The unending story. Paper presented at the National Reading Conference, Scottsdale, AZ.

Flood, J., & Lapp, D. (in press). C.A.R.S. (Center-Activity Rotation System): A model for grouping students for effective learning. In R. Indrisano & J. Squire (Eds.), *Theoretical models of writing.* Newark, DE: International Reading Association.

Flood, J., Lapp, D., Flood, S., & Nagel, G. (1992). Am I allowed to group?: Using flexible patters for effective instruction. *The Reading Teacher, 45,* 608–616.

Flournoy, V. (1995). *The patchwork quilt*. New York: Puffin Books.

Gambrell, L. B. (1996). Creating classroom cultures that foster reading motivation. *The Reading Teacher, 50,* 14–25.

Griffith, P., & Olson, M. (1992). Phonemic awareness helps beginning readers break the code. *The Reading Teacher, 45,* 516–523.

Hickman, J. (1983). Classrooms that help children like books. In N. Roser & M. Frith (Eds.), *Children's choices: Teaching with books children like* (pp. 1–11). Newark, DE: International Reading Association.

Huck, C., Hepler, S., & Hickman, J. (1993). *Children's literature in the elementary school* (5th ed.). Fort Worth, TX: Harcourt Brace.

Indrisano, R., & Parratore, J. R. (1991). Classroom contexts for literacy learning. In J. Flood, J. Jensen, D. Lapp, & J. Squire (Eds.), *Handbook of research on teaching the English language arts* (pp. 477–488). New York: Macmillan.

Jordan, M. (1989). *Losing Uncle Tim*. New York: Whitman.

Katz, L., Sax, C., & Fisher, D. (1998). *Activities for a diverse classroom: Connecting students*. Colorado Springs, CO: PEAK.

Kirk, D. (1994). *Miss spider's tea party*. New York: Scholastic.

Kuklin, S. (1992). *How my family lives in America*. New York: Bradbury Press.

Lapp, D., & Flood, J. (1992). *Teaching reading to every child* (3rd ed.). New York: Macmillan.

Lapp, D., Flood, J., Fisher, D., & Cabello, A. (in press). An integrated approach to the teaching and assessment of language arts. In J. Tinajero & S. Hurley (Eds.), *Literacy assessment for bilingual learners*. Boston: Allyn & Bacon.

Lord, B. (1984). *In the year of the Boar and Jackie Robinson*. New York: Harper & Row.

Marshall, N. (1996). The students: Who are they and how do I reach them? In D. Lapp, J. Flood, & N. Farnan (Eds.), *Content area reading and learning: Instructional strategies* (pp. 79–94). Boston: Allyn & Bacon.

Power, B. M., & Hubbard, R. S. (1996). *Language development: A reader for teachers*. Englewood Cliffs, NJ: Prentice Hall.

Purves, A. (1994). On honesty in assessment and curriculum in literature. In J. Flood & J. Langer (Eds.), *Literature instruction: Practice and policy* (pp. 153–169). New York: Scholastic.

Rosenblatt, L. M. (1990). Retrospect. In E. J. Farrell & J. R. Squire (Eds.), *Transactions with literature: A fifty-year perspective* (pp. 97–107). Urbana, IL: National Council of Teachers of English.

Roser, N. (1994). From literature to literacy: A new direction for young learners. In J. Flood & J. Langer (Eds.), *Literature instruction: Practice and policy* (pp. 71–108). New York: Scholastic.

Roser, N., & Hoffman, J. (1992). Language charts: A record of story talk. *Language Arts, 69,* 44–52.

Roser, N., & Martinez, M. (Eds.). (1995). *Book talk and beyond: Children and teachers respond to literature*. Newark, DE: International Reading Association.

Ruddell, R. B., & Ruddell, M. R. (1995). *Teaching children to read and write: Becoming an influential teacher*. Boston: Allyn & Bacon.

Say, A. (1993). *Grandfather's journey*. New York: Houghton Mifflin.

Shaw, C. G. (1947). *It looked like spilt milk.* New York: Harper & Row.
Shyer, M. F. (1988). *Welcome home, Jellybean.* New York: Macmillan.
Thomson, P. (1991). *City kids in China.* New York: HarperCollins.
Tunnell, M. O., & Jacobs, J. S. (1989). Using "real" books: Research findings on literature based reading instruction. *The Reading Teacher, 42,* 470–477.
Whitney, A. (1997). *Uncle Max's secret.* New York: Macmillan McGraw-Hill.
Woodson, J. (1995). *Between Madison and Palmetto.* New York: Delacorte.

Chapter 9

AND IN THE CENTER RING, BASAL READERS, ATTEMPTING THE ULTIMATE BALANCING ACT

Nancy L. Roser
James V. Hoffman

We were both basal reader kids. Both of us are from the Midwest, from neighborhoods where the trees, houses, cars, dogs, and people looked almost like the ones in our "readers." (We say "almost" because Dick's short pants were dorky even by 1950s standards.) The "readers" themselves guided our introduction to literacy. The methodology seemed uncomplicated: Our teachers read aloud an enlarged version of our preprimer, using a chart stand and pointer to focus our task. We echoed the reading, "practicing" the text. We talked about the story and the wildly funny Baby Sally. Our teachers helped us focus on the sounds and patterns of words we could read. We worked in a *Think and Do* book. Perhaps because the basals one of us experienced offered Dick and Jane's walls configured with religious pictures and crucifixes (a publisher's accommodation to a large parochial market), we each found our own reality reflected. All in all, we did well. We were basal kids.

When we took our first teaching positions, we were "basal teachers," at least at first. Because we had been taught with the basal, because we had learned to use a basal in student teaching, and because our cooperating teachers had used basals as well, we followed the pattern. This was the late 1960s. Sally, Dick, and Jane were still players, but there were changes in the basals to reflect the social reality: Characters of color (or at least characters who were shaded) began to appear. We used basals as part of a nongraded structure, drawing from a variety of published series. No sooner had our students finished the first preprimer in one series than we returned from the book room with our arms overflowing with yet another publisher's preprimer. They read horizontally (across series) until fluent, and only then vertically, moving through preprimers, primers, and the graded readers, giving extended practice in these leveled texts. We didn't use the teacher guides much. And, although we were basal reader teachers at the beginning, we were trying hard to energize the teaching and individualize the learning. From the vantage point of today, we remember planning for lively discussions, dramatic presentations, child-initiated questions, independent reading, cross-curricular units, and book clubs.

Now, as university professors of teacher education, we face the constant dilemma of providing our students with enough buoying and lifeline so they can stay afloat upon the rough (and often uncharted) waters of day-to-day instruction, but not so much help that they fail to negotiate the shoals for themselves. We want our undergraduates to recognize that there is more to effective teaching than blindly following a basal; we hope they also recognize there is no honor in rejecting the security basals offer neophytes who are overwhelmed with the challenges of teaching. Our own struggle is to provide our students both with the strength to hang on and the courage to let go.

We have carried the same struggles into our work as basal "authors." (The real authors of basal series are the countless poets, songsters, artists, word crafters, and illustrators who create what the children read.) Our own work is really advisory. For example, we have been asked to recommend and react to texts being considered for inclusion in basal anthologies; we have helped to design the organization of program, units, and plans; we have reacted to and made suggestions for minilessons, special features, projects, and discussions. Our struggles are often between providing "too much" or "too little"—plans too prescriptive or too ambiguous, too linear or too redundant, too obvious or too likely to be overlooked.

We also carry the questions surrounding basals into our roles as university-based researchers, studying basals and their use. Over a decade ago, we edited a volume of the *Elementary School Journal* (January 1987) which focused on basal readers in American reading instruction. In preparation for that task, we read all we could find on the history, prevalence, use, and criticisms of basals. In the years that followed, one of us investigated trends in new basals (Hoffman et al., 1994).

We tell you all this by way of explaining the background, stance, and potential for bias we bring to this chapter. In the pages that follow, we tell you the story of how basals came to be; we recount the criticisms levied against basals' form, content, and use; and we summarize the changes in today's basals, drawing upon the considerable analytic and comparative studies of basals. We then take you into the classrooms of three teachers who are all struggling to be better at their craft. One has adapted the basal; another has abandoned it; the third takes pride in never having used it at all. Through them, perhaps, we offer perspective on the basal as *a* tool rather than *the* tool of effective practice. Finally, we look closely at the tenuous balancing act that basal readers are called upon to perform as they attempt to serve needs both by reflecting trends (but not too much) and guiding practice (but not too far).

THE BIRTH OF BASALS

The First Instructional Materials

It seems that throughout recorded history the shortcomings of the "texts" with which children have been taught to read have been remarked upon. William V. Harris (1989), in his exploration of *Ancient Literacy,* noted that "if we may judge from a third-century Greek collection of school-texts from Egypt, there were . . . apparently no readings for children between single words on the one hand and Homer on the other" (p. 137). From ancient times until colonial America, one of the most prevalent teaching materials was a set of alphabet letters. English and colonial American children met their letters on a hornbook, a paddle-shaped piece of wood just a few inches across, with a card of print tacked to it containing letters, syllables, and the Lord's Prayer. A thin sheet of transparent horn protected the letters from smudges (Huey, 1908/1968). Children repeated the letters and sounds (combining the sounds into syllables) forward and backward until they could name each of them (C. Hoole, cited in Mathews, 1966, p. 29). According to John Locke, born in 1632, the first English schoolbooks for children were the hornbook, primer, psalter, testament, and Bible (Venezky, 1997).

The first "primers" for children, according to Nila Banton Smith's *American Reading Instruction* (1934/1965), were actually church books. The dominant text in our colonial history, *The New England Primer,* presented the alphabet, syllables, and lists of words increasing in length, all introductory to the simple prayers and religious material that followed (see also Venezky, 1987). Beyond the primer, it was the family Bible that served colonial America as the pervasive "instructional material."

Following the colonial period, children's reading texts were called "spellers." That may have been in reference to the way children learned to read, first by spelling and then by pronouncing the words. The bestselling speller for about a half century was Noah Webster's famous "Blueback," nicknamed for its pale blue cover. The Blueback had word lists organized by number of syllables, but also reading selections with decided moral and patriotic tones. Webster's goal was to standardize the pronunciations and spellings of words in the young, diverse, and disconnected United States (Roser, 1984).

The First Graded Series

Smith (1934/1965) cites the 19th century as the first time "authors" began to prepare series of books for students, with each book intended to be more difficult than the one preceding it. By the end of the Civil War, Venezky (1987) describes the reading series as beginning to appear much as they do in modern times, with five or six books preceded by a primer. So, it was about 150 years ago that basal readers were "born." The 20th century brought the assignment of graded readers to grade levels, the introduction of the preprimer to teach the vocabulary of the primer, and eventually the kind of basal reader configuration that persisted for many decades: five or so books at first grade, and books for each semester thereafter. From the outset, the books produced for beginners tried to make the text "manageable" by introducing fewer words, providing repetition, and illustrating more plentifully. Books for older students carried information, speeches, and other pieces of literature useful for oral interpretation, or elocutionary performances. The most popular readers in terms of sales were the *McGuffey Eclectic Readers,* which offered students rules for reading, pronunciation guides, comprehension questions, and words for spelling (Venezky, 1987).

Perhaps from the beginning, publishers of school texts, fighting for a market share, began the balancing act. For example, the early McGuffey readers, prepared for a post–Civil War southern market, avoided mention of Abraham Lincoln and slavery.

Teacher Guides and Directives

The first guides for teachers were simple lesson outlines, or questions tucked in the margins and footers of the children's books. An Illinois principal, writing an eight-page guide in 1893 titled *How to Teach Reading,* waxed eloquent on approach:

> Pupils cannot afford to waste their entire time pronouncing words, as it has little to do with developing thought—the end and object of school life. If you let your pupils go on thus, you will never develop a taste for good literature, which some think the prime object of school reading. Were the

salt taken from our food, we would soon cease to relish it and finally pine away and die. Thought is more than the salt of our reading. Take it away and you take everything. Pupils in the higher grades are not automatons by nature, but only so by defective teaching. But you say I have uttered nothing new on teaching—a fact I candidly admit. Educationally speaking of this secular age, we believe the old proverb "nothing is new under the sun" is certainly true. The so-called New Education is a myth. But things can be new to you or to me, and they can be new to the pupils—when, strictly speaking, they are not new. In a restrictive sense, we should have two new things in every lesson—they are LIFE and THOUGHT. (Marlin, 1893, p. 8)

The earliest graded readers, such as Watson's *Independent Fourth Reader* (1868), provided brief notes "To Instructors," followed by a Treatise on Elocution, the Reading Lessons, and the Accessory Aids. Directives to teacher were precise:

Before the final reading, be sure that the pupils *understand* the lesson. Adopt a simple Order of Examination, and let them give the leading thoughts in their own language, *without formal questions*: For example, *first,* the title of the piece; *secondly,* the words liable to mispronunciation, both in the notes and the reading; *thirdly,* the objects mentioned, and the facts concerning these objects; *fourthly,* the narrative or connected thoughts, and the portion illustrated by the picture, if any; and *fifthly,* the moral or what the lesson teaches. (Watson, 1868, n.p.; italicized as in the original)

Over the decades that followed, guidebooks and manuals for teaching reading have expanded considerably. Venezky (1987) notes wryly that as teacher education and opportunities for professional growth have increased, so too have the unabashed sizes of teacher guides, with some 500-page manuals available for guiding the teaching of a single text. Basal publishers would no doubt contend that guides would be thinner if basals were called upon to do only what they did in McGuffey's day: present the orthography, list the vocabulary, provide comprehension questions, and offer principles of elocution.

Prevalence of Basal Use

When Austin and Morrison (1963) surveyed practices of teaching reading in all U.S. communities with populations over 10,000, they found that "despite discordant views over its value, the basal reader is unquestionably the predominant tool of instruction in most of the school systems sampled throughout this study. . . . In only one school system visited during the original field study were basal readers not used as the major tools of reading instruction" (p. 54). Austin and Morrison discovered that administrators who were most committed to basals were those most convinced that use of a basal series was the only way to ensure that all skills would be developed and a progression of vocabulary instruction ensured. Over twenty-five years later, the National Council of Teachers of English (1989), through its Commission on Reading, issued "Basal Readers and the State of American Reading Instruction." The statement began by noting that basal readers dominate reading instruction in roughly 90% of the elementary classrooms in the United States.

HOW BASALS ARE DEVELOPED

Suzanne Singleton (1997), a former vice president of Macmillan/McGraw-Hill School Division, described the creation of basal readers as a process of collaboration involving hundreds of people in multiple roles, including program authors, consultants, editors, writers, teacher advisors, student advisors, designers and artists, technology developers, sales' representatives, as well as public input. According to Singleton, the complex process of constructing a basal program takes approximately 3 years. Typically, a diverse author team selected based on "curricular expertise, gender, geographical location, and cultural background" (p. 869) helps to shape the program's pedagogical framework. Experts in many areas, ranging from multicultural literature to cooperative learning, provide input. Teacher users and student advisors register needs and wishes and react to prototype offerings along the way. The process of basal building includes field testing instructional designs, as well as the lengthy process of reviewing, selecting, and field testing literature selections. A team of artists and designers work to ensure that the instructional materials have usable and appealing layouts. Other teams may develop technology or work to obtain permission to reprint trade books.

Publisher Roger Rogalin (1997) argues that the California Reading Initiative had major impact on the preparation of basals in the late 1980s. Because California is a "state-adoption" state (i.e., it approves published materials at the state level for purchase in local districts), and because it has 11% of the U.S. student population, when then-State Superintendent William Honig (1988) led the charge for more integrated language arts instruction, more "authentic" literature selections, and more diversity in content, basal publishers listened and complied. A part of the balancing act for basal publishers became including fine literature, unabridged, without offending some portion of the taxpaying public:

> The first backlash came as parents reacted to some of the content in the now unabridged passages. The world was not always "politically correct" as

we define that concept today. Mark Twain included racist words and content in his portrayal of 19th century life along the Mississippi River. Judy Blume described young girls' curiosity about brassieres in novels for middle school readers. The myriad special interests had specific concerns about specific passages or artwork included in programs. The concerns were often in direct conflict with each other, placing publishers squarely in the middle of contentious arguments based on some people's strong personal values and opinions. (Rogalin, 1997, p. 865)

A second balancing act that publishers faced was arraying "real" literature in ways that helped children manage the texts. When beginners' texts, for example, were constructed from a corpus of words that were repeated for practice, the argument was made that the difficulty of the texts could be controlled. When children's earliest books became the finest examples of trade literature with no attempt to "control" for the repetition of vocabulary, it became necessary for the natural and repetitive language patterns of the text to support the beginners. Further, publishers were also challenged to provide for skills instruction that grew out of but did not violate the artistry of the literature.

BASAL READERS AND THEIR CRITICS

Admittedly, early "readers" had contrived and insipid real-life adventures, and spoke a "sub-Tonto" grammar of "Go. Go. Go." and "Funny, funny Sally." These oft-lampooned patterns of "preprimerese" have fed the pens and pockets of cartoonists and T-shirt designers over the decades that followed. But there were even more serious criticisms: Basals of the 1960s were chastised for their flatness in depicting the world of readers. Children and adults in our "readers" of the 1950s were only white. In a kind of flurry to rectify that, one basal series rushed into print with a new series that literally imported children of color into depicted scenes. Others quickly "tinted" the faces; settings and plots were not immediately affected. Flesch (1955) produced a popular-press attack on the "whole-word" methodologies promulgated by these basals.

In her "Introduction" to the special "basal reader" issue of the *Elementary School Journal* (1987), Jeanne Chall wrote from a 20-year vantage point on her own basal inspection (Chall, 1967/1983). She summarized the mid-1980s discomfort and antipathy against basals as questioning the following: the methodology (whether their suggested practices are true to existing research and true to principles of effective learning and teaching); the degree of use (or overuse, as critics argued) of basals; their complexities (e.g., length, detail, number of components); and their "sameness" within historical periods. Among Chall's recommendations was a challenge to consider both the content and literary quality of basals' selections. It was this concern, echoed broadly across the country, that changed basals in decided ways.

Toward the end of the 1980s came a demand for "real" (meaning well-crafted, published, recognizable trade) literature with which to teach children. Researchers who analyzed the content of basals (e.g., Flood, Lapp, & Flood, 1984), made recommendations for increased breadth and quality of selections. Others argued that "real" texts promoted literacy as well as or better than basals (Tunnell & Jacobs, 1989). Criticism of basals included antipathy toward adaptations, revisions, and excerpts as destructive of a legitimate art form—children's literature—and of the natural language patterns that support children's efforts to read (Babbitt, 1990; Goodman, Maras, & Birdseye, 1994). Venezky (1987) argued that textbooks today "as they have [been] since textbook publishing began in this country, tend to be conservative, representing a narrow, sterilized view of society and the child's role in it" (p. 248).

Other critics have charged basals with sustaining the status quo by encouraging teachers to do what they have always done, "deskilling" teachers by undermining their voice and power (Shannon, 1989). There is considerable concern and dissatisfaction with public policy, including decisions about assessments and textbooks that emanate from power brokers and government officials rather than from communities, classrooms, and students.

Hoffman and his colleagues (1994) contend:

> Publishers must anticipate changes in teaching practices if they are to remain viable; they must walk the fine line between not offering a product that is so new and different that it appeals only to the high "risk-takers" and something that is so conservative and traditional that it is viewed as outdated. In the past, the safe position for most of the successful publishers has been to take a rather conservative stance toward change. (p. 48)

RECENT CHANGES IN BASALS

Although our field tends generally to ignore historical perspective as a valuable reference point for understanding change, Chall's (1967/1983) description of the commonalities of reading instruction in the early 1960s suggests a central role for the basal and its common features (e.g., vocabulary control, leveling of texts, a privileging of narratives). As we have attempted to show, these commonalities, evolving over decades of development and use, have been seriously challenged in recent years by both theoretical trends (e.g., literature-based philosophy and pedagogy) and political trends (e.g., the California Initiative of the late 1980s).

Basals have undergone remarkable changes over the past decade. We (Hoffman et al., 1994) have documented some of these changes in a study comparing the basals of the mid-1980s with those of the mid-1990s. We critically analyzed both student texts and teacher guides from the most popular basals (in terms of sales and marketing) in the United States. The comparative findings related to the student texts suggest the following differences as important: The total number of words in the new (1993) programs was considerably less than in the old (1986/1987) programs, but the new programs contained substantially more unique words than did the old. Evidence of vocabulary control and repetition had been significantly reduced if not abandoned in the new programs. In contrast to the old series, the adaptations of the literature in the new texts were minimal and the new basals had more engaging qualities in terms of content, language, and design than did the old series. Additionally, the text in the new series was substantially more predictable on features such as repeated patterns, rhyme, rhythm, and match of print and text than the old series. These new texts were more demanding in terms of decoding than the old ones.

The findings related to the teacher guides suggest the following differences as important: The new teachers' editions were found to be different from the old in terms of their underlying instructional design features, replacing a directed reading model with a shared reading model. Vocabulary was introduced more in the context of the story in the new teacher's edition; fewer questions were offered with a greater attempt to include more higher-level questions. The high degree of focus on skills and isolated skills instruction had decreased from the old to the new, though skills were still prevalent. Features such as pacing, entry levels, and grouping differed from the old to the new. Assessment tools had been broadened considerably from a testing-only mentality in the new basals. The tone of the manuals was less prescriptive than the old, moving in the direction of a teacher-as-decision-maker model.

These changes in basal reading programs have come in response to a number of factors, including (1) a changing political climate in which policy makers have assumed a bolder stance in prescribing pedagogy; (2) new theoretical directions in reading, as well as findings from research on reading acquisition, reading instruction, and teacher development; and (3) changes in the resource needs of teachers in planning for instruction. It would be impossible to sort out the degree of these influences on change if for no other reason than they interact directly with one another.

However, we focus our discussion on the last point: Teachers are changing in terms of teaching practices and are demanding changes in the materials they need to support this instruction. The challenge for basal publishers is to develop materials that meet these needs insofar as they represent or project the future. The question for all of us to ponder is what teachers need as they represent the future of reading instruction.

Who are these cutting-edge teachers that basals must consider? In the following sections, we describe three representatives of this group: one has never used a basal series in her classroom; one abandoned the basal after several years of frustration; and the third uses a basal but diverges from it. We describe them in terms of the challenges they face in everyday teaching and the innovations they are exploring. Finally, we discuss the issue of whether basals can/should/will serve a range of teachers who think, explore, create, weigh, and inquire.

ROSA HERNANDEZ

Rosa Hernandez is a fourth-grade teacher in an urban school district that serves an ethnically diverse working community. Rosa is one of those teachers who lives in her classroom. She arrives by 7:00 in the morning and seldom leaves before 7:00 in the evening. Her district recently instituted a year-round school calendar, although anyone who knows Rosa believes that year-round is the only way she has ever worked. When she is not teaching or getting ready to teach, she volunteers, serving meals at shelters, building houses for low-income families, or pinch-hitting in the church nursery.

Her classroom is a special place. Each time we visit, it changes. On one visit, for example, we found the room has been transformed into a cave with stalagmites and stalactites "growing" strategically. Multiple copies of *Trapped in Death Cave* (Wallace, 1988) sat near a display of information books, evidence of book clubs that had spawned inquiry. Additional evidence of reading, writing, and learning abounds: models, projects, displays, photos, articles, experiments, graphs, notebooks, charts, reports. On the next visit we found ourselves in a Mayan village, and then in a space station. The environment never stops changing.

Rosa uses the basal unit themes to center her cross-curricular planning. She finds the unit titles such as "Viewpoints," "Communities," and "Challenges" broad enough and ambiguous enough to be interpreted in multiple ways. The space station followed children's interests but fit within a theme of "Exploration" she selected (out of "sequence") from the basal. She relies on basals for multiple copies of good literature. She uses basal selections to illustrate a host of understandings about language use. She treats basals as an instructional choice that opens a further set of instructional decisions.

Not long ago, Rosa received a teaching award. During the awards ceremony, each teacher acknowledged appreciation to friends, family, and coworkers to the misty-eyed audience. They commented on their dedication to children and the privilege of touching the future. Rosa was the last to be recognized that day, and her message was different. She confessed her embarrassment at not being able to join with the other teachers in attributing her quest for excellence in teaching to her dedication to children. She explained her driving force in terms of a selfish motivation, what she labeled her "addiction." "I am addicted to learning," she explained. "It is in my nature to wonder, question, and inquire. The quest for knowledge has become a habit for me that I cannot break. It is only in teaching that I find my habit satisfied. I learn with my students. That is my reward and my challenge. When I cease to be excited about learning, I will cease to be a teacher."

PAM STILLWELL

Pam Stillwell teaches first grade. We have been observers in her classroom and had many long chats with her about teaching. Several years ago she "threw out" (her words) the basal from her classroom. She told us she decided that if she had to teach one more idiotically contrived story, she was going "to get sick right there on the floor." And so, she made a plan. First, she sat down with her principal to arrange a teaching schedule that would allow her 3 hours of uninterrupted instructional time every morning with her students—no "pull-outs," no "specials," no services—just Pam and her class from 8:30 to 11:30 focusing on the hard work and great joys of becoming literate. Second, she went to work to make it work.

Fortunately, a renewed focus on instruction didn't place a ban on quiet observers. We observed Pam orchestrating her students through 3 hours of integrated reading/language arts/social studies instruction. Now, she uses only trade books in her classroom. As we watch, we are caught up in the new "routines"—the rhythms of journal writing and sharing, the entrenchment of skills through "warm-ups" for reading, the discussions of old favorites and new stories, the problem solving and inquiry that lead children into information texts.

Pam is "direct" and "explicit" in her teaching without disrupting the flow of activity and experience. She has a "meta" lexicon all her own for the written code of language that never fails to get giggles and attention: She points out "garbage words" (words that have vowel combinations that are irregular) or "peanut butter and jelly words" (those with vowel combinations that kids can count on because they "stick" together). At work with new texts, she consistently models and makes reading strategies explicit. All of this is done without distracting or distorting the experience of message or story or text. In addition, she focuses the students' attention on code at every turn—in reading and in writing and across the curriculum. By challenging her students to look more carefully, to search for patterns, and to share their insights, her students are intent upon determining how the writing system works. The code instruction is internalized by students and used with great enthusiasm.

New literature enters Pam's classroom daily. The first experience with a new piece of literature is typically under storytime conditions—but this is only the first experience. The story (or whatever text) is read again and again under different types and degrees of support and for different purposes: shared reading, repeated reading, dramatization, small-group guided reading, pocket-chart work, paired reading, and so on. Gradually, students gain independence with the text. Eventually, it will become part of the classroom library for independent reading time and part of the take-home library for family sharing.

Pam favors literature that causes her children to laugh. She loves the theatrical and hardly ever shares a book aloud without adding some dramatic flair. Music is a key part of Pam's teaching. The students sing the traditional rhymes and popular children's songs, as well as Pam's creations of new lyrics to popular "rock" songs that fit whatever theme they are exploring.

Observations in her classroom reveal the "intake" and "output" periods of a day described by Sylvia Ashton Warner in *Teacher* (1964), or the intensity and rhythms of Vivian Paley's classroom—as though the instructional day is synchronized with the heartbeats of the children. There is a sense of "flow" (Csikszentmihalyi, 1990) in Pam Stillwell's first-grade language arts period, described by psychologists as those moments of intensity and engagement that sweep us up and almost take over consciousness.

CATHY CICHANTEK

Step outside a classroom like Pam's, however, and you often find this synchrony in conflict with a different set of expectations and realities. Cathy Cichantek is another teacher who "teaches against the grain." She does things differently than most of her colleagues. Already an innovative teacher in an urban setting, Cathy was recruited by a new principal in a suburban district. Committed to change, the new principal wanted the kindergarten teachers to break away from traditional forms of instruction and offer more integrated language instruction. But change was to be slow. The extant kindergarten team took comfort in teaching the same content every day. Their lesson plans were exactly the same. The letter of the week was exactly the same. There were uniform expectations for the art projects and products. Even bulletin boards were the same. Cathy was told by her new team that the thematic units of instruction were already established for the year by the basal plan.

The message from her new team was clear: Join us. Every variation or deviation on Cathy's part was viewed as undermining what the team had developed over the years. Even so, Cathy initiated an experience-oriented kindergarten in which the need for literacy was "critical." In her classroom, print was unavoidable. Print began the day with class stories, songs, and rhymes; print made magical announcements ("Gina has a surprise to tell us!"); print communicated the important business of school ("M-m-m-m. Soup for lunch today!"); it directed the rabbit's feeding, recorded the hamster's weight, and compared the children's favorite foods. Print announced, invited, and remembered in her classroom. Pam's children were given time for just reading and just writing. Book publishing was so heroic that it competed with construction and gardening. During the first year, she was forced to defend (1) her choices of read alouds ("But *Charlotte's Web* is a fourth-grade book"); (2) her investigative projects ("But hatching eggs is for second grade"); (3) her views on instruction ("But opportunities to write 'real messages' don't prepare children adequately for first-grade penmanship"); and (4) her views on learning ("But children's reversed letters indicate referral for dyslexia intervention").

Cathy has been at the school for 3 years now. Things have changed. She has moved into a multiage teaching setting with a combined group of kindergarten and first-grade students. Three of her colleagues have joined with her in considering the primacy of children rather than curriculum, but it has been a struggle. Step inside the classroom, though, and you cannot feel the heat. The students are excited and engaged and learning about their world through language. And they don't use basals.

THE BASAL DILEMMA

Pam, Cathy, and Rosa, collectively, have read more books, attended more conference sessions, and conducted more in-service sessions than imaginable. They struggle to solve the problems of teaching. None sees the current basals as a solution. They want something else, something that provides greater flexibility for them to use in a responsive teaching environment.

Do these three teachers represent the future? Or do these teachers represent the exceptions who will always be teaching against the grain? What (if anything) can basals provide them? Is it possible for a basal series to assist teachers who want to redefine the instructional paths in their classrooms? Can a basal series capture and transmit the strategies of the best teachers without codifying and rendering those strategies lifeless?

It is unlikely that any set of instructional materials, including basal readers, will ever again have to carry the entire weight of the past. Given the prevalence of print, the basal is no longer the protector/transmitter of the mores/norms/culture. Perhaps it never was. Some of our friends and contemporaries, also basal kids, tell us they never "identified" with the basal that looked like our Midwestern 1950s world. Laughingly, they recall that their basal's suburban settings, with their pale-skinned and light-haired populace, their picket fences and unleashed dogs, never depicted their world. Its stories were never theirs.

But if one role of the basal may be to continue to reflect society's memories, hold onto a "communal past" through which novitiates are inducted both into literacy and culture, another role may be to point at the present. Today's basal has much help: There are approximately 90,000 children's books in print, about 6,000 additional titles published each year, as well as periodicals and on-line sources. But the issues are never even as simple as what book, for whom, and when. In his *History of Reading*, Manguel (1996) contends that the methods (and, by implication, the materials) with which we learn to read embody the conventions of a society's stance on literacy, including the "channeling of information, the hierarchies of knowledge and power, [and the] . . . ways in which [the] ability [to read] is put to use" (p. 67). Manguel, himself, muses that in the Argentina of his youth, learning to read was neither for pleasure or for knowledge, but merely for instruction.

Singleton (1997), writing from the perspective of a producer of basal materials, describes the difficult task basals are expected to perform: "Teachers ask for the latest research translated into manageable classroom practice. They ask for instructional designs that are clear, concise, and easy to follow, and for options that allow them flexibility and decision-making power. The publisher's job is to create instructional plans that translate theory into practice effectively" (p. 870).

Given that basals can be primarily designed and selected by those who may not actually use them, the question may be whether basals can serve well the teachers who strive to move beyond them. What do the best and most effective teachers want them to do? Cathy wants nothing at all. Her children, though, have a wealth of materials to learn from, supplied by her own budget, the school's resources, and willing parents. Pam needs more multiple copies of books that the children can and want to read from the beginning of the year, but she is not so worried about a slow and steady buildup of sound–symbol patterns. She feels competent to take care of code instruction through the myriad ways she works with her children to make all texts manageable. The state in which she teaches, however, has in its latest call for new textbooks the expectation that publishers provide her first graders with "decodable texts," described as those with "an accumulating sequence of letter–sound correspondence being taught" (Texas Proclamation, 1997). Rosa wants broad, inviting themes, more complete texts, and easily implemented strategy lessons not embedded in hundreds of pages of summary, guide, adaptation suggestions, and questions. She would be happier with a thin eight-page guide.

Textbook selection committees, charged with the serious task of making recommendations for classrooms and children, determine how competing basal series measure up against agreed-upon criteria. Ultimately, basals are products of private enterprise. They follow the "proclamations" and "initiatives." Because expense prohibits (currently) basals being produced for regions or states, the largest "state-adoption" states have advantages over those states with local adoptions in that the features and factors that big states call for are passed on. As basal series grow fewer in number, as the expenses of production escalate, and as the survival of publishing houses depends upon marketing, publishers walk the line, most arguing for a "balanced perspective" (Pearson, 1996). To borrow from the terms of high school chemistry, we hope the balance is not just a "mixture" (or combination of elements) but a true "compound" (or new substance) perfectly assimilating its contributing features. And in the center ring. . . .

REFERENCES

Austin, M. C., & Morrison, C. (1963). *The first R: The Harvard report on reading in elementary schools*. New York: Macmillan.

Babbitt, N. (1990). Protecting children's literature: On preserving the fragile medium of fiction. *Horn Book Magazine, 66*(6), 696–703.

California Department of Education. (1986). *A balanced, comprehensive approach to teaching reading in prekindergarten through grade three*. Sacramento, CA: State Superintendent of Public Instruction.

Chall, J. (1983). *Learning to read: The great debate*. New York: McGraw-Hill. (Original work published 1967)

Chall, J. (1987). Introduction. *Elementary School Journal, 87*, 243–245.

Csikszentmihalyi, M. (1990). *Flow: The psychology of optimal experience*. New York: HarperCollins.

Flesch, R. (1955). *Why Johnny can't read*. New York: Harper & Row.

Flood, J., Lapp, D., & Flood, S. (1984). Types of writing included in basal reading programs: Preprimers through second-grade readers. In J. A. Niles & L. A. Harris (Eds.), *Changing perspectives on research in reading/language processing and instruction*. Rochester, NY: National Reading Conference.

Goodman, K. S., Maras, L., & Birdseye, D. (1994), Look! Look! Who stole the pictures from the picture book?: The basalization of picture books. *The New Advocate, 7*(1), 1–24.

Goodman, K. S., Shannon, P., Freeman, Y. S., & Murphy, S. (1988). *Report card on basal readers*. Katonah, NY: Owens.

Harris, W. V. (1989). *Ancient literacy*. Cambridge, MA: Harvard University Press.

Hoffman, J. V., McCarthey, S. J., Abbot, J., Christian, C., Corman, L., Curry, C., Dressman, M., Elliott, B., Matherne, D., & Stahle, D. (1994). So what's new in the new basals? *Journal of Reading Behavior: A Journal of Literacy, 26*(1), 47–73.

Honig, W. (1988). The California Reading Initiative. *The New Advocate, 1,* 235–240.

Huey, E. B. (1968). *The psychology and pedagogy of reading.* Cambridge, MA: MIT Press. (Original work published 1908)

Manguel, A. (1996). *A history of reading.* New York: Viking.

Marlin, E. A. (1893). *How to teach reading.* Epworth, IL: Epworth Schools.

Mathews, M. M. (1966). *Teaching to read: Historically considered.* Chicago: University of Chicago Press.

National Council of Teachers of English (1989). Basal readers and the state of American reading instruction: A call for action. *Language Arts, 66*(8), 896–898.

Pearson, P. D. (1996). Reclaiming the center. In M. F. Graves, P. van den Broek, & B. M. Taylor (Eds.), *The first R: Every child's right to read.* New York: Teachers College Press.

Rogalin, R. (1997). The changing face of literacy: A publisher's perspective. In J. Flood, S. B. Heath, & D. Lapp (Eds.), *Handbook of research on teaching literacy through the communicative and visual arts.* New York: Macmillan.

Roser, N. L. (1984). Teaching and testing reading comprehension: An historical perspective on instructional research and practice. In J. Flood (Ed.), *Promoting reading comprehension.* Newark, DE: International Reading Association.

Shannon, P. (1989). *Broken promises.* Granby, MA: Bergin & Garvey.

Singleton, S. (1997). The creation of a basal program: A collaborative effort. In J. Flood, S. B. Heath, & D. Lapp (Eds.), *Handbook of research on teaching literacy through the communicative and visual arts.* New York: Macmillan.

Smith, N. B. (1965). *American reading instruction.* Newark, DE: International Reading Association.

Texas Proclamation (1997). *Reading, English language arts, K–1.* Austin: Texas Education Agency.

Tunnell, M. O., & Jacobs, J. S. (1989). Using "real" books: Research findings on literature-based reading instruction. *The Reading Teacher, 42,* 470–477.

Venezky, R. L. (1987). A history of the American reading textbook. *Elementary School Journal, 87,* 247–266.

Venezky, R. L. (1997). The literary text: Its future in the classroom. In J. Flood, S. B. Heath, & D. Lapp (Eds.), *Handbook of research on teaching literacy through the communicative and visual arts.* New York: Macmillan.

Wallace, B. (1988). *Trapped in Death Cave.* New York: Holiday House.

Warner, S. A. (1964). *Teacher.* New York: Bantam Books.

Watson, J. M. (1868). *Independent fourth reader.* New York: American Book.

Chapter 10

KEY COMPONENTS OF SOUND WRITING INSTRUCTION

Karen Bromley

Over the years, writing instruction has changed in response to new ideas that have evolved from research, theory, and practice. These changes are like the sweep of a clock's pendulum. Simply put, the teaching of writing shifted from a focus on skills and the written product to a focus on writing process, and most recently to a balanced approach that embraces both product and process. But recent calls for "back to basics" in teaching to ensure higher achievement suggest that the writing pendulum is moving again in the direction of skills and product.

Where is the safe, sound, and prudent place to be? How can you avoid the pendulum and invite students to write, enjoy writing, learn as writers, and write well in a range of forms for a variety of purposes and audiences? Good teachers of writing find themselves somewhere in the middle, borrowing the best from both product and process approaches to develop writers who are fluent, competent, and independent.

This chapter identifies key components of sound writing instruction (see Figure 10.1) that span both approaches. It examines several classrooms where practices reflect each component and provides suggestions for good writing practices in K–8 classrooms.

STANDARDS AND ASSESSMENTS THAT GUIDE TEACHERS AND STUDENTS

Donna Evans, a fourth-grade teacher, feels she is a better teacher of writing because of the New York State Education Department's (1996) publication of *Learning Standards for English Language Arts*. Donna says,

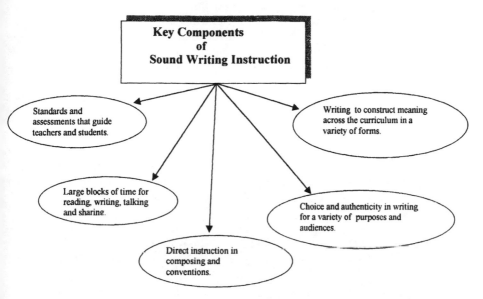

FIGURE 10.1. Consider these components in planning your writing program.

"After the standards came out and we started using them in our curriculum planning and teaching, I began to think I had short-changed students in the past. It wasn't intentional, but when you don't include the full range of language uses in your program and you don't pay attention to assessments that measure student progress, then you don't give them the experiences they need to become fully literate. I saw this especially in writing. Although we always did a fair amount of writing, it was separate from content learning and I always graded and corrected it."

Donna realizes that standards are controversial. Critics say standards narrow teaching, restrict learning, and take curriculum control away from teachers. While these concerns are valid, Donna believes in their benefits:

"The standards have helped my faculty talk about what we value in our students as writers. They've given us guidelines and a common language to use with each other, our students, and parents. The standards have made us more accountable and more definitive about what we teach. We had to decide what a good writer looks like at each grade level. We had to set higher standards for our students and change our assessment practices. We've begun to use rubrics and portfolios."

Donna is positive about the changes in her teaching as a result of the adoption of standards. But she is also cautious and says continued growth is important:

"I am more intentional now about including writing that helps kids analyze and think in science and social studies. I give them many more choices, and they can work together on more assignments and on revising their own writing. We talk about what a good finished piece looks like. We've started creating checklists and rubrics they can use to guide their writing and for self-evaluation after writing.

"I feel more confident in my teaching because of the conversations we've had around the standards. I know there is lots more to do and I'll continue to question and modify my teaching of writing. But I don't feel that I'm shortchanging my students as I was. I know I have better writers this year because I've changed my expectations and practices."

Donna is like many other teachers who struggle with how to help students develop into effective writers. She and her faculty have begun a dialogue that includes creating a writing curriculum and developing assessment tools. They know that good instruction begins with goals and a vision of exemplary student performance. They also know that assessment drives good instruction and has an enormous effect on what students produce.

Assessment for you as a teacher of writing should begin with an examination of your own beliefs and practices. Answers to questions such as "What do I believe about writing?" and "How do students become good writers?" will help shape your philosophy of writing. You can also examine your classroom practices with questions like the following ones, adapted from Marino (1997), to see how your teaching reflects your philosophy:

- For what purposes are students writing?
- Who are the audiences for their writing?
- Am I giving students choices in what they write?
- Are they writing in a variety of forms in all content areas?
- How am I helping them understand and use the writing process?
- What direct instruction am I providing?
- How am I using literature to inspire and model good writing?
- How am I helping students understand how conventions affect meaning?

Assessment should also include a regular examination of the climate for writing in your classroom and your students' perceptions of themselves as writers. Hansen (1996) suggests having students answer questions like the following:

- What do I do well?
- What's the most recent thing I've learned as a writer?
- What do I want to learn next to become a better writer?
- What do I plan to do to work on this?

Bottomley, Henk, and Melnick (1998) suggest using the Writer Self-Perception Scale, which appraises students' self-perceptions so you can adjust instruction and curriculum appropriately. Of course, you can use observation, conferences, interviews, and self-assessment checklists to regularly gauge student interest and attitudes.

After taking a year-long in-service course on the language arts standards and new assessments, Donna often talked with her class before they began writing to decide what a good finished product should look like. For example, before writing letters to chambers of commerce in other states as part of a study of the United States, students brainstormed characteristics of a good letter and organized them into categories. Donna added levels of use, and then her fourth graders had a rubric to guide their writing (see Figure 10.2).

Creating rubrics with students before writing has a dramatic effect on the quality of the finished product. Helping students make a check-

Letter Rubric

	Needs Work	Getting there	Almost there	Got it
Content				
Message /meaning				
Organization				
Details				
Complete sentences				
Word use				
Mechanics				
Inside address				
Date + greeting				
Body / paragraphs				
Closing + name				
Capitals + punctuation				
Neatness				
Spelling				

FIGURE 10.2. Rubrics guide writing and make assessment more objective.

list of criteria to include in a written piece is also helpful. Not only do these practices make assessment easier for you, but they show students and parents why a piece received a particular grade. Then a student's areas of strength can be noted and you know what to reteach. Of course, teachers don't use rubrics for every piece of student writing. Many teachers use a rubric only for a large project or final piece of written work, but they might well introduce rubrics to their students like the one that Donna's class used.

LARGE BLOCKS OF TIME FOR READING, WRITING, TALKING, AND SHARING

Donna and other teachers find that extending classroom time devoted to writing often has a positive effect. These teachers set aside large blocks of time for reading, writing, talking, and sharing during Writing Workshop. Of course, students also do other kinds of writing during the day for other purposes. In Writing Workshop, a regular time is set aside, usually daily, for writing by each student on a topic of the student's choice (Atwell, 1987; Calkins, 1994; Graves, 1994). Calkins (1994) suggests the following components of Writing Workshop: minilessons; work time for writing and conferring; also time for peer conferring and/or response groups, share sessions, and publication celebrations. Atwell (1987) spends an hour a day in Writing Workshop, about one-third of which is brief lessons focused on a demonstrated need of a group of students. She also spends time sharing and discussing a well-written piece of literature at the end of the workshop to help students improve their writing and learn to respond to each other's work.

Tonya Dauphin, a third-grade teacher, uses Writing Workshop and experiments each year with its organization and delivery. Through professional reading (Sudol & Sudol, 1995; Zaragoza & Vaughn, 1995) and talk with colleagues, Tonya has come to realize the importance of listening to her students, reflecting on what works and doesn't work, and developing and changing her approach each year. This year, Tonya uses Writing Workshop 3 days a week and begins each workshop with a lesson on a skill she has noticed that the class or several students need. Then students write for 30 minutes and there is a 10 minute sharing time when a student sits in the Author's Chair (Graves, 1994) and reads his/her work to the class. Tonya uses a wall calendar on which students sign up in advance to share a finished story, and she requires students to share at least twice a month.

Tonya's room shows evidence of her commitment to writing. Posters about each aspect of the writing process adorn the walls, and student writing is posted on bulletin boards. For Tonya's students, Writing Workshop was a new idea. One of the things she did early in the year to help children develop good habits was to have a discussion about the workshop. Tonya and her students created the accompanying T-chart she posted in the classroom as a reminder.

Our Writing Workshop

• Looks like—	• Sounds like—
• People being polite	• Quiet but not silent
• Working not talking	• No put-downs
• Sharing ideas quietly	• Clean language
• Cooperation	• No unpleasant noises
• People writing	• Listening during sharing time
• People reading	• Asking good questions

Stefan Zappey's second graders typically do Writing Workshop for 45 minutes every day. When he omits or shortens the workshop for any reason, his students notice the omission or abridgement and may voice their disappointment. Moreover, he says groans of frustration often accompany the signal to stop writing.

In Writing Workshop, not every piece of writing proceeds through the entire process. Students choose the story they are most proud of or want to bring to completion. In Stefan's school, parents run a project called "Books from Boxes" in which they use cereal boxes and other materials to make blank books for the best student work.

In her first year using Writing Workshop, Karen Wassell, a third-grade teacher, uses several strategies to manage it successfully. To help her students keep track of where they are in the writing process, Karen made a pocket chart with a tagboard pocket for each step of the process and with student names on tagboard strips (see Figure 10.3). Each day, students put their names in the pocket that shows where they are in the writing process. Then, Karen knows who is ready for a conference with her or prepared to share in Circle Time during the last 10 minutes of the workshop. Other charts remind students how to use a web (concept map) and story grammar (setting, characters, problem, events, resolution, and theme) to plan for writing.

Many teachers include the reading of literature during Writing Workshop so students are reading good models as they compose. To help manage the reading that is part of her workshop, Karen and her class created the list of Rules for Buddy Reading (see Figure 10.3). Pairs of students use these rules as they read books together, work at the computer to gather ideas for writing, or respond to each other's written drafts.

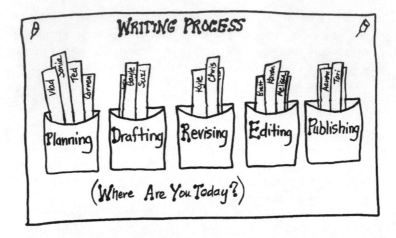

FIGURE 10.3. Karen Wassell posts these charts to help manage writing workshop in third grade.

Karen has found buddy reading and collaborative writing particularly helpful for students who may have ideas to contribute but who may not yet have the language skills. Both ESL (English as a Second Language) students and struggling readers are supported in their work and encouraged to develop their abilities when they work in pairs with proficient English speakers. And native English speakers can learn about other cultures and languages of their buddies.

Both self-selection and guided selection of literature help develop readers with wide reading experiences and familiarity with a variety of language models and forms. In Figure 10.4, Alex keeps a record of each book he reads in his literature response journal and evaluates it using a sports-related symbol system he has created. With records like this to examine, Lisa Rieger, his teacher can see whether her fourth graders are reading a variety of genres and if necessary suggest other genres.

Many teachers introduce students to authors of children's books to help them see how authors use the writing process in their own composing (Calkins, 1994; Harwayne, 1992). You can help your students read and look at written products with new eyes—the eyes of writers—and help your students write with an audience in mind, as a reader would read the piece. As children are alternately readers and writers, they begin to observe how authors hold the reader's attention and how authors use conventions. When this happens, students often begin to use this knowledge in their own writing.

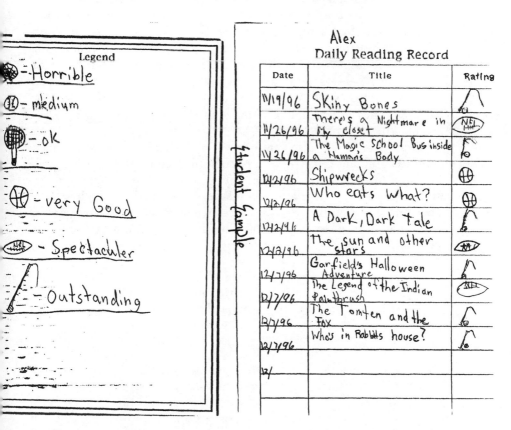

FIGURE 10.4. Alex's Reading Record shows the variety of books he has read.

Just as Lancia (1997) suggests, Stefan encourages his second-grade students to engage in *literary borrowing*. He finds that literature is an effective model for writing and that in a Writing Workshop where reading occurs students make natural connections between their reading and writing. Jesse had read several of R. L. Stine's books where he incorporates "THE END" into the final sentence, for example, "It doesn't really matter in . . . THE END." Jesse borrowed this technique, concluding his nonfiction report on volcanoes with "Volcanoes are very cool but when they erupt it's . . . THE END." Stefan's feeling is that reading all types of literature can have a positive impact on student writing.

DIRECT INSTRUCTION IN COMPOSING AND CONVENTIONS

In the past, some teachers who adopted a writing process approach believed that students would become good writers when they chose topics themselves and had many opportunities to plan, draft, revise, and publish. Direct instruction that emphasized the finished product and skills was replaced with a focus on the writing process. But an overreliance on process doesn't always yield students who can write in different forms for a variety of purposes and audiences. Good teachers of writing have learned that writers need direct and systematic instruction in writing as well as time to write (Routman, 1996).

Shanahan (1997) also reminds teachers that in classrooms where integrated thematic instruction occurs and reading and writing are linked within the context of meaning, students still need "opportunities for enough instruction, guidance, and practice to allow them to become accomplished" (p. 18). Good teachers of writing have learned to strike a balance between the writing process and the written product, honoring each in their writing programs. Good teachers of writing:

- Celebrate and encourage individuality, creativity, meaning, standard form, and the conventions of language.
- Grow and change in their philosophies and practices from year to year.

Many teachers incorporate direct instruction in composing and the conventions of grammar, spelling, form, and handwriting into Writing Workshop. Bromley (1998) suggests ways to do this both directly and indirectly in situations that make sense to students without engaging in isolated skill instruction. She believes that knowing grammar terms gives students a common vocabulary for discussing and improving their writing. Routman (1996) suggests teaching and discussing word usage and sentence construction in the context of writing for a specific audience. Kane (1997) uses sentences from real literature that students know, rather than "fix-the-error exercises," to teach specific grammar skills. And you can use your own writing and student writing to demonstrate how quotations, commas, and periods are used, for example.

Like Tonya and Stefan, Karen begins her workshop with a 10- to 15-minute lesson on a specific aspect of writing. Her lessons may focus on organization, run-on sentences, adjectives, verbs, punctuation, or other things she has identified through assessment that her third graders need or are ready to learn. Karen uses the term *focus lesson* because she agrees with Routman (1996) that *minilesson* may appear to trivialize the direct instruction she feels is so important in Writing Workshop. Karen began a recent workshop with a lesson on common and proper nouns after she noticed the overuse of pronouns in several stories. Part of the lesson included revising the work of a student who wanted help with her story. Karen often uses her own writing in these lessons because she believes this is a meaningful way to teach revising.

To extend her students' writing beyond topics they select themselves, Karen incorporates Calkins's (1994) idea of a genre study into the workshop. In a genre study, students immerse themselves in a particular kind of literature and then write in this form themselves. For example, during recent Writing Workshops and in conjunction with a social studies unit, Karen's students read nonfiction books about animals, gathered information from a CD–ROM encyclopedia, took an electronic field trip to a zoo, and then created their own informative report about an animal. These were compiled into a book of chapters, each about a different animal, to share with a first-grade class and as a culminating activity for the unit. Karen encourages students to coauthor at least one book together because she believes that collaboration can be a catalyst for learning. From the talk, shared decisions, and joint creation, Karen has seen some students acquire skills, knowledge, and confidence.

Diane Leskow is a special education teacher who finds that students with learning disabilities need direct instruction and modeling to support their writing. In teaching persuasive writing, Diane first shared a paragraph she wrote to her husband to convince him to try her favorite sport, roller blading. She had students brainstorm a list of their favorite hobbies and identify someone to whom they would like to write to convince him/her about their hobby's attractiveness. Then, they analyzed

Diane's paragraph and identified the persuasive writing frame she used in planning:

Persuasive Writing

Introduction (Position or Purpose)

Facts and Reasons
  1.
  2.
  3.

Conclusion (Restate Position)

Next, students planned their writing using the frame, composed rough drafts, and self-checked to revise and edit (see Figure 10.5). Then, Diane used a volunteer's rough draft and had a whole-class lesson on revising and editing, which she followed with student revision and then peer editing before final copies were made. The classmate Amy chose to write to (Sha-tobbya) was so important that Amy included Sha-tobbya's name in her writing even though it was not suggested. Each finished paragraph went to the person for whom it was intended, who then wrote a response.

At all grade levels, besides conferring with students themselves, teachers use peer conferences to give students real and immediate audiences for their work. Often, when a student reads work to a peer, the student can see and hear what needs to be revised. In sixth grade, Michelle Lehr often has students work in pairs or in small groups to give each other feedback on writing. She introduced the acronym PQS (Bromley, 1998) to her students as a way to give constructive responses.

P—Praise
Q—Question
S—Suggest

The classroom examples included here show how Tonya, Stefan, Karen, Diane, and Michelle combine direct instruction in composing and conventions, analysis of a model, and peer interactions to help students become competent writers. Where does handwriting fit in these classrooms? Many of these teachers teach handwriting and spelling together. Some have set standards for neatness in their students' written work, refusing to accept a *sloppy copy* for a rough draft, believing this term gives students the wrong message. Other teachers have students regularly self-assess their own handwriting.

In many of these classrooms, there are a variety of tools for writing available for student use, including the computer.

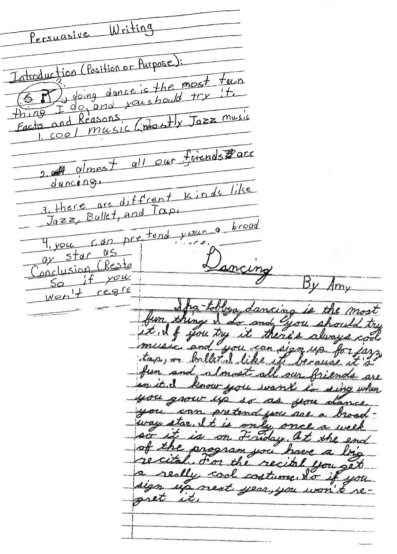

FIGURE 10.5. A paragraph frame helps a fourth grader plan for persuasive writing.

CHOICE AND AUTHENTICITY IN WRITING FOR A VARIETY OF PURPOSES AND AUDIENCES

Writing for a variety of purposes and audiences builds students' fluency, competence, and independence. This chapter contains many examples and references to student writing for different purposes (to persuade, inform, entertain, and narrate) and for different audiences (adults in other states, peers, parents, teachers, and self). Does giving students a choice in what they write and making it authentic or genuine build competence? Yes, choice and authenticity invite writers, especially reluctant writers, to write by giving them a personal reason to write and building ownership for the task and product.

For many students, technology is intriguing and it provides choice and authentic opportunities for writing for a variety of purposes and audiences. Electronic literacy has replaced what was meant by being literate in the past. Leu (1997) says we should think of ourselves and our students as *becoming literate,* rather than *being literate,* as we learn to use the navigational strategies and critical thinking necessary for electronic literacy. He believes electronic literacy is a necessity for today's teachers and students (Leu & Leu, 1997).

Most often in schools today, students use computers to search for information to include in written reports and presentations. Teachers use computers to find ideas and information and prepare lessons. Both students and teachers use CD–ROM encyclopedias and primary sources on the World Wide Web (WWW) such as historical documents or secondary sources like museum or observatory web sites.

Using computers, CD–ROM, or the Internet extends literacy beyond traditional print to viewing and evaluating hypertext composed of pictures, animation, and sounds. Students learn to search for information, interpret and analyze data, and think critically about the validity of sources. But be careful about which sites are valuable and appropriate for school use. Sites like "Thinking Critically about World Wide Web Resources"* provide criteria to consider in evaluating the usefulness of WWW resources.

Examples follow for using the computer to develop student writers. First, many teachers establish electronic key pal exchanges with students and classes in other states or countries. Sometimes the exchanges are social, and sometimes they are related to a science or social studies unit. Second, classes take electronic field trips to places around the world to extend learning in a particular content area. During these field trips, students can often ask questions of experts and get answers that might not yet appear anywhere in print. Third, many teachers and students participate in collaborative projects with other schools. For example, middle school teachers Mickie Flores-Ward and Tricia Normile invite K–12 classes to create a virtual tour of a local historical landmark with electronic graphics to post on their Historical Landmark Website (for more information, contact hilites@gsn.org). Fourth, students publish their own

*http://www.library.ucla.edu/libraries/college/instruct/critical.htm

original writing in *e-zines,* electronic magazines that include opportunities to write poetry, book reviews, and stories, enter contests, chat with others, and submit original artwork.

A variety of Internet sites offer student-writers choice in the kind of writing they do and in what they compose. The web sites for writers in Table 10.1 were selected according to several criteria: appearance, ease of use, content, and suitability for K–8 students. No matter which opportunities for writing with technology you and your students decide to pursue, there are rich opportunities for developing and refining both their writing and your own.

Writing on the Internet integrates reading and writing. It requires skills in viewing, gathering, interpreting, and analyzing information; keyboarding and navigating with browsers and search engines; and word processing. The skills required for writing with technology prepare students to be better learners in school and for the world beyond school.

WRITING TO CONSTRUCT MEANING ACROSS THE CURRICULUM IN A VARIETY OF FORMS

Paul Walens, a sixth-grade teacher, believes it is important for teachers of writing to be writers themselves. He keeps a personal journal, uses e mail, and writes curriculum, lesson plans, and grant proposals for his classroom and school. He believes, as do Vacca and Vacca (1999), that writing regularly is a powerful strategy for learning subject matter. Paul says:

"From my own writing, I've learned that writing is a process of constructing meaning. I never realize what I know until I start writing. Then I make connections and come up with ideas that I didn't have before. When I understood the power of writing for me, I began to realize what it could do for my students. I make writing a conscious part of science, social studies, and math now. My students keep journals that we use for a lot of different reasons at different times of the day. I've found that it's pretty amazing what my students can relate about their thinking when they write. It's a totally personal quiet time in our classroom when students reflect and make insights about a unit we are studying, for example, or make connections between math and social studies or relate it to the world."

Paul and many other teachers like him have discovered that when students write in a variety of forms in the content areas, they construct new meaning and demonstrate their content knowledge too. Like Paul, Arline Drann, a fourth-grade teacher believes strongly in the importance of writing as a learning tool across the curriculum. In a unit on Native

TABLE 10.1. Web Sites for Writers

1. Internet Public Library—world-reading@ipl.org
   Kids can post class book reviews or individual student book reviews and read about good books. Includes formats for review.

2. Scholastic Network—http://www.scholastic.com
   Ask the Author—http://ipl.org.youth/AskAuthor
   Kids can ask authors questions and read answers from them.

3. MidLink Magazine—http://longwood.cs.ucf.edu/~Midlink/
   An electronic magazine for kids where they can write articles and poetry, participate in projects, exchange art and writing, view projects from other kids worldwide in grades 4–8.

4. Global Heinemann Keypals—http://www.reedbooks.com.au/
      heinemann/global/global1.html
   Intercultural e-mail Classroom Connections—http://www.stolaf.edu/
      network/iecc/
   Kidlink: Global Networking for Youth 10–15—http://www. kidlink.org/
   Kids can exchange letters, do joint projects, enter contests, and play games with teachers and classes from other countries and cultures around the world.

5. The Quill Society—http://www.quill.net
   Encourages kids to explore their imaginations through writing advertisements, fantasy, mystery, science fiction, and poetry. Kids receive comments from the "Board of Critics" and discuss topics on a Bulletin Board.

6. The Book Nook for Kids—http://i-site.on.ca/booknook.html
   Publishes student reviews of books and provides interactive book conferences.

7. Inkspot for Young Writers—http://www.inkspot.com/~ohi/inkspot
      young/
   Publishes writing tips, interviews, contests, markets for kids' writing, and loads of other writing information.

8. Kids' Space—http://www.kids-space.org/
   Kids can share original writing with kids from other countries, improvise music, submit original stories, participate in a Bulletin Board, and find links to other kids' sites around the world.

9. Internet Public Library Youth Division—http://ipl.sils.umich.edu/youth
   Kids can enter contests, share stories, do experiments with "Doctor Internet," tour a museum, read about books other kids are reading, talk to authors, and find resources for science projects and science facts.

10. Mind's Eye Curriculum Projects—http://www.csnet.net/minds-eye/
    KIDPROJ—http://www.kidlink.org:80/kidproj/
    These sites let kids share language arts and science projects with other kids.

(*continued*)

TABLE 10.1. (*continued*)

11. Math:Kidsweb "Ask Mr. Math"—http://www.npac.syr.edu/textbook/
    kidsweb/math.html
    Kids can find answers to math questions, solve math problems and puzzles
    alone, or collaborate with other students.
12. WRAL Postcard Shop—http://www.wral-tv.com/mall/cards/
    Blue Mountain Arts—http://www.bluemountain.com/index.html
    Kids can design, send, and receive custom-made postcard messages.
13. Girl Tech—http://www.girltech.com/
    Girls can write stories, read women's history, chat with other girls, give
    and get advice.
14. Children's Book Creation Station—http://www.cybermail.net/~kjcbooks
    A place to read, write, illustrate, and review children's books in progress.
15. Looking Glass Gazette—http://www.cowboy.net/~mharper/LGG.html
    Publishes stories, poems, artwork, book reviews, and creative work of kids
    up to age 13. Includes writing contests, kids' columns, and a "Kids Speak
    Out Against Drugs" column.
16. Little Planet Times—http://www.littleplanet.com
    An interactive online newspaper for K–5 kids that publishes letters to the
    editor, movie reviews, stories, creative ideas for and by kids.
17. Kidworld—http://www.bconnex.net/kidworld/
    Kids under 16 can write stories, play games, or visit a bulletin board.
18. Positively Poetry Website for Kids & Teens—http://www.advicom/net/
    ~e-media/kv/poetry1.html
    Publishes poems from other kids around the globe. Each month an "Edi-
    tor's Choice" poem is selected to highlight one poet's creative work.
19. Stone Soup—http://www.stonesoup.com
    This international magazine contains stories, poems, and book reviews
    written and illustrated by kids through age 13.
20. The Young Writers Club—http://www.cs.bilkent.edu.tr/~david/deya/
    ywc.html
    Publishes *Global Wave*, a monthly online magazine of writing by kids ages
    7–15 that includes story suggestions, stories to finish, book reviews, and
    more.

Americans, small groups of Arline's students researched different tribes.
After reading a story about the Cheyenne, she asked groups to write what
they had learned on a partially constructed web. In Figure 10.6, Arline's
main categories are in bold print and the student wrote what he remembered. Students could add information to the web as they learned more
about the tribe. Near the end of the unit, Matt created the acrostic poem

in Figure 10.6, showing that he had learned about the Cheyenne people's respect for the environment and pondered about their undeserved fate.

Writing across the curriculum takes many forms. In first grade, Jane Hores linked math, social studies, and language arts in a unit called Quilt Connections. After students read and heard many stories about quilts, researched other cultures' quilts in the library and on the Internet, visited a museum exhibit, and learned about shapes, equal parts, and fractions, a final activity involved creation of a classroom quilt. The finished quilt, made of special fabrics and designs contributed by each student, went home each day with a different student. A journal accompanied the

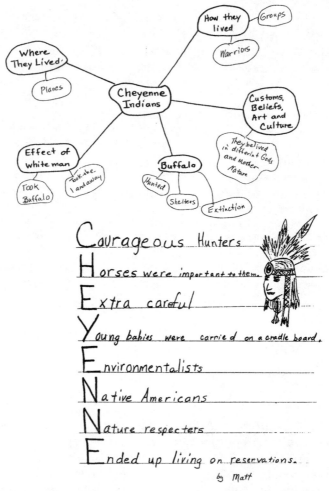

FIGURE 10.6. Webs and poetry writing have a place in social studies.

quilt in which each student wrote an entry about the experience and parents wrote responses. In Figure 10.7, Tyler says, "It is warm. Everybody made it. We had to tie it to keep it together. My pattern has green iguanas. Some patterns have bats. They are cool." While Jane's writing activity had students write to explain and inform their parents, it also gave parents an opportunity to be involved in a small way in their child's classroom learning.

Like other teachers, Rebecca Beers finds that graphic organizers support student research and writing (see Figure 10.8). In a study of Mexico, her second graders read and gathered information using Venn diagrams to show similarities and differences between two things and data charts to gather information from several sources.

There are many other types of organizers that show important ideas and information and relationships among concepts in text, providing helpful structures for student writing (Bromley, Irwin-DeVitis, & Modlo, 1995). As part of a unit on immigration, Michelle Lehr's sixth graders were better prepared to write about the characters' feelings in *How Many*

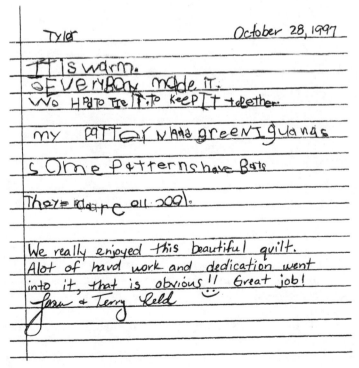

FIGURE 10.7. Writing for a real audience gives Tyler an incentive to write clearly to inform everyone about the class quilt.

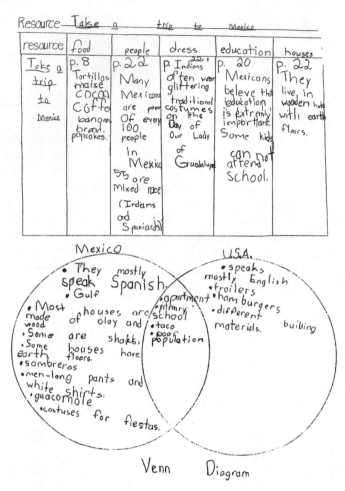

FIGURE 10.8. Rebecca Beers's second graders find that graphic organizers aid their research on Mexico.

Days to America?, by Eve Bunting (1990), and *Molly's Pilgrim,* by Barbara Cohen (1990), often creating graphic organizers. The character map and character relationships map in Figure 10.9 are straightforward ways to help students take the perspective of a character or focus on relationships among characters.

Today, writing is used in math class, a content area traditionally ruled by numbers. Gordon and Macinnis (1993) say that dialogue journals in math add a personal dimension to learning and provide "a window on students' thinking." Colleen Schultz regularly asks her eighth graders to write to her in their journals about what they enjoy and are having trouble with

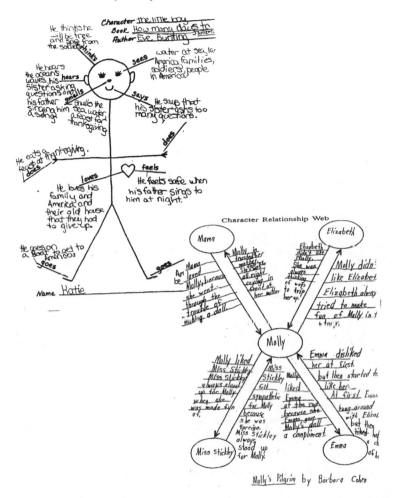

FIGURE 10.9. Michelle Lehr's sixth graders use graphic organizers to gain insight into characters and their relationships.

(see Figure 10.10). Colleen also has students explain answers to incorrect test items for extra credit. This lets her see students' reasoning so she can reteach a concept if necessary. For Colleen, writing is an assessment tool that shows math learning and misconceptions (see Figure 10.10).

Teachers of younger students use journal writing in math as well. Venita Dibble says it helps her second graders clarify, extend, and document their thinking. Macail drew and labeled a Venn diagram to show the results of research with her classmates about sports (see Figure 10.11). Venita encourages her students to draw pictures to help them figure out

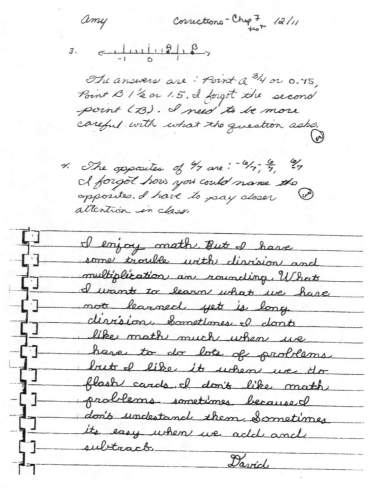

Amy   *Corrections - Chap 7   12/11*

3.

The answers are : Point A 3/4 or 0.75,
Point B 1½ or 1.5. I forgot the second
point (B). I need to be more
careful with what the question asks.

4. *The opposites of 4/7 are : -4/7, 6/7, 2/7*
I forgot how you could name the
opposites. I have to pay closer
attention in class.

I enjoy math. But I have
some trouble with division and
multiplication an rounding. What
I wants to learn what we have
not learned yet is long
division. Sometimes I dont
like math much when we
have to do lots of problems
but I like it when we do
flash cards. I don't like math
problems sometimes because I
don't undestand them. Sometimes
its easy when we add and
subtract.
                        David

FIGURE 10.10. Colleen Schultz uses math journals to assess her eighth graders' math learning and misconceptions.

problems and write their own problems as well. Sarah Evans's third-grade students explain their computations to demonstrate understanding of a concept. From his writing, Sarah knows that Kyle can teach subtraction to another student (see Figure 10.11).

IN CONCLUSION

The key components of sound writing instruction and the practices examined in this chapter provide ideas for balancing your teaching to include both the written product and the writing process. Avoiding the

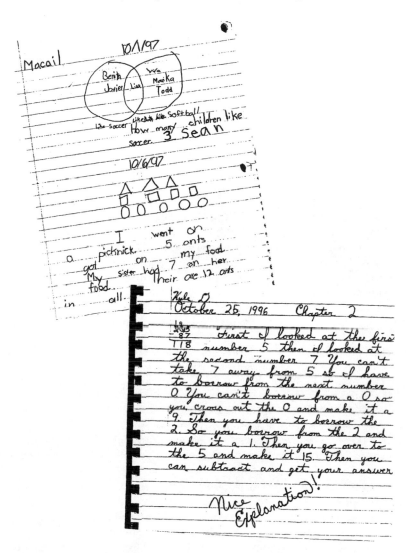

FIGURE 10.11. Venita Dibble encourages her second graders to draw Venn diagrams, and Sarah Evans checks her students' conceptual understanding through their writing in math journals.

pendulum swings overemphasizing one and excluding the other in teaching writing means that you can borrow the best from both approaches in order to develop writers who are fluent, competent, and independent. Good teachers of writing use a variety of practices that invite students to engage in and enjoy writing, learn as writers, and write well in a range of forms for a variety of purposes and audiences.

REFERENCES

Atwell, N. (1987). *In the middle: Writing, reading and learning with adolescents.* Portsmouth, NH: Heinemann.

Bottomley, D. M., Henk, W. A., & Melnick, S. A. (1998). Assessing children's views about themselves as writers using the writer self-perception scale. *The Reading Teacher, 51*(4), 286–296.

Bromley, K. (1998). *Language arts: Exploring connections.* Boston: Allyn & Bacon.

Bromley, K., Irwin-DeVitis, L., & Modlo, M. (1995). *Graphic organizers.* New York: Scholastic.

Bunting, E. (1990). *How many days to America?: A Thanskgiving story.* New York: Clarion.

Calkins, L. (1994). *The art of teaching writing.* Portsmouth, NH: Heinemann.

Cohen, B. (1990). *Molly's pilgrim.* New York: Dell/Yearling.

Gordon, C. J., & Macinnis, D. (1993). Using journals as a window on students' thinking in mathematics. *Language Arts, 70,* 37–43.

Graves, D. (1994). *A fresh look at writing.* Portsmouth, NH: Heinemann.

Hansen, J. (1996). Evaluation: The center of writing instruction. *The Reading Teacher, 50*(3), 188–195.

Harwayne, S. (1992). *Lasting impressions.* Portsmouth, NH: Heinemann.

Kane, S. (1997). Favorite sentences: Grammar in action. *The Reading Teacher, 51*(1), 70–72.

Lancia, P. J. (1997). Literary borrowing: The effects of literature on children's writing. *The Reading Teacher, 50*(6), 470–475.

Leu, D. J. (1997). Exploring literacy on the Internet: Caity's question—Literacy as deixis on the Internet. *The Reading Teacher, 51*(1), 62–67.

Leu, D. J., & Leu, D. D. (1997). *Teaching with the Internet: Lessons from the classroom.* Norwood, MA: Christopher-Gordon.

Marino, J. (1997). *Questions and answers about the new ELA standards.* Presentation to area educators, Board of Cooperative Educational Services, Binghamton, NY.

New York State Education Department. (1996). *Learning standards for the English language arts.* Albany, NY: Author.

Routman, R. (1996). *Literacy at the crossroads: Crucial talk about reading, writing and other teaching dilemmas.* Portsmouth, NH: Heinemann.

Shanahan, T. (1997). Reading–writing relationships, thematic units, inquiry learning: In pursuit of effective integrated literacy instruction. *The Reading Teacher, 51*(1), 12–19.

Sudol, D., & Sudol, P. (1995). Yet another story: Writers' workshop revisited. *Language Arts, 72*(3), 171–178.

Vacca, R. T., & Vacca, J. L. (1999). *Content area reading* (6th ed.). New York: HarperCollins.

Zaragoza, N., & Vaughn, S. (1995). Children teach us to teach writing. *The Reading Teacher, 49*(1), 42–49.

Chapter 11

CONTENT AREA
LITERACY INSTRUCTION

Thomas W. Bean
Paul Cantú Valerio
Lisa Stevens

You are in Mrs. Azner's tenth-grade Algebra II and Trigonometry II class. It's Wednesday, third period, and today's topic from Chapter 7 of your textbook, *Algebra and Trigonometry: Structure and Method,* Book 2 (Brown, Dolciani, Sorgenfrey, & Kane, 1990) will be introduced the same way as always.

Mrs. Azner, standing by the whiteboard at the front of the room says, "Today we'll be dealing with quadratic functions and their graphs. We'll start by learning how to graph parabolas where equations have the form $y - k = a(x - h)^2$, and how to find the vertices and axes of symmetry." She writes the equation, $y - k = a(x - h)^2$ and the vocabulary terms "vertices" and "axes of symmetry" on the whiteboard.

It's early fall, and the room is stuffy. You fight to stay awake, copying the equation in your notebook. The room is decorated with commercial math posters that stay there, as far as you can tell, forever. No student work is displayed. Your desk and the others are arranged in carefully ordered rows.

If you can stay awake, you can figure out parabolas. So far, you've got a solid C going in Mrs. Azner's honors class and, at this point, you'd just like to maintain it. Mrs. Azner allows no talking during her lecture and most of the class time. She drones on in a dull monotone and you hope that reading the textbook, the only book used in the class, will help you get these new concepts tonight when you get home after swimming practice. You're not sure what parabolas are good for, but you know that someday you'd like to be an engineer and design power plants. And, based on the discussions you've had with others, you know that you'll have to be able to use a lot of math.

You pull yourself out of your daydreaming about being a high powered female executive in a major engineering firm and hear Mrs. Azner say, "The y-axis is called the axis of symmetry, or the axis of the parabola."

Time passes, and some students daydream. Others like yourself take notes on the upcoming problems for tonight's homework. The problems seem to exist for the sheer purpose of torturing you every night, seemingly unrelated to anything outside the textbook. You imagine they will be useful in design work, but this is the only book used in the class and no projects are undertaken with other students that might shed some light on this mystery.

Your friend Kyle wakes up from a catnap and says, "Mrs. Azner, I don't get it. What's a parabola do?" Your other friends giggle at Kyle, and Mrs. Azner's deep-creased frown gets even more dour as she replies, "I already explained that, Kyle. If you were awake you'd know. Just make sure you understand this material by next Monday when we have the end of the chapter test."

You cringe, knowing that this will be a series of problems like those from the book and all you can do is go home and practice solving them. Somehow, these equations will be important for solving problems sometime in the future. For now, you just want to maintain your C grade, a deflating raft in a sea of obscure mathematical concepts that you think could be taught more effectively but you have no power to change the situation.

In this chapter we briefly review the literature on content area literacy and best practices. We then illustrate our view of best practices in content area literacy by taking the reader into middle school classrooms where a core team of teachers incorporate strategies and classroom climates conducive to in-depth inquiry across four content areas: (1) U.S. History; (2) English; (3) Reading; and (4) Mathematics. Following this example, we discuss implications of this model and offer additional resources designed to help other content teachers and literacy professionals develop classrooms that truly exemplify best practices.

RESEARCH ON CONTENT AREA LITERACY

Content area literacy instruction once centered almost exclusively on learning from text strategies. Now, writing, critical discussion, the integration of technology, and the infusion of fiction and nonfiction trade books to illuminate concepts receive attention at conferences and in our professional journals (Bean, 1999). Despite this effort to broaden the lens so as to include adolescents' interest in themselves, each other, and the value of talk as a means of shaping personal and cultural identities (Alvermann, Moore, Phelps, & Waff, 1998), single texts and little discussion remain the realities in many classrooms (Stahl, Hynd, Britton, McNish, & Bosquet, 1996). When students work with a single text in a content area, it becomes the authority and limits their opportunities to critically evaluate ideas across multiple sources (Geisler, 1994). In a survey of 44 high school students' opinions about the texts used in their content area classes, math and social studies textbooks were viewed as confusing, despite almost daily use (Lester & Cheek, 1998). Additionally, diverse learners may struggle with classrooms that ignore their unique cultural experiences in favor of mainstream ideas and a transmission style of teaching (Bean & Valerio, 1997; Hynds, 1997). Content classrooms that pigeonhole students based on tracking or labels adhere to a social determinism perspective where the rich get richer and the poor get poorer (Mehan, Villaneuva, Hubbard, & Lintz, 1996).

It really isn't hard to find content classrooms where students read, listen to lectures, and copy rote information in their notebooks similar to Mrs. Azner's Algebra and Trigonometry class in the vignette at the beginning of this chapter. Mrs. Azner most likely cared a great deal about her subject and was probably perplexed by the lack of student learning and involvement. But this transmission style of content delivery is the antithesis of best practices for today's students. Lifelong strategies of inquiry, critical analysis, and synthesis of information from multiple texts seem curiously absent in these settings. Yet, these are exactly the higher-order thinking skills students need as they move into various careers (Bean, 1999; Texas Education Agency, 1994; U.S. Department of Education, 1996).

Newell (1996) contrasted teacher-centered and reader-based tenth-grade literature classrooms where students read and considered a short story. Students in the reader-based setting made far more personal and high-level interpretive associations based on their story reading than did their peers in the teacher-centered classroom. The teacher-centered classroom was characterized by excessive control of the direction, pace, and organization of classroom discussion and writing (Newell, 1996). In this context, students spent much of their time trying to figure out what the teacher wanted while largely ignoring their own critical voices.

Middle and secondary school classrooms are places where time is frozen long enough to read and discuss compelling literature and nonfiction that can be used to illuminate textbook concepts. Issues of human rights, ethnic identity development, protection of the environment, and the accelerating progress of science can be explored in depth. In classrooms orchestrated by truly influential teachers, students are engaged in reading and discussion of challenging content area concepts (Ruddell, 1996). High-level questions and ample time for discussion of key concepts in English, science, social studies, mathematics, and other subjects characterize classrooms of influential teachers (Ruddell, 1996). In this setting, students learn how to find their critical voices.

It is no longer enough to preteach vocabulary, guide students' textbook comprehension, and teach independent study strategies. These are still important, but expectations for students expressed in the standards established by our content area professional associations set the bar much higher. For example, current standards for student performance in the English language arts specify the following requirement: "Students [should] apply a wide range of strategies to comprehend, interpret, evaluate, and appreciate texts" (Emig et al., 1996, p. 3). Comprehension involves the learner's construction of new understanding influenced by the dimensions of interpretation, evaluation, and appreciation of texts (McCormick & Pressley, 1997). Moreover, texts now encompass novels, multimedia, compact discs (CDs), and Internet printouts.

These new forms of learning in content classrooms call for newer forms of assessment. Although content area teachers labor under the obvious constraints of large numbers of students and expectations about content coverage, alternative assessments have been successful (Moje & Handy, 1995). For example, portfolios, projects, cooperative lab problems in science, and oral presentations can supplement and extend traditional multiple-choice and essay assessments (Moje & Handy, 1995). One chemistry teacher slowly phased in more student-centered assessments by introducing and modeling graphic organizers for the lab portion of her exam to supplement multiple-choice questions (cf. Moje & Handy, 1995). In a great example of student inquiry, this chemistry teacher had students read two articles on the use of DDT as a pesticide. One article supported its use, and the other argued for a ban on DDT. Following intensive note taking on the articles and feedback from the teacher, students completed a written exam where they had to vote for or against the use of DDT and write letters to government officials explaining their votes (Moje & Handy, 1995). Forming and supporting opinions is a missing ingredient in many content classrooms and assessments of student learning.

While we cannot expect a rapid shift toward classrooms that encourage student inquiry and assess this higher-order learning through portfolios, creative writing, and oral presentations, we can call for a gradual shift in this direction. In the section that follows, we describe an integrated unit cooperatively developed by a core team of teachers. The unit is designed to foster students' comprehension and independent learning. We place you, the reader, in the role of a seventh grader experiencing the integrated unit in history, reading, English, and mathematics. This student's teachers collaborated in the creation of the month-long integrated unit on slavery with attention to guiding students' learning before, during, and after reading (Readence, Bean, & Baldwin, 1998). As you read and experience the unit, note how the following characteristics contribute to students' comprehension and independent learning: (1) use of multiple resources; (2) cooperative learning; (3) classroom environment; (4) interdisciplinary teaching; and (5) transfer of decision making to the student.

BEFORE READING

History

As you enter Mr. Jones's classroom for first period U.S. History, you notice that two of the bulletin boards have been changed and now contain information, pictures, and artifacts about slavery. You take your seat and read the directions on the board for the beginning activity. The directions tell you to look at the two bulletin boards and then freewrite associations with what you see. You are familiar with this activity; Mr. Jones often introduces new topics by asking the class to first reflect upon what they know or associate with the subject. After about 5 to 10 minutes of writing time, Mr. Jones asks the class to divide up into small groups to discuss and compare what they have written. You move your desk closer to two of your classmates. While comparing written responses, you find that you all wrote about slavery but each student had different details. While you focused on slavery being one of the major causes of the Civil War, Jackie was reminded of more basic crimes against humanity committed during the time of slavery, and Tom wrote about how slavery still exists in the modern world. Mr. Jones then asks for volunteers from the groups to share their findings. Tom volunteers first, and while he is sharing what the three of you wrote about and discussed, Mr. Jones makes a semantic map of the topics on the markerboard. You are familiar with some of the topics raised and others sound fairly new to you, but the classroom discussion helps show how they are all related to the larger issue of slavery. By the end of the class discussion, a large and detailed map has been drawn on the markerboard. While you finish copying down the map, you listen to Mr. Jones as he explains that some of these issues and topics will be explored in school during this unit on slavery and the Underground Railroad. He also tells the class to keep in mind all the issues, as they may come in handy as the unit unfolds. The bell rings and you're off to English class.

English

Since this is Monday, you are not surprised to see a list of spelling and vocabulary words on the board. However, you are a bit relieved to see that all the words were brought up in the U.S. History discussion of slavery. You feel pretty confident that you will be able to master these words, since you'll also be studying and using them in History. Mr. Welch asks the class to make verbal–visual vocabulary squares (Readence et al., 1998) for each word. You've done this before, so you quickly take out some sheets of paper, fold them in half, and use each half for one word. You write the word in the middle of the half and leave the corners empty for the definition, part of speech, sentence, and image (Figure 11.1).

Then Mr. Welch asks you to take out your history books. You look around to make sure that you are in English, but Mr. Welch seems pretty clear in his directions, so you take out *The American Nation* (Davidson & Stoff, 1995) and open up to Chapter 13. Mr. Welch now tells the class that they may work in small groups to come up with possible definitions for the words on the board. All of the words are used in the chapter. He encourages you not to use the glossary and to put the definitions in your own words. He also instructs you to write the definitions on a piece of scratch paper, not on the vocabulary cards. As you work in your small group, you find that it is harder to come up with your own definitions than copying the glossary definitions, but your definitions do make sense, instead of being groups of words from the book. When small-group time is up, Mr. Welch leads the class through each word. Suggestions for the definition are taken from each group. Mr. Welch writes down all the

Someone who is running away from or escaping authority

noun

Fugitive

stop!

The fugitive fled from the police

FIGURE 11.1. Verbal–visual vocabulary square.

possible definitions, and then the class discusses similarities between them. In most cases, it is easy and logical to see what the definition should be, based on the context clues in the book. When a word arises that poses some difficulty, Mr. Welch asks you to consult the glossary in the back of the textbook or use the dictionary. When you encounter the strange word "antebellum," you look at the glossary and it says, "existing before the civil war."

Mr. Welch asks you to complete your verbal–visual squares (Figure 11.1) that are due tomorrow. Along with your classmates, you start on the homework in class and the verbal–visual squares are actually kind of fun to do. Mr. Welch is comfortable with students asking each other for help, too. Since the definitions were done in class, the parts of speech are pretty easy to figure out. Next come the sentences. These are easy too, because there are lots of examples in the book. You use these to create sentences of your own. But the best part is the image. Like most teenagers, you like to draw, and this part of the verbal–visual square lets you communicate the meaning of the word through a simple picture or image. You know that Mr. Welch also enjoys these, because the wall behind his desk is plastered with detailed, artistically colorful and creative verbal–visual squares. You smile as you glance at one of yours on the wall. As the bell rings, you pack up your stuff and head to your Reading class.

Reading

Even though you like all your teachers pretty well, you always look forward to Mrs. Seivers's reading class. The main reason is that she always reads aloud to the class. No matter what else has to get done that day or how poorly the day is going, you can count on some reading time in Mrs. Seivers's class. She always puts on the special lamp on her desk and lets everyone sit on the floor around her reading chair. One time you even got to sit in the reading chair and share a part of a Chris Crutcher book about a high school girl who joined a wrestling team.

Today, Mrs. Seivers asks everyone to bring their reaction journals with them when they come to sit around the reading chair. She shows everyone the cover of the book and reads the title aloud: *Christmas in the Big House, Christmas in the Slave Quarters* (McKissack & McKissack, 1994). The book tells the story of preparations for Christmas from two perspectives: one account is of festivities as seen from the slave owner's house; the other is from the viewpoint of those in the slave quarters. The book is very connected to issues about slavery considered in your History class. After reading one episode aloud and showing the pictures, Mrs. Seivers asks the students to react and respond in their reaction journals. You write about the obvious and stark differences between the two sets of lives on the plantation. But you also write about the common experiences that the plantation dwellers share: the joy of the season, the simple pleasures of family, and the sounds and smells of holiday cooking. You note how remarkable it is that these people are so fundamentally the same in their feelings and experiences; it even reminds you of some of your own experiences during the holidays. Yet, the white slave owners were firmly convinced that their slaves were not at all human, let alone created equal.

Mrs. Seivers finishes reading aloud the final portion for today and instructs everyone to choose a book for silent reading. Some students have brought their own reading material from home, but you decide to choose something from the classroom. On a table at the back of the room, Mrs. Seivers has on display many books about slavery and the underground railroad. You choose a biography of Harriet Tubman (Burns, 1992). You have just finished reading about an injury Harriet sustained as a child that led to frequent blackouts throughout her adult life when you hear Mrs. Seivers instruct everyone to clean up for the bell. You make another quick entry in your reaction journal about Harriet's injury and then return the book to the display table. During lunch you run into Alexis, a friend and classmate, and you talk about other teens in your group but also about what you are reading in the slavery unit. Alexis is reading Gary Paulsen's (1993) *Nightjohn* about a very brave slave who escaped to freedom but returned to teach others how to read at a time when reading was banned for slaves. Lunch goes by too fast, and Math class is next.

Mathematics

In Mr. Owen's Math class, you go over your homework from the day before. Math is not your best subject, but you're managing to maintain a C in his class. When the homework papers are handed in, Mr. Owens asks everyone to take out their history books. Huh? This is Math. Again, you wonder what is the fascination with the history books today but are glad that you still have yours with you. Many of your friends have already put their books away in their lockers since this is the last class of the day, so you share your book with two students sitting next to you. Mr. Owens says, "Flip through chapters 13 through 15 and scan for numerical information." Everyone makes some notes on a piece of scratch paper of the statistics they find. You are surprised at all the numbers there are in a history book. Mr. Owens asks for students to go up to the board to write down examples of different data found in the book. You read all the statistics, including Sylvia's, which says that enslaved African Americans made up one-third of the South's population by 1860. Mr. Owens explains that the class will be using statistics to create graphs and charts about the slavery era. He then explains and shows several different kinds of charts and graphs while you and the rest of the students take notes.

DURING READING

History

It is now 1 week into the unit on slavery, and you are accumulating quite a few concepts about this era. To go along with the readings, you have taken notes using graphic organizers (Readence et al., 1998). At first, Mr. Jones supplied the models for the graphic organizers, as he did with the prereading discussion on the first day of the unit. But gradually you have learned to make your own graphic organizers for the readings you do in class. You now can look at the titles, subtopics, pictures, and charts in reading, and sketch a graphic organizer to use while reading and taking notes. You have notes covering the textbook and the class lectures and videos. Yesterday and today have been devoted to creating a large graphic organizer to include all of the important facts found in the readings and the lectures (see Figure 11.2).

You have been working with a partner on this project and together have sifted out four major topics associated with slavery. Together, you have organized the more detailed information under these topics. Actually, the activity has reminded you a bit of the List–Group–Label activity (Readence et al., 1998) you did in Mr. Welch's English class on Friday. That day, everyone in class brainstormed vocabulary words associated with slavery. Then the class decided on five categories for the words and made lists of words under the five categories. This reworking of the graphic organizers is basically a more detailed version of the List–Group–Label strategy. While you are finishing adding details to the slave trade circle on the graphic organizer, Bryan, your partner, adds a border and some color to the graphic organizer.

After everyone hands in their graphic organizers, Mr. Jones spends the last part of class explaining the next activity. He says, "You will gather ideas and information for a week and then spend about two weeks producing your group project. You will be working in small groups to make the final project. Each group needs to choose one issue of slavery to explore in-depth and share with the rest of the class." Mr. Jones gives out the names of the group members and asks everyone to come to class tomorrow with some suggestions for possible topics. After class, you go up to Mr. Jones because you are upset. He assigned you to work with Bryan, who is great, and with Jesseca, whom you don't like because she wants to

FIGURE 11.2. Graphic organizer.

do everything herself. You say, "Mr. Jones, I have a problem with our group. Jesseca hogs everything and wants to do everything herself." Mr. Jones listens patiently to your objection to Jesseca. He says, "Each group member has a specific task each day. Try working with Jesseca, and if you feel the group members can't maintain their assigned jobs, then I'll see what I can do. But at this point, I'd like you to give it a try." You reluctantly agree to this arrangement.

English

You pick up a copy of *Escape to Freedom* (Davis, 1990), a play about Frederick Douglass. You have been reading this play for the past few days, and today the class is scheduled to finish the play. Mr. Welch starts the class by asking today's readers to prepare for the skit. Each day, different students are chosen to read the parts and they rehearse their respective sections the night before they perform them. Only the readers have a copy of the section being read, in the fashion of Radio Reading (Tierney, Readence, & Dishner, 1995). The rest of the class must listen carefully and ask questions later if clarification is needed. Your turn was yesterday. You did pretty well reading the words of a bigoted white man in the play. You tried to use intonation (which Mr. Wells calls reading as though you mean it) and gestures.

After today's skit is finished, the class has discussion time. During this time, anyone can ask questions about what was not clear or just say what they thought about the reading based on their close listening. You raise your hand and say, "I hadn't thought about the right to read until hearing Frederick Douglass's struggle to learn to read." This must have occurred to a lot of the other students, because many of them nod in agreement while you talk about how hard Frederick Douglass had to fight to learn to read. Christine asks, "Why were the whites so afraid of the blacks learning how to read, if they truly believed that blacks were too ignorant to learn that ability?" Jordan replies, "White people during this time convinced themselves that black people were inferior. But they knew deep down that learning how to read and write would eliminate inequality." Dylan adds, "Keeping the slaves from reading and writing also prevented them from communicating with each other outside of verbal communication."

As you pack up to leave English, your mind is filled with all the different obstacles confronted by Frederick Douglass in his successful fight for literacy. You think about how easy and accessible literature is to you as you enter your reading class.

Reading

Today, Mrs. Seivers is giving the class more time to read silently. However, she asks the students to choose something related to slavery, since many are still adding to their graphic organizers for U.S. History. Before you retrieve the Harriet Tubman biography, you read Mrs. Seivers's comments in your reaction journal. She is interested in your thoughts about the book. You answer her questions in the journal, including the one about choosing a biography. No, you tell her, you have never before chosen to read a biography on your own. It's more interesting than you thought it would be because it's still like reading a story, only it's the real story of a person's life. You set aside your reaction journal to continue with your reading of the Harriet Tubman biography. The part you are reading right now is kind of boring. It's about the time in Harriet's life after she escapes from slavery but before she becomes a conductor for the Underground Railroad. In your journal, you write that you are a bit bored with the biography but will stick with it until is gets more exciting again. That's another thing you like about Mrs. Seivers's class: It's okay to say you don't like a book. It's even okay to stop reading it before the end if you really don't like it. But you decide to stick with this biography to find out about Harriet's life as a conductor. All too soon, it's time to head for Math class.

Mathematics

Just when you get to Mr. Owens's Math class at the end of the day, you remember that you are still working on your chart of the numbers of African Americans who fought during the Civil War. You run back to your locker to retrieve your history book and barely make the dive into your seat before the bell rings. After today's assignment has been corrected and the homework for tomorrow has been explained and assigned, the rest of the class time is given to working on the graphs. You are especially thankful that you made the mad dash to your locker for the book. As you take out your list of numbers and add to it from the book, Mr. Owens walks around the room, looking at students' work. He stops at your desk and asks, "How's it going?" You reply, "It's going OK, but I'm having trouble finding more numbers and data for my graph." He looks at your list of statistics about the numbers of African Americans fighting in the Civil War at various times. "Have you looked at any other books besides the history book?" You're thinking, yeah, that makes sense, but you haven't done it. "No," you answer. Mr. Owens suggests a book that you've seen on Mrs. Seivers's display table in Reading class. You write down the name of the book and pack up your other math materials as the bell rings.

In the next few classes, the unit on slavery will be concluded and you look forward to seeing all the different projects your classmates have been working on.

AFTER READING

History

You rush to your seat in U.S. History and scramble to get out your materials for the group project. Time is running out—only two more days before the entire project is due. The project is turning out great, and you want to be sure that the final product is fantastic. You, Bryan, and Jesseca decided to focus on the Underground Railroad. After gathering information and data for a week, and after conferring with Mr. Jones about final project ideas, you and your group decided to create a typical but fictional journey on the Underground Railroad. Your project includes a map of the eastern United States, complete with a legend showing stops and events along the way. You have also decided to include a journal written by a character on the journey, using a real journal of an escaped slave, *From Slave to Abolitionist: The Life of William Wells Brown* (Warner, 1976). He tells, in the first person, of the dangers and risks that surrounded his life, especially when he became an abolitionist. This book is hard to read, and you get some help at home from your older sister, who is in high school.

In class, the hardest part of the project has been deciding what not to include. Between the readings and information gained through U.S. History, research in the library and Internet sources, and literature read in Reading and English classes, your group has collected a lot of information that might be included. Mr. Jones has helped your group to decide on the number of journal entries to include on the map, and that has helped narrow down the most essential experiences. You were able to use information gained not only in U.S. History but from all of the classes. For example, the biography of Harriet Tubman from Mrs. Seivers's class helped you come up with authentic situations for the journey.

Today, you are writing the final journal entry, which will be about the former slave's celebrated arrival at Frederick Douglass's house in Canada. Meanwhile, Bryan and Jesseca are working together on drawing a legend for the map. You have to admit that you have been continually impressed with Jesseca's cooperation. At first, Mr. Jones did give daily assignments for each member of each group, but he gradually stopped doing that as each group took more control of its daily activities. It was easier for you, Bryan, and Jesseca to decide how to spend class time since your project is different than everyone else's. You haven't had much time to look around, but you know that you are anxious to see the play written and acted out by the group in the corner about Nat Turner's slave rebellion (Oates, 1975).

As the class draws to a close, you give the final journal entry to Bryan and Jesseca to read while you look at the legend they have drawn. Each member of the group has suggestions to make the project better. The group decides what work each person will do at home so that there will be very little to do tomorrow in class. Tomorrow is the final day of the project. You are going to rewrite the journal entries, trying to write them as a barely literate escaped slave would. Bryan is going to make some parchment with burnt edges for the cover of the journal. Jesseca is going to finish adding the legend and color to the map. You are excited to see the finished journal, and you are confident that you and your group have put together a polished product that shows expertise about the Underground Railroad.

English

In Mr. Welch's English class, you finish the rough draft of your square for the whole-class patchwork quilt. Each member of the class was assigned one of the slavery words. Yours was "emancipation," and you are creating a patchword square using green construction paper with five sections (Figure 11.3).

The middle section contains the word, and each of the four flaps covers four aspects of the word: the definition, the part of speech, an original sentence, and an image. You are glad that you kept all your ver-bal–visual vocabulary squares, since you had already done much of this work for the "antebellum" vocabulary card and others like "fugitive" (Figure 11.1). But since this patchword square is going to be combined with everyone else's to make the big patchwork quilt for the hallway, you are redoing the image to make it catchy and original. You finish the last journal entry and get it approved by Mr. Welch just before the bell rings.

Reading

In Mrs. Seivers's class, time is being devoted to reading and writing for the U.S. History projects. It is during this class that you have been able to make many trips to the library for research. And now that you have fin-

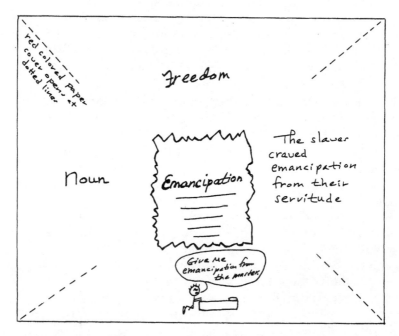

FIGURE 11.3. Patchword square for the whole-class patchwork quilt.

ished the Harriet Tubman biography, you choose to look again at *Christmas in the Big House, Christmas in the Slave Quarters* (McKissack & McKissack, 1994). As you open your reaction journal to write about this change in reading material, you notice Mrs. Seivers's comments to you. You smile at her compliments for sticking with the biography. And she agreed that the adventures of Harriet Tubman could rival the escapades of any thriller movie. When making your entry today, you note that you have never before looked at so many different books on the same topic. But you also write that you have never gotten into a subject as much as you did these past few weeks in school.

During the reading share time today, you sit with other students in front of the reading chair while Mrs. Seivers reads *Pink and Say* (Polacco, 1994). By the time Mrs. Seivers finishes the story of two young Civil War soldiers (one black and one white) and their cruelly interrupted friendship, most of the students are close to tears. You wonder if this story would have affected you this much if you hadn't learned so much about the people of this time. It sure would have been harder to relate to the young boys in the book. You find it hard to leave Reading class to move to Math when the bell rings.

Mathematics

When you get to Math class, you are glad you finished your three graphs on the computer during computer lab fifth period. Mr. Owens says, "Try to finish your graphs—and when you are finished, take a look at other students' graphs." He adds, "If you finish early, you can write math problems based on other students' graphs for extra credit. The problems must have the correct solutions written on a separate sheet of paper." Your heart does a dance of joy, for you surely could use the extra credit in this class. Since you have spent so much time looking at graphs and making your own, you feel pretty confident as you spend the class creating math problems from the other graphs on the walls. You hand in the work for extra credit at the end of class and reflect a little about your day. Even though it was hard to tell where the subject of one class separated from another, it sure made it easier to tackle a big issue like slavery. You hope that your teachers do more units like this in the future.

BEST PRACTICES THEMES FROM THE UNIT

Teacher Planning

These four teachers decided to undertake the integrated unit described in this chapter after much reflection and introspection about their teaching and students' learning. They were frustrated at the disparity between

their past efforts to engage middle school students in content area topics and the low level of student involvement and achievement. They decided that work would be done in each class to contribute to the unit,
with Mr. Jones's U.S. History class as the anchoring point for the unit.
Although Mr. Jones used the text *The American Nation* (Davidson & Stoff,
1995) as a key reference, he supplemented the book with lectures, videos, and a research scavenger hunt to the library to locate additional
biographies and stories about slavery.

The thematic unit on slavery, integrated across History, English,
Reading, and Math classes, represented the culmination of careful core
team planning on the part of these four content area teachers. This transition from more typical didactic teacher-centered lesson delivery is never
easy (Hynds, 1997). As you followed our seventh-grade student into the
initial days of this unit, you could see his surprise at instances of history
teaching in math and other classes. While he went along with this, somewhat reluctantly at first, many students take a while to adjust to the change
when teachers organize core teams and expect their students to suddenly
work comfortably in small, cooperative groups (Hynds, 1997). Indeed,
our student, who appeared to go with the flow initially, balked when told
that Jesseca, who normally preferred to hog the show, would be in his
small group. Teacher and student self-doubt are very real any time you
institute something new in the curriculum, but thematic teaching across
content fields represents a fairly radical departure from territorial depart-
mental structures. Indeed, it is rare to find this occurring at the high
school level, but we know of some school settings where a similar model
operates successfully. Many of the teaching and learning strategies demonstrated in the unit on slavery lend themselves to content area classrooms
at both middle and secondary levels. You undoubtedly noticed that these
four teachers provided a high degree of guidance in the early stages of
the unit. Then, they slowly phased themselves out to provide students with
more independent choice and strategy use in the latter stages of the unit.
This model is important for helping students develop independence in
reading and synthesizing concepts from multiple sources.

Teaching and Learning Strategies in the Unit

In the Before Reading section of the unit (above), these teachers endeav-
ored to tap and add to students' prior knowledge about slavery through
brainstorming, semantic mapping, verbal–visual vocabulary squares, reaction journals, sustained silent reading, scanning for information, and
timelines (cf. Buehl, 1995; Readence et al., 1998; Tierney et al., 1995).
During reading, students explored multiple texts, used note-taking strategies, graphic organizers, List–Group–Label tasks for vocabulary learning,

Radio Reading for read alouds, small-group collaboration, and group projects (Readence et al., 1998; Tierney et al., 1995). They increasingly made their own choices about how to undertake various tasks in the four classrooms.

By the final stage of the unit, after reading and researching their project topics, students independently collaborated on map drawing, a large vocabulary patchwork quilt made from all their individual patchword art, and they finished reading self-selected trade books related to the slavery unit. Most importantly, the unit assessment involved actual performances of plays and sharing a journal created to demonstrate the hardships experienced along the arduous journey as the slaves fled to Canada.

In the reference list we have included various professional resources and a listing of the books used for the unit on slavery. We do not claim that the transition from comfortable teacher-centered instruction to the model presented in this chapter is easy. But the alternative, the status quo, places the reading and discussion of books in content classrooms in an all too familiar stultifying atmosphere. Hynds (1997) said that books in our classrooms are often "treated rather like stone tablets, on which the great wisdom of the world was stored, rather than occasions for reconsidering, challenging, or making an impact on that world" (p. 160). For the students engaged in the unit on slavery, books took on a life that affected their emotions. This is all too rare in content area classrooms, and that needs to change.

REFERENCES

Alvermann, D. E., Moore, D. W., Phelps, S., & Waff, D. (1998). *Toward reconceptualizing adolescent literacy.* Mahwah, NJ: Erlbaum.

Bean, T. W. (1999). Reading in the content areas. In M. L. Kamil, P. B. Mosenthal, P. D. Pearson, & R. Barr (Eds.), *Handbook of reading research* (Vol. III). Mahwah, NJ: Erlbaum.

Bean, T. W., & Valerio, P. C. (1997). Constructing school success in literacy: The pathway to college entrance for minority students. (Review of the book: *Constructing school success: The consequences of untracking low-achieving students.*) *Reading Research Quarterly, 32,* 320–327.

Brown, R. G., Dolciani, M. P., Sorgenfrey, R. H., & Kane, R. B. (1990). *Algebra and trigonometry: Structure and method* (Book 2). Boston: Houghton Mifflin.

Buehl, B. (1995). *Classroom strategies for interactive learning.* Schofield, WI: WSRA Publications.

Burns, B. (1992). *Harriet Tubman.* New York: Chelsea Junior.

Davidson, J. W., & Stoff, M. B. (1995). *The American nation.* Englewood Cliffs, NJ: Prentice Hall.

Davis, O. (1990). *Escape to freedom: A play about young Frederick Douglass.* New York: Puffin Books.

Emig, J., et al. (1996). *Standards for the English language arts.* Dubuque, IA: International Reading Association.

Geisler, C. (1994) *Academic literacy and the nature of expertise.* Hillsdale, NJ: Erlbaum.

Hynds, S. (1997). *On the brink: Negotiating literature and life with adolescents.* New York: Teachers College Press.

Lester, J. H., & Cheek, E. H. (1998). The "real" experts address textbook issues. *Journal of Adolescent and Adult Literacy, 41,* 282–291.

McCormick, C. B., & Pressley, M. (1997). *Educational psychology: Learning, instruction, assessment.* New York: Longman.

McKissack, P. C., & McKissack, F. L. (1994). *Christmas in the big house, Christmas in the slave quarters.* New York: Scholastic.

Mehan, H., Villanueva, I., Hubbard, L., & Lintz, A. (1995). *Constructing school success in literacy: The pathway to college entrance for minority students.* New York: Cambridge University Press.

Moje, E. B., & Handy, D. (1995). Using literacy to modify traditional assessments: Alternatives for teaching and assessing content understanding. *Journal of Reading, 38,* 612–625.

Newell, G. E. (1996). Reader-based and teacher-centered instructional tasks: Writing and learning about a short story in middle-track classrooms. *Journal of Literacy Research, 28,* 147–172.

Oates, S. B. (1975). *The fires of jubilee.* New York: New American Library.

Paulsen, G. (1993). *Nightjohn.* New York: Bantam.

Polacco, P. (1994). *Pink and say.* New York: Philomel.

Readence, J. E., Bean, T. W., & Baldwin, R. S. (1998). *Content area literacy: An integrated approach* (6th ed.). Dubuque, IA: Kendall/Hunt.

Ruddell, R. B. (1996). Researching the influential literacy teacher: Characteristics, beliefs, strategies and new research directions. In D. J. Leu, C. K. Kinzer, & K. A. Hinchman (Eds.), *Forty-Sixth Yearbook of the National Reading Conference.* Chicago, IL: National Reading Conference.

Stahl, S. A., Hynd, C. R., Britton, B. K., McNish, M. M., & Bosquet, D. (1996). What happens when students read multiple source documents in history? *Reading Research Quarterly, 31,* 430–456.

Texas Education Agency. (1994). *Raising expectations to meet real-world needs: Report of the State Panel on Student Skills and Knowledge to the State Board of Education.* Austin, TX: Author.

Tierney, R. J., Readence, J. E., & Dishner, E. K. (1995). *Reading strategies and practices: A compendium* (4th ed.). Boston: Allyn & Bacon.

U.S. Department of Education. (1996). *Building knowledge for a nation of learners: A framework for education research, 1997* (a Report by Sharon P. Robinson, the Assistant Secretary, Office of Educational Research and Improvement, and the National Educational Research Policy and Priorities Board). Washington, DC: Author.

Warner, L. S. (1976). *From slave to abolitionist: The life of William Wells Brown.* New York: Dial.

Chapter 12

TEACHING LITERATURE AND COMPOSITION IN SECONDARY SCHOOLS

Judith Diamondstone
Michael W. Smith

Controversies abound in the field of literacy education, whether one is talking about teaching young children or teaching students in secondary schools. But it seems to us that the controversies change as students get older. The controversies surrounding the literacy education of young children understandably center on how teachers ought to teach. They presume a shared belief that the goal of instruction is to make sure that young children are able to read and write. And while there are undoubtedly significant differences in opinion about what it means to learn to read and write and how those abilities can be measured, such disputes take a backseat to those surrounding instruction. In contrast, the controversies surrounding teaching older students more often center on what the teaching is for. The public debate surrounding the Ebonics controversy in the Oakland schools provides a case in point. The original resolution by the school board was a "symbolic manifesto" validating Ebonics as a language and recommending that teachers gain an awareness of it so that they could more effectively teach African American students (Chronicle East Bay Bureau, 1997). But that recommendation was buried in the ensuing controversy, which transmogrified the intent of the recommendation (improving students' academic performance, including their Standard English) into that of validating students' home language use. As such, the recommendation was attacked by those who argued that the purpose of education is to prepare students to succeed in the culture of power, both within and outside of school. And this is just one example. If one looks at the furor surrounding Stanford's decision to change its Western civilization requirement and the uproar about E. D. Hirsch's (1987) *Cultural Literacy,* they have the same character.

What this means for us is that we can't write about what the best practices for the teaching of literature and composition to secondary students are until we explain what we think they are for. And after this rather long-winded introduction, we'd like to offer a succinct statement of our shared goal: to engage students in developing an understanding of how texts work so that they can effectively assert their textual power. In the first and second sections of this chapter, Michael will consider what this goal means for the teaching of literature and will then explain instructional strategies to achieve it. In the third and fourth sections, Judith will do the same for the teaching of composition.

WHAT READERS SHOULD KNOW
ABOUT HOW LITERARY TEXTS WORK

Understanding how literary texts work begins by recognizing that they were produced by someone and for someone. This seems like a simple idea, but it's a radical challenge both to traditional instruction informed by the New Criticism and the response-centered instruction that's often suggested as a progressive alternative to traditional instruction. Why think about authors and their intended audience? Literary theorist Peter Rabinowitz (1987; see also Rabinowitz & Smith, 1998) has argued that although the characteristics of every individual reader are different from those of any other reader, writers have to base their efforts not on those differences but rather on their sense of what most readers of their text will likely have in common. That is, in addition to imagining characters, plot, language, and so on, authors have to imagine the audience they are writing for. Rabinowitz calls the audience for whom a writer has written the *authorial audience.*

To help illustrate the kinds of things authors count on, I'd like you to try a little thought experiment. Imagine two comic strips, one that is centered around a single joke each day (I'm thinking of "Dilbert") and one that is a serial that at least occasionally takes on a serious subject (I'm thinking of "For Better or for Worse"). What does Scott Adams, the creator of "Dilbert," count on? He counts on a whole range of knowledge and beliefs, most notably his readers' understanding of bureaucracies and their suspicion of them. But perhaps most importantly, he counts on our understanding of how jokes work and our knowing that our job is to get them. I've been seeing the power of this expectation when I read the comics with my 8-year-old daughter. When we finish a strip, she either laughs or, as is usually the case with "Dilbert," says, "I don't get it." She doesn't get it because she doesn't have the knowledge and beliefs that Adams counts on. But she knows that there is something to get, and she looks to me for a succinct explanation of what that is. When we read a book together, she never asks for that kind of explanation. She may not understand the motivation for a character or some turn of the plot, and she'll ask about them. But she knows that stories can't be reduced to a succinct explanation. She knows that getting a joke is entirely different from reading a story.

On the one hand, then, authors count on our knowledge of the world and knowledge of texts. But authors count on more than just what's in our heads. They also count on what's in our hearts. Recently Lynn Johnston devoted several weeks of her "For Better or for Worse" strip to chronicling the death of the mother of one of her characters. During those weeks, she counted on lots of knowledge: knowledge of who the characters are, knowledge of hospitals, and so on. But she also counted on our caring about those characters as we read the strip. Every serial does. She may not have wanted us to lose sleep over the death of Elly's mother, but she also certainly didn't want us to say, "Well, she's only ink on paper. No need to be concerned." She counted on our playing what Rabinowitz (1987; Rabinowitz & Smith, 1998) calls the narrative audience. That is, while we are reading the strip, she counted on our pretending that her characters are more than ink on paper. She counted on our reading as though they are people worthy of our attention and concern.

Reading authorially, then, has at least two dimensions. It means pretending while we are reading that the characters about whom we are reading are people who are worthy of our attention and concern. And it means applying as best we can the knowledge of texts and the world that the author seems to be inviting us to apply. I want to stress that reading authorially does not mean simply accepting the knowledge and beliefs an author counts on. It means *provisionally* adopting them. After I've provisionally adopted the beliefs that Adams counts on, I can critique them. Once I've gotten the joke, I could criticize his cynicism or dismiss a joke as, for example, silly or sexist.

I don't want to be reductive, but one way to illustrate the difference between what I've called authorial reading and other theories is to pose the central question of each. The question implied in my discussion of "Dilbert" and "For Better or for Worse" is this: "What attitudes, knowledge, reading behaviors, values, and so on is the author counting on, and how do I feel about that?" The New Criticism, the theory that still informs most instruction about literature at least in the secondary schools, seems to me to ask: "What does this text mean?" In contrast, most response-centered theories seem to me to pose a different question: "What does this text mean to me?"

I believe that preparing students to grapple with the authorial reading question has the potential to transform the classroom for two fundamental reasons: (1) It encourages the possibility of ethical and political discussions, and (2) in so doing, it allows classes to develop a common project in which differences are resources—a situation that is, in my view, at the heart of democratic teaching. As I explained, a crucial dimension of authorial reading is playing the narrative audience. That's one reading behavior that virtually every author of a narrative counts on. What that means is pretending while we read a narrative that the people about whom we are reading are real people—people who have something to say to us.

When I taught in high school, I didn't always give characters a voice. Let me explain. Like many teachers, I taught *To Kill a Mockingbird* (Lee, 1960/1962) in my ninth-grade classes. A minor but important character in that novel is Dolphus Raymond. Let me quickly set the scene. *To Kill a Mockingbird* is set in Maycomb, Alabama, in the 1930s. The central episode of the novel is the trial of Tom Robinson, an African American unjustly accused of raping a white girl. The novel is narrated by Scout, the daughter of the man who's defending Tom. Readers are introduced to Dolphus Raymond during the trial. Townspeople are gathering to enter the courthouse. Dolphus Raymond, who the children know as the town drunk, is the only white person sitting with the black townspeople. Jem explains that Raymond has a "colored woman" and "all sorts of mixed chillun" (p. 163). During the course of the trial Dill, Scout's best friend, is so upset by the scornful cross-examination of Tom Robinson that Scout takes him from the trial. As they leave, they see Dolphus Raymond, who offers Dill a drink from the bottle he carries in a sack—it turns out to be Coca-Cola. When the children ask him about his pretense, he explains:

> "Why do I pretend? Well it's very simple. . . . Some folks don't—like the way I live. Now I could say the hell with 'em, I don't care if they don't like it. I do say I don't care if they don't like it, right enough—but I don't say the hell with 'em, see. . . .
>
> "I try to give 'em a reason, you see. It helps folks if they can latch onto a reason. When I come to town, which is seldom, if I weave a little and drink out of this sack, folks can say Dolphus Raymond's in the clutches of whiskey—that's why he won't change his ways. He can't help himself, that's why he lives the way he does. . . .
>
> "It ain't honest but it's mighty helpful to folks. Secretly, Miss Finch, I'm not much of a drinker, but you see they could never, never understand that I live like I do because that's the way I want to live." (p. 203)

When Scout asks him why he shared his pretense, he explains, "Because you're children and you can understand it . . . and because I heard that one— . . . Things haven't caught up to that one's instinct yet" (p. 203).

When I taught this novel, I asked the New Critical question: What does this mean? This brief episode was a key to my interpretation of the novel, for it established that children are naturally good, and that idea was central to my understanding of what the novel suggested about how change can come to societies. But because of the hindsight that Rabinowitz's ideas provide and because my life is different now, I have a different response to this episode. My wife and I have adopted two biracial daughters. I don't want to be helpful to those who don't understand or who disapprove of our decision. I want them to have to confront their racism. So I wonder why Dolphus Raymond was content to do so little. It seems to me that Tom Robinson was doomed to die because people like Raymond didn't challenge the status quo.

Maybe it's unfair of me to bring a 1990s' point of view into a 1930s' setting. Maybe I don't understand the risks that came from challenging the status quo. Maybe I'm basking in a morally superior position. But what's important for my discussion here is that my teaching didn't allow talking about such issues. My students never heard my feelings about the moral choices Dolphus Raymond or the other characters made. I believe that we didn't talk about them because I treated Dolphus Raymond as a tool Harper Lee was using to develop an idea rather than as a human being about whom I ought to care and with whom I could dispute. That is, we didn't talk about those issues because I lost sight of playing the narrative audience.

Then why not ask the reader-response question? Why not ask, "What does the text mean to me?" I would argue that if class members regard responses as manifestations of the uniqueness of individual readers, they are likely to listen to them uncritically. They will be much less likely to push for articulation and to challenge assumptions that they believe are poorly grounded or unfair to the characters or to the text. I neglected the opportunity to have a discussion with my students about how Dolphus Raymond responded to the racism of his society. That discussion could have led to a consideration of the comfort and cost of taking a morally superior position to people of other times and other cultures. It could have led to a greater understanding of the personal risk involved in making change. It could have led to a more careful scrutiny of others who seem on the surface to have a more appealing attitude toward race relations. But none of these discussions could have ensued if my students simply regarded my response as a function of my adopting two biracial children.

Authorial reading not only brings an ethical dimension to discussions, it brings a political dimension as well, for it allows readers to resist the politics of the author. The New Critical question "What does this mean?" doesn't allow students to resist authors because their energies are devoted to discovering meaning. The reader-response question ("What does this text mean to me?") doesn't allow resistance because it does not provide anything to resist. In contrast, the authorial reading question ("What attitudes, knowledge, reading behaviors, values, and so on is the author counting on, and how do I feel about that?") encourages resistance both because it provides something to resist and because it gives students something to resist with: what Eli Goldblatt (1995) calls their home institutions. Ethical and political discussions are not grounded in literary knowledge. Rather, they are grounded in the knowledge of how humans behave and in families and churches and whatever else helps us think about how humans ought to behave.

This brings me to my second major point: When we allow students to bring their home institutions into class in order to inform their authorial reading, we are enacting a Deweyan vision of democracy. Dewey (1916/1944) explains: "A democracy is more than a form of government; it is primarily a mode of associated living, of conjoint communicated experience" (p. 87). Dewey challenges teachers to consider the impact of their teaching on their students' immediate experience rather than on some future goals. Accepting his challenge requires teachers to create contexts that engage students in meaningful associated living.

Authorial readings can assist in achieving this goal. Dewey believed that healthy communities "possess members whose unique functions . . . complement one another" (Fishman, 1993, p. 319). My research on patterns of discourse in discussions of literature suggests that discussions that work to develop authorial readings can be the kind of occasion that Dewey urged teachers to provide.

In my study of the discourse of two adult book clubs (a description I use to designate the age of participants, not the reading material they discussed), I found that one of the primary benefits that the adults recognized was the way their discussions allowed them to draw upon each other's lives. One man put it this way: "And you get pieces of the strong points of other people's backgrounds that can help bring more into those ideas, can help those ideas grow, you know, a knowledge base that somebody else has that, that maybe I don't have, I'm able to tap into."

His comment suggests the complementarity of which Dewey speaks. I want to stress here that he talks about more than hearing from others about their lives. Rather his comment illustrates that he came to appreciate others' lives because he used them to work on the common project of doing an authorial reading.

INSTRUCTIONAL IMPLICATIONS

So what to do? I've argued that reading authorially has at least two dimensions. It means pretending while we are reading that the characters about whom we are reading are people who are worthy of our attention and concern. And it means applying as best we can the knowledge of texts and the world that the author seems to be inviting us to apply. I think that our instruction should encourage students' to engage in both of these dimensions.

If teachers want to encourage students to provisionally regard characters as human beings worthy of their attention and concern, drama can play an important part in classroom instruction. Wilhelm (1997) quotes Heathcote's contention that in drama you "put yourself into other people's shoes and by using personal experience to help you understand their point of view you may discover more than you knew when you started" (p. 100). I know that advocating the use of drama in the classroom is hardly a radical suggestion, but it's important to note that the notion of authorial reading suggests that not all uses of drama are equal. If teachers want students to play the narrative audience, they can use drama to help students imagine the lives of the characters about whom they are reading rather than engaging them in doing improvisations inspired by the text but centered on their own lives. For example, students might take on the perspective of a character in a scene in which that perspective wasn't specified. They could act out what Eco (1979) calls ghost chapters, that is, the scenes that authors omit but that we have to write in our minds. Another possibility would be to take the characters outside the story world and place them in a new context, for example, by asking Atticus Finch from *To Kill a Mockingbird* to comment on the O. J. Simpson trial and its aftermath. (See Wilhelm, 1997, and Wilhelm & Edmiston, 1998, for detailed suggestions on how to incorporate a wide variety of dramatic activities designed to achieve the goal of activating students' ethical imaginations.)

Further, if the goal of drama is to encourage students to play the narrative audience, drama ought to be a regular (as opposed to a culminating) activity, one that all students take part in. That would mean rather than assigning a few students a part for an ongoing dramatic reading, teachers ought to assign lots of short minidramas. For example, teachers could divide the class in half and assign half of the class to play one character and the other half to play another character. In a class of 30, students could pair up for 15 simultaneous dramas.

The second dimension of playing the authorial audience is applying the textual knowledge that authors count on their readers applying.

I'd like to share a unit on unreliable narrators (Smith, 1991b) that I've developed to do just that.

I'd like to start with another thought experiment. As you read the following short monologue, try to be aware of the strategies you employ to read it authorially:

> "Of course, I'm upset. Anyone would be. She leaves me for no reason. To take up with that slime. I break into a sweat whenever I think about it. And I think about it. Always. I was so good to her. Three, four, five phone calls a day. Flowers twice a week. And all this after only one date. What more could any woman ask? Now I sit in my car outside her door, watching, waiting, hoping to catch even a glimpse of her. But she's with him. I know that she is. It makes me sweat just to think about it."

Does the author share the narrator's view that the woman left the narrator for no good reason? I hope that it's clear that the answer is no. I worked to create a narrator who is unbalanced, as evidenced by his breaking into a sweat and watching the woman's house. I included the flowers and the phone calls to reveal that he is obsessed. My little story, then, is not one of man who was wronged, but rather of a woman who is being harassed.

We make this reconstruction by first recognizing that I deliberately distanced myself from my narrator. This guy is obsessed. I certainly wouldn't want readers to identify such a person with me. Authors may distance themselves in other ways, among them by making their narrators immoral, inexperienced, inconsistent, self-interested, or uneducated. Second, we determine the facts of the situation. In this case, while we question the speaker's interpretation of events, we believe certain things about his story. We believe that he calls. We believe in the flowers. We believe that he's sitting in the car watching and waiting. And because of our knowledge of the world, we know what that means. When we put it all together, we understand the harassment and may even fear for the woman's safety.

Unfortunately, students may not adjust their reading to meet the demands of stories told by an unreliable narrator (Smith, 1991a). What I'm proposing, therefore, is that teachers should design instruction to give students directed practice in the strategies experienced readers employ to read authorially.

For example, my unit on unreliable narrators begins by having students generate criteria for evaluating the reliability of narrators through a discussion of cartoons, songs, and little monologues like the one above. Such an introduction helps students identify the strategies they use. Instead of seeing the strategies as another thing that the teacher is making them do, they recognize that they, in fact, make use of them in their lives.

Once students have been introduced to the concept of unreliable narrators and to the strategies experienced readers use to recognize them and to reconstruct their judgments, they should be ready to apply these strategies to their reading of stories. However, because the strategies are new, it's unreasonable to expect that students will be able to apply them without help in doing so. To give them that help, I suggest having them discuss a series of stories with the aid of questions that highlight the strategies that experienced readers employ in assessing a narrator's reliability and in reconstructing the meaning if they find the narrator to be unreliable. In order to keep discussions of literature from becoming recitation sessions, it's important to identify questions that engage students in the important issues of the stories. If students are to use the strategies, they have to feel a reason to do so. That is why I worked to devise questions that make it clear that the strategies are a means to an important and enjoyable end, the grappling with the underlying issues that makes us lovers of literature.

Ultimately, however, it is important for students to exert their own textual power. Consequently, the instruction continues by asking students to develop and debate their interpretations of stories without the benefit of a teacher's questions. Finally, because there is no better way to have students exert their textual power than making them authors, I also ask the students to create their own unreliable narrators.

The model of instruction I'm suggesting, then, has these steps:

1. Analyze the strategies that authors count on readers' applying when they read a particular kind of literature.
2. Introduce those strategies so that students recognize their importance.
3. Give students directed practice in applying the strategies toward some significant end.
4. Move students to independent application of the strategies.

Most teachers of literature take as an article of faith that literature provides students a unique and compelling way of knowing. But most teachers also understand that all students don't share that faith. Creating contexts to engage students in working together to read authorially seems to me to be the best way to help students experience the power of literature.

WHAT WRITERS SHOULD KNOW ABOUT HOW WRITTEN TEXTS WORK

What does it mean for a teacher concerned about writing to care about how texts work? To address this question in a chapter that is also concerned with the teaching of literature obliges me to draw attention to the differences between the two subjects. Composition and literature were, in fact, taught separately for much of the history of schooling. Consider the different meanings of the term "text" in each subject. For a teacher of literature, a text ordinarily means a literary text. But while we may wish for all students to become readers of literature, it would not be realistic to imagine all of them as literary authors. A teacher of writing must keep in view all manner of written texts: In addition to stories and poems (literary texts), students must learn to write essays, reports, letters, articles, etc. Writing *something* has utilitarian overtones; it is connected to the immediate world in a way that reading a novel may not be.

What is important for a teacher of writing to keep in mind is that texts are produced not only by someone and for someone but also for a purpose; the purpose implies a social situation, a setting, a context for the writing. To write is to write something for a reason. We write letters to "keep in touch" with friends and relatives, to complain about products to manufacturers, to request services from providers, or to the editor to make our strong opinions public. We write memos to coordinate our work and scheduling with that of colleagues. If we have studied a problem, we might write a report to others who are, or who ought to be, concerned about it. In all these cases, writing means writing *to* someone *for* a given purpose.

All of these activities could be called specifically communicative. There are other functions that writing serves. If we are in school, we usually write papers to and for the teacher, which serves the function of exhibiting what we know so that someone else can evaluate it. We may also write to keep a record of events and transactions so that we and others can refer back to it. We may use writing to "hold" our thoughts in place so that we can think more *about* them, so that we can sort out and reconsider what we know, believe, and value. And we can write in order to challenge or change the way things are (Clark & Ivanic, 1997).

Except perhaps when writing "for ourselves" as an aid to our own thinking, writing always serves some social function. It means using language in ways that are tailored to particular audiences and purposes. In this sense, it is closely tied to rhetoric, the art of persuasion traditionally associated with spoken language—with oratory. Writing has not typically been taught this way in composition courses or in English classes in the public schools. However, the study of how language works and how it can be used to influence people always did occur in private grammar schools—academies for middle- and upper-class children who needed to learn the specialized uses of language required for government, the professions, and the military (Hunter, 1997). Learning to write and to speak in these specialized ways meant learning to participate in civic activities, to take on public responsibilities. It was not for "commoners" or for girls.

Times have changed! Or have they? Are we really teaching as if all our students may take up civic and professional responsibilities? And what would it mean to do so?

It should be clear by now that by "writing" I mean more than putting pen to paper (or fingertip to keyboard). Composition cannot be reduced to a set of skills and competencies that we want our students to develop. All written texts, literary or not, have to be considered in relation to the context that gave rise to them. That's part of what my colleague Michael means when he talks in the first section of this chapter about reading authorially—imagining the context that motivated the author to write a particular text. For teachers of writing, it means helping our students to read the sociocultural and situational contexts that they intend to influence.

The sociocultural context implies a world of other, related texts. Consider what a writer knows before a text is finished—sometimes before it is even begun. We first have to determine *what* the writer intends to write. Imagine, then, the author of a cookbook (whether regional, dietary, or "general"); if he/she intends to be successful, he/she will be aware of current and/or historical trends in cooking that sort of cuisine; he/she will know of related successful cookbooks that already exist, and maybe the current news about nutrition and the latest technologies for specialty cooking. Learning to *read the world that is relevant to one's writing* is a critically necessary part of learning to write authorially (i.e., influentially, with authority). The content of a text is necessarily addressed to that world, and the structure of a text generally represents how such a task (instructing others on how to cook certain kinds of meals) is accomplished. The cookbook usually begins with a table of contents, followed by an introduction to the kind of cookbook it is, and then presents a set of recipes, often divided by food group (vegetables, meats) or by parts of a meal (appetizers, main dish, deserts). These are all options, by virtue of the cookbooks that already exist, that are readily available to someone who wants to write a cookbook.

There is another sense of "context" that is a salient concern for writers—the rhetorical context. This is the immediate situational context that determines the audience and purpose for the text. To write authorially means to write in a way that is effective, that works within the immediate situational context to do what the writer intends. That means keeping in mind what is situationally *appropriate,* even if one decides to do something different—to flout conventions. A good writer knows that an important part of the meaning of an unconventional choice is that it is unconventional: The meaning will be made in relation to what was expected. The rhetorical context includes the setting, the purpose of writing, the participants, and their relations to one another.

To illustrate a rhetorical context, I will turn from cookbooks to the work I did with a student who chose the pseudonym "Zan" for publication purposes. I spent a year observing Zan's seventh-grade classroom before he was admitted to a Master's program at Harvard on the basis of his outstanding performance as a teacher, not his shaky, previous performances as a student. Zan asked me for help on his writing, and I agreed to help him as much as he wanted on the condition that I could audiotape our sessions in order to study the teaching and learning process.

When we first began to work together, Zan expressed his anger at "the man" and the institutions that excluded any discourse other than "the man's" (Zan's speech and writing showed signs of Black English Vernacular, otherwise known as African American English or Ebonics). He often spoke through the words of Malcolm X, calling for a revolution that would change the consciousness of those in power; he also referred to black artists and to the work of Paulo Freire (1970, 1973) to support his vision of cultural transformation. In these ways, Zan showed his understanding of the world in the first sense of the term "context:" He interpreted the sociocultural milieu from a particular position, which informed his stance as an educator.* He made his commitment to transforming urban education the topic of all his coursework.

However, Zan's reading of the world in the second sense of the term "context" was less astute. He insisted that his professors should meet him halfway in making meaning—that they could understand his language if they wanted to. When I insisted that they might not be able to "hear" his poetic, revolutionary texts, Zan asked, "Am I writing to idiots?" Idiots or not, Zan's professors had authority to accept or reject what Zan wrote; in fact, it was their job to evaluate his written texts in academic terms. Understanding the rhetorical context means knowing what terms of discourse are expected, that is, knowing—or guessing wisely—just who the audience is, and judging what the relative status of reader and writer require to make a particular point. A writer is foolish to write the same way to professors as to peers or to write the same way to those who are likely to see things differently as to those who agree.

To write authorially requires that the writer understand the context of writing—both the immediate situation of the writing and the wider sociocultural context—because this is the ground of an authorial iden-

---

*As an observer in Zan's classroom, I can attest that his analyses of power relations had informed the decisions he made in the classroom when he was in charge. For instance, he performed a project twice so that students had shied away from participating with the "smartest" of their peers could (in at least one case, at his urging) take up leading roles alongside these same peers.

tity. Because Zan felt threatened by the demand to use an "alien" discourse (Bakhtin, 1981), my role as tutor became that of mediator, engaging Zan's concerns while representing academic requirements, an arrangement that enabled him after a number of sessions to resolve his dilemma, as follows:

> ZAN: I NEVER wanted to use the man's words, but I did want to let the man hear. And I wanted to do in my writing what he did to us.
>
> JUDITH: You have to do it with his words.
>
> ZAN: I will use his words. I will use his words. BUT! I will use my words too. . . . I will use the language that black folks are used to . . . IN the man's words. . . . So it's [i.e., the struggle is] how to not compromise, but how to have those commingle. (cited in Cazden, 1992, p. 204; also Diamondstone, 1992, p. 188)

Of course, reading the world that is relevant to one's writing is not all that is required to write, and the full story of my work with Zan makes this point well. Together with me, Zan wrote the course papers that were most demanding; I supplied the grammatical and textual resources for writing an academic text. Zan supplied the content and the reasoning, but the substance of his texts had to be elaborated and "repackaged" in academic discourse, making the terms of argument and the relations between parts of the text linguistically explicit.

So finally I get to the last point of what it means to write authorially. It means knowing written language tools—the linguistic and textual resources that can be used to do different tasks—and knowing how to use them. This is *not* the same kind of knowledge that underlies the technical approach to writing instruction, knowledge about the desired features of a written product and the ability to produce those features. What distinguishes this knowledge (i.e., of how linguistic tools can be used to make texts that work in the world) is its connection to the other kinds of understanding a writer needs. The technical approach makes no connection to the world of the writer; it does not hold out any promise, nor can it motivate the student to do the hard work of learning.

Let me give an example of what it would mean to teach linguistic and textual resources in a way that connects to a rhetorical context and to the world of the writer. I will use one of the units developed by the Disadvantaged Schools Project in Erskineville, New South Wales, Australia, which produced instructional resources for English/Language Arts classes informed by linguistic theory (systemic functional grammar). The unit focuses on reading and writing film reviews (Gereige & Knight, 1995). Most of the recommended techniques are familiar to teachers—brainstorming, concept mapping, providing multiple models of film reviews. What is distinctive about the unit is its attention to linguistic features. Students are asked to list words that reviewers use to write about films in general (the language of "what this is about," such as *flick, action, rating, nominations, or viewing*), and the words they use to evaluate the films (the language of judgment, such as *funny, obscure, lighthearted, not the best, predictable, terrific, or fresh*). They are given words that characterize different types of films and are asked to sort them into categories (Westerns, horror films, musicals, martial arts movies, etc.). Other activities, such as small-group discussions and questionnaires, are designed to develop students' understanding of the purposes of film reviews and to elicit students' own criteria for evaluation (what makes a comedy, a thriller, etc., entertaining). Finally, the teacher works with students to name the "parts" of a film review—a catchy heading; background information about the film (the title, director, scriptwriter, where the film is showing, its rating, who is starred); a description or storyline; and then the writer's judgment of the film and recommendation to readers—typically presented in just that sequence. Students label the parts of a review of a film they are familiar with and add their own judgment and recommendation. Only then are they asked to review a film on their own, including all the parts they have identified. By then they have familiarity with the genre and language of a film review, and they can write their own evaluation of the film with authority. (Of course they are expected to draft, revise, and edit what they write as well. But notice how the unit represents a departure from the workshop arrangement described by Atwell (1987) in that it does not set the students up to invent the form of a film review entirely on their own.)

I am suggesting by this example that literacy instruction can and should be organized around activities that matter to students and that, in such a context, the formal and structural features of written language *should* be made a focus of instruction. A discussion of linguistic forms and textual structures suggests a kind of formalism, but that is because linguistic forms have historically been considered out of their contexts of use or, in the New Critical approach to literary texts, in terms of a single text, dislodged from its sociohistorical setting. A discussion of how language works in a sociocultural and situational context is necessarily political and ethical. It obliges us to look at how lexical and grammatical choices create a kind of world, naming its features, and how these choices also perform the authorial voice of the text and position its readers.

Of course, a film review draws on language that is generally familiar to students, not the kind of language that seems alien and difficult, which is the kind that many academic texts require. When Zan needed a syntactic hinge to link the pieces of his sentences together, I supplied it. But if I were to design a program of writing instruction that would prepare high school students to do the kind of writing required in college, I would incorporate units that focused on the grammatical features that characterize an academic text. And I would teach these formal devices in functional terms, in the context of challenging literacy activities that required students to position themselves as social actors.

INSTRUCTIONAL IMPLICATIONS

I have so far said that writing always means writing something to someone for a purpose and that whatever the purpose, before (and during) the act of writing, writers must read the sociocultural and situational contexts that they intend to influence. Reading implies both gathering knowledge about the world and viewing it in perspective, that is, taking an evaluative position. Reading the sociocultural context means familiarizing oneself with related texts, especially those that are relevant to one's own purposes and interests, and knowing how the task one sets out to do has been accomplished by others (i.e., knowing the functional parts of a type of text, like a cookbook or a film review). Reading the situational context means knowing what is expected, who the audience is, and the kind of language that is appropriate for the circumstances. Reading the world in both these senses precedes the kind of writing that matters to anyone.

An act of writing is an authorial act, a way of using language to make meaning. It is a way of construing a kind of world, naming its features, participants, and goings-on, and a way of projecting an authorial identity (a "voice") and positioning an audience. Different situations require different kinds of text, different kinds of language. Certain kinds of text require a language that is unfamiliar to most students, language that may seem alien and difficult. How can we introduce students to academic literacy in a way that engages them in purposive work? How can we integrate the different kinds of understandings that students need to act like critical readers and writers on a seemingly alien academic task?

One way is to incorporate reading and writing activities in a program of inquiry into how language works in the world—identifying and discussing linguistic and textual patterns within and across a range of literary and functional texts; discussing the similarities and differences across written and spoken texts produced for different purposes in various formal and informal situations; discussing linguistic and textual features in terms of the writer's projected identity, the way the texts position readers, the kind of worlds the texts construe and how those worlds are seen from the perspectives of our students; inviting students to challenge, in terms of their own home institutions, the representational, actual, and moral worlds of the texts they read and are asked in school to write; and systematically building up with students a common language for talking about language and texts in situational and sociocultural contexts. In other words, the aim should be to bring rhetoric and democratic critique into the foreground of literacy education.

These are my instructional recommendations:

1. Investigate language. Compare and contrast texts of different kinds. Identify the features that distinguish them.

2. Assign writing in the context of challenging activities that focus on a particular genre. "Chunk" various examples of texts within that genre into stages. How does each text start? How does each one end? How many parts count as the middle? What do the different parts do? How does the language vary across functional parts of the text? What is common across all the examples? What is the range of variation within the genre? Discuss the reasons for differences across the texts.

3. Draw attention to linguistic features that are characteristic of the genre, including the evaluative language that positions the writer and the readers of the text.

4. Provide opportunities for students to practice "languaging" in different ways. Provide opportunities for students to experiment with variations on a genre. Have students produce the same text from different social positions. Draw attention to the linguistic features that students themselves use to signal authority, tentativeness, enthusiasm, and other aspects of a writer's stance.

5. Discuss the effects that different linguistic and textual choices have on different readers.

6. Have students produce a text on their own only after much discussion and activities that familiarize them with the kind of text they will be writing and the range of options that already exist to write that kind of text.

Both of us believe that teaching about literary and other sorts of text in secondary schools should enable students to enter textual practices with confidence and a critical eye. We believe that if English Education is to provide the occasion for democratic critique, teachers need to provide students many opportunities to experience the power of language and to become authoritative users of language—whether they are making sense of existing texts or making texts of their own.

REFERENCES

Atwell, N. (1987). *In the middle: Writing, reading and learning with adolescents.* Portsmouth NH: Boynton/Cook.

Bakhtin, M. M. (1981). Discourse in the novel. In M. Holquist (Ed.), *The dialogic imagination: Four essays by M.M. Bakhtin* (pp. 259–422). Austin: University of Texas Press.

Cazden, C. (1992). *Whole language plus: Essays on literacy in the United States and New Zealand.* New York: Teachers College Press.

Chronicle East Bay Bureau. (1997, January 8). At Northern Arizona University, Jim Wilce's Internet Homepage. http://jan.ucc.nau.edu/~jmw22/Ebonics. html

Clark, R. & Ivanic, R. (1997). *The politics of writing.* New York: Routledge.

Dewey, J. (1944). *Democracy and education.* New York: Free Press. (Original work published 1916)

Diamondstone, J. (1992). Doing the do at a tête-à-tête: A portrait of struggles over academic texts. In A. Branscombe, D. Goswami, & J. Schwartz (1992), *Students teaching: Teachers learning* (pp. 179–191). Portsmouth NH: Boynton/ Cook.

Eco, U. (1979). *The role of the reader: Explorations in the semiotics of texts.* Bloomington: Indiana University Press.

Fishman, S. M. (1993). Explicating our tacit tradition: John Dewey and composition studies. *College Composition and Communication, 44,* 315–330.

Freire, P. (1970). *Cultural action for freedom* (Monograph No. 1). Cambridge, MA: Harvard Educational Review.

Freire, P. (1973). *Pedagogy of the oppressed.* New York: Seabury Press.

Gereige, J., & Knight, M. (1995). *Write it Right Project, English: Film review.* (Disadvantaged School Program, no. 7013). Erskineville, New South Wales, Australia: Department of Education.

Goldblatt, E. (1995). *'Round my way: Authority and double-consciousness in three urban high school writers.* Pittsburgh: University of Pittsburgh Press.

Hirsch, E. D. (1987). *Cultural literacy: What every American needs to know.* Boston: Houghton Mifflin.

Hunter, I. (1997). After English: Toward a less critical literacy. In S. Muspratt, A. Luke, & P. Freebody (Eds.), *Constructing critical literacies: Teaching and learning textual practice* (pp. 315–334). Cresskill, NJ: Hampton Press.

Lee. H. (1962). *To kill a mockingbird.* New York: Popular Library. (Original work published 1960)

Rabinowitz, P. 1987. *Before reading.* Ithaca, NY: Cornell University Press.

Rabinowitz, P., & Smith, M. W. (1998). *Authorizing readers: Resistance and respect in the teaching of literature.* New York: Teachers College Press.

Smith, M. W. (1991a). Constructing meaning from text: An analysis of ninth-grade reader response. *Journal of Educational Research, 84,* 263–272.

Smith, M. W. (1991b). *Understanding unreliable narrators: Reading between the lines in the literature classroom.* Urbana, IL: National Council of Teachers of English.

Wilhelm, J. (1997). *"You gotta BE the book": Teaching engaged and reflective reading with adolescents.* New York: Teachers College Press.

Wilhelm, J., & Edmiston, B. (1998). *Imagining to learn: Inquiry, reading, ethics, and integration through drama.* Portsmouth, NH: Heinemann.

Chapter 13

BEST PRACTICES IN LITERACY ASSESSMENT

Peter Winograd
Harriette Johns Arrington

One of the most powerful examples of good assessment that we have encountered comes from a primary classroom in Kentucky where the teacher and students were working on writing. The children had been writing stories for a while and discussing what they liked and didn't like about what they had written. After a couple of weeks of discussion, the teacher introduced a very simple form of self-evaluation to the children. The children were asked to pick their favorite piece and tell why they liked it. One of the writing prompts the teacher used asked the children to write about their favorite wish. A boy whose parents were in the midst of a divorce had written about his wish for his parents to quit fighting and get back together. He picked that piece of writing as his favorite. When the teacher asked him why, he replied, "Because I opened up my heart." This child's insight into the nature of writing will serve him well as he develops into a lifelong writer, especially if he is fortunate enough to encounter good teachers and a strong curriculum in literacy during the rest of his school career.

This vignette is important because it illustrates how far we have come in rethinking the notion of testing. We have moved from simply using tests as a way of ranking and sorting students to exploring how students can use assessment to become more competent and self-reflective; how teachers can use assessment to improve teaching and learning; and how parents, policy makers, and other stakeholders can use assessment as an integral part of a systemic approach to ensure that their schools and communities are thriving.

We will begin this chapter by trying to answer the question of what are the best practices in literacy assessment. Then, we will focus on four particular assessment strategies that teachers will find useful. We will close with some thoughts about the future of literacy assessment.

WHAT ARE THE BEST PRACTICES
IN LITERACY ASSESSMENT?

One way to answer this question is by placing literacy assessment within the larger context of the national debate on the need to reform the entire system of public education in the United States.

Since the early 1980s, *A Nation at Risk* (National Commission on Excellence in Education, 1983) and a host of other reports have warned about two related crises in American education. The first is the low levels of academic achievement of American students, in general, and the need for higher "world-class" standards of learning so that the United States can remain economically competitive in the future. The second is the continued low academic achievement of many African American, Hispanic, Native American, inner-city, and poor rural students, and the importance of helping *all* children obtain an equitable and effective education.

More recently, national attention has refocused on the crisis in the teaching profession. The National Commission on Teaching and America's Future (NCTAF; 1996), for example, examined the uneven and often dismal quality of the teaching profession and argued eloquently for the need to improve teacher preparation, teacher recruitment, teacher induction, professional development, and the ways that schools are organized. The NCTAF also argued that, next to the family, what teachers know and are able to do is the most important influence on what students learn, and that recruiting, preparing, and retaining good teachers is the central strategy for improving the nation's schools. The seriousness of this issue becomes apparent when one considers that approximately 2 million teachers will need to be hired in the next 7–8 years.

In an attempt to address these crises in education, policy makers, educators, and other stakeholders have engaged in a variety of reforms since the mid-1980s. In the last few years, we have witnessed a more comprehensive and systemic approach to education reform. Systemic reform, in this context, refers to efforts that include several key components: (1) the promotion of meaningful goals and standards for all students; (2) the increased focus on accountability and assessment of students, teachers, and schools; (3) alignment of policy approaches and the coordination of a wide variety of educational, economic, social, and health institutions and stakeholders to support student achievement: (4) the restructuring and aligning of public education governance to support student achievement; (5) an increase in the funding and other resources needed to support student achievement; and (6) an increased appreciation for the role of the classroom teacher.

Let us consider, for a moment, some of the latest evidence behind the concerns over excellence, equity, and the importance of teachers. These data are drawn from a number of crucial sources including the National Education Goals Panel (NEGP; 1998), the *Quality Counts* reports published by Education Week (1997, 1998), Kids Count Data Book (1997), the U.S. Department of Education (1998), and the National Assessment of Educational Progress (NAEP; 1998).

Here are some of the national statistics related to reading and writing:

- Twenty-eight percent of fourth-grade students scored at the proficient or advanced reading level on the NAEP in 1994.
- Forty-one percent of fourth-grade students scored below the basic reading level on the NAEP in 1994.
- The average reading score of 17-year-olds has improved slightly over the last 25 years, but the reading scores for 1996 were not significantly different from reading scores for 1973.
- Thirteen-year-olds have shown moderate gains in reading from 1971 to 1996.
- The performance in reading for 9-year-olds improved from 1971 to 1980 but have declined slightly since that time. However, the average score for 9-year-olds in 1996 was higher than that for 9-year-olds tested in 1971.
- An overall pattern of declining performance is evident in the average writing scores of eleventh-grade students from 1984 to 1996.
- The writing performance of eighth-grade students and fourth-grade students has not changed significantly from 1984 to 1996.

But here are some other U.S. statistics that are equally important that let us take a look at the larger picture:

- Some 40% of 3- to 5-year-olds were not enrolled in nursery school or kindergarten in 1993.
- Some 21% of children were in poverty in 1994.
- Some 15% of children lived with parents who were high school dropouts in 1994.

- Some 43% of minority children attend urban schools. Most of them attend schools in which half of the students are poor and that are predominately, often completely, minority.
- In about half of the states with large cities, a majority of urban students fail to meet even minimum standards on national tests.
- The poorest students are at greatest risk. In urban schools where most of the students are poor, two-thirds or more of children fail to reach even the "basic" level on national tests.
- Schools in urban districts tend to be larger, have higher truancy rates, and less involvement from parents than other schools. Urban teachers are twice as likely as other teachers to report that violence is a problem in their schools.
- Big-city districts are twice as likely as nonurban ones to hire teachers who have no license or who have only an emergency or temporary license.
- Some 12% of all newly hired teachers enter the workforce without any training at all, and another 15% enter without having fully met state standards.
- Some 23% of all secondary teachers do not have a college minor in their main teaching field.
- Most elementary teachers have only 8.3 minutes of preparatory time for every hour they teach, and high school teachers have just 13 minutes of preparation time for every hour they teach.
- School districts spend only 1–3% of their resources on teacher development, as compared to much higher expenditures in most other professions and in other countries' schools.
- Student drug use and attempted sales of drugs have increased since 1996.
- Threats and injuries to public school teachers have increased since 1996.
- More teachers are reporting that disruptions in their classrooms interfere with their teaching.

These statistics, as well as those from other reports produced by national, state, or local organizations, are powerful tools in helping us understand what education is about and what our priorities should be. We see the debates about meaningful goals and standards, the use of multiple indices to measure progress, the disagreements about what these measures really mean, the arguments over resources, and the struggles to reform teaching and learning as a sign of health in American education. Although the process can be frustrating, it does show a country coming to grips with the reality of public education. One way to measure best practices in assessment at the national level, then, is to see how well they motivate and guide us in improving the lives of all our students.

We can also argue that the best practices in literacy assessment are those that help us understand the larger issues, frame important goals, gather multiple kinds of evidence, and engage us in rich discussions about how to help children become better readers, writers, listeners, and speakers. To put it another way, no particular assessment is a best practice in and of itself; rather, the quality of assessments lies largely in how wisely they are used. Here are some thoughts about using assessment wisely.

The most effective practices in literacy assessment are those that occur in the classroom between a competent teacher and a confident student. The most effective practices in literacy assessment happen when teachers and students can work side by side in a trusting relationship that focuses on growth, nurturing, and self-evaluation. Indeed, the most important change in the way we think about assessment is the move toward more teacher- and student-controlled evaluations and away from more standardized tests controlled by individuals outside of the classroom. But this shift in thinking is a fundamentally radical one, and we must understand some of the powerful influences that must be addressed if we are to turn new ways of thinking about assessment into widespread practice in real classrooms.

One of the most difficult challenges we face is ensuring that there is an adequate supply of teachers who are well prepared in the instruction and assessment of literacy and that these teachers work in contexts enabling them to focus on meeting the needs of their students. This is no small problem when one considers the nation's need for so many new teachers and that, in too many states, prospective teachers may take only one course in reading. What is even more frightening is that some teachers who enter the classroom through alternative routes may take no classes in reading at all. Professional organizations like the International Reading Association, the American Federation of Teachers, the National Council on Measurement in Education, and the National Education Association have developed thoughtful standards about what teachers should know and be able to do in terms of evaluation and assessment, but it will take serious revision of teacher preparation programs and professional development opportunities to ensure that the majority of teachers can meet these standards.

Moreover, we need to ensure that when new teachers obtain their licenses, they begin to work in schools that are better organized for and more supportive of student and teacher success. When teachers have too heavy workloads and too little time, to ask them to engage in more intensive evaluation and instruction with individual children is unrealistic and unfair. We want to stress that we are not blaming teachers. We are fortunate that the majority of teachers are competent, caring, and committed. What we are saying is that if we truly believe that teachers should engage in the assessment of literacy, then we must strengthen the ways teachers are prepared and improve the ways schools are organized.

Another challenge we face is thinking more wisely about how to meet the needs of the children in the classrooms. For example, we must understand that when teachers teach reading or writing, they often face issues that are not just educational in nature. The fact that 41% of America's fourth graders scored below the basic level on the 1994 NAEP reading exam is a social, political, economic, *and* educational problem. Keeping this context in mind is vital because the best practices in literacy assessment are those that help us understand these broader issues and how to deal with them systemically so that all students receive an excellent and equitable education. Assessments that focus on a narrow or isolated aspect of literacy are not as effective as those that give us a richer picture of the whole child and the world in which he/she lives.

We must also understand that assessments are a very limited tool in dealing effectively and fairly with children and the world they live in. Madaus (1994) makes this point most eloquently when he cautions us about becoming too enchanted with assessments and overlooking the needs to attend to student health, nutrition, and living conditions, teacher training, and other critical components in the system of education: "[T]here is a danger that technological solutions, such as alternative educational assessment, will blind policymakers and the public to the reality that we Americans cannot test, examine, or assess our way out of our educational problems" (National Commission on Testing and Public Policy, as cited in Madaus, 1994, p. 79).

The National Council on Education Standards and Testing (NCEST; 1992) raises a similar point when it states, "particularly for [those children] who have historically experienced less success in schools, such as the poor, ethnic minorities and students with disabilities, schools should ensure the opportunity to learn as a critical condition for valid and fair use of assessment results" (p. 6). Note that this is not just concern voiced by a few advocates in the field; rather, it is a specific standard for the fair use of educational and psychological tests developed by the American Educational Research Association, the American Psychological Association, and the National Council on Measurement in Education (AERA, APA, & NCME; 1985). The issue of fairness in assessment, especially for students whose first language is other than English, is one of critical importance that has yet to be addressed in any systematic fashion across the nation (e.g., King, 1993; LaCelle-Peterson & Rivera, 1994; Linn, 1994; Valdés & Figueroa, 1994; Winograd, Blum Martinez, & Noll, in press).

We need to understand the larger issues in education and education reform because we often find ourselves torn between the demands for assessment for accountability and the need for assessment to improve instruction. We need to understand why there is such a demand for assessment for accountability and how to deal with that demand in a constructive fashion. We find it useful to think about assessment by identifying what kinds of audience it can serve. For example, assessment can help:

- Students become more self-reflective and in control of their own learning
- Teachers focus their instruction more effectively
- Educators determine which students are eligible for Chapter 1, programs for the gifted, or special education
- Parents understand more about their children's progress as learners
- Administrators understand how groups of students in their schools are progressing
- Legislators and citizens understand how groups of students across the state or nation are progressing
- Policy makers and stakeholders monitor the implementation and effectiveness of various reform initiatives including those that deal with school finance and resource allocation, governance and policy issues, or changes in curriculum

The best practices in literacy assessment, then, are those that use a variety of appropriate indices to address the needs of different audiences. Thus the choice does not have to be assessment for accountability versus assessment for instruction. Some states like Vermont, Kentucky, or Maryland have attempted to develop assessment systems that are performance based, linked to clear standards, support important curricular goals, and useful for both accountability and instructional purposes. In addition, these assessments are viewed as part of an overall approach to reform that includes professional development, curriculum development, and other key changes to the system. As Darling-Hammond (1994) notes, the fundamental question "is whether assessment systems will support better teaching and transform schooling for traditionally underserved students or whether they will merely reify existing inequalities" (p. 7).

Unfortunately, too many states, too many districts, and too many schools continue to use assessments in ways that do reify existing problems and inequalities. The misuse of tests continues despite the large body of research that indicates traditional forms of assessments have the following drawbacks: (1) they are based upon outdated and inappropriate models of learning; (2) they narrow the curriculum in destructive ways; (3) they provide results that are misinterpreted and misused; and (4) they often produce invalid results that vary widely for individuals and reflect confounded effects related to socioeconomic status, home experiences, or testing conditions (e.g., Darling-Hammond, Ancess, & Falk, 1995; Haney & Madaus, 1989; Winograd, Paris, & Bridge, 1991).

Fortunately, the large body of research on assessment has produced some principles for using assessments wisely. Here are some of our favorites drawn from a number of sources including the National Center for Fair and Open Testing (1998), Fairfax County Public Schools (1998), Harp (1996), Johnston (1991), Stiggens (1997), Tierney (1998), and Winograd and Perkins (1996); the best practices in literacy assessment are those that:

- Focus on important goals and support meaningful student learning
- Are based on our most current and complete understanding of literacy and children's development
- Are based in the classroom rather than imposed from outside
- Involve students in their own learning and enhance their understanding of their own development
- Use criteria and standards that are public so that students, teachers, parents, and others know what is expected
- Start with what the students currently know
- Involve teachers (and often students) in the design and use of the assessment
- Empower teachers to trust their own professional judgments about learners
- Nourish trust and cooperation between teachers and students
- Focus on students' strengths rather than just reveal their weaknesses
- Provides information that is used to advocate for students rather than to penalize them
- Support meaningful standards based on the understanding that growth and excellence can take many forms
- Are integral parts of instruction
- Gather multiple measures over time and in a variety of meaningful contexts
- Provide educators and others with richer and fairer information about all children, including those who come from linguistically and culturally diverse backgrounds
- Are part of a systemic approach to improving education that includes strengthening the curriculum, professional development for teachers, and additional support for helping those children who need it

- Provides information that is clear and useful to students, teachers, parents, and other stakeholders
- Continually undergo review, revision, and improvement

WHAT ARE SOME OF THE BEST CLASSROOM STRATEGIES FOR LITERACY ASSESSMENT?

Trying to identify which literacy assessments are "best" in some absolute sense is a task fraught with perils because the field of literacy has a huge array of classroom assessment methods and strategies that can be used either effectively or inappropriately. For example, we have informal reading inventories; running records; concepts about print tests; assessments for emergent literacy; tests for book-handling knowledge; miscue analysis; portfolios; conference guides; anecdotal records; guides for evaluating metacognitive awareness; holistic and analytic evaluations of writing; interview, attitude, and disposition surveys; retellings; basic skills tests; decoding skills tests; comprehension checklists; spelling checklists; vocabulary tests; student self-assessments of reading and writing; observational checklists for reading and writing; checklists and surveys for parents; literacy profiles; language records; developmental scales for emergent reading and writing; performance tasks, rubrics, and benchmarks for literacy; instruments for placing students in programs; instruments for taking students out of programs; and methods for teachers to evaluate the teaching of literacy.

And, of course, the general field of education has all kinds of performance-based assessments, standardized tests, diagnostic tests, norm-referenced tests, criterion-referenced tests, constructed response tests, psycho-educational batteries, achievement tests, minimum-competency testing, group tests, individual tests, graduation examinations, or college entrance examinations, all of which involve the assessment of literacy. Please note that we have not even mentioned issues like report cards, computer-based assessments, assessments for special populations, or other many of the other assessment-related topics. (Here is an interesting factoid: The National Center for Fair and Open Testing [1998], estimates that more than 100 million standardized exams are administered in America's public schools each year, including IQ, achievement, screening, and readiness tests. Clearly one best practice would be to reduce the amount of testing that takes place, especially for young children!)

Because our space is limited, we will focus on a few assessment strategies that we find particularly helpful for students, teachers, and parents. These strategies grow out of the national debates about excellence and equity and the concerns surrounding the limitations of traditional, multiple-choice tests. A number of researchers have attempted to develop forms of assessment that are based on current models of learning, enhance and strengthen the curriculum, are easily understood by stakeholders, and produce valid results and positive educational consequences for all children. The class of approaches loosely labeled alternative assessments, performance assessments, or authentic assessments is the result of these efforts (U.S. Congress, Office of Technology and Assessement, 1992; Wiggins, 1989).

Alternative assessment is assessment that occurs continually in the context of a meaningful learning environment and reflects actual and worthwhile learning experiences that can be documented through observation, anecdotal records, journals, logs, work samples, conferences, portfolios, writing, discussions, experiments, presentations, exhibits, projects, performance events, and other methods. Alternative assessments may include individual as well as group tasks. Emphasis is placed on self-reflection, understanding, and growth rather than responses based only on recall of isolated facts. Alternative assessments are often called performance-based or authentic assessments because they are intended to involve learners in tasks that require them to apply knowledge faced in real-world experiences, rather than a test given after and disconnected from instruction. Alternative assessments are also intended to enhance teachers' professional judgment, rather than weaken it, and to provide teachers with systematic opportunities to engage in linguistically and culturally appropriate evaluation and instruction.

In the remainder of this chapter, we will examine four recommended authentic assessment strategies for use in classrooms: (1) performance tasks and rubrics; (2) portfolios; (3) observation strategies: anecdotal records and developmental checklists; and (4) student–teacher conferences. It is important to note from the beginning that these strategies are interrelated. Portfolios will contain, among other things, evidence of each student's performance in writing and reading, records of the teacher's observations, and conferences with students. Portfolios, performance tasks, anecdotal records, and developmental checklists provide important starting points for conferences between teachers and students.

It is also important to note that our discussion of these strategies in only an introduction to what is available. The field of literacy has benefited from a long list of outstanding educators and researchers who have made and are making critical contributions to the field of assessment. Here are a few sources of assessment instruments and approaches that will provide you with a flavor of what is available: Clay (1985); Darling-Hammond et al. (1995); De Finan (1992); Gambrell and Almasi (1996); Goodman, Goodman, and Hood (1989); Goodman, Watson, and Burke (1987); Harp (1994, 1996); Hill and Ruptic (1994); Johnston (1991); Morrow and Smith (1990); Rhodes (1993); Rhodes and Shanklin (1993); Sharp (1989); Stiggins (1997); Tierney, Carter, and Desai (1991); and Valencia, Heibert, and Afflerbach (1994).

Performance Assessments and Rubrics

Performance assessments are those assessment strategies that require students to demonstrate what they know and are able to do. Performance assessments usually require a student to perform a task rather than select an answer. Performance assessments come in many forms including writing different kinds of essays, narratives, expository texts, letters, or short answers; completing mathematical computations; making oral presentations; conducting an experiment; or working cooperatively in a group. One of the most common kinds of performance assessment is assembling a portfolio (like those that will be described in the next subsection).

Performance tasks are usually coupled with rubrics or other sets of criteria so that the teachers and the students can judge the quality of the performance. A rubric is a set of descriptions or characteristics identifying the qualities of good work. Rubrics can range from simple statements to elaborate lists of explicit criteria that distinguish between levels of performance ranging from poor to outstanding. Note that rubrics can be used at any level of sophistication and in a variety of assessment situations. For example, Figures 13.1–13.3 are some rubrics for writing that teachers use in Kentucky: Figure 13.1 is one that teachers can use to evaluate the quality of students' stories; Figure 13.2 is the writing rubric developed by the State of Kentucky; and Figure 13.3 is a more student-friendly version developed by teachers so that their upper-primary students would have a better sense of what was expected of them.

Baron (1991) offers five criteria that are useful for thinking about performance tasks. Three of her criteria are applicable to most performance tasks: (1) the task is meaningful to both teachers and students; (2) the task requires the student to locate and analyze information as well as draw conclusions about it; and (3) the task requires the student to communicate results clearly. In addition, Baron (1991) offers two other criteria that are often, but not always, applicable to performance tasks: (4) the task is framed by the student and (5) the task requires students to work together for at least part of the task.

The attraction of performance assessments is that they offer tremendous potential for evaluating students' ability to achieve the kinds of authentic and complex learning, thinking, and doing envisioned in our richest descriptions of our most valued learning goals. In addition, good

WRITING STORIES

Name_____ Date_____ Grade _____

Characteristics of student's writing
  0 = no evidence   1 = poor   2 = fair   3 = good   4 = excellent

Title_____

RATING

Focus/Purpose —————————————————— 0 1 2 3 4

  * **The introduction to the story creates interest.**   Comments:
    a. *The reader is put right into the action.*
    b. *The setting creates suspense.*
    c. *The characters are faced with a problem.*

  * **The reader can predict conflicts and consequences.**
    a. *The characters may be endangered by the power of nature.*
    b. *A conflict between characters may end in the loss
       of something very important.*
    c. *Making the wrong decision or taking the wrong action may make
       the characters feel bad about themselves.*

  * **The reader can predict possible story endings.**
    a. *The setting gives clues to what might happen.*
    b. *The characters give hints to what they will do.*
    c. *The story's conflict or problem has predictable solutions.*

Content/Organization ——————————————— 0 1 2 3 4

  * **The action in the story builds toward an exciting
    event, or an important decision (the climax).**   Comments:
    a. *The action leads logically to the climax.*
    b. *Characters act predictably.*
    c. *The writer is always giving clues to what will happen next.*

  * **All details are used to develop the *story's* conflict.**
    a. *Details make the action more exciting.*
    b. *Description makes characters more interesting and believable.*
    c. *The description of the setting makes the action more believable.*

  * **Only characters important to the story's
    action are used.**

  * **The story's problem faced, the writer
    concludes with:**
    a. *a moral or lesson learned.*
    b. *the characters thinking or talking about their experience.*
    c. *the characters returning to life before the start of the action.*

Grammar, Mechanics, Usage —————————— 0 1 2 3 4

  * **Errors in punctuation and spelling do not interfere**   Comments:
    with reading the story.
  * **Words are used that fit the characters and the
    action in the story.**

NOTES AND COMMENTS ————————————————————————

FIGURE 13.1. A rubric for evaluating story writing. Reprinted with permission
of Richard Williams.

KENTUCKY WRITING ASSESSMENT
Holistic Scoring Guide

Portfolio ID _____

NOVICE	APPRENTICE	PROFICIENT	DISTINGUISHED
• Limited awareness of audience and/or purpose • Minimal idea development; limited and/or unrelated details • Random and/or weak organization • Incorrect and/or ineffective sentence structure • Incorrect and/or ineffective language • Errors in spelling, punctuation, and capitalization are disproportionate to length and complexity	• Some evidence of communicating with an audience for a specific purpose; some lapses in focus • Unelaborated idea development; unelaborated and/or repetitious details • Lapses in organization and/or coherence • Simplistic and/or awkward sentence structure • Simplistic and/or imprecise language • Some errors in spelling, punctuation, and capitalization that do not interfere with communication	• Focused on a purpose; communicates with an audience; evidence of voice and/or suitable tone • Depth of idea development supported by elaborated, relevant details • Logical, coherent organization • Controlled and varied sentence structure • Acceptable, effective language • Few errors in spelling, punctuation, and capitalization relative to length and complexity	• Establishes a purpose and maintains clear focus; strong awareness of audience; evidence of distinctive voice and/or appropriate tone • Depth and complexity of ideas supported by rich, engaging, and/or pertinent details; evidence of analysis, reflection, insight • Careful and/or subtle organization • Variety in sentence structure and length enhances effect • Precise and/or rich language • Control of spelling, punctuation, and capitalization

INSTRUCTIONAL ANALYSIS

Examining instructional strengths can assist in improving writing and learning in your school. Student portfolios can provide evidence of instructional practices. This section of the Holistic Scoring Guide is provided to assist teachers in identifying sustained evidence of instructional practices through examination of student products. When scoring a student portfolio, scorers may identify any number of the instructional strengths listed below.

The sustained performance in this portfolio demonstrates that the student has applied instruction in the following areas:

O Establishing focused, authentic **Purposes**

O Writing for authentic **Audiences**, situations

O Employing a suitable **Voice and/or Tone**

O Developing **Ideas** relevant to the purpose

O Supporting ideas with elaborated, relevant **Details**

O **Organizing** ideas logically

O Using effective **Transitions**

O Constructing effective and/or correct **Sentences**

O Using **Language** effectively and/or correctly

O **Editing** for correctness

COMPLETE/INCOMPLETE PORTFOLIOS

A portfolio is **Incomplete** if any of the following apply:

- Table of Contents does not contain required information
- Table of Contents does not note study area information (including the letter to the Reviewer)
- There are fewer than 7 different entries, including Table of Contents and the Letter to the Reviewer
- One or more entries are plagiarized (must be proven)
- One or more entries are different than those listed in the Table of Contents
- One or more entries are written in a language other than English
- One or more entries demonstrate only computational skills, or consist of only diagrams or drawings
- Portfolio contains a group entry
- Entries are out of order without clear descriptors on the Table of Contents

A portfolio is **complete and will be scored** according to how well it fulfills the criteria of the Holistic Scoring Guide if one or more entries are:

- out of order with clear descriptors on the Table of Contents
- questionable concerning fulfillment of the purpose for which it is intended
- questionable concerning plagiarism, but the plagiarism cannot be proven

SCORING CRITERIA

CRITERIA	OVERVIEW
PURPOSE/AUDIENCE	The degree to which the writer • establishes and maintains a purpose • communicates with the audience • employs a suitable voice and/or tone
IDEA DEVELOPMENT/SUPPORT	The degree to which the writer provides thoughtful, detailed support to develop main idea(s)
ORGANIZATION	The degree to which the writer demonstrates • logical order • coherence • transitions/organizational signals
SENTENCES	The degree to which the writer includes sentences that are • varied in structure and length • constructed effectively • complete and correct
LANGUAGE	The degree to which the writer exhibits correct and effective • word choice • usage
CORRECTNESS	The degree to which the writer demonstrates correct • spelling • punctuation • capitalization

FIGURE 13.2. Kentucky State Department of Education's rubric for evaluating writing. Reprinted with permis-

	NOVICE.	APPRENTICE.	PROFICIENT.	DISTINGUISHED.
AWARENESS OF AUDIENCE PURPOSE.	(face, no expression)	(face with eyes)	(smiling face)	(smiling face with freckles)
IDEA DEVELOPMENT.	HUH?	OK. I DON'T SEE THE LIGHT I NEED MORE DETAILS...	MESSAGE IS CLEAR NOW I SEE THE LIGHT.	I SEE THE BRIGHT LIGHT THE MESSAGE SHINES.
ORGANIZATION:	LOOSE PIECES THAT DO NOT ALWAYS FIT TOGETHER	SOME IDEA PIECES FIT TOGETHER BUT NEED MORE PIECES TO COMPLETE.	THE IDEAS FIT TOGETHER... A COLORFUL PICTURE FORMS.	ALL IDEAS TIGHTLY FIT TOGETHER. A COMPLETE, COLORFUL PICTURE FORMS.
SENTENCE WORDING...	AND MY DOG.	I LOVE MY DOG. HE IS MY BEST FRIEND.	"SNOOPY IS MY BEST FRIEND," I SAID "I LOVE HIS FRIENDLY BARK AND LARGE FLOPPY EARS."	"MY BEST FRIEND IS NOT AN ORDINARY COMPANION, I EXPLAINED. "HE HAS LONG FLOPPY EARS, A FRIENDLY BARK AND WIGGLES ALL OVER EVERYTIME HE SEES ME!"
SURFACE FEATURES..	USES •	USES • ?!	USES • ?! " ",	USES • ?! " ", : ; — ...

FIGURE 13.3. Teacher-made rubric for evaluating writing based on Kentucky writing assessment. Reprinted with permission of Kentucky Department of Education.

performance assessments are intended to be both an integral part of the curriculum and a way to assess student performance at the same time, thus reducing the traditional tension between testing and teaching.

Performance assessments can range from simple to complex. Here is a description from the Kentucky Department of Education's (1994/95) KIRIS assessment for eighth graders. Students are asked to read two poems about basketball ("Two Points," by Lillian Morrison, and "Foul Shot," by Edwin Hoey) and then asked to write a response to the following question: "How doe the language by the two poets help create images? Support your answer with examples from both poems."

The students' responses were scored on a 5-point rubric:

Level 4—Student describes a variety of ways in which poets create images through the use of language, citing several strong examples from each poem.

Level 3—Student describes at least two ways in which poets create images; examples are strong but focus on most obvious aspects of language use.

Level 2—Student discusses the action taking place in the poem(s) and correctly identifies the poets' intentions but does not focus on the use of language to achieve their goals. References to use of language is only general (e.g., playful language) without specific examples.

OR

Student describes the effect of poem(s) on the reader. Reference to the use of language in only general.

Level 1—Student discusses the poems in vague or personal terms and does not include description of the use of language to achieve effect.

Level 0—Response is totally incorrect or irrelevant.

Marzano, Pickering, and McTighe (1994) provide a thoughtful framework and a useful guide for teachers interested in developing performance assessments. Here is a step-by-step approach they suggest that involves teachers and students in the development of performance assessments:

Step 1. Have students identify a question related to something in the current unit of study that interests them.

Step 2. Help students develop a first draft of a task that requires them to extend and refine their knowledge and then to use that knowledge in a meaningful way.

Step 3. Help students think about what kinds of criteria or standards will be used to evaluate the quality of the performance. Marzano and his colleagues (1994) suggest that students identify standards from the categories of information processing, effective communication, habits of mind, and collaboration/cooperation listed below:

1. Complex thinking standards
   - Effectively uses a variety of complex reasoning strategies
   - Effectively translates issues and situations into manageable tasks that have a clear purpose
2. Information processing standards
   - Effectively uses a variety of information-gathering techniques and information resources
   - Effectively interprets and synthesizes information
   - Accurately assesses the value of information

- Recognizes where and how projects would benefit from additional information
3. Effective communication standards
   - Expresses ideas clearly
   - Effectively communicates with diverse audiences
   - Effectively communicates in a variety of ways
   - Creates quality products
4. Collaboration/cooperation standards
   - Works toward the achievement of group goals
   - Effectively uses interpersonal skills
   - Contributes to group maintenance
   - Effectively performs a variety of roles
5. Habits of mind standards
   - Self-regulation
     a. Is aware of his/her own thinking
     b. Makes effective plans
     c. Is aware of and uses necessary resources
     d. Is sensitive to feedback
     e. Evaluates the effectiveness of his/her own actions
   - Critical thinking
     f. Is accurate and seeks accuracy
     g. Is clear and seeks clarity
     h. Is open-minded
     i. Restrains impulsively
     j. Takes a position when the situation warrants it
     k. Is sensitive to the feeling and level of knowledge of others
   - Creative thinking
     l. Engages intensely in tasks even when answers or solutions are not immediately apparent
     m. Pushes the limits of his/her own knowledge and abilities
     n. Generates, trusts, and maintains his/her own standards of evaluation
     o. Generates new ways of viewing a situation outside the boundaries of standard conventions

Step 4. Help students rewrite the task so that it highlights the standards identified in Step 3.

Step 5. Help students write the rubrics for the standards they have been built into the task.

Marzano et al. (1994) illustrate their steps by describing how a student studying the life of John F. Kennedy might develop a performance task:

Step 1. Identify the question: What would have happened if John F. Kennedy had not been assassinated?

Step 2. Write the draft of the task: "I'm going to examine what might have happened if John F. Kennedy had not been assassinated. I will identify what other people have written about this possibility and then take and defend my own position."

Step 3. Identify the standards: The student decides he/she wants to accurately assess the value of information, express ideas clearly, and assesses and monitors his/her own performance in a group.

Step 4. Rewrites the task: "I'm going to examine what might have happened if John F. Kennedy had not been assassinated. I will identify what other people have written on this topic. Working with two other people who have identified similar topics, I will gather information from various sources. While working with my research partners, I will keep track of how well I monitor my behavior in the group. As I collect my research information, I will keep track of the most relevant information and the information that is interesting but not as relevant and report on this. After I have collected enough information, I will take a position and defend it, taking special care to express my ideas clearly."

Step 5. Develop a rubric for evaluating the performance task: The student develops a rubric that identifies four levels of performance:

> *Level 4*—"I have communicated my position clearly. In addition, I have provided support that is very detailed and rich."
> *Level 3*—"I have presented my position clearly. I have provided adequate support and detail."
> *Level 2*—"I have presented some important information, but I have no clear position."
> *Level 1*—"I have communicated only isolated pieces of information."

These are two examples of performance assessment involving literacy, and this subsection is only a brief introduction to the potential richness of such assessments. Fortunately, there are a large number of useful references available including Stiggins (1997), Marzano et al. (1994), the ERIC Clearinghouse on Assessment and Evaluation (1998), and the National Center for Research on Evaluation, Standards, and Student Testing (CRESST; 1998) which has an extensive web site that includes newsletters, research articles, guidebooks, videos, and a data bank of performance assessment items. As we noted earlier, performance assessments can range from very simple to more complex. We suggest you start with some of the simple tasks and see what you and your students can learn.

Portfolios

Portfolios come in a variety of forms and each serves a different purpose. One of the most popular types is a *best-pieces portfolio,* which contains examples of work that the student (sometimes with help from the teacher) considers to be his/her best efforts. Best-pieces portfolios are popular because they encourage students to become more reflective about and involved in their own learning. Indeed, some writers have argued that what makes such portfolios significant learning and assessment tools is that these collections include "student participation in selecting contents, the criteria for selection, the criteria for judging merit, and evidence of student self-evaluation" (Paulson, Paulson, & Meyer, 1991, p. 60). Tierney et al. (1991) also stress that such portfolios represent the students' abilities to engage in the processes of selecting, comparing, self-evaluation, sharing, and goal setting.

Setting the criteria for selection, setting the criteria for judging merit, and showing evidence of student self-evaluation is perhaps the most important aspect of best-pieces portfolios. One of the most powerful strategies in the teachers' repertoire for developing these crucial self-assessment skills in students is pairing portfolios with rubrics like those described in the previous subsection.

Here is a step-by-step introduction to using best-pieces portfolios and rubrics in your classroom:

• Start by identifying some of your most effective instructional activities in literacy. Do you teach the students the writing process, have them develop neat stories, engage them in literature-response groups, oral presentations, sustained silent reading, literary analyses, and the other best practices in literacy instruction? Pick one instructional strategy that really works well for you and your students.

• After students have gained some experience with this particular instructional activity, begin to discuss what make a good piece of work in this context. For example, after students have written some stories, ask, "What makes a good story?" After making presentations, ask them, "What makes a good presentation?" Other key questions include "What makes someone a good writer?" and "What makes someone a good reader?"

• During these discussions, the teacher and the students develop a set of criteria for what makes a good piece of work. These criteria should be recorded on charts on the walls or other public places and used as the basis for rubrics that students will use (and revise) to help them internalize standards of quality.

After the students have become comfortable with discussions about what makes a good piece of work, move on to the next set of steps:

• Introduce the concept of portfolios to the students. Discuss with students why they are creating portfolios—so that the students, their teachers, and their parents can see how they have grown as readers and writers.
• Confer with the students to identify what kinds of work samples should be included in the portfolios and how those materials will be stored. Student work samples that could be included in portfolios include literature-response logs, writing samples, story retellings, drawings, and so forth. Some ways of storing these samples include large envelops, notebooks, folders, boxes, or baskets.
• Develop some simple forms for helping students evaluate the pieces of work they include in their portfolios. Many teachers produce a simple form that asks students questions like the following:

What does your portfolio show that you can do?
What is your favorite piece in your portfolio? Why?
Which pieces show that you have made improvement?
What changes would you like to see in your portfolio?

This is also a good time to have students develop a table of contents for the portfolio.

• Work with students to set up a regular schedule for making additions to their portfolio. Make sure there are regular times in class when students can select the work samples, evaluate and record why they have been chosen as best pieces, and update their portfolios.
• Use the portfolios regularly to inform classroom discussions about what makes for a good piece of work. Take time for students to compare their earlier work samples with later ones to reflect on how they have grown as readers and writers.
• Use the portfolios for student–teacher conferences, as well as for student–parent–teacher conferences. Enjoy!

Helping children reflect on their own work forms the crucial interplay between assessment and instruction. Consider this example from an experienced first-grade elementary teacher who had her class come up with ideas of what they thought makes a piece of writing a "best piece." Her students generated the following list:

• Uses imagination
• The words make good pictures in your mind

- Uses things that happen in your own life
- Uses writing rules like periods and capitals
- Spaces between words
- Makes you want to keep on reading

The teacher reported, "After writing down these ideas, the children were able to evaluate the work in their portfolios with some focus. The audience for this best piece was their own classmates. When they realized that their best pieces would truly circulate among their friends, they became very self-motivated and diligent in their efforts to present their best pieces to their friends in the best possible light. Now when someone reads his best piece in the classroom, the author isn't satisfied unless he is getting laughs, gasps, or smiles from the audience. We now choose a best piece about once every 2 months, which has added a lot of enthusiasm to our writing workshops."

Experienced teachers understand that the ability to engage in self-reflection does not just appear fully developed in children. Students need to see teachers and other students modeling self-assessment. Students also need support and structure as they learn to evaluate themselves as learners.

We should note that best-pieces portfolios often grow to include other kinds of student work, teacher records, and other kinds of evidence that can be used as additional sources of information for evaluating a student's progress. The diverse evidence that goes into such expanded portfolios can be gathered by both students and teachers and often includes the following:

- Table of Contents
- Samples of daily work including student responses to reading journals, anecdotal records of reading conferences, graphs showing progress during running records, sight words, or other developmentally appropriate instructional activities
- Drafts and revisions of written work
- Dictionary of the words the student is working on
- Lists of written work and/or ideas for future writings
- An "I can do" list showing progress on different aspects of writing
- Anecdotal records/editing notes from writing conferences
- Records of student's self-evaluation
- Summaries of Running Records or Informal Reading Inventories
- Logs of books read
- Audio and/or videotapes
- Lists of goals identified by students
- Lists of goals identified by the parents

- Lists of goals identified by the teacher
- Records of student–teacher or parent–teacher conferences
- Observational checklists.

It is important to note that *not all of these contents are necessary for all students at all times*. Teachers and students need to adapt portfolios so that they are useful sources of information, not extra burdens of busy work! But the key thing to keep in mind about portfolios is the point that Paulson et al. (1991) made when they stated that a portfolio is something done *by* the child rather than *to* the child.

Observation Strategies: Anecdotal Records and Developmental Checklists

Most of the information that teachers gather about their students comes from observation. Yetta Goodman (1978) coined the term "kidwatcher," and it is clear that good teachers are constantly watching their kids. "Kidwatching" can take many forms—from informal observation on the playground to systematic keeping of anecdotal records to more structured observations using checklists. In this subsection, we'll examine how teachers can use anecdotal records and developmental checklists to assess students' growth in literacy.

The use of observation as a means of assessment has a number of advantages. For example, anecdotal records, developmental checklists, and other forms of observation:

1. Provide teachers with a way of assessing how students interact with a complex environment both in and out of classrooms; teachers thus gain a more valid understanding of what each student really knows and can do.
2. Provide teachers with an efficient method of assessing students in many different situations over longer periods of time, thus increasing the reliability of the assessment data.
3. Focus the teacher's attention on what the student can do, rather than on what the student has yet to learn.
4. Provide a relatively stress-free form of evaluation for students, especially those students who become anxious when they take standardized tests.

Anecdotal Records

Anecdotal records are informal observations about what students are learning, how students are responding to instruction, or any other student behaviors, actions, or reactions that might provide teachers with some insight. The best time to take anecdotal records is while observing the students, and it is often helpful to focus on questions such as the following:

What can this child do?
What does this child know?
How does this child read, write, work on projects, work with others, or deal with other important aspects of the school curriculum?
What kinds of questions does the child have about his/her work?
What does the child's attitude reveal about his/her growth and progress?

In addition, anecdotal records often include teacher comments and questions that are particularly useful in helping teachers become more reflective about their teaching. Experienced teachers record their observations of the student over time and then analyze their anecdotal records for patterns of what the student knows and can do. This information is then used to plan appropriate instruction.

Occasionally, some teachers find anecdotal records a bit overwhelming and difficult to keep. In our experience, that happens when teachers are making anecdotal records more complex than they need to be. The purpose of anecdotal records is to provide teachers with a tool for sharpening their professional judgments. One school system (Fairfax County Public Schools, 1998) suggests using a focused approach to anecdotal records:

- Select a focus for your anecdotal record keeping. In reading, for example, the focus may be on fluency, comprehension, response, or interests. In writing, the focus may be on voice, organization, or mechanics.
- Develop a simple form that includes space for the date of the observation, the names of the students being observed, and the focus of the observation.
- Observe the students you are most concerned about, and take notes about what you see in terms of the focus area.
- Use the anecdotal records, along with any other evidence you have gathered, to plan instruction. As you work with the students, continue to observe how they perform and grow in the areas you identified.

The Fairfax County Public Schools (1998) suggest a simple format (see Figure 13.4) for keeping track of anecdotal records for individual students.

Individual Anecdotal Record

Name _____

Date	Reading	Writing	Oral Language

FIGURE 13.4. Fairfax County Public Schools' individual anecdotal record. Reprinted with permission of Fairfax County Public Schools.

Checklists

Checklists are a common and useful way of evaluating students' growth in literacy. A major reason for their appeal is that checklists can be used in a wide variety of instructional contexts. Teachers interested in looking at examples of checklists will find lots of good ideas in the literature on assessment (e.g., Clay, 1985; Goodman et al., 1989; Harp, 1994, 1996; Kemp, 1989; Routman, 1988, 1991; Sharp, 1989).

Figures 13.5–13.7 are some checklists for observing students' use of reading strategies before, during, and after reading. Figure 13.5 comes from some of our earlier work, while the Figures 13.6 and 13.7 come from Fairfax County Public Schools' *Expanding Expectations: Assessing* (1998).

Conferences

Conferences between teachers and students are another powerful tool in the repertoire of teachers adept at authentic assessment. Conferences can be quick and informal, or they can be a bit more structured and systematic. Informal conferences may last from 3 to 4 minutes and may focus on something interesting that the teacher has seen or overheard. More structured conferences may take a bit longer and follow a predictable pattern where students have a good idea of what is expected of them. For example, if the conference concerns books read or papers written,

Reading Strategies Assessment

Name _____ Date _____

Directions: As you observe each student, place a check mark beside each behavior in the appropriate column: Most of the Time, Working On, or Not Yet. You may wish to note the circumstances or activity in which observation occurred, write in additional criteria or notes about the evaluation, and write ideas for next instructional steps.

Circumstances or Activity				
Behavior	**Most of the Time**	**Working On**	**Not Yet**	**Notes/Next Steps**
THINK AHEAD				
Previews the reading text				
Recalls prior knowledge				
Sets purposes for reading				
Understands different ways of reading				
THINK WHILE READING				
Checks and clarifies comprehension				
Understands different kinds of meaning				
THINK BACK				
Reviews comprehension				
Applies different kinds of reading				
Additional Criteria:				

FIGURE 13.5. Checklist for evaluating the use of reading strategies before, during, and after reading.

Reading Individual Checklist:	Name: _____		
		Date	Comments
Before Reading:			
Chooses reading as a free-time activity			
Has book ready during reading workshop			
Chooses appropriate reading material			
Previews text before reading			
During Reading:			
Connects background knowledge to information in the text			
Predicts and confirms or revises predictions			
Discusses explicit and implied information			
Stops and reviews reading with longer texts			
Reads familiar material with clarity, using punctuation appropriately			
When confronting unfamiliar words: Cross-checks one cue with another (phonics, language structure, and meaning)			
Rereads			
Uses chunks within multisyllable words to read			
Skips, reads on, and goes back to check word			
Asks another person for help			
Self-corrects to preserve meaning			
Uses features of informational text to aid comprehension			
Uses the context to determine meaning of new or unfamiliar vocabulary			
After Reading:			
Retells, including important information or events			
Relates what is read to personal knowledge			
Makes comparisons			
Categorizes and classifies appropriately			
Summarizes			
Draws conclusions based on reading			
Shows understanding using graphic organizer			
Uses information in the book to justify a response, confirm a prediction, or discuss elements of fiction or important information			
Written response shows evidence of critical thinking and a reflective stance towards reading			
Evaluates use of author's craft			

FIGURE 13.6. Fairfax County Public Schools' individual checklist for evaluating the use of reading strategies before, during, and after reading. Reprinted with permission of Fairfax County Public Schools.

then students are familiar with the kinds of questions that will be asked. The important point with conferences of all sorts is that they should be conducted in a secure and comfortable manner so that students feel encouraged to take risks and share their ideas.

Student–teacher conferences are an important method of authentic assessment because they provide information about (1) what the student is learning; (2) the student's understanding about reading, writing, mathematics, and other aspects of the primary program curriculum; (3) the student's interests; (4) the areas where the student needs help; (5) what things the teacher is doing that the student feels is particularly helpful; and (6) what things the student would like to learn next.

Reading Group Checklist:	Names							
Before Reading: Dates→								
Chooses reading as a free time activity								
Has book ready during reading workshop								
Chooses appropriate reading material								
Uses text structure to preview								
Connects background knowledge to information in the text								
During Reading:								
Predicts and confirms, or revises predictions								
Stops and reviews reading with longer texts								
Reads familiar material with clarity, using punctuation appropriately								
When confronting unfamiliar words: Cross-checks one cue with another (phonics, language structure, and meaning)								
Rereads								
Uses chunks within multisyllable words to read								
Skips, reads on, and goes back to check word Asks another person								
Self-corrects to preserve meaning								
Uses features of informational text to aid comprehension								
Uses the context to determine the meaning of new or unfamiliar vocabulary								
After Reading:								
Retells, including important information or events								
Relates what is read to personal knowledge								
Makes comparisons								
Categorizes and classifies appropriately								
Discusses explicit and implied information								
Summarizes								
Draws conclusions based on reading								
Shows understanding using graphic organizer								
Uses information in the book to justify a response, confirm a prediction, or discuss elements of fiction or important information								
Written response shows evidence of critical thinking and a reflective stance towards reading								
Evaluates use of author's craft								

FIGURE 13.7. Fairfax County Public Schools' group checklist for evaluating the use of reading strategies before, during, and after reading. Reprinted with permission of Fairfax County Public Schools.

Conferences are often centered around something specific—a book being read, a paper being written, a performance task being developed, a project being completed. Here are some examples of different kinds of conferences and the kinds of information that teachers can learn.

Reading Conferences

The teacher can listen to the student read, discuss a book previously read, or talk about the student's book log. These activities enable a teacher to learn about (1) the strategies that the student uses; (2) whether the student reads for meaning; (3) whether the student is developing fluency; (4) the student's interests; (5) whether the student selects reading materials of appropriate difficulty; (6) whether the student is reading a variety of genre; (7) the student's progress in comprehending and re-telling what has been read; and (8) the student's ability to justify an opinion about what has been read.

Writing Conferences

The teacher can help the student brainstorm topics to write about, discuss early drafts, listen to a student read a paper, or talk about which piece of work the student considers his or her best work and should be included in the best-pieces portfolio. These activities enable teachers to learn (1) how the student is progressing in the use of the writing process; (2) what the student knows about organization, topic development, mechanics and spelling; (3) whether the student can effectively verbalize opinions, ideas, and feelings; (4) whether the student can write for a variety of purposes; and (5) whether the student can edit drafts to a point where others can understand them.

Clearly, conferencing can be a useful form of assessment in any aspect of the curriculum. As students talk about mathematics, social studies, art, and other activities and projects, teachers can learn (1) what students need to learn next; (2) whether students can communicate what has been learned; (3) whether students can use appropriate terminology; (4) whether students can use strategies to solve real-life situations; and (5) whether students can provide reasonable explanations for solutions and strategies.

Paris (1995) suggests a very useful framework for conferences that works well with reading and writing conferences, as well as those conferences that take place around portfolios. He suggests that teachers ask questions about performance, processes, and perceptions. Performance questions focus on the actual work the student has completed. Process questions focus on reading and writing strategies. Perception questions focus on the students' motivational and affective perceptions about literacy and include the dimensions of effort, confidence, independence, and self-evaluation. Here are some sample performance questions:

What do you like about this paper?
Tell me why you included this piece in your portfolio?
What books did you read this last month?
Did you meet your writing (reading, learning) goals this month?

Here are some sample process questions:

How did you get the idea for writing this?
What do you do when you read something you don't understand?
How did you change your writing as you made drafts?

Here are some sample perception questions:

What is the hardest part about reading (writing) for you?
Who are your favorite authors?
What kinds of books do you read at home?
What is the best part of your writing?
What makes you a good reader? A good writer?
What should we work on this year to make you a better reader (or writer)?

Paris (1995) also reminds us of the key guidelines to keep in mind about conferences: Do not ask too many questions; let the student do most of the talking. Be interested, enthusiastic, and brief. Celebrate the students' strengths and be constructive about areas of growth. Record pertinent comments that will be useful information for later review. Remember that the goal of the conference is student self-reflection.

THE FUTURE OF BEST PRACTICES
IN LITERACY ASSESSMENT

When we identify any practice as a "best practice," we run the risk of assuming that the particular practice has reached the peak of its development. Nowhere is this risk more dangerous than in the area of assessment. While we have made major progress in terms of improving assessment, we have so much farther to go (e.g., Darling-Hammond, 1994; Linn, 1994; Winograd, 1994; Worthen, 1993). Here are some questions that face educators interested in continually improving the assessment of literacy:

- How do we ensure that literacy assessments are viewed as an integral part of a systemic approach to educational reform rather than as a panacea to cure all of education's ills?
- How do we ensure that literacy assessments meet rigorous standards of validity, reliability, authenticity, relevance, responsiveness, and flexibility?
- How do we ensure that literacy assessments meet rigorous standards for fairness, particularly for those students with diverse language or cultural backgrounds?

- How do we ensure that the consequences of literacy assessments are positive for all students?
- How do we set standards of student performance that are clear, fair, and achievable, and then ensure that assessment and instruction are integrated in constructive ways that improve teaching and learning?
- How do we ensure that all teachers receive adequate initial preparation and continued professional development in the ethical, technical, and instructional uses of educational assessments?
- How do we involve parents, school-board members, legislators, and other stakeholders in the process of changing assessments from a process of ranking and sorting students to one of helping all students reach their full potential?

Given American education's love–hate relationship with testing in general, given the long history of literacy assessment in particular, given the large number of approaches for literacy assessment, given the broad range of functions these assessment serve, and given the number of issues to be solved, it is important to ask, "What is the future of literacy assessments?"

We believe that the future of literacy assessments can be positive and we are cautiously optimistic. Educators, researchers, and policy makers interested in literacy have shown a willingness to explore new forms of assessment because we do recognize the limitations and problems inherent in our traditional and current approaches. We are making a genuine effort to reconceptualize the purpose of assessment from a process of classifying children into winners and losers to a process for providing students with opportunities to gain ownership of and insight about their own learning and providing teachers with a rich basis for making professional judgments about instruction. Many of the forms of literacy assessment that have been developed recently do have the capacity to provide rich, descriptive evidence of students' literacy understandings and growth, and the potential to provide educators with ways to engage in linguistically and culturally appropriate evaluation and instruction, particularly for students whose knowledge is poorly reflected in traditional standardized testing.

But we must be realistic. The overuse and misuse of testing and evaluation is still a major problem, and the current national emphasis on accountability is likely to exacerbate the problem. This situation is not going to change until Americans have more trust and confidence in teachers and in public schools.

In summary, our current practices in literacy assessment have the potential to strengthen or weaken the ways we teach reading and writing in schools. Whether the effects of literacy assessment will be positive or negative depends upon our ability and willingness to ask the right questions about our priorities, our schools, our teachers, our students, and ourselves.

REFERENCES

American Educational Research Association, American Psychological Association, and National Council on Measurement in Education. (1985). *Standards for educational and psychological testing.* Washington, DC: American Psychological Association.

Baron, J. (1991). Strategies for the development of effective performance exercises. *Applied Measurement in Education, 4,* 305–318.

Clay, M. (1985). *The early detection of reading difficulties* (3rd ed.). Portsmouth, NH: Heinemann.

Darling-Hammond, L. (1994). Performance-based assessment and educational equity. *Harvard Educational Review, 64,* 5–30.

Darling-Hammond, L., Ancess, J., & Falk, B. (1995). *Authentic assessment in action: Studies of schools and students at work.* New York: Teachers College Press.

De Fina, A. (1992). *Portfolio assessment: Getting started.* New York: Scholastic.

Education Week. (1997). *Quality counts.* www.edweek.org.

Education Week. (1998). *Quality counts.* www.edweek.org.

ERIC Clearinghouse on Assessment and Evaluation. (1998). www.ericae.net/main.htm.

Fairfax County Public Schools. (1998). *Expanding expectations: Assessing.* Annadale, VA: Author.

Gambrell, L., & Almasi, J. (1996). *Lively discussions!: Fostering engaged reading.* Newark, DE: International Reading Association.

Goodman, K., Goodman, Y., & Hood, W. (1989). *The whole language evaluation book.* Portsmouth, NH: Heinemann.

Goodman, Y. (1978). Kidwatching: An alternative to testing. *Journal of National Elementary Principals, 57*(4), 41–45.

Goodman, Y., Watson, D., & Burke, C. (1987). *Reading Miscue Inventory: Alternative procedures.* New York: Richard C. Owen.

Haney, W., & Madaus, G. (1989). Searching for alternatives to standardized tests: Whys, whats, and whithers. *Phi Delta Kappan, 70,* 683–687.

Harp, B. (1994). *Assessment and evaluation for student centered learning.* Norwood, MA: Christopher-Gordon.

Harp, B. (1996). *The handbook of literacy assessment and evaluation.* Norwood, MA: Christopher-Gordon.

Hill, B., & Ruptic, C. (1994). *Practical aspects of authentic assessment: Putting the pieces together.* Norwood, MA: Christopher-Gordon.

Johnston, P. (1991). *Constructive evaluation of literate activity.* New York: Longman.

Kemp, M. (1989). *Watching children read and write: Observational records for children with special needs.* Portsmouth, NH: Heinemann.

Kids Count Data Book. (1997). www.aecf.org.

King, D. (1993). Assessment and evaluation in bilingual and multicultural classrooms. In B. Harp (Ed.), *Assessment and evaluation in whole language classrooms* (pp. 159–176). Norwood, MA: Christopher-Gordon.

LaCelle-Peterson, M., & Rivera, C. (1994). It is real for all kids?: A framework of equitable assessment policies for English language learners. *Harvard Educational Review, 64,* 55–75.

Linn, R. (1994). Performance assessment: Policy promises and technical measurement standards. *Educational Researcher, 23*(9), 4–14.

Madaus, G. (1994). A technological and historical consideration of equity issues associated with proposals to change the nation's testing policy. *Harvard Educational Review, 64,* 76–95.

Marzano, R., Pickering, D., & McTighe, J. (1994). *Assessing student outcomes: Performance assessment using the dimensions of learning model.* Alexandria, VA: Association for Supervision and Curriculum Development.

Morrow, L., & Smith, J. (1990). *Assessment for instruction in early literacy.* Englewood Cliffs, NJ: Prentice Hall.

National Assessment of Educational Progress (NAEP). (1998). www.nces.ed.gov/naep.

National Center for Fair and Open Testing. (1998). www.fairtest.org.

National Center for Research on Evaluation, Standards, and Student Testing (CRESST). (1998). //cresst96.cse.ucla.edu.

National Commission on Excellence in Education. (1983). *A nation at risk: The imperative for educational reform.* Washington, DC: U.S. Government Printing Office.

National Commission on Teaching and America's Future (NCTAF). (1996). *What matters most: Teaching for America's future.* New York: Columbia University.

National Council on Education Standards and Testing (NCEST). (1992). *Raising standards for American education: A report to Congress, the Secretary of Education, the National Education Goals Panel, and the American people.* Washington, DC: U.S. Government Printing Office.

National Education Goals Panel (NEGP). (1998). www.negp.gov.

Neill, D., & Medina, N. (1989, May). Standardized testing: Harmful to educational health. *Phi Delta Kappan, 70,* 688–697.

Paris, S. (1995). *Coming to grips with authentic instruction and assessment.* Presentation sponsored by the Education Center, Torrance, CA.

Paulson, F., Paulson, P., & Meyer, C. (1991). What makes a portfolio a portfolio. *Educational Leadership, 48,* 60–64.

Rhodes, L. (1993). *Literacy assessment: A handbook of instruments.* Portsmouth, NH: Heinemann.

Rhodes, L., & Shanklin, N. (1993). *Windows into literacy: Assessing learners K–8.* Portsmouth, NH: Heinemann.

Routman, R. (1988). *Transitions: From literature to literacy.* Portsmouth, NH: Heinemann.

Routman, R. (1991). *Invitations: Changing as teachers and learners K–12.* Portsmouth, NH: Heinemann.

Sharp, Q. (1989). *Evaluation: Whole language checklists for evaluating your children.* New York: Scholastic.

Stiggens R. (1997). *Student-centered classroom assessment.* Upper Saddle River, NJ: Merrill.

Tierney, R. J. (1998). Literacy assessment reform: Shifting beliefs, principled possibilities, and emerging practices. *The Reading Teacher, 51,* 374–391.

Tierney, R. J., Carter, M. A., & Desai, L. E. (1991). *Portfolio assessment in the reading–writing classroom.* Norwood, MA: Christopher-Gordon.

U.S. Congress, Office of Technology Assessment. (1992). *Testing in American schools: Asking the right questions* (OTA-SET-519). Washington, DC: U.S. Government Printing Office.

U.S. Department of Education. (1998). www.ed.gov.

Valdés, G., & Figueroa, R. (1994). *Bilingualism and testing: A special case of bias.* Norwood, NJ: Ablex.

Valencia, S., Hiebert, E., & Afflerbach, P. (1994). *Authentic reading assessment: Practices and possibilities.* Newark, DE: International Reading Association.

Wiggins, G. (1989). A true test: Toward authentic and equitable forms of assessment. *Phi Delta Kappan, 70,* 703–713.

Winograd, P. (1994). Developing alternative assessments: Six problems worth solving. *The Reading Teacher, 47*(5), 420–423.

Winograd, P., & Perkins, F. (1996). Authentic assessment in the classroom: Principles and practices . In R. Blum & J. Arter (Eds.), *Handbook for student performance assessment* (pp. 8:1–8:11). Alexandria, VA: Association for Curriculum Development.

Winograd, P., Blum Martinez, R., & Noll, E. (in press). Alternative assessment of learning and literacy: A U.S. perspective. In D. Wagner, B. Street, & R. Venesky (Eds.), *Literacy: An international handbook.* Westminster, CO: Westview Press.

Winograd, P., Paris, S., & Bridge, C. (1991). Improving the assessment of literacy. *The Reading Teacher, 45,* 108–116.

Worthen, B. (1993, February). Critical issues that will determine the future of alternative assessment. *Phi Delta Kappan, 74,* 444–454.

Part III

SPECIAL ISSUES

Chapter 14

MEETING EACH CHILD'S LITERACY NEEDS

Dixie Lee Spiegel

Envision a classroom of children you have taught or whom you hope to teach. Are all the children alike? Do they all look alike? Surely not. Are they all on grade level in every subject? In your dreams. Do they all learn in the same ways? Of course not. A few consistently learn everything easily and make us feel like superteachers. A few struggle with almost every new task and haunt our dreams. But most students have days filled with both successes and struggles, easy tasks and challenges, topics they are interested in and topics they avoid at all costs. Most breeze through some tasks with no help from us at all, need our guidance and coaching on some new tasks, and occasionally need very explicit help in order to succeed with other tasks. And as teachers most of us wouldn't want it any other way. I can't think of anything more boring than teaching a class of 25 clones in Lake Woebegon. The wondrous diversity and uniqueness of children makes teaching interesting and challenging to many of us.

The focus of this chapter will be on meeting the literacy needs of each child, teaching Jameria and Bill and Hannah, not third graders or writing or American History. Each child in every classroom is unique, and each child deserves a teacher who acknowledges these differences by modifying instruction and tasks and materials based on an understanding of what each child needs. This is not a simple challenge, but it is a challenge we can meet.

This book is about *best practices,* not *best practice,* and this chapter is not going to offer one silver bullet that makes it easy for teachers to meet children's individual literacy needs. This is a chapter for teachers who are flexible, reflective kidwatchers, who are willing to try new ideas in thoughtful ways, who are willing to modify or even abandon comfortable practices that don't seem to be working with some children, and who are not blinded by what "ought" to be, what they hoped would be, or what used to be, but who are aware of what is.

THE ISSUES

The choices are legion; the issues are many. Each day teachers make many decisions, including the following:

- Between student- and teacher-selected materials (Hiebert & Colt, 1989)
- Between trade books and basals (Baumann & Ivey, 1997; Canney, 1993; Fisher, Flood, & Lapp, Chapter 8, this volume; Roser & Hoffman, Chapter 9, this volume)
- Between whole group and small group interactions (Reutzel, Chapter 16, this volume; Strickland, 1994/1995)
- Between planned and unplanned instruction (Durkin, 1990; Yatvin, 1991)
- Between authentic assessment and standardized, norm-referenced instruction (Spiegel, 1994; Strickland, 1996; Winograd & Arrington, Chapter 12, this volume)
- Between teacher-directed instruction and learner-directed discovery (Baumann & Ivey, 1997; Carroll, Wilson, & Au, 1996; Delpit, 1988; Dudley-Marling, 1996; Hiebert & Colt, 1989; Pikulski, 1994; Purcell-Gates, 1996; Spiegel, 1992, 1994; Strickland, 1994/1995, 1996)
- Between isolated strategy emphases and use of whole texts (Baumann, & Ivey, 1997; Duffy & Roehler, 1987; Freppon & Headings, 1996; McIntyre, 1996; McIntyre, Kyle, Hovda, & Clyde, 1996; Roehler, Hallenbeck, McLellan, & Svoboda, 1996; Spiegel, 1992, 1994; Strickland, 1994/1995, 1996)

Whew! But take heart: In this chapter, I will focus only on the last two issues: (1) teacher-directed instruction and learner-directed discovery, and (2) isolated strategy emphases and use of whole texts. I will use these two issues to focus on the need for and process of making decisions about individual children's literacy needs. For each issue, I will suggest guidelines to help teachers make these decisions, with the hope that these exemplar guidelines can be extrapolated for decisions regarding other issues. I will end the chapter with a quick strategy for managing the process of making daily decisions about 25 important people.

OUR MODEL STUDENTS

To help us keep the diversity of real classrooms in mind, I want you to think about three students: Jameria, Bill, and Hannah. As we explore teacher-directed instruction and learner-directed discovery and isolated strategy emphases and use of whole texts, these children will serve as model students for our decisions.

Jameria is a first grader. Both her kindergarten teacher and her first-grade teacher used a lot of Shared Book Experiences (Holdaway, 1979) and Language Experience (Van Allen, 1976). She began first grade with a fairly secure understanding of consonant letter–sound relationships. Now that she is spending more time reading by herself, she uses initial and final consonants somewhat consistently to help her identify unknown words and to spell new words. Jameria tends not to pay much attention to medial consonants yet and vowels are alien territory, yet to be mentioned by her teacher. Jameria is a confident reader and a good meaning maker. She tended not to use context at first, but once her teacher showed her how to use meaning plus letter sounds to figure out a word, Jameria embraced this strategy and now uses it often. Jameria spends much of her free time reading and writing.

Bill is a fourth grader. His comprehension of "big ideas" is generally excellent, and his journal responses and discussions of what he has read show a sophisticated depth of understanding of all kinds of text. Bill's decoding skills, however, have not advanced beyond the identification of two-syllable words. When Bill faces an unknown polysyllabic word, he often pronounces the first syllable correctly and then guesses a word that more or less makes sense and has the same beginning syllable. He has an outstanding meaning vocabulary and even stumbles on the correct word occasionally through this first-syllable-plus-context strategy. Thus Bill is able to maintain a broad understanding of what he reads, but his comprehension of details is often incorrect because of his frequent "almost right" substitutions. Because Bill reads for meaning, he enjoys reading a great deal, but when he reads aloud this enjoyment disappears and he reads in a boring monotone.

Hannah is a struggling sixth grader. Like Bill, she does not have a reliable strategy to get past first syllables. Unlike Bill, she does not have a rich meaning vocabulary to fall back on and she does not read voluntarily, so her meaning vocabulary continues to be restricted. Her comprehension is generally poor because she cannot read enough of the words to construct meaning. Even when reading text for which she can identify the words, Hannah tends not to focus on meaning; she is so used to not finding meaning that she tends to forget to look for it.

ISSUE ONE: TEACHER-DIRECTED EXPLICIT INSTRUCTION AND LEARNER-DIRECTED DISCOVERY

The issue of teacher-directed explicit instruction and learner-directed discovery has been the focus of much debate, rhetoric, and dispute. It is important that we recognize that this issue is not about either/or, although that is what the discussion has often been limited to (Doake, 1987; Goodman, 1986; Spiegel, 1992). One main point of this chapter is that thoughtful teachers do not play the either/or game. They decide what is best practice for each child each day. It is likely that for some children on some days for some tasks, teacher-directed explicit instruction will be best. On other days and with other tasks, with the same or other children, learner-directed discovery is likely to be the most effective.

To avoid the either/or game, we need to quickly dispense with false perceptions that the extremes of this continuum typify that point of view. The extreme direct instruction point of view is that instruction should be prescribed, sequenced, and presented in a lockstep manner, usually through skilling and drilling. Conversely, the extreme learner-centered perspective is that children should be left alone to explore reading and writing and eventually they will figure literacy out for themselves. Both extremes are unrealistic and fortunately rare. However, a tendency for us to focus on these extremes may prevent us from identifying the best practice needed for each child, to see that perhaps for this child at this moment moving a bit toward the other end of the continuum may have value.

With the moderate perspective of teacher-directed explicit instruction, the teacher selects what strategy will be learned and provides direct instruction on why that strategy is important and how learners might put that strategy into practice. Instruction is followed by guided practice as the teacher observes how students interpret the instruction. Then learners practice what they have learned independently in authentic texts so that they can quickly see the value of what they have just learned. Duffy and Roehler's work (1986, 1987) has shown that developing lessons around "what," "why," and "how" leads to increased learning. *Direct* instruction provides the sustained and focused practice that allows children to use strategies effectively to solve new problems. Yatvin (1991) describes how direct instruction can be used in a very learner-centered way: "It is a teacher's job to support inductive learning by focusing children's attention on significant features of language and helping them through the language problems they need to solve in order to achieve their purposes" (p. 80).

In *systematic* instruction, teachers have in mind some literacy goals they want their students to meet and consciously set up opportunities to observe children's progress toward meeting these goals. If observation or more formal assessment shows that some children have not met a particular goal, instruction is provided. Instruction and practice are followed by formal or informal assessment to determine if the children now can meet the specified goal. If they cannot, modified instruction is provided, followed by practice and assessment.

I do think that a teacher should have a sense of *a* curriculum, a set of goals for the year for students so that he/she has some touchstone against which to assess progress. Without at least a loose curriculum, children's literacy development is likely to be haphazard, within and across grades. Further, Yatvin (1993) makes the point that all teachers do have at least an unconscious curriculum that dictates what they notice needs to be taught. If "story grammar" is not part of the teacher's unconscious curriculum, then he/she will never notice the opportunity to seize the teachable moment to assist children in gaining control over this aspect of story structure.

Some have criticized direct instruction as antichild or as not showing respect for the child. However, it is far more antichild to assume that all children can attain literacy in the same manner. It does not show respect for the child to restrict his/her opportunity to learn by insisting on maintaining practices that are not resulting in the success all children deserve. For many reasons, including their home environments, some children come to school already knowing a great deal about books and writing and the kinds of interactions that take place in most schools, but others do not (Delpit, 1988; Heath, 1982; McGill-Franzen, 1992). Some children therefore have a head start. These same children are likely to have a continued "home advantage" (Lareau, 1989) because their parents understand schools and schooling and can step in with assistance at home when their children experience difficulties with their school curriculum. On the other hand, if children who come to school knowing little about literacy are left to explore literacy primarily on their own, they may stay behind, both because they lack the rich literacy foundations on which to base explorations and because their parents do not have the knowledge to assist them in their learning. School is not automatically a level playing field for all children, and to deny children information that will help them accelerate their literacy learning is unfair and may only widen the gap between those children who have a wealth of home literacy experiences from which to draw and those who do not. Best practice does not mean all children receive the same education. Best practice means that when a child needs explicit, systematic instruction in order to progress, the teacher provides this guidance.

What about the value toward the other end of the continuum? In learner-directed instruction, children identify what needs to be learned and through exploration they use trial and error to learn that. Through authentic, not contrived, experiences children focus on issues of interest and seek to explore those topics through various means, including texts written by others and by themselves. The teacher's role is to lead from behind, to support the efforts of learners, and to step in *only as needed—but certainly when needed.* Those who have a moderate learner-centered perspective heed Field and Jardine's words to be "wary and watchful" (1994, p. 259) that encouraging children to take charge of their own learning does not mean abandoning them. Advocates of a more learner-centered approach often talk about seizing the *teachable moment,* that is, the moment when the children themselves have come to a roadblock and cannot move forward without new strategies. That may be the time for coaching or for a minilesson that focuses the children on an aspect of literacy that will help them move forward in their present literacy quest. The children are motivated to learn the new strategy because it is their own quest that is stymied and they can perceive the need for the strategy.

Best practice means that teachers need to acknowledge learner needs and interests and take advantage of them. Why would you not want to make use of that enthusiasm? Allowing children to help design their own curricula gives them ownership and a much-needed sense of control and should also help foster responsibility. Metacognition, awareness of one's own understanding and strategy usage, should be enhanced because children who have selected their own topics and tasks are likely to want to understand and to find ways to understand. Teachers should seize teachable moments when a need is made evident by a learner's inability to complete an authentic task and therefore his/her interest is high. Teachers who kidwatch are ready to seize these opportunities.

These descriptions show that there is both room and necessity for moving back and forth across the continuum of teacher-directed instruction and learner-centered discovery. Both approaches have value. So how can a teacher decide what is best practice for each child for each literacy situation? The following guidelines may be useful:

Looking at the Learner

Move more toward teacher-directed instruction if:
- The child has tended to fall behind peers without teacher direction.
- The child runs the risk of a cumulative deficit because he/she never quite learns what the others do.
- The joy of self-directed discovery is tarnished by loss of confidence and interest because the child "never quite gets it" on his/her own.

Move more toward learner-directed instruction if:
- The child has been able to induce learning strategies primarily through his/her own explorations of literacy.
- The child will be held back by having to listen to suggestions for accomplishing a task he/she already knows how to do.
- The child's interest will flag by having to listen to the "how" when he/she wants to get on with the doing.

Looking at the Task

Move more toward teacher-directed explicit instruction if:
- Most readers need to know this strategy or concept.
- The ability to use a particular strategy is needed now.

Move more toward learner-directed instruction if:
- The concept or strategy is easily learned through exploration.
- The concept does not provide a foundation for other concepts and therefore doesn't need to be learned at a particular time.
- Children are not engaged in the curriculum.
- Children are not taking responsibility for their own learning.

Let's apply these guidelines to our three children. Jameria seems to be doing just fine with minimal teacher guidance. When the teacher modeled the use of letter–sound relationships, Jameria profited and was able to transfer this knowledge to authentic reading situations. When given a little coaching on the use of context-plus-phonics, Jameria made the strategy her own. Most importantly, she is now able to construct meaning as she reads. If we apply our guidelines to Jameria, we see that best practice for her at the moment seems to be to promote learner-directed discovery. She is learning what she needs to know with minimal individual guidance and she has no important weaknesses.

Bill presents a more mixed profile. He has made good progress in the past, especially in the important area of reading for meaning. However, he has not yet developed an effective strategy for dealing with large words and his comprehension is likely to suffer as he needs and wants to read increasingly sophisticated text. The development of an effective strategy for dealing with polysyllabic words is an important task that Bill has not been able to fulfill on his own. Therefore, it would seem that best practice in this case would be teacher-directed explicit instruction. The Bills I have worked with have become successful decoders of large words once they have received a few explicit lessons on polysyllabic compare/contrast (Cunningham, 1980) or Making Big Words (Cunningham, Moore, Cunningham, & Moore, 1995).

On the other hand, Bill's monotone oral reading does not meet the criteria for intervention. Reading with expression is not that important. I would tend to continue modeling appropriate expression for oral reading when I read to the class, but I wouldn't involve Bill in direct instruction in "reading with expression."

For Hannah, best practice is likely to involve a great deal of teacher-directed explicit instruction. Hannah has not been able to develop effective strategies on her own and she is falling progressively behind. There is absolutely no reason to believe that she will suddenly figure out effective strategies on her own when she has not been able to do so in 6 years of schooling. It's time to sit down with her, with materials at her instructional level, and teach her the strategies she needs. I would start with a strategy for decoding large words. At the same time I would work with her in easy materials on refocusing her on meaning making. Then as Hannah becomes able and confident in identifying large words, I would carefully "up the ante" on her comprehension guidance and show her how to maintain the meaning focus regained through easy text when she is reading more difficult text.

How will the teacher find time to offer all the Hannahs the direct instruction they need? The answer is inherent in an approach dedicated to meeting individual needs: Because many children are like Jameria, those children will need little teacher guidance. They can explore and practice relatively easily on their own, freeing up the teacher for more face-to-face interaction with Bill and Hannah. On the other hand, if the majority of the children in the class need direct instruction, then whole-group lessons with small-group follow-ups provide a solution. Individual needs for teacher-directed instruction and learner discovery can both be met.

ISSUE TWO: ISOLATED STRATEGY EMPHASES AND USE ONLY OF WHOLE TEXTS

Strategies are not synonymous with skills. Strategies are procedures used to solve a problem. They have value only as tools. Strategies pull skills together (Pikulski, 1994). Knowing *about* strategies is of no use. Being able to *use* them is what is important. Table 14.1 gives an example of a decoding strategy that makes use of multiple cue systems simultaneously and provides a reader with a plan when he/she can't identify a word in whole text.

Skills, on the other hand, are entities in themselves and are taught isolated from utility. Using the consonant–vowel–consonant pattern to determine if a vowel has a short *a* sound is a skill.

TABLE 14.1. A Decoding Strategy

Look at the picture.
Spell the word out loud to yourself.
Read the rest of the sentence.
Go back to the beginning of the sentence.
Reread the sentence, putting in a word that makes sense and starts with the right sound.
Double-check for meaning.

The most extreme examples of isolated skill emphases are found in commercially packaged programs that teach each skill in isolation, often using worksheets and workbooks and rarely using extended or authentic text. Reading is equated with completing a worksheet (either a paper or computer version). Unfortunately this skilling and drilling approach is not all that rare and even programs not intended to be used in that way are sometimes shattered into isolated fragments. Allington, Stuetzel, Shake, and Lamarche (1986), among others, found that many remedial programs tend to use isolated skill approaches.

At the other end of the continuum is the perspective that any isolation of or focus on strategies or skills will fragment the reading process and make it unnatural. Therefore, advocates of this position do not want the child ever to deal with parts of text, including in some cases single words or letters.

More moderate perspectives can be found along the continuum. Those with a strategy-based, focused instruction perspective want children to receive instruction that identifies a particular strategy, usually separating it from the "whole" process of reading. This instruction often takes the form of using whole text to identify a strategy need, examination of and practice with the strategy in isolation, and then transfer of the strategy through practice again with whole texts.

On the other hand, classroom teachers who tend to take a more holistic perspective make adjustments every day when it becomes clear that children cannot induce strategies and their uses from interacting solely with whole texts. As one teacher who described herself as a whole language teacher said to me, "Of course I teach phonics! I just deal with individual letters and sounds as little as possible to get the job done."

The moderate members of both perspectives acknowledge the importance of sustained reading of connected, authentic text. It is through this kind of reading that the reader pulls strategies together, tries them out, and develops fluency. Teachers who are somewhere in the middle of this continuum seem to use the following guidelines in seeking best practice for each child:

Move more toward a strategy focus if:
- The child cannot move around roadblocks met when interacting with whole text.
- The child has only one way of moving around a roadblock.
- The child needs to focus on the strategy long enough to learn it.

Move more toward a holistic focus if:
- The child is practicing the strategy only with artificial texts.
- The child cannot transfer the strategy to authentic whole texts.
- The child cannot utilize the strategy spontaneously and simultaneously with other strategies when reading in authentic texts for his/her own purposes.

Let's revisit Jameria, Bill, and Hannah and apply these guidelines. Jameria has been able to find and use effective strategies primarily through interactions with whole texts. When she did need to learn about the use of context, Jameria's teacher briefly focused her on the sentence level of text but quickly showed her how to apply this strategy to larger sections of text. And that brief isolation was all that Jameria needed.

Bill seems to be doing fine with comprehension and response to what he reads, dealing with meaning making in a holistic manner. But Bill needs to have his attention drawn to a strategy for identifying large words. Because he depends too much on context and thus misidentifies words, Bill should have some isolated work with a new strategy. Then his teacher should let Bill practice the strategy in whole texts.

Hannah is likely to need a great deal of strategy work with small segments of text. Right now she is overwhelmed by text, even when it is easy for her to decode. She needs to gain strategic use of a way to identify large words and then gradually gain confidence in applying this strategy to increasingly larger segments of text.

MAKING MEETING INDIVIDUAL NEEDS MANAGEABLE

It is easy for someone else to tell teachers to take all of these things into consideration each day for each child. But this is not a completely unworkable task. Yet, neither is it simple. To make this manageable, let's examine the hypothetical but rarely real classroom of 25 students. Each day, the teacher should target five children to focus on, perhaps using the grid shown in Figure 14.1. Under "Evidence," the teacher should put notes about how he/she came to the conclusions listed in the first column. Then for "What Next?" the teacher should consider changes, rebalancing, both for the successes and the roadblocks. If a child is

NAME: DATE:	EVIDENCE	WHAT NEXT?
What successes did _____ have today?		
What roadblocks did _____ have trouble with today?		

FIGURE 14.1. Progress record.

at last successful with a previously troublesome task, "What Next?" might be additional practice opportunities. In this case, the balance remains about the same for a little longer. However, if a successful experience has come easily to the child, "What Next?" might be more challenging work or less teacher direction and more learner-initiated exploration.

Similarly, with roadblocks, "What Next?" might include grouping with children who have similar needs or regrouping. "What Next?" might include teaching, if direct instruction has not yet been used, or reteaching if it has. It might involve focusing, if the child has not yet been fully focused on a strategy, or refocusing. Usually "What Next?" will involve change.

"What Next?," like "What Is?," should always be considered temporary. Groups are ad hoc. They change daily as children's needs change. Emphasis on strategies ebbs and flows as children's literacy develops or fails to prosper.

CONCLUSION

I am discouraged when asked, "What is the best way to teach this or that?" A person who asks that question is rarely satisfied with my answer: "There is no best way. It depends on so many things." Helping each child each day reach toward his/her potential is truly a balancing act. It requires teachers who have the courage to make decisions, to look critically at their own practices, and to trust in their own competence to build their own philosophies.

REFERENCES

Allington, R. L., Stuetzel, H., Shake, M., & Lamarche, S. (1986). What is remedial reading?: A descriptive study. *Reading Research and Instruction, 26,* 15–30.

Baumann, J., & Ivey, G. (1997). Delicate balances: Striving for curricular and instructional equilibriums in a second-grade, literature/strategy-based classroom. *Reading Research Quarterly, 32,* 244–275.

Canney, G. (1993). Teachers' preferences for reading materials. *Reading Improvement, 30,* 238–245.

Carroll, J., Wilson, R., & Au, K. (1996). Explicit instruction in the context of readers' and writers' workshops. In E. McIntyre & M. Pressley (Eds.), *Balanced instruction: Strategies and skills in whole language* (pp. 39–63). Norwood, MA: Christopher-Gordon.

Cunningham, P. (1980). Applying a compare/contrast process to identifying polysyllabic words. *Journal of Reading Behavior, 12,* 13–23.

Cunningham P., Moore, S., Cunningham, J., & Moore, D. (1995). *Reading the writing in elementary classrooms: Strategies and observations.* New York: Longman.

Delpit, L. (1988). The silenced dialogue: Power and pedagogy in educating other people's children. *Harvard Educational Review, 8,* 280–298.

Doake, D. (1987). Learning to read: It starts in the home. In D. Tovey & J. Kerber (Eds.), *Roles of literacy learning* (pp. 2–9). Newark, DE: International Reading Association.

Dudley-Marling, C. (1996). Explicit instruction within a whole language framework: Teaching struggling readers and writers. In E. McIntyre & M. Pressley (Eds.), *Balanced instruction: Strategies and skills in whole language* (pp. 23–38). Norwood, MA: Christopher-Gordon.

Duffy, G., & Roehler, L. (1986). *Improving classroom reading instruction: A decision-making approach.* New York: Random House.

Duffy, G., & Roehler, L. (1987). Teaching reading skills as strategies. *The Reading Teacher, 40,* 414–418.

Durkin. D. (1990). Dolores Durkin speaks on instruction. *The Reading Teacher, 43,* 472–476.

Field, J., & Jardine, D. (1994). "Bad examples" as interpretive opportunities: On the need for whole language to own its shadow. *Language Arts, 71,* 258–263.

Freppon, P., & Headings, L. (1996). Keeping it whole in whole language: A first grader teacher's phonics instruction in an urban whole language classroom. In E. McIntyre & M. Pressley (Eds.), *Balanced instruction: Strategies and skills in whole language* (pp. 65–82). Norwood, MA: Christopher-Gordon.

Goodman, K. (1986). *What's whole in whole language?* Portsmouth, NH: Heinemann.

Heath, S. (1982). What no bedtime story means: Narrative skills at home and school. *Language in Society, 11,* 49–76.

Hiebert, E., & Colt, J. (1989). Patterns of literature-based reading instruction. *The Reading Teacher, 43,* 14–20.

Holdaway, D. (1979). *The foundations of literacy.* Sydney, New South Wales, Australia: Ashton Scholastic.

Lareau, A. (1989). *Home advantage: Social class and parental intervention in elementary education.* Philadelphia: Falmer Press.

McGill-Franzen, A. (1992). Early literacy: What does "developmentally appropriate" mean? *The Reading Teacher, 46,* 56–58.

McIntyre, E. (1996). Strategies and skills in whole language: An introduction to balanced teaching. In E. McIntyre & M. Pressley (Eds.), *Balanced instruction: Strategies and skills in whole language* (pp. 1–20). Norwood, MA: Christopher-Gordon.

McIntyre, E., Kyle, D., Hovda, R., & Clyde, J. (1996). Explicit teaching and learning of strategies in whole language classrooms. In E. McIntyre & M. Pressley (Eds.), *Balanced instruction: Strategies and skills in whole language* (pp. 231–250). Norwood, MA: Christopher-Gordon.

Pikulski, J. (1994). *Exploring the balance in comprehension development.* Paper presented at the annual meeting of the Balanced Reading Instruction Special Interest Group, the International Reading Association, Toronto, Ontario, Canada.

Purcell-Gates, V. (1996). Process teaching with direct instruction and feedback in a university-based clinic. In E. McIntyre & M. Pressley (Eds.), *Balanced instruction: Strategies and skills in whole language* (pp. 107–127). Norwood, MA: Christopher-Gordon.

Roehler, L., Hallenbeck, M., McLellan, M., & Svoboda, N (1996). Teaching skills through learning conversations in whole language classrooms. In E. McIntyre & M. Pressley (Eds.), *Balanced instruction: Strategies and skills in whole language* (pp. 193–212). Norwood, MA: Christopher-Gordon.

Spiegel, D. L. (1992). Blending whole language and direct instruction. *The Reading Teacher, 46,* 38–44.

Spiegel, D. L. (1994). Finding the balance in literacy development for all children. *Balanced Reading Instruction, 1,* 6–11.

Strickland, D. (1994/1995). Reinventing our literacy programs: Books, basics, balance. *The Reading Teacher, 48,* 294–302.

Strickland, D. (1996). In search of balance: Restructuring our literacy programs. *Reading Today, 14,* 32.

Van Allen, R. (1976). *Language experiences in education.* Boston: Houghton Mifflin.

Yatvin, J. (1991). *Developing a whole language program.* Newark, DE: International Reading Association.

Yatvin, J. (1993). *When literacy learning breaks down: Adapting whole language to children's needs.* Unpublished manuscript.

Chapter 15

CREATING CONTINUITY IN EARLY LITERACY: LINKING HOME AND SCHOOL WITH A CULTURALLY RESPONSIVE APPROACH

Susan B. Neuman

Three-year-old Kalief is trying to open a box of toy cars while his mother, Sakema, is folding laundry:

> KALIEF: Open, open, open.
>
> SAKEMA: You want to open this box?
>
> KALIEF: Other open.
>
> SAKEMA: You want to open it the other way?
>
> KALIEF: (*Getting a bit frustrated*) Uuuuuuhh.
>
> SAKEMA: That's right. You have to get it right on top where the sign says "up." That's right. Oh, look at that. You're opening up the box all by yourself.

Children learn to read and write in the context of their closest personal relations—their family. Their earliest attempts may include reading signs, pretending to read stories, scribble-writing a special thank-you letter to a distant relative, or trying to spell "I love you" to a parent. Even the most trivial events or activities can provide occasions for parent–child interactions. Everyday activities, such as eating or playing, create opportunities for children to ask questions and for parents to relay language information. From these routine, collaborative experiences, children of all cultures learn about written language and how to use it for a wide variety of purposes.

For example, the foregoing simple exchange between Sakema and Kalief reveals several important aspects of language and literacy that are characteristic of home learning. Sakema listens thoughtfully to her son's words before responding. She then probes, attempting to interpret the child's statement and offering her own understanding of the situation. Also, she naturally refers to the written language in her explanation. Catherine Snow (1983), as well as other colleagues (e.g., Rogoff, 1990), describes this parental pattern as "motherese"; Sakema encourages Kalief to take the initiative, then supports and assists his language attempts.

None of these efforts are consciously educational. In fact, learning in such informal settings at home is often incidental to other ongoing activities. During these everyday events, however, parents demonstrate what is involved in spoken and written language. And from these rich, contextualized activities, children develop ideas about the functions and uses of language and literacy, internalizing many of the roles and routines long before coming to school.

A DIFFERENT WORLD

As the primary education context moves from home to school, however, the child enters a different world. Language and literacy experiences in the classroom may differ dramatically from the informal shared learning environment of the home. At school, teachers must often try to organize and engage in discussion with whole classes or small groups, rather than individual children. Sometimes teachers may not understand the child's particular "ways of speaking" or communicating as the parent does in the home. Further, different expectations, derived from culturally distinctive "speech communities" (Gumperz, 1968) may lead to systematic and recurrent communication difficulties between teacher and children. Language learning strategies that once served the child so effectively at home may seem less successful and sometimes even counterproductive in the school context.

This mismatch in communication styles has important implications for literacy instruction, especially in the early grades. Ferdman (1990) argues, for example, that children who perceive reading and writing as reaffirming their cultural identity become more engaged in literacy tasks. By contrast, if written tasks devalue children's identity, the gap may only widen between home and school contexts. In this case, children may become increasingly disenfranchised, regarding what they are learning in school strictly as "school-defined" literacy practices.

How might these observations relate to creating more effective language and literacy learning environments in classrooms? It suggests the importance of building bridges between home and school literacies. As Courtney Cazden (1992) has demonstrated in working with children of many cultures, the hard work for teachers comes in discovering what children already know about writing and reading, and helping them make connections with what the schools want them to know.

In order to make these connections, in this chapter I argue for the importance of "culturally responsive instruction." In this approach, teachers build on children's home culture and patterns of language learning to further develop their literacy skills. Culturally responsive instruction that actively engages our increasingly diverse community of learners may help children build upon their own sense of identity and extend their emerging language and literacy abilities (Neuman & Roskos, 1994). At the same time, a culturally responsive approach builds connections beyond the classroom and into the community, as teachers demonstrate a connectedness with all children and their families.

A number of studies have highlighted the importance of culturally responsive instruction. Philips (1972), for example, found that Native American children were more comfortable working together in small groups, a pattern of participation typical of their community, rather than being singled out from others. Au (1980) also demonstrated the power of a culturally responsive approach. She developed a "talk-story," an adaptation of the oral reading lesson that engaged children in cooperatively responding, and found that this strategy enhanced Native Hawaiian children's oral language learning and subsequent reading achievement. Further, in two provocative case studies, Gloria Ladson-Billings (1994) and Lisa Delpit (1995) reported that when children's real-life experiences were legitimized and when curriculum was connected to their background knowledge, children were capable of learning complex ideas and skills that far exceeded their reading grade level expectations.

FEATURES OF CULTURALLY RESPONSIVE INSTRUCTION

In a previous article, Kathy Roskos and I characterized culturally responsive instruction as focusing on three essential features (Neuman & Roskos, 1994); in this chapter, I highlight a fourth distinguishing feature.

First, culturally responsive instruction acknowledges and appreciates *children's home cultures* and attempts to build upon the uses of language and literacy with which children are already familiar. Taylor and Dorsey-

Gaines (1988), for example, followed a number of families in culturally diverse homes and found that their cultures were rich in literacy, yet not necessarily in book form. Families used literacy to structure their daily lives, to provide moral and religious guidance to children, and to effectively organize activities.

Second, a culturally responsive approach promotes *collaboration among children* and between children and adults as they learn through social interaction. Social play, for example, affords young children a clear example of collaboration in learning. In this context, each young player's cultural and individual differences contribute to the context and the narratives of satisfying play (Roskos, 1988). Likewise, Morrow's (1997) independent reading and writing periods foster an opportunity for children to socially collaborate over books and writing activities. In these settings, children engage in creating stories and play with books using puppets and dramatic play activities. By involving children in language and literacy activities that foster collaboration, we invite the sharing of cultural perspectives. Through this process, children from all cultural backgrounds engage in the construction of new knowledge, ensuring that each participant's learning is enhanced.

Third, a culturally responsive approach shares the same *standards of achievement* for children of diverse backgrounds as for those from the mainstream. Literacy teachers have a responsibility to enhance all children's literacy skills—to build bridges that help children understand how to behave with print and to point them toward new linguistic possibilities. Thus, although the discussion of Ebonics in recent years was interpreted as lowering the standards, it was originally conceived of as a way to accept and build on children's language and previous experiences. However, setting standards for children of diverse backgrounds, which are different from the mainstream, will only marginalize them and set them at a severe disadvantage.

But while the goals must remain the same for all children, the means of achieving these goals may be different for children from nonmainstream cultures. These different means may be accomplished by adjusting some instructional practices and providing a range of multicultural literacy experiences. In this respect, cultural diversity becomes a strength, a central feature of cultural pluralism in which children may function well in their own culture as well as that of the mainstream.

Fourth, a culturally responsive approach acknowledges the importance of *continuity* between the child's experiences with literacy and home and those encountered in school. As Shirley Brice Heath (1983) and others (Delgado-Gaitan, 1994; Goldenberg & Gallimore, 1991) have reported, some children will have experienced a far different set of literacy practices in their home than those traditionally honored in the school.

Even so, educators must recognize that the power that literacy holds in young children's lives ultimately depends on whether writing and reading become meaningful to them in daily practices. This, in turn, will depend on the people who are most central to children—their family, caregivers, and their kinship networks outside of school—and on the messages these people communicate about the children's development as writers and readers. Thus, it becomes imperative to involve parents in children's language and literacy learning in schools. In fact, the accumulation of evidence is now beyond dispute: when schools work together with families to support learning, children tend to succeed not just in school but throughout life.

EXAMPLES OF CULTURALLY RESPONSIVE INSTRUCTION

Many fine teacher resource books and textbooks today focus on cultural responsive activities in classrooms (see Diamond & Moore, 1995, for additional references). They include—but are certainly not limited to—the necessity of including culturally diverse reading experiences that provide rich potentials for sharing understanding about people and their cultures. In addition, teachers may celebrate cultural pluralism by making classroom Big Books of favorite sayings, jingles, or holiday family traditions which suggest to all that diversity is welcome and prized in the classroom community. Sharing time, once a staple in early childhood classrooms, can be an excellent resource for teachers to encourage children to share important events and activities from their own culture, enriching the experiences of all children in the classroom.

But far less addressed has been the attention to the fourth feature of cultural responsiveness—one that focuses on the continuity between home and school practices. In the following subsections, I highlight three kinds of activities that have been used successfully in early childhood classrooms.

A Family Album

Too often, parents' participation in children's schooling is relegated to peripheral activities such as bake sales, clerical tasks, and field trips. In fact, substantive parental involvement in children's school learning appears to be quite rare. This is usually a terrible loss since parents often have great talents and "funds of knowledge" that they can contribute to the diverse experiences in classrooms.

Several years ago, Kathy Roskos and I developed a portfolio project that we described as a "family album" and was a strategy devised to encourage greater parent–child–teacher partnerships in literacy activities (Neuman & Roskos, 1993b). The project began as a home-based learning experience in which children could share their outside literacy activities in their classrooms. Caregivers and children were encouraged to make homemade books from Zip-loc bags (which we provided to each family) filled with pictures of the child drawn at home or school, photographs, assorted memorabilia, and magazine pictures. Each item was glued onto colored paper. Parents were asked to help convey their children's ideas by writing simple captions under each picture and creating stories about their life experiences together.

We found that these homemade books reflected the cultural values, activities, and expressions of their authors and became an ongoing part of classroom life—as contributions to shared reading time, centerpieces of a literature theme, additions to the classroom library collection, and causes for celebration. Also, they were an excellent resource for "buddy reading" during the independent reading and writing period in the library settings in classrooms. We found that teachers paired children of diverse backgrounds and encouraged them to "read" to each other, helping students share the special events of their lives together.

For example, here are Traycee and Wanda reading together:

TRAYCEE: That's my Aunt Patty, who was 10 and had on a cape and was acting like superman.

WANDA: Where did she get that idea from?

TRAYCEE: She jumped so hard and far that her head hit the floor. First we thought it was funny, but she started bleeding. We had to take her to the hospital.

WANDA: She OK now?

We have since used family albums as language and literacy portfolios (Roskos & Neuman, 1994). Unlike typical portfolios, which are largely developed and maintained by teachers and children, here we involved the family. Since much of children's learning activities typically occurs outside of the classroom, we believed that it was important for parents and other caregivers to become active participants in the creation of the album.

Letters were sent to parents requesting them to gather items that might display their child's growth in language and literacy over the year. Such items might include the following: drawings; scribble messages; a list of favorite books, poems, and songs; favorite games; and reports of "firsts" (first written phrase, first talking, etc.). Next, we invited parents and children to a get-together to personalize a holder for these memories. In one classroom, for example, all portfolio cases were pocket folders with a strip for punched inserts. We had materials available for them to design their folders, including glue, yarn, and construction paper. As several parents and their children worked together at tables, we found that they all got to know one another. These conversations created a sense of community in the class and stimulated an acceptance of cultural diversity.

As the time for parent conferences approached, we invited parents to stop by and review their children's portfolios with them in a casual way, much as they would look at a family photo album. In the course of this portfolio sharing, parents become witnesses to their children's language and literacy learning activities and processes and could recognize their own contributions to their child's development. They could also add items to the portfolio, informing teachers of important events occurring outside of school. As a result, both parents and teachers became better informed about what their children were capable of doing both in and out of school.

Literacy-Related Prop Boxes

Parents may also become actively involved in their children's language and literacy learning through literacy-related "prop boxes" (Neuman, 1995). These theme boxes contain sets of related objects that are designed to stimulate literacy-related activities from a multicultural perspective. They typically include four sets of materials, described next.

A Chant, Jingle, Song, or Finger Play

Each prop box contains a chant, jingle, song, or finger play related to a particular theme. For example, our African American literature prop box included the following (with hand motions):

> Imani
> I have faith in myself
> I have faith in my parents
> I have faith in my teachers
> I have faith in my people

Storybooks

The literacy prop box includes about three to five books, all related to the theme. Some of these books are narrative, others are informational, but regardless of genre they all encourage active responses from the children. For example, *The Adventures of Spider* (Arkhurst, 1964) encourages children to play with rhymes and sounds as the adult and the child read together. Other books enhance children's reading along by including predictable stories and repetitive phrases. Still others extend children's labeling of objects that may be central to the theme, like the words *spider* or *letter*. Such a variety of books also provide parents with many different options for reading, allowing them to select materials appropriate to their own reading level as well.

Play Objects

Included in the literacy box is a set of play objects related to the theme. For example, in our African American box we included *kente* cloth, small doll figures, and musical cans to add sound effects to the story. These inexpensive objects are designed to encourage children to reenact many of the scenes from the books as well as to generate new creative ideas of their own. Based on research by Neuman and Roskos (1992, 1993a), literacy play objects have been found to assist children in conveying meaning, making the language of literacy their own.

Writing Books

Each literacy box includes blank writing books in which children can write about the theme. In some cases, children may scribble and "tell" their story; in other cases, they may attempt to write a favorite line from the storybook. Still other children may combine pictures or stickers with their writing. All writing books are eventually sent home, providing parents with evidence of their children's writing development (see Figure 15.1).

These basic components in the prop boxes—chants, storybooks, play objects, and writing books—focus on receptive and expressive language and are designed to approximate many of the activities that naturally occur in literacy-rich environments. Prop boxes were sent home on a rotating basis, and parents were invited to contribute items that reflected their own cultural heritage, including special food boxes, signs, and currency. These activities became the source of reading and writing for a week in the child's home. One Hispanic parent, for example, included a piñata in a birthday prop box to demonstrate her child's particular cultural experiences and traditions. Thus, through a culturally responsive approach, activities are structured to build on strengths the children gain through their home experiences, thereby linking school activities to home and community life.

FIGURE 15.1. Parent and children engaged in activities using a literacy-related prop box.

A Book Club

One of the most popular (and ongoing) activities in our early childhood classes have been our parent–child book clubs (Neuman, 1996; see Table 15.1). Designed to be a meeting place for conversations about children's books and a time for parents and children to read together, book clubs are held weekly at each school, over a 12-week period. Together, along with the librarian and a bilingual specialist, parents read popular children's literature together and talk about the texts (see the book list in Table 15.1 for examples). Coffee and donuts are always available for parents who may not have had time for breakfast.

Generally, about 20 parents come to the book club in each school site. Each week begins with a choral reading of a children's book (which is available in either Spanish or English). The facilitator dramatizes the action, emphasizes repetitive phrases, and sometimes stops to ask questions as she reads. Following the reading, the facilitator then engages parents in a discussion of the story, focusing on three key questions:

• What would you want your child to take away from this book? Acting as a recorder, the parent leader lists common themes, distinctive qualities about the book, descriptive phrases, and unusual vocabulary.

TABLE 15.1. Some Book Club Favorites

Belpre, P. (1968). *Santiago.* New York: Warner.
Brown, M. (1972). *The runaway bunny.* New York: Harper & Row.
Carle, E. (1969). *The very hungry caterpillar.* New York: Philomel.
Freeman, D. (1968). *Corduroy.* New York: Viking.
Galdone, P. (1975). *The little red hen.* New York: Scholastic.
Greenfield, E. (1975). *Honey I love: And other poems.* New York: Harper & Row.
Guarino, D. (1989). *Is your mama a llama?* New York: Scholastic.
Keats, E.J. (1976). *The snowy day.* New York: Puffin Books.
Keats, E.J. (1971). *Over in the meadow.* New York: Scholastic.
Mayer, M. (1975). *What do you do with a kangaroo?* New York: Scholastic.
Piper, W. (1954). *The little engine that could.* New York: Platt & Munk.
Solbert, R. (1971). *I wrote my name on the wall.* Boston: Little, Brown.
Slobodkin, E. (1947). *Caps for sale.* Reading, MA: Addison-Wesley.
Sonneborn, R. (1970). *Friday night is Papa night.* New York: Viking.
Young, E. (1989). *Lon Po Po.* New York: Scholastic.
Zolotow, C. (1972). *William's doll.* New York: Harper & Row.

• What kinds of questions or comments would you use to stimulate a discussion of the story? Discussion includes questions that ask children to predict, recall, and clarify story events.

• How would you help your child revisit this book? Parent suggestions such as rereading or activity extensions like visiting a zoo, making cookies, or going for walks together were described.

Conversations are designed to engage parents in analyzing events and ideas presented in the story, relating stories to their own personal experiences as well as helping to bridge these experiences to their children's early educational needs. In this respect, then, the discussion format assumes that parents have had rich experiences to share with others and that can be applied to children's literature selections (see Figure 15.2).

Library pockets and small index cards are provided so that parents can write down questions they believe are most useful for guiding discussions with their children. Some of the parents then continue to discuss the book; others who want additional practice can reread the text along with a facilitator. Following the discussion of approximately 40 minutes, parents visit their child's classroom and read their new book together for about 15 minutes, depending on the level of interaction. Parents who are less proficient readers might opt to tell their child the story as they remember it, using the pictures as guides, if they can't easily read it aloud.

Parents are given a new book each week to add to their home libraries (books that are ordered through book clubs cost approximately $2.00

FIGURE 15.2. Father and son reading together in a book club.

apiece). No specific guidelines, however, are given regarding when, how often, or in what ways to read to their child. Rather, the goal of our book clubs is to provide opportunities for parents to talk about and share ways in which storybooks might enable them to spend enjoyable time with their children. In addition to helping their children, however, we are both learning from and giving to families, tying the two different worlds of young children together.

CONCLUSIONS

I would argue that bridging home and school is a metaphor (and a strategy) for connecting two different learning environments. While both are contexts for language and literacy learning, each has its unique goals and different ways of achieving those goals. The culturally responsive approach ultimately seeks to bridge these two powerful learning contexts. This approach views the cultural and language differences of home and school as contributors to the development of young children's motivation to learn about literacy (Neuman & Roskos, 1994).

Infusing the elements of home learning into language and literacy instructional activities brings home and school contexts closer together. Activities that foster understanding between teachers and children, children and children, and parents and teachers allow the contributions of many cultures to be woven into solutions of common problems, invention of new ideas, and expansion of imagination. By assisting children in using what they already know and can do as speakers, listeners, readers, and writers, we expand their spoken and written language competencies while affirming their capabilities and cultural identity. Thus, we can approach the language and literacy instruction of all children, respecting, responding, and advancing the learning and culture of each individual child.

REFERENCES

Arkhurst, J. C. (1964). *The adventures of spider*. Boston: Little, Brown.

Au, K. H. (1980). Participation structures in a reading lesson with Hawaiian children: Analysis of a culturally appropriate instructional event. *Anthropology and Education Quarterly, 11*, 91–115.

Cazden, C. (1992). *Whole language plus*. New York: Teachers College Press.

Delgado-Gaitan, C. (1994). Sociocultural change through literacy: Toward the empowerment of families. In B. Ferdman, R. M. Weber, & A. Ramirez (Eds.), *Literacy across languages and cultures* (pp. 143–170). Albany: State University of New York Press.

Delpit, L. (1995). *Other people's children*. New York: New Press.

Diamond, B., & Moore, M. (1995). *Multicultural literacy: Mirroring the reality of the classroom*. New York: Longman.

Ferdman, B. (1990). Literacy and cultural identity. *Harvard Educational Review, 60*, 179–204.

Goldenberg, C., & Gallimore, R. (1991). Local knowledge, research knowledge, and educational change: A case study of early Spanish reading improvement. *Educational Researcher, 20*, 2–14.

Gumperz, J. (1968). The speech community. In D. Sills (Ed.), *International encyclopedia of the social sciences* (pp. 381–386). New York: Macmillan.

Heath, S. B. (1983). Ways with words: Language, life, and work in communities and classrooms. New York: Cambridge University Press.

Ladson-Billings, G. (1994). *The dreamkeepers*. San Francisco: Jossey-Bass.

Morrow, L. M. (1997). *The literacy center*. York, ME: Stenhouse.

Neuman, S. B. (1995). Reading together: A community-supported parent tutoring program. *The Reading Teacher, 49*, 120–129.

Neuman, S. B. (1996). Children engaging in storybook reading: The influence of access to print resources, opportunity, and parental interaction. *Early Childhood Research Quarterly, 11*, 495–514.

Neuman, S. B., & Roskos, K. (1992). Literacy objects as cultural tools: Effects on children's literacy behaviors in play. *Reading Research Quarterly, 27*, 202–225.

Neuman, S. B., & Roskos, K. (1993a). Access to print for children of poverty: Differential effects of adult mediation and literacy-enriched play settings on environmental and functional print tasks. *American Educational Research Journal, 30,* 95–122.

Neuman, S. B., & Roskos, K. (1993b). *Language and literacy learning in the early years: An integrated approach.* Fort Worth, TX: Harcourt Brace Jovanovich.

Neuman, S. B., & Roskos, K. (1994). Bridging home and school with a culturally responsive approach. *Childhood Education, 70,* 210–214.

Philips, S. (1972). Participant structures and communicative competence: Warm Springs children in community and classroom. In C. Cazden, V. John, & D. Hymes (Eds.), *Functions of language in the classroom* (pp. 370–394). New York: Teachers College Press.

Rogoff, B. (1990). *Apprenticeship in thinking.* New York: Oxford University Press.

Roskos, K. (1988). Literacy at work in play. *The Reading Teacher, 41,* 562–567.

Roskos, K., & Neuman, S. B. (1994). Of scribbles, schemas, and storybooks: Using literacy albums to document young children's literacy growth. *Young Children, 49,* 78–85.

Snow, C. (1983). Literacy and language: Relationships during the preschool years. *Harvard Educational Review, 53,* 165–189.

Taylor, D., & Dorsey-Gaines, C. (1988). *Growing up literate: Learning from inner-city families.* Portsmouth, NH: Heinemann.

Chapter 16

ORGANIZING LITERACY INSTRUCTION: EFFECTIVE GROUPING STRATEGIES AND ORGANIZATIONAL PLANS

D. Ray Reutzel

It's the first day of school for 20 excited and somewhat frightened first-grade children. Like most young children, they arrive fully expecting that this is the year, perhaps even today will be the day, when they learn to read and write! Ms. Songi, first-grade teacher at Sunset Elementary School, greets the children with a warm smile as they rambunctiously enter a classroom carefully crafted to support a variety of literacy teaching and learning situations.

The classroom is organized into several areas, each thoughtfully designed to meet the needs of whole-class, small-group, and individual learning activities. The classroom is filled with print—labeled objects, posters, charts, daily schedules, message centers, books, Word Walls, environmental print collections, signs, etc. A carpeted area in the front of the room near the chalkboard, with an electronic music keyboard and an easel, is ready to be used for whole-class instruction. A small horseshoe-shaped table in a distant corner of the classroom awaits a variety of instructional activities organized for small groups of children.

Learning centers are placed around the perimeter of the classroom. A publishing center runs along one side of the room opposite the windows; on a cupboard top in this area, a full line of writing tools and materials awaits anxious but willing hands for writing and publishing. A small carpeted reading nook, complete with a large rocking chair for one-to-one reading and several bean bag chairs for independent reading by children, is neatly organized in a quiet area of the room. Near the front is a play office area complete with typewriter, adding machine, telephone, desk, writing tablets, pencils, pens, erasers, markers, rubber stamps, dictionary, speller, liquid Wite-Out, and a dry-erase board for business planning and messages. Across the room sits a small center stocked with everything from stencils and magnetic letters to Alpha-Bits cereal, a center designed to enable children to explore letters of the alphabet and engage in word play. Near the classroom door is a listening center complete with cassette tape recorder, headphones, cassette tapes of books, multiple copies of selected children's book titles, and a computer loaded with children's books on compact discs (CDs). A storage area with 20 large plastic trays is located on the other side of the classroom door. Each child will place his/her name on a tray to be used as a place for keeping individual books and supplies. The classroom has no desks, only tables and chairs organized into many interesting and exciting learning areas. Children are instructed to each find a chair with his/her own name tag carefully written in manuscript on a cartoon bookworm character, a name tag to be pinned to each child's shirt. School is ready to start.

As Ms. Songi would tell us, much study, reading, planning, thought, and preparation has preceded this momentous day. It is common knowledge that effective classroom environments, grouping strategies, and organizational structures do not occur by accident. These environmental components, like so much of effective literacy instruction, are the products of teacher knowledge, skill, and creativity.

ORGANIZING FOR INSTRUCTION: AN OVERVIEW OF GROUPING STRATEGIES

Because teachers' experience and expertise in coping with the complexity of classrooms vary greatly, and because students' needs are equally complex and challenging, the question of grouping in a classroom is critical for all teachers—novice and experienced. Using a variety of grouping plans adds to the complexity of coping with the management concerns of the classroom while providing necessary attention to student needs. Although a teacher's choice to use a particular grouping strategy may reduce the complexity in a classroom, the potential moral consequences of such a choice may be that individual student needs may not be met or, worse yet, that some children may be denied access to knowledge, instruction, and opportunity to learn (Goodlad & Oakes, 1988; Oakes, 1986, 1988). Thus the decision to use a particular grouping strategy should be made in full appreciation of the potential social, instructional, psychological, and moral outcomes, not just for the ease or convenience of the teacher. A workable model for most teachers is to begin with a simple and manageable grouping strategy and gradually expand toward effectively using a wide range of grouping strategies to provide for individual differences, allow for free choice, foster collaboration, provide access to knowledge, support individual readers as they develop, and encourage social interaction.

Organizing classrooms into smaller groups of children fills the moral imperative often felt by teachers to meet individual student needs. However, somewhere between meeting individual needs and managing a classroom filled with children lies a wide gulf to be bridged by grouping strategies and organizational plans. Individualized instruction in classrooms filled with 20–30 children, while ideal, is also virtually impractical. On the other hand, the use of whole-class instruction fails to address students as individuals whose needs, skills, performance, and dispositions differ greatly. It is through the use of a variety of grouping strategies that teachers address students' needs, skills, and motivations in learning literacy. This chapter will begin by considering the positive and negative aspects of whole-class grouping for instruction. Next, a discussion on ability grouping will be presented, followed by suggestions of a variety of grouping strategies that provide classroom teachers workable and effective alternatives to whole-class and ability grouping. Finally, an organizational strategy will be developed for planning daily literacy instruction, incorporating a variety of grouping strategies on a daily basis.

WHOLE-CLASS INSTRUCTION

Whole-class grouping can be use to effectively address the *general developmental* needs of a group of children in a given classroom. No attempt is made to subdivide the group into smaller or more focused instructional groups along any dimension of learning, need, or skill.

Whole-class grouping has become an increasingly popular organizational format in recent years (Reutzel & Cooter, 1996). It is an effective means for safety-netting young learners as they develop conventional and increasingly sophisticated literacy learning strategies. Whole-class grouping shields the individual within a community of learners from potentially harsh emotional and psychological consequences that may result from the risks associated with *solo reading*. Whole-class grouping can also reduce some of the negative effects of labeling young learners as "slow," "special needs," or "disabled."

Because becoming literate is a social endeavor, whole-class grouping engages teachers and children in community-based or socially shared discussions, as well as reading, writing, and performance activities. Shared literacy learning activities generally provided in whole-class groups need to be a regular and integral part of every literacy classroom. Just a few examples of potentially effective literacy learning activities that can be used in connection with whole-class grouping are the following: telling stories; dramatizing; reading books aloud and sharing student-authored stories, poems, songs; reading big books together; reading the enlarged texts of songs, poems, raps, and jingles; participating in an experiment or some other active-learning experience; and creating language experience charts. On the down side, whole-class grouping used exclusively clearly fails to meet the needs of individual children.

ABILITY GROUPING

Ability grouping places children in several homogeneous groups for instruction as determined by their performance on a reading achievement test or some other form of norm-referenced or criterion-referenced measurement (Hiebert, 1983; Pallas, Entwisle, Alexander, & Stluka, 1994; Slavin, 1987). Typical ability grouping practice has resulted in three achievement groups: high, medium, and low. The groups are generally given names to mask the leveled nature of the grouping scheme. But children often uncover the meaning of being in the Eagles, the Robins, or the Buzzards group—or in the Roses, the Daisies, or the Weeds group! Ability grouping has often been characterized by critics *as running a three-ring reading circus.*

Although most teachers have relied heavily upon standardized reading achievement test scores in assigning children to an ability group, other factors such as personality attributes, general academic competence, work habits, and home background are also weighed in the decision (Haller & Waterman, 1985). Also, ability grouping has been associated with the use of graded basal readers, workbooks, and skill lessons designed to follow a published scope and sequence of skill development.

Teachers' continued reliance upon ability grouping has likely been rooted in the worthwhile goal of attending to individual student needs. Unfortunately, very often the instruction offered to students in ability groups has failed to meet student needs and, in some cases, has been harmful to both teachers and students.

Numerous negative outcomes have been associated with the use of ability grouping despite its intuitive appeal and longevity. For example, children in low-ability groups spend more time in oral *round-robin* reading and reading workbook assignments than do their peers in high-ability groups (Allington, 1983; Harp, 1989a, 1989b; Leinhardt, Zigmond, & Cooley, 1981; Pallas et al., 1994). Teachers tolerate more outside interruptions in low-ability groups than in high-ability groups (Allington, 1980). In the spring of the school year, children assigned to low-ability groups for reading instruction exhibited three times the number of inattentive behaviors exhibited by their counterparts assigned to high-ability groups (Felmlee & Eder, 1983). Children in low-ability groups tend to have lowered academic expectations and self-concepts (Eder, 1983; Hiebert, 1983; Rosenbaum, 1980). Time devoted to decoding instruction and practice is fully double for low-ability group readers as compared to high-ability groups (Gambrell, Wilson, & Gnatt, 1981). Teachers tend to interrupt low readers more often for miscues while reading than they do high readers (Allington, 1980).

Weinstein (1976) found that as much as 25% of the variation in reading achievement at the end of first grade can be attributed to group assignment. Kulik and Kulik (1982) analyzed the results of 52 studies and determined that (1) ability grouping generally has small effects on achievement, (2) high-ability readers profit from ability grouping in terms of achievement, and (3) the effects of ability grouping on average- and low-ability children's achievement is only trivial. On the other hand, children's friendships tend to be increasingly influenced by continuing membership in an ability group (Hallinan & Sorensen, 1985; Sorensen & Hallinan, 1986). Eder (1985) showed that even 1 year in an ability group caused some children to begin to question the reasons underlying their group membership. Thus reading achievement may be minimally affected by ability grouping, but children's self-images and social circles appear to be profoundly affected (Harp, 1989a, 1989b; Oakes, 1988; Wuthrick, 1990).

In short, the use of ability grouping is not recommended to promote effective literacy instruction. In defense of ability grouping there are those who suggest that its negative effects are largely associated with the static nature of the groups and with the teacher's attitudes and expectations. They also maintain that if groups were changed at least monthly and the teacher were aware of and resisted the expectations often invited by ability grouping, the ability grouping strategy might not constitute as harmful a practice to teachers and children as has been suggested (Worthy & Hoffman, 1996).

However, given the pervasive use of ability grouping in the past, which has given way to the pervasive use of whole-class grouping of late, many teachers are prompted to ask, "If whole-class grouping is insufficient to meet student needs and ability grouping is or can be harmful, just what do we put in the place of ability grouping?" The discussion that follows is intended to provide teachers an answer to this question by suggesting multiple grouping alternatives for organizing effective classroom literacy instruction.

ALTERNATIVE GROUPING STRATEGIES

Flexible Groups

Flexible grouping is a partial answer to the question of what to put in the place of whole-class or ability groups. In flexible grouping, children are placed into *temporary* groups based on their level of independence as learners and their personal interests that sustain independence. Flexible groups are formed and reformed on the basis of a set of principles articulated by Unsworth (1984, p. 300):

1. There are no permanent groups.
2. Groups are periodically created, modified, or disbanded to meet new needs as they arise.
3. At times there is only one group consisting of all pupils.
4. Groups vary in size from 2 or 3 to 9 or 10 depending on the group's purpose.
5. Group membership is not fixed; it varies according to needs and purposes.
6. Student commitment is enhanced when students know how the group's work relates to the overall program or task.
7. Children should be able to evaluate the progress of the group and the teacher's assessment of the group's work.
8. There should be a clear strategy for supervising the group's work.

It is clear from these principles that flexible grouping strategies can be used to accommodate student interests, learning styles, and social needs such as friendship groups in addition to meeting instructional needs and goals. For flexible grouping to function effectively, the organization, purpose, and tasks must be clearly understood by students.

Concerns such as what is to be accomplished and how it is to be accomplished must be clearly stated and understood by students. The potential for unproductive chaos is high in flexible grouping arrangements if the teacher has not carefully prepared the learning tasks and the environment for success. For example, a classroom in which flexible grouping is used to provide for participation in multiple centers or stations might operate something like the one described next.

This hypothetical classroom has six literacy learning centers, established in various locations around the classroom. The first center is an alphabet and word-building station where children use magnetic letters and word pattern cards (rimes/word families) to build words, sort words, and store words in personalized word banks. A second center houses listening stations where students have multiple copies of a single title to be read with a read-along cassette tape. A third center provides a quiet, comfortable area for reading self-selected books, magazines, comics, etc. A fourth center seats children around a horseshoe-shaped table for guided reading and interactive writing sessions with the teacher. A fifth center is a Writing Workshop where students can have peer conferences, get and give editing assistance, and prepare student-authored products from greeting cards, recipes and calendars, to newspaper ads, books, and story murals. Finally, there is a center for individual student conferences that are scheduled in advance with the teacher.

Flexible groups of children are formed to participate in these six designed center activities. Each flexible group includes a mix of reading and writing ability levels, called heterogeneous grouping, to avoid the pitfalls associated with ability grouping. Flexible groups may also have an elected or appointed group leader to oversee cleanup of centers, operation of necessary equipment, management of supplies, and other tasks. In any case, these groups have assigned tasks to complete in each center. Behavioral and instructional guidelines and goals are clearly established and communicated to each group prior to center time. And most importantly, students are helped to know what they may do as follow-up work should they finish before the others. All of this requires extraordinary instructional planning and management skill on the part of the teacher, but the busy and productive activity and learning that come from the flexible grouping strategy make it well worth the effort!

Visiting Basal Reader Selection Groups

In visiting basal reader selection groups, students are invited to spend about 20 minutes browsing through the basal reader table of contents, looking at the pictures throughout the book, and scanning the stories. This requires that teachers and students think about the basal reader as an anthology of literature to serve as a resource. Following this browsing time, the teacher might read each title in the table of contents aloud. Students indicate their interest in each story title read aloud by raising their hands, and the teacher records interest levels in the teacher's manual table of contents. This process provides a quick means of gauging interest for each selection in the basal reader. Following this initial interest assessment, the teacher looks at selection titles in the table of contents for common themes or topics so that basal stories can be grouped by theme, genre, or author to provide several related units for organizing visiting basal reader selection groups.

To get the visiting basal reader selection groups launched, the teacher describes the themes or topics for groups of selections, as well as each selection related to the theme or topic. Students pick their first or second basal selection choices for group membership. The remaining steps for forming visiting basal reader selection groups are the same as described in the next subsection outlining literature circles. Visiting basal reader selection groups, recommended by the Commission on Reading in the report *Becoming a Nation of Readers* (Anderson, Hiebert, Scott, & Wilkinson, 1985), represent a potentially effective grouping strategy to be used in conjunction with published basal reading programs.

Literature Circles

In literature circles, teachers and children use trade books or literature books, both narrative and expository, as the core for reading instruction. To form literature circles, the teacher has children look through several selected titles of trade books available for small-group instruction. (This will mean that multiple copies of each will be needed! It is recommended that teachers purchase about eight copies of each book rather than purchasing classroom sets.) At the conclusion of this exploration period, the teacher reads available book titles aloud and asks how many students would like to read each book. In this way teachers can get a quick idea of which available books seem to interest the students most and which engender no interest. The teacher selects from the high-interest trade books three to four titles, depending on how many literature circles he/she can reasonably manage and how many copies of each book are available. Next, the teacher works up a "book talk" on each of the selected books to present to the students the following day. A book talk is a short, interesting introduction to the topic, setting, and problem of a book. After presenting a book talk on each of the books selected, the teacher asks older children to write down the titles of their first two choices. The teacher asks the younger children to come to the chalkboard and sign their names under the titles of the two books they like best of those presented. Only one literature circle meets each day with the teacher to discuss and respond to a chapter or predetermined number of pages to have been read in a trade book. It is best if the teacher meets with each literature circle after children have indicated their choices to determine how many weeks will be spent reading the book and how many pages per day need to be read to reach that goal. The remaining steps for organizing literature circles are summarized in the following list:

1. Select three or four books children may be interested in reading from the brief interest inventory of literature available in the school or classroom, as described.

2. Introduce each of the books by giving a book talk on each.
3. Invite children to write down the titles of their two top choices.
4. Depending on the number of multiple copies of trade books available, fill each group with those children who have indicated the book as their first choice. Once a group is filled, move the remaining children to their second choice until all children have been invited to attend the group of their first or second choice.
5. Decide on how many days or weeks will be spent reading this series of book choices.
6. Meet with each of the literature circles and determine the following:
   a. How many pages per day will need to be read to complete the book in the time allowed.
   b. When the first group meeting will be held. (The teacher meets with only one group per day.)
   c. How children will respond to their reading. This may involve a reading response log, character report cards, or wanted posters.
7. Help children understand when the first or next meeting of their literature-response group will be, how many pages in the book will need to be read, and which type of response to the reading will need to be completed before the meeting of the literature-response group.
8. Near the completion of the book, the group may discuss possible extensions of the book to drama, music, art, and other projects.

Peterson and Eeds (1990), in their book entitled *Grand Conversations,* suggest a checklist that may be used by teachers to track student preparation for and participation in literature response groups. I have modified this form to be used with literature circles as shown in Figure 16.1.

When the literature circle book has been completed, literature circles are disbanded and new groups are formed for selecting and reading a new series of books. Thus, students' interests are engaged by encouraging choice, and the problem of static ability-grouping plans can be avoided.

Cooperative Learning Groups

Another grouping strategy for effective reading and writing instruction is called cooperative learning. This grouping strategy makes use of heterogeneous groups ranging from two to five children working together to accomplish a *team task* (Harp, 1989a; Opitz, 1992; Slavin, 1987). Harp (1989a) indicates four characteristics of cooperative learning groups. First, each lesson begins with teacher instruction and modeling. Second, the

Name _____   Date _____

Author _____   Title _____

Preparation for Literature Study

- Brought book to the literature circle.   Yes ___ No ___
- Contributed to developing group reading goals.   Yes ___ No ___
- Completed work according to group goals.   Yes ___ No ___
- Read the assigned pages, chapters, etc., for the goals.   Yes ___ No ___
- Noted places to share (ones of interest, ones that were
  puzzling, etc.)   Yes ___ No ___
- Completed group response assignments before coming
  to the day's discussion.   Yes ___ No ___

Participation in the Literature Circle Discussion

- Participated in the discussion.   Weak ___ Good ___ Excellent ___
- Gave quality of verbal responses and
  contributions.   Weak ___ Good ___ Excellent ___
- Used text to support ideas and assertions. Weak ___ Good ___ Excellent ___
- Listened to others.   Weak ___ Good ___ Excellent ___

FIGURE 16.1. Record of goal completion and participation in literature circles. Adapted from Peterson and Eeds (1990). Copyright 1990 by Scholastic. Adapted by permission.

children in the group work together to accomplish a task assigned by the teacher to the group. Third, children work on individual assignments related to a group-assigned task. Each student must be willing to complete his/her part of the group shared assignment. Finally, the team is recognized by averaging individual grades and assigning a group grade to each member of the group.

Much research indicates that children in cooperative learning groups have consistently shown greater achievement than children who participate in traditional grouping schemes (Johnson, Maruyama, Johnson, Nelson, & Skon, 1981; Jongsma, 1990; Opitz, 1992; Radencich, 1995; Slavin, 1988; Stevens, Madden, Slavin, & Farnish, 1987a, 1987b; Topping, 1989; Webb & Schwartz, 1988; Wood, 1987). In a synthesis of research on cooperative learning, Slavin (1991) found that cooperative learning not only increased student achievement but also increased student self-concept and social skills.

Manarino-Leggett and Saloman (1989) and Wood (1987) describe several different grouping alternatives that can be applied with the concept of cooperative learning. A few of these group alternatives are briefly described in Table 16.1.

Needs Grouping

Needs groups are determined by careful observation as teachers assess and work with children in a variety of literacy learning activities. Through the use of assessment strategies like running records, anecdotal records, group participation records, and observation, teachers determine individual student learning needs. Needs groups are formed when this careful assessment and observation process indicates several children with similar learning needs. Typically, a needs group will include as few as two students or as many as half the class, 10–15 students. The purpose of a needs group is to teach a temporary group of students a particular procedure, literary stylistic device, skill, or strategy they have yet to learn and apply. The vehicle for instruction within needs groups is minilessons.

Minilessons can occur with an entire class or with small needs groups. They are not always meant to be lessons for which outcomes are required. Sometimes minilessons are simply invitations to engage in some literate behavior or process. Hagerty (1992) describes three types of minilessons that may be taught in a needs group setting: (1) *procedural,* (2) *literary,* and (3) *strategy/skill.*

A procedural reading minilesson, for example, might involve the teacher and students in learning how to care for new books to be placed into the classroom library, as well as how to repair worn older books already found in the classroom library. The teacher may demonstrate how to break in a new book's binding by standing the book on its spine and opening a few pages on either side of the center of the book, carefully pressing them down. Cellophane tape and staplers may be used to demonstrate how to repair tears in a book's pages or covers. A heavy duty stapler can be used to reattach paperback book covers in another demonstration on caring for books.

Another example of a literary minilesson for early readers might involve a child presenting the teacher with a small booklet written at home in the shape of a puppy and that retells favorite parts from the book *A Taxi Dog Christmas* (Barracca & Barracca, 1994). This may present an opportunity for the teacher to share the book with his/her students as one demonstration of how another student shared his/her ideas using the writing process.

A typical strategy/skill minilesson might occur during the reading of a big book entitled *Who's in the Shed?* (Parkes, 1986), with the teacher mak-

TABLE 16.1. Alternative Grouping Plans for Encouraging Cooperative Learning

Dyads

Wood (1987) assigns roles to each student in a dyad or pair of readers. Each student reads two pages of text silently, or in some cases the two students read orally in unison. After reading these two pages, one student acts as the recaller and verbally recounts what the two have read. The other student acts as listener and clarifier for the recaller. Dyad reading is an effective means for supporting young children's reading development, especially for at-risk readers (Eldredge & Quinn, 1988).

Focus trios

Children may be randomly assigned or may form social groups of three students for the purposes of summarizing what they already know about a reading selection and developing questions to be answered during reading. After reading, the trio discusses answers to the questions and clarifies and summarizes their answers.

Group retellings

Students read different books or selections on the same topic. After reading, each student retells to the other group members what he/she has read. Group members may comment on or add to the retellings of any individual.

Groups of four

Groups of four are randomly assigned task completion groups. Each individual is given a responsibility to complete some phase of a larger task. For example, when writing a letter, one student might be the addresser, another the body writer, another the checker, etc. In this way, all students contribute to the successful completion of the task. Roles should be exchanged regularly to enable students to experience all aspects of task completion.

Jigsaw

Students in a group are each assigned to read a different part of the same selection. After reading, each student retells to the others in the group what he/she has read. A discussion usually ensues in which students may interview or question the reteller to clarify any incomplete ideas or correct misunderstanding. After this discussion concludes, students can be invited to read the rest of the selection to confirm or correct the retellings of other group members.

Metacomprehension pairs

Students alternate reading and orally summarizing paragraphs or pages of a selection. One listens, follows along, and checks the accuracy of the other's comprehension of the selection.

(continued)

TABLE 16.1. (*continued*)

Problem-solving/project groups

Having children work together cooperatively in pairs or small groups to solve reading or writing problems is another effective classroom practice involving the collaboration of children to enhance classroom instruction. Small problem-solving groups are initiated by children who wish to work collaboratively on a self-selected reading or writing problem.

In project groups, children are encouraged to explore a wide variety of possible reading and writing projects (e.g., plays, puppetry, reader's theater, research, student-authored books, poetry, lyrics to songs, notes, invitations, or cards). The products resulting from project groups are to be of publishable quality. The culmination of a project group is sharing the project or product with an authentic audience.

Think–pair–share

Lyman (1988) recommends that students sit in pairs as the teacher presents a reading minilesson to the class. After the lesson, the teacher presents a problem to the group. The children individually think of an answer; then with their partners they discuss and reach a consensus on the answer. A pair of students can be asked to share their agreed upon answer with the class.

Turn-to-your-neighbor

After listening to a student read a book aloud, share a book response, or share a piece of published writing, students can be asked to turn to a neighbor and tell one concept or idea they enjoyed about the presentation. They should also share one question they would like to ask the reader or author.

---

ing note of the fact that many of the words in the book rhyme but the rhymes are not spelled the same (*shed* and *said*). Noticing this irregularity in the text, the teacher draws the children's attention to these words and to the fact that these words rhyme but are spelled differently. For example, while rereading the big book the next day, the teacher may cover the words "shed" and "said" with small self-adhesive notes. During the group rereading of the book, the teacher reveals the *covered words*. On subsequent readings, the teacher invites students to join in the reading while emphasizing the target words. Children use the /ed/ rime to produce rhyming words written on cards to be displayed on the Word Wall. Children add other rhyming words to the Word Wall as they think of them.

A minilesson for more advanced readers might pertain to patterns used by nonfiction writers to make abstract information easier to understand (e.g., cause–effect, description, problem solution, or comparisons). The lesson could involve (1) describing the patterns used; (2) searching for examples in science, mathematics, and social studies materials; then (3) having students write/create their examples of these patterns pertaining to a topic of choice.

In summary, needs groups are formed to meet specific learning outcomes formulated through careful observation and assessment by the classroom teacher. These groups are not simply formed to teach a skill or strategy to a group of children because these appear in the curriculum guide or the scope and sequence chart of the basal reader; rather they are only formed specifically to address student needs discerned through careful teacher assessment.

Guided Reading Groups

Guided reading is an essential part of an effective reading program. The practice of guided reading focuses on reading *with* and *by* children when texts would present too many challenges if children were to take full responsibility for the initial reading. Thus the purposes of guided reading are (1) to develop reading strategies and (2) to move children toward independent silent reading (Mooney, 1990; Fountas & Pinnell, 1996).

In practice, the use of guided reading groups looks very similar to the practices of ability grouping. Since ability grouping has already been discussed, it is appropriate to examine the practices of guided reading groups and contrast these with ability grouping.

Children in guided reading are grouped homogeneously by developmental levels, reflecting a range of competencies, experiences, and interests (Mooney, 1990). The most important consideration centers on the child's ability to successfully manipulate and process leveled books. Developmental guided reading groups are composed of six to eight children who will be working together for a period of time with the assistance of the teacher. Groups change as children make progress during the year—usually changing by months rather than by weeks or days.

Prior to guided reading, great care is taken to match a leveled book and child to ensure that children can enjoy and control the book throughout their first reading. Texts chosen for each level should present children with a reasonable challenge but also with a high degree of success. Typically, children should be able to read 90–95% of the words correctly in a leveled book chosen for use in a guided reading group. During guided reading, teachers use questions and comments to help children employ strategies and resources available to them from within themselves and from within the text.

Children should *not* be placed in guided reading groups until they have had ample opportunities to listen to stories, poems, songs, etc. and to participate in shared or community-based whole-class reading experiences. A gradual release of responsibility from teacher to child for the first reading of a guided reading book generally occurs as teachers observe that children understand basic print concepts and have acquired a basic sight word vocabulary. As teachers work with children in guided reading groups, they lead them to understand and use strategically three important cuing systems that good readers use to unlock text: the meaning and organization of text, grammatical elements, and visual/letter–sound cues. Guided reading groups provide a context for systematic skill instruction related specifically to the language, literary devices, and content of each leveled book read in the group. Guided reading is a time to focus instruction directly on student reading skill development rather than on appreciating and responding to superb literature. In fact, the use of leveled books in guided reading does not always allow for the use of recognized literature of enduring quality, but rather necessitates books that are written to support individual readers in their development of self-extending reading strategies.

USING LANGUAGE ROUTINES TO PLAN FOR LITERACY INSTRUCTION IN THE PRIMARY GRADES (K–2)

Children develop a sense of security when the school day revolves around an established daily routine. One effective means for organizing early reading instruction is called *language routines*. Language routines have been used extensively and successfully in New Zealand, Australia, Canada, and the United States.

Language routines are specific, short, teacher-organized language learning opportunities. In effective literacy learning classrooms, teachers establish a variety of daily routines for organizing daily literacy instruction. While past instructional organization has focused on teacher-directed skill instruction, current effective literacy organization focuses on teacher and student shared-skill application. Holdaway (1984) describes five language routines for working with young children, routines that have undergone years of extensive field testing by teachers in Australia, New Zealand, the United States, and Canada. I have added a sixth daily language routine called *closing sharing time*. An outline of these six language routines is presented in Table 16.2.

Language Routine 1: Tune-In

Each school day is begun by warming children up or tuning them in to language. The purpose of the *tune-in* routine is to provide a time for the teacher to help children focus on language and acquaint them with the

TABLE 16.2. Six Language Routines for Organizing Daily Literacy Instruction

Tune-in (10% of allocated reading time or about 10 minutes). The teacher selects and reads aloud books, big books, cartoons, poems, songs, and jingles, etc., displayed on enlarged text. There is likely to be a new piece for the day or a new activity, such as movement, added to an old familiar piece.

Old favorites (10% of allocated reading time or about 10 minutes). Children select an old favorite story, chart, poem, etc. which they have enjoyed in the enlarged format before during Tune-in.

Learning about language (15% of allocated reading time or about 15 minutes). During this very brief period something useful (a skill or strategy) is taught, or something previously taught is reviewed in connection with the New Story routine (below).

New story (10–15% of allocated reading time or about 10–15 minutes). A new story is introduced generally in an enlarged format, or a new story is composed from an old favorite.

Independent reading/writing (50% of allocated reading/writing time or about 50 minutes). This routine is the reason for all of the previous language activity. Children and the environment are now ready for independent language output activities. Center activities and small group instruction are often the focus of student involvement.

Closing sharing time. Students share books they have read or seek responses to books they have completed or writing projects they have published. These are often shared in the setting of special "chairs" or "corners."

Note. Based on Holdaway (1984).

language learning opportunities for the day. The teacher reads aloud or sings poems, jingles, chants, word games, or songs to the children as models of language use and enjoyment. Often the teacher selects songs and chants to support specific reading instruction goals, such as learning the alphabet, recognizing words, and understanding letter–sound relationships. When using the tune-in routine to introduce new songs, poems, or chants on a daily basis, the teacher is seeking to expand the children's literary horizons while fanning the fires of their language enjoyment.

Language Routine 2: Old Favorites

The *old-favorites language routine* provides daily time for children and their teacher to return to and reread favorite enlarged texts of songs, poems, chants, and books for enjoyment or to deepen understanding. In this way, the old-favorite routines provides children with regular practice of familiar texts. Because old-favorite books have been introduced by the teacher for enjoyment on previous *tune-in* occasions, Holdaway (1981) suggests that this may be an appropriate time for students to choose what will be read.

Language Routine 3: Learning about Language

Holdaway (1984) describes the *learning about language* routine as a time for teaching a "very brief *skill* lesson" (p. 36; emphasis mine). Such a skill lesson should not be an isolated skill and drill session; rather, it should be a short lesson provided in a meaningful situational and language context. Most important, teachers should remember that when skill lessons for reading and writing are provided, four criteria should be considered and met if at all possible:

1. The lesson should grow out of an observed need or a desire to enrich children's literacy horizons, not merely to teach the next skill on the basal or district skill list.
2. A minilesson rather than a maxilesson is preferred: 5–10 minutes maximum.
3. The skill selected for instruction should be one that helps young children read better and with greater enjoyment. Lessons focusing on syllabication rules, diacritical marks, the schwa, finding the accent, and the like do little to meet this criterion.
4. Finally, any skill selected for instruction should be demonstrated with real texts and/or books the children have been reading or writing, thus providing a meaningful language context for instruction.

Language Routine 4: New Story

The *new-story routine* is often the highlight of the day: a time for children to discover a brand-new story. In selecting the new story, the teacher should look for a book that contains interesting illustrations and language. Books like *My Little Sister Ate One Hare* (Grossman, 1996) and *The Napping House* (Wood, 1984) are effective because the illustrations match the text and the language is predictable, playful, and interesting. Many teachers are selecting nonfiction/information books for sharing during the new-story routine, as well-written and beautifully illustrated nonfiction books become increasingly available. The *new story* may become a book to be reread if selected by children during the *old-favorites* language routine at some later time.

Language Routine 5: Independent Reading/Writing Activities

The *independent reading/writing activities* routine is aimed at involving individual children in reading, writing, and other language-output activities. Providing independent reading and writing opportunities, allowing students to select from a wide range of possibilities, is the ideal. Teachers often create stations or centers around the room to offer a variety of reading and writing activities. During this time, the teacher may be occupied in a single center with a group of children conducting a minilesson or a guided reading or interactive writing group. When not occupied with a single group of children, the teacher is free to move about the classroom during independent reading/writing time to engage in conferences with individual students—offering help and suggestions or conducting informal assessment of individual progress.

Language Routine 6: Closing Sharing Time

As a concluding language routine, *closing sharing time* enables children to gather together as a classroom community to share the things they have been reading or writing during the day. Several types of language sharing strategies have been developed and used successfully. For example, a chair in the classroom can be designated, even decorated, as the *author's chair*. Children who have published their writing in one form or another can be given an opportunity to sit in that chair and share their work with the class. Although a single author's chair is useful, I have found that as more and more children began writing and publishing in my own classroom, a single author's chair was insufficient. Thus my students proposed authors' corners. Similarly, providing a time and place for children to read their favorite book aloud to an audience is accomplished by a reader's chair or readers' corners.

The sharing circle allows children time to share in abbreviated form how they have spent their independent time that day. Children briefly share the title of the book they have read or written or the play they have been working on; occasionally they may perform a play for the entire group when scheduled with the teacher. Typically, individual sharing progresses rapidly around the entire circle of participants. The only recurrent difficulty experienced with the closing sharing time is the children's apparent enjoyment of it. Stopping is always difficult!

A FINAL NOTE ON GROUPING

Grouping children for instruction has always been grounded in a teacher's desire to accommodate individual student needs. Throughout the history of classroom literacy instruction, several variations on ability grouping and whole-class instruction have persisted as dominant forms of instructional grouping for literacy instruction, despite a large body of relevant research pointing to several negative outcomes for students and teachers related to these grouping strategies. In recent years, a number of alternative grouping strategies have emerged including flexible groups, visiting basal reader selection groups, literature circles, cooperative learning groups, needs groups, and guided reading groups; these strategies offer teachers a wider array of possibilities. By using the language routines for organizing daily literacy instruction, teachers not only access a variety of grouping strategies but also have an instructional framework that has proven effective. The best advice for the use of alternative grouping strategies may be the same as for many other aspects of human endeavor: Variety is the spice of life. For literacy instruction, a variety of grouping strategies may be the spice of literacy!

REFERENCES

Allington, R. L. (1980). Teacher interruption behaviors during primary grade oral reading. *Journal of Educational Psychology, 72,* 371–372.

Allington, R. L. (1983). The reading instruction provided readers of differing reading ability. *Elementary School Journal, 83,* 255–265.

Anderson, R. C., Hiebert, E. F., Scott, J. A., & Wilkinson, I. A. G. (1985). *Becoming a nation of readers: The report of the commission on reading.* Washington, DC: National Institute of Education.

Barracca, D., & Barracca, S. (1994). *A taxi dog Christmas.* New York: Dial.

Eder, D. (1983). Ability grouping and student's academic self-concepts: A case study. *Elementary School Journal, 84,* 149–161.

Eldredge, J. L., & Quinn, D. W. (1988). Increasing reading performance of low-achieving second graders with dyad reading groups. *Journal of Educational Research, 82,* 40–46.

Felmlee, D., & Eder, D. (1983). Contextual effects in the classroom: The impact of ability groups on student attention. *Sociology of Education, 56,* 77–87.

Fountas, I., & Pinnell, G. S. (1996). *Guided reading: Good first teaching for all children.* Exeter, NH: Heinemann.

Gambrell, L. B., Wilson, R. M., & Gnatt, W. N. (1981). Classroom observations of task-attending behaviors of good and poor readers. *Journal of Educational Research, 74,* 400–404.

Goodlad, J. I., & Oakes, J. (1988). We must offer equal access to knowledge. *Educational Leadership, 45*(5), 16–22.

Grossman, B. (1996). *My little sister ate one hare.* New York: Crown.

Hagerty, P. (1992). *Reader's workshop: Real reading.* New York: Scholastic.

Haller, E. J., & Waterman, M. (1985). The criteria of reading group assignments. *The Reading Teacher, 38*(8), 772–781.

Hallinan, M. T., & Sorensen, A. B. (1985). Ability grouping and student friendships. *American Educational Research Journal, 22,* 485–499.

Harp, B. (1989a). What do we know now about ability grouping? *The Reading Teacher, 42*(6), 430–431.

Harp, B. (1989b). What do we put in the place of ability grouping? *The Reading Teacher, 42*(7), 534–535.

Hiebert, E. H. (1983). An examination of ability grouping for reading instruction. *Reading Research Quarterly, 18,* 231–255.

Holdaway, D. (1981). Shared book experience: Teaching reading using favorite books. *Theory into Practice, 21,* 293–300.

Holdaway, D. (1984). *Stability and change in literacy learning.* Portsmouth, NH: Heinemann.

Johnson, D. W., Maruyama, G., Johnson, R. T., Nelson, D., & Skon, L. (1981). Effects of cooperative, competitive and individualistic goal structures on achievement: A meta-analysis. *Psychological Bulletin, 89,* 47–62.

Jongsma, K. S. (1990). Collaborative learning (questions and answers). *The Reading Teacher, 43*(4), 346–347.

Kulik, C., & Kulik, J. A. (1982). Effects of ability grouping on secondary students: A meta-analysis of evaluation findings. *American Educational Research Journal, 19,* 415–428.

Leinhardt, G., Zigmond, N., & Cooley, W. (1981). Reading instruction and its effects. *American Educational Research Journal, 18,* 343–361.

Lyman, F. (1988). Think–pair–share, wait time two, and on. . . . *Mid-Atlantic Association for Cooperation in Education Cooperative News, 2,* 1.

Manarino-Leggett, P., & Salomon, P. A. (1989, April–May). *Cooperation vs. competition: Techniques for keeping your classroom alive but not endangered.* Paper presented at the Thirty-Fourth Annual Convention of the International Reading Association, New Orleans, LA.

Mooney, M. E. (1990). *Reading to, with, and by children.* Katonah, NY: Owen.

Oakes, J. (1986). Keeping track, Part 1: The policy and practice of curriculum inequality. *Phi Delta Kappan, 68*(1), 12–17.

Oakes, J. (1988). Beyond tracking. *Educational Horizons, 65*(1), 32–35.

Opitz, M. F. (1992). The cooperative reading activity: An alternative to ability grouping. *The Reading Teacher, 45*(9), 736–738.

Pallas, A. M., Entwisle, D. R., Alexander, K. L., & Stluka, M. F. (1994). Ability-group effects: Instructional, social, or institutional? *Sociology of Education, 67*(1), 27–46.

Parkes, B. (1986). *Who's in the shed?* Crystal Lake, IL: Rigby.

Peterson, R., & Eeds, M. (1990). *Grand conversations: Literature groups in action.* New York: Scholastic.

Radencich, M. C. (1995). *Administration and supervision of the reading/writing program.* Boston: Allyn & Bacon.

Reutzel, D. R., & Cooter, R. B., Jr. (1996). *Teaching children to read: From basals to books.* Columbus, OH: Merrill, Prentice-Hall.

Rosenbaum, J. (1980). *Making inequality: The hidden curriculum of high school tracking.* New York: Wiley.

Slavin, R. E. (1987). Ability grouping and student achievement in elementary schools: A best-evidence synthesis. *Review of Educational Research, 57*(3), 293–336.

Slavin, R. E. (1988). Cooperative learning and student achievement. *Educational Leadership, 45*(2), 31–33.

Slavin, R. E. (1991). Are cooperative learning and "untracking" harmful to the gifted? *Educational Leadership, 48*(6), 68–71.

Sorensen, A. B., & Hallinan, M. T. (1986). Effects of ability grouping on growth in academic achievement. *American Educational Research Journal, 23*(4), 519–542.

Stevens, R. J., Madden, N. A., Slavin, R. E., & Farnish, A. (1987a). *Cooperative integrated reading and composition: A brief overview of the CIRC program.* Baltimore: Johns Hopkins University, Center for Research on Elementary and Middle Schools.

Stevens, R. J., Madden, N. A., Slavin, R. E., & Farnish, A. M. (1987b). Cooperative integrated reading and composition: Two field experiments. *Reading Research Quarterly, 22*(4), 433–454.

Topping, K. (1989). Peer tutoring and paired reading: Combining two powerful techniques. *The Reading Teacher, 42*(7), 488–494.

Unsworth, L. (1984). Meeting individual needs through flexible within-class grouping of pupils. *The Reading Teacher, 38*(3), 298–304.

Webb, M., & Schwartz, W. (1988, October). Children teaching children: A good way to learn. *PTA Today,* pp. 16–17.

Weinstein, R. S. (1976). Reading group membership in first grade: Teacher behaviors and pupil experience over time. *Journal of Educational Psychology, 68,* 103–116.

Wood, A. (1984). *The napping house* (illustrated by D. Wood). San Diego, CA: Harcourt Brace Jovanovich.

Wood, K. D. (1987). Fostering cooperative learning in middle and secondary school classrooms. *Journal of Reading, 31*(1), 10–19.

Worthy, J., & Hoffman, J. V. (1996). Critical questions. *The Reading Teacher, 49*(8), 656–657.

Wuthrick, M. A. (1990). Blue jays win! Crows go down in defeat! *Phi Delta Kappan, 71*(7), 553–556.

Chapter 17

BEST PRACTICES IN LITERACY INSTRUCTION FOR CHILDREN WITH SPECIAL NEEDS

Richard L. Allington
Kim Baker

Not all children, unfortunately, acquire literacy easily. While there has always been much debate as to just why some children struggle mightily to become readers and writers, in this chapter we focus on how exemplary instructional support might be provided to such children and largely leave the issue of etiology of learning difficulties for others to discuss. In our view, children who find learning to read and write more difficult are best served not by identifying some label for them but by designing and delivering sufficient and appropriate instruction and substantial opportunities to actually engage in real reading and writing activity. Thus, we draw upon our experiences in two long-term school-based research projects to offer detailed descriptions of interventions that we consider exemplary in nature and outcomes.

In our view, efforts to intervene productively begin in the general education classroom. In other words, providing all children with exemplary classroom literacy instruction is an essential first step in addressing the needs of children who find learning to read and write more difficult. In our studies of exemplary first-grade teachers (Pressley et al., 1998), for instance, we found the greatest impact of the exemplary teachers we studied was on the development of reading and writing proficiency in the lowest-achieving children. In other words, in the classrooms of the exemplary first-grade teachers there were far fewer children who ended first grade still struggling with reading and writing. Likewise, Mendro, Jordan, and Bembry (1998) studied the effects of 3 consecutive years of high-quality teaching on student reading development. They compared the achievement of children who were placed in high-quality classrooms with students who were unfortunate enough to have attended lower-quality classrooms over the same period. While the children's average standing on national norms rose consistently year after year in the high-quality classrooms, the standing of children in the lower-quality classrooms dropped each year. After 3 years, the achievement of children who had similar initial achievement now differed by almost 40 percentile ranks! The results of this large-scale study mirror the findings that Snow, Barnes, Chandler, Goodman, and Hemphill (1991) had reported earlier.

Now, it would not have seemed necessary, in some senses, to actually conduct studies to show that access to high-quality teaching is important—essential, in fact. Who would argue against providing high-quality classroom instruction? But then, who argues for it? How often are resources allocated to improving classroom instruction from funding provided by either the Title 1 program of the Improving America's Schools Act (IASA) or special education under the Individuals with Disabilities Education Act (IDEA)? How often are such funds allocated for the purchase of needed classroom instructional materials, for instance, to purchase a supply of tradebooks at an appropriate level of complexity for use by the learning disabled students included in the classroom? Or how often are funds allocated for providing professional development opportunities for classroom teachers to learn how to better document the development of children who are struggling with literacy learning?

Instead, these programs more often fund additional personnel including specialist support teachers (reading teachers, learning disabilities teachers, speech and language teachers), school psychologists, social workers, or paraprofessional personnel. There may be a role for any and all of these extra personnel, but in our view a necessary first step is ensuring that children have access to high-quality instruction regardless of their label or their participation in a special program. One question that we now routinely pose is whether there exists evidence that specialized personnel enhance the quality of classroom instruction. In other words, what evidence is available that points to the ways that the school psychologist has improved classroom teaching? The same question might be asked as to the roles of the social worker, the learning disability specialist, the reading teacher, or the paraprofessional. In most schools such evidence is often slim, if available at all. But if the presence of specialized personnel is not improving classroom instruction, then perhaps we should consider whether it makes more sense to use the funding for these positions in other ways. At the very least we should reconsider the role demands for such positions so that improving the quality of classroom teaching becomes a central attribute of each specialists' role (Walmsley & Allington, 1995).

However, even exemplary classroom teachers cannot do it all. While such teachers dramatically reduce the incidence of reading difficulties, a few children typically continue to struggle even in these exemplary classrooms. Some children have enormous instructional needs that simply cannot be met in the day-to-day bustle of the classrooms. Their needs for close and personalized teaching simply exceed the capacity of even exemplary teachers. It seems to be both a quantity and quality problem. Most of these children simply need closer and more explicit teaching than can be accomplished by a teacher with the responsibility for a classroom filled with 25 children. These children need, for instance, larger amounts of guided reading opportunity. Most will need a supply of books at appropriate levels of difficulty—typically levels different from those of the books used in the daily classroom lessons and activities. And some will need particularized instruction—an emphasis on hearing sounds in words, for instance, that may require not only more time to provide than the classroom teacher has available but may also require a particular instructional expertise that classroom teachers do not routinely acquire, even exemplary classroom teachers. Thus, a second feature of exemplary intervention efforts is the useful and targeted deployment of special support teachers and personnel who provide the intensive and personalized instruction that those few children need in order to thrive in school.

Unfortunately, it is common today to also find that a school employs paraprofessional staff in attempting to meet the instructional needs of children who find learning to read difficult, usually funding such personnel with monies allocated by Title 1 IASA or IDEA. In other words, huge numbers of paraprofessionals are employed in remedial and special education programs (International Reading Association, 1994). Unfortunately, the weight of the evidence indicates that the use of paraprofessionals lessens the likelihood that children with difficulties will be well served. In other words, when high-poverty schools use paraprofessionals in an instructional intervention, the achievement of children with learning difficulties is rarely enhanced (Allington & Cunningham, 1996; Anderson & Pellicier, 1990). In fact, the use of paraprofessionals in classrooms of any sort of school has been shown to have no positive effect on student achievement (Boyd-Zaharias & Pate-Bain, 1998). The key to understanding these findings is located in the need children have for access to expert instruction. Too often, it seems, school programs are designed such that children who find learning to read difficult are paired with paraprofessional staff for instruction and practice. Paraprofessionals should not be criticized for their failure to offer expert instruction; they are the least expert of all school personnel when it comes to providing appropriate instruction. The criticism should fall on those who design programs that place paraprofessionals in the untenable position of being the person least well prepared to work with children with the greatest instructional needs. There are useful and important roles that paraprofessionals may be able to play in the design of an exemplary intervention program, but those roles are limited and require paraprofessionals with substantially better preparation than is now usually the case.

So, what might an exemplary intervention program look like? It would, of course, begin with exemplary classroom teaching. Support for exemplary classroom teachers would be available in the form of expert specialists who provide appropriate and intensive services for children who need such added attention. This support might be offered during the school day or after school or during the summer. It might be offered in the classroom or in another location. There might be paraprofessional support for either the classroom teacher or the specialist teacher, or for both. But the efforts of the specialist and any paraprofessionals would be targeted at fostering student success on the classroom curriculum and the enhancement of classroom instruction in as short a period of time as possible.

A grand scheme, you say, but what exactly would it look like in practice? In the following sections you will meet (1) an exemplary first-grade teacher and spend a day in her classroom, and (2) an exemplary support teacher—certified and experienced in both reading and learning disabilities—and spend a day with her as she goes about supporting teachers and children as they learn to read and write.

EXEMPLARY CLASSROOM INSTRUCTION FOR CHILDREN WHO FIND LEARNING TO READ AND WRITE DIFFICULT

Georgia teaches in a small rural district in northern California. Nearly two-thirds of the children come from low-income families, and one-sixth of the children are members of an ethnic minority group. Seasonal employment in agriculture supports a mobile, low-wage work force in this community. Because of the transient nature of agricultural work, Georgia's class membership had a 50% changeover during the last school year.

However, when you walk into Georgia's first-grade classroom, the mood is one of a community that is actively engaged and interested in what it is doing. Students are working in groups and alone, reading and writing, sharing and exchanging ideas and information. Georgia integrates reading and writing throughout the day and across subjects. Print surrounds the students on all four walls, including student stories, students' artwork with labels, charts of songs and poems, and a pocket board for sentences about the basal story from guided reading.

Georgia's language arts program involves a weekly schedule of varied reading and writing activities, not the more common daily schedule. At least three times a week the students have independent reading time while Georgia holds individual reading conferences. A literature-based basal reader is used twice weekly for guided reading, supplemented with appropriately leveled little books at these sessions for more guided reading. The class is divided by reading ability into four groups for these twice-a-week sessions, but it is heterogeneously grouped for daily independent reading time. While Georgia meets with guided reading groups, the other students have center activities. Friday is an independent reading day for all groups. Each day after lunch the students have leisure reading time. Georgia also reads aloud daily offering a chance for predictions, sharing of personal knowledge and experiences, and vocabulary building. Often she chooses books that enhance a math, science, or social studies concept the class is working on. Writing Workshop is a vital component in the planned weekly literacy program. Twice a week students are composing for at least 45 minutes. Other writing assignments, responses to their reading, personal journals, and whole-class-generated big books offer diverse writing opportunities. The students have cubbyholes and are encouraged to write notes to each other all the time.

A Day in First Grade

Students enter school at 8:20, quickly hang up their jackets, put away lunches, and group on the rug. On Mondays there is oral sharing time, when students have the opportunity to participate in telling an experience. Georgia quickly takes the lunch count, attendance, and has two helpers writing the day of the week and the date. (At the beginning of the school year she modeled this, and by January she handed it over to students to do on their own.) While this is going on she engages the rest of the class in "reading the room"—reading words from the Word Wall, reading words from the poems and songs around the room. When the students finish their calendar information, the class reads it silently and then in unison. Then the pledge of allegiance is said and a patriotic song is sung with a student pointing to the large printed words on a chart. Again, this is an activity that Georgia did at first but has now been taken over by the students. This usually takes 15 minutes, and by 8:35 the class is engaged in guided reading and centers, independent reading, or Writing Workshop. Georgia has organized a 90-minute block of time for literacy activities. Over two-thirds of this period involves students daily in individual reading and writing. Writing Workshop, guided reading and centers, independent reading, and conferences are included throughout the week.

Guided reading revolves around a basal selection for the week. Georgia had all the students on the rug as she did a prereading activity. With this week's story, *Over in the Meadow* (Keats, 1993), she had the children close their eyes and think about animals and plants in a meadow. She told them, "There is a creek not as big as our local creek, and a tree trunk nearby with ants crawling on it. Up in the blue sky are clouds. If you are sitting back in this meadow, you would be smelling things, seeing things, and hearing things." Georgia then directed the students to the story, illustrated by Ezra Jack Keats. A discussion about the fact that this is an old story, he didn't write it, and that they had read other retold stories ensued. Georgia read it aloud from a big book edition, and the students commented that it is a counting book, a rhyming book, a repeating book. *Muskrat, snug,* and *chirp* were discussed as vocabulary as she read because they were hard to determine from the pictures. Georgia asked questions about the muskrat; she just elaborated on *snug* by saying, "I like snug. It reminds me of being warm and comfortable"; and she demonstrated "chirping" when asked "What is chirp?" by a student.

Georgia had the written numbers *one* through *ten* on cards and arranged them, using a pocket chart, in a column and placed blank cards across from them in another column. As the students worked on remembering which animal matched which number, students flipped the cards to reveal the correct names. Georgia also used this exercise to stress sounds and words. She used the word numbers *one* and *eight* to talk about how *one* starts with the *w* sound, not *o*, and how *e* and *i* says *a* in *eight*. As students matched the animals to the number from the story, they silently—in their heads—read. Then in unison they read it again, with all the students appearing to be able to read. At their seats they all found the story in individual books using the table of contents and read chorally.

Then, Georgia directed her students to write in their journals about their favorite baby animal and why it was their favorite. During this time Georgia and her aide circulated, helping students sound out words. With *cheetah,* Georgia directed a student to look at her mouth as she said it, stretching it out. The student said, then wrote, *ch—e—ta.* This sound stretching was a common feature in the classroom during writing. Both Georgia and her aide linked the students' sound spelling to developing phonemic segmentation by modeling stretching a word in segments and encouraging the students to do this on their own.

The next day in the students' smaller guided reading groups Georgia worked with the pocket chart using sentences from the story but leaving blank the animals and their activity. The students filled in these missing words by reading the sentence in their head, talking with each other, and deciding what should fit. Afterward, they read it silently or whisper-read, then read it aloud together. Finally, in individual books, Georgia directed the students to read it loud enough for her to hear when she moved around, but not loud enough to disturb their neighbor.

The reading teacher, who provides instruction to five students in a pullout program, did so at this time. She coordinates what she is working on with Georgia. Next, she pulls one student for a Reading Recovery lesson. She has trained Georgia's aide to work with another student, using the one-on-one daily instruction and general Reading Recovery practices. This understanding of reading strategies and decoding is helpful when the aide works with any student in the Writing Workshop, when working with students who are practicing for author's chair, in literacy activities at the centers, and during independent reading time. The aide is there all morning, spending most of her time working with students individually while Georgia monitors her interactions and offers bits of advice about each student.

Next, the students who have been with the reading teacher have a discussion with Georgia about what they heard in the story and saw outside (the class went for a walk in the meadow to observe and gather data the day before). Georgia shares pages from several books about bees. Then she introduces the Storybox book *The Bee* by Joy Cowley (1990), preparing the students by activating their background information about bees, previewing the cover and the following pages, and setting the readers up to successfully whisper-read on the first try. She then has them reread two times, stressing that the sentences make sense. Next she gives a minilesson on the double *ee* sound, starting with *bee* and making a list with *see, meet, beet,* and *bees,* all words from this story and a recently read book. The students think of sentences about what bees can do: *Bees can sting. Bees can collect nectar. Bees can drink.* Although they know only the beginning letter of *collect,* the students spell everything else as Georgia writes. As Georgia writes *collect,* she models stretching out the sounds of the word to better be able to hear and spell them. Students whisper-read the chart, read all the sentences together, and then each student picks a sentence to read alone.

Guided reading is alternated with independent reading of books chosen from the book baskets. The baskets are filled with teacher-selected books that the students have encountered during previous lessons. This is a quiet reading time, but students share with each other or sometimes read with partners, taking turns. With the groups heterogeneously mixed and a variety of leveled books available, students model good reading strategies and fluency for each other. During this time

Georgia has individual reading conferences, takes running records, jots down notes, and offers personal instruction in reading strategies to encourage self-monitoring, multiple strategy use, and independence. In one reading conference with a student, Georgia encourages his use of multiple strategies: self-monitoring, decoding, and—most importantly— meaning making. *The Comstock Farm* is a new book for this reader, so Georgia encourages talking about it a little bit, looking at the title, and discussing the opening illustration and what he thought was going on. When the student reads "country farm" instead of "Comstock Farm," Georgia praises the try, saying it is a really good word that made sense. She then claps out the syllables in *Comstock,* directing the student to look closely at the letters, and he is able to sound it out by syllable. Early in the story the student reads "greens and chickens" for "geese and chickens." Georgia draws attention to the mistake, asking, "Does that make sense?" The student quickly rereads the phrase correctly. She then encourages the use of multiple strategies, using picture cues, making sense, use of letter–sound relationships and word patterns, and reading on to find out what happens. The student slowly but successfully reads, "The geese and chickens and a big fat turkey walked with us on our way to the . . . . . . where the apples grow." The word skipped is *orchard.* Georgia builds upon the student's knowledge, asking, "Where do apples grow? What do we call a lot of trees? What parts of the word look familiar?" until the student uses existing prior knowledge and the word structure to correctly pronounce "orchard." As the student reads on he became more fluent. Another mistake, "for me vine"/"for the vine"/"from the vine" is a quick succession of readings. The student is self-correcting as Georgia asks, "Does that make sense?" Another self-correction leads Georgia to ask, "How did you figure out that it was 'carry?'" The student doesn't know how to verbalize what strategies he has used, so Georgia suggests some: "Did you look at the pictures? Did you go on?" For a final mistake, "fake" for "face," Georgia again stresses making sense: "Read it again and see if that makes more sense to you, from the beginning," encouraging another strategy, rereading along with meaning making, in cross-checking. The student successfully reads, "At home we carve a jack-o'-lantern face on our big orange pumpkin." Georgia praises him for his use of multiple strategies and for sticking to the reading even though the book has many hard words.

The days students have reading for 30 minutes from the literature baskets are also Writing Workshop days. The teacher and aide give individual attention and encouragement to the writers. There are checklist cards for editing that encourage final punctuation, capitals, and spelling. Most of the students spell phonemically, sounding out words and stretching the sounds. Back in January, Georgia added a priority word list of 25 nonphonemic and high-frequency words. The students have a list of them on their tables and are expected to refer to it whenever they need to use these words in writing. After 3 months, students were spelling them correctly without looking at the lists. Today, there is much use of the Word Wall for spelling other words. Typical is one boy who is adding to a story on giant sea turtles. He is reading from a book about sea turtles to gather new information. He has already written two drafts that have been revised and edited. As he writes, he uses the Word Wall and the information and spelling from the turtle book he is using as a resource. Another student is working on a chapter in a book about animals because she has decided to combine two works in progress, one on horses and one on dogs.

After recess, Georgia has a math lesson on telling time on the hour and on the half hour. It starts as a whole class discussion on the rug as she models with a large yellow clock with movable hands, indicating the time for reading, for recess, and for leisure reading. Again literacy is stressed. To tie in with this unit on telling time, she reads aloud *The Bear Child's Book of Hours* by Anne Rockwell (1987). Students then proceed to more individualized work back at the tables, each writing *My Book of Hours and Half Hours*. With the assistance of Georgia and her aide, scaffolding when necessary, each student fills in clocks and composes sentences that match his/her personal experiences. Lunchtime and another recess end this busy morning.

When students return from lunch they settle down for independent leisure reading time. Crates of books of different reading levels are available, including many easy ones, as well as magazines and student-published books. Students share responses with each other, partner read, or read segments to each other from the books they have chosen. There is a very low hum to this reading time. Twenty-five minutes later students go to the gym.

When Georgia picks them up from the gym she comes prepared with clipboards, paper, and pencils. They discuss the various sights and smells they envisioned earlier on the rug before reading *Over in the Meadow*. Then Georgia directs them to write down anything they observe as they go on their meadow walk. Students are busy, talking, smelling, looking, and sharing ideas as they gather data and write their own observations.

This day the students have written in response journals, in their individual "books of hours," and now on clipboards about their trip to the meadow, writing in their own words everything they have seen, smelled, or heard. Georgia teaches both reading and writing skills explicitly, typically in the context of a reading or writing activity. She is opportunistic, selecting multiple occasions daily to provide explicit skill information, during whole-group, small-group, and individual meetings. But Georgia is also systematic, incorporating much of her strategy and skill instruction into her guided reading lessons, Writing Workshop conferences, and reading conferences. All of these activities offer students instruction on a personalized basis.

EXEMPLARY INSTRUCTIONAL SUPPORT FOR CHILDREN WHO FIND LEARNING TO READ AND WRITE DIFFICULT

Joyce is a reading teacher in an old mill town on a river in the Northeast. The school serves significant numbers of at-risk students, with 40% of the children eligible for free or reduced-price lunch. Joyce starts her day at 8:30, snatching small conferences with the various teachers whose rooms she pushes into, getting plastic baskets ready with books for the various first-grade rooms she enters, and setting up her small, cozy room for the two pullout sessions she does a day. At 9:00 she is entering the first of five first-grade classrooms she visits on a daily basis.

The "warm-up" involves 10 students who come over immediately as Joyce spreads multiple copies of eight little books. These are all rereads that students quickly engage in with such comments as "I can read this one" (e.g., *The Ghost*; Cowley, 1990) or "Let's read this one together" (e.g., *In a Dark, Dark Wood*; Ross, 1990). Joyce works with and listens to each student as he/she reads in a whisper, their silent reading. As they finish one book, they take or trade for another. After 10 minutes she collects those texts and gives each child a copy of *Where's the Halloween Treat?* (Ziefert, 1985), introduced yesterday.

Joyce starts the guided reading with "Where are your eyes going to be?" The students chime, "On the words." Working on the title, one student knows the word *the,* another *Halloween,* another guesses *trick.* Noting that *trick* makes sense, Joyce asks, "Is that trick or treat?" The student answers, "Treat because of the *t* at the end." Students read the text together, misreading *us* for *me.* When asked "Is that *us?*" they reread, voicing the word starting with an *m* and self-correcting to *me.* Joyce points out, "I hear a rhyme. Listen for two rhyming words," and then rereads the pages. Students quickly pick out and say, "Eat/treat." Sharp-eyed young detectives are asked to find more rhyming words as the story progresses. Joyce picks up the pace and so does the group, self-correcting individually as they go along. When they finish the story Joyce has them turn back to page 6 to find the words *good, eat,* and *six.* She cues each word with "What's it going to start with?" This reread with a minilesson on rhymes takes 10 minutes.

For the final 10 minutes Joyce introduces a new book, *Going Up?: The Elevator Counting Book* (Cummins, 1995). Finger pointing to the first word she asks, "What does it say?" As she covers the *ing,* students quickly chant *go*; then they chant *going* as she uncovers the word. From the title students predict where the character is—in an elevator. Joyce asks the students, "Why is this a good name for a book about an elevator, and how does it know when to stop?" Students have various responses, which are all accepted positively. Then they begin to read as Joyce finger-points to each word. The elevator stops at floor number five. She then asks them to predict what will happen next: The numbers go down as the elevator goes down. Then all read the rest of the text together. Before leaving, Joyce shares with them that they will work on writing books tomorrow.

She quickly goes back to her small room, where she picks up the next basket of books and hurries on to her second first-grade class. In this class, they start their warm-up with *Jack-o'-Lantern* (Frost, 1990). Each student has his/her own copy. Joyce has extra copies for those children who took it home and forgot to bring it back. Other books for the warm-up are spread out with the instruction, "Everyone find one page to read to me. When I hear your page take a different book." Joyce encourages rereading, thinking of a word that makes sense and starts with the beginning sound, and voice–print match. One student, who picked the first page of *Scarecrow* (Bacon, 1993), reads. Joyce asks him how the book ends, which he doesn't know. She directs him to find the end and together they read the last pages, working on self-correcting and understanding. After the 12-minute warm-up, the students are directed to put the books in the middle and are told they can keep *Jack-o'-Lantern* and take it home.

In this group she is introducing *Where's the Halloween Treat?*. Looking at the title, students are directed to the *H* and asked, "What sound does it make?" Students all say /h/ and start thinking of a word that makes sense with the cover picture. Students offer *haunt, house, Halloween*. Another student reads, "Where's the," and everyone choruses, "Halloween." Joyce begins the book, her finger pointing to the words as she goes along. By the second page students are chiming in and predicting a good thing to eat behind the door. *Sandwich* and *apple* are accepted, but *skeleton* is confronted with "Is that something good to eat?" By the third page the students are using the repetition and their knowledge of numbers to read with no assistance. When asked how they know it is *seven*, one student says it starts with an *s* and another student adds that it ends with *n*. Near the end of the book, Joyce asks the students to predict, "What do you think they did when the ghost said, Boo?" Answers varied from "They stayed," to "They ran," to "They were afraid." They finish the story to see what happens and revise their predictions as needed.

With 5 minutes left, Joyce starts them on writing their own book modeled after the book they have just read. The classroom teacher allows them to continue writing as Joyce leaves.

Joyce's third first-grade class does a warm-up reading time for 10 minutes. Then *Where's the Halloween Treat?* is read chorally, a reread for three students and new to two others. With this group, Joyce brings out *My Journal* books from her basket with each child's name at the bottom of the covers. In it they are working on patterns and words they can make from them to use in writing. The students are directed to make a box, then a *u* in the box, then a wall, and then an *s*. Joyce asks, "What's that word?" Students respond, "Us." After writing it under the box, Joyce asks, "What would rhyme with us?" Students think of *bus*. Joyce models on a pad writing *us* and putting a *b* in front of it, while she thinks aloud, "If we can write *us*, we can write *bus*. We need to put the *b* first, then *us*." Students are now directed to write *give* on the bottom of their page; then students and Joyce spell it. Next they are asked to write *us* from above and read the two words and add a number, *Give us 7*. Then they spell together *good things to eat*, the students spelling the beginning and ending sounds and the *ing*. Joyce ends her half hour telling the students, "When I come back tomorrow we will cut up these sentences and do a new book."

It is now 10:30 and time for Joyce's fourth first-grade class. Six in this group quickly dive into the warm-up books she brought in a plastic basket. As Joyce comments positively to one student, "I like the way you are finger-pointing," other students start finger-pointing. Joyce works individually with each student. Then a new book for this group is introduced, *Jack-o'-Lantern*. The end of the lesson revolves around the word *made*. "We are going to write the word *made*. Think about it. How big a box?" Joyce uses a small easel blackboard to model a box with three spaces, the last divided with a dotted line. The students fill in *m*, *a*, *d*, as Joyce ends with "There is a letter we don't hear at the end." Students predict *n* or *t*, and Joyce tells them *e*. They add the *e*, going over there are three sounds, but four letters. This leads to writing in their journal about the kind of face they would make on a pumpkin. Joyce has each student say the sentence they want to write, concentrating on adjectives. Students quickly write, "I made a," then Joyce helps them sound out *vampire, scary, wolf, happy,* or *mad*. She then directs them to the word *face* in their book. On a blank piece of paper she writes each sentence, cuts it up, puts it and a copy of *Jack-o'-Lantern* in a Zip-lock bag for each student to take home.

Joyce is a little behind schedule, arriving in the fifth classroom at 11:10. They do warm-up reading and then the new book, *Jack-o'-Lantern*. She says, "Look at the cover. What do you see?" Students say, "Pumpkin." Joyce responds, "Do you think that word says *pumpkin?*" The students reply, "No." Her "Why?" is answered, "Because it starts with a *j*." Joyce prompts them: "What is another name that starts with *j*?" They answer, "jack-o'-lantern." Different students take turns finger-pointing and reading with

Joyce. Then the students read in pairs with their own copies. Joyce then has each student pick one page to read out loud to her after first practicing it in pairs.

Joyce now has a prep time and lunch, which she spends preparing the different baskets for the five first-grade lessons tomorrow. She talks with the fourth grade teacher over lunch, whose room she will be in for an hour.

At 12:30 Joyce provides a one-on-one pullout session with a first grader. She is giving daily intensive tutoring to the two first graders who are struggling the most with reading. Joyce picks up the student, quickly walking to her small room. The student picks *The Monster's Party* (Cowley, 1990) herself out of a packet with her name on it kept in the reading room. She reads it, finger-pointing as Joyce listens. Then Joyce picks *Sing a Song* (Melser, 1990) out of her packet. As the student reads it, she takes a running record. When stuck on *about,* Joyce prompts, "What can you do if you don't know it?" The student says, "Read on," and does. Although she does not self-correct here, she does so later on when reading *together* for *bed* and *tuck* for *us.* In both cases she appears to use meaning and the first letter to help self-correct. As she completes the book Joyce asks, "Can you tell me one thing in this story you liked?" The girl likes the splashing. Joyce continues by asking, "What else happened in the story?" The student replies, "They got out." Joyce asks, "How did they get out?" "Jump," which she is asked to find as a word and does. The next book read is *Hairy Bear* (Cowley, 1990), where they discuss that *we* and *together* mean more than one tiger. Up on the blackboard they work on the word *out,* making a box with one wall and one segment divided with a dotted line. The student fills in the *t,* Joyce the *o* and *u.* They then work on a box for *about,* the word she missed in her reread for the running record. The student hears and writes each sound, then practices writing *about.* Then she writes *out* and *about* on 3 × 5 cards that will be added to her word box, a recipe box. For two minutes they practice words from the box. Then as the student picks another story to read, Joyce writes a sentence on jumping from *Sing a Song:* "Out, Out, Out we jump." The student reads the sentence, Joyce cuts it up, has her assemble it, and read it again. Into a bag go the cut-up sentence, the book, and the 3 × 5 cards *out* and *about* to go home for practice. In the last 3 minutes they discuss real and make-believe as a new book, *Dan the Flying Man* (Cowley, 1990), is introduced. Joyce starts reading it, having the book in front of the student and having the student finger-point to the words. Joyce leaves blanks at the end of the sentence and the student correctly supplies *trees* and *train.* Halfway through, the student takes over. Joyce joins in again at the ending, which has a change of wording. The student goes back to her classroom, while Joyce goes on to fourth grade.

Joyce is working with a fourth-grade teacher this year because of the teacher's request that Joyce work with her to enhance her writing instruction. In September, Joyce had modeled the writing process, brainstorming, rough drafts, revising, conferencing, editing, and publishing. She and the teacher worked on modeling peer conferences that sensitively gave feedback, constructive criticism, and specific ideas to the writer. With the writing process smoothly working in late October, Joyce continued to help with writing conferences but also was available for reading conferences and small heterogeneously grouped work. Language arts time was structured so that remedial aid included students with special needs who were working on reading and writing material that was at their independent and instructional levels. More frequent conferences in reading and writing were provided for them.

Joyce enters the room as the teacher is reading the beginning of *The Eerie Canal* (Reber, 1991). The introduction to the book had taken place before. Joyce points out at the end of the chapter, "I met a lot of characters. They keep mentioning Tom. I think he will be important." A student adds that another character, Sandy, is being described in detail and must be important too. As the teacher reads, Joyce and the children discuss the opening chapters, and inferences and predictions flow. Questions like "I'm getting a funny feeling. What do you think right now?"; "What do you feel?"; "Can you picture that?"; "What made you think it?" all encourage response, sharing of different ideas, and predictions. The discussion is then led by both teachers to important characters and significant events that happen to them. In groups of two or three the students discuss, share ideas, and write about the two main characters and important events that they had experienced in the opening chapters. Joyce and the teacher circulate among the students, listening, prompting, and asking questions to expand ideas and encourage examples. Coming back for whole-class discussion and a composite list of events, the conversation also includes the author's style and how he jumped the reader right into the story. They contrast it to Cynthia DeFelice's style in *The Light on Hogback Hill* (1992), the current read-aloud book, which has a much slower beginning and drew the reader in slowly. As this discussion is continuing, Joyce leaves.

It is now 2:00 and time to pick up the other first grader for intensive one-on-one tutoring. After that Joyce has a prep period, which she uses to prepare for the individualized tutoring she will do tomorrow and further preparation for the five first grades she pushes into.

Joyce and her school have participated in a variety of studies with a nearby university for 10 years. Organizational support from a former administration allowed and even encouraged change, involving teachers and their ideas. Earlier, some 12 years ago when Joyce was a special education teacher, she started pushing into the classrooms. She started with one teacher: "It was contagious. People were upset I couldn't come into their room. Part of that was they were getting something back. They were learning how to teach with literature, and they really wanted to have their special education kids with them more of the time. We were learning together how to best do this."

When Joyce became a reading teacher 9 years ago the program was completely pullout. At that time an administrator wanted to start a brand new kindergarten and first-grade reading program that was a push-in model. Joyce: "The K–1 teachers never had exposure to working with someone in their rooms before. . . . They might not have invited me in, but I just couldn't feasibly do a pullout in K–1. Plus it was really successful with the way my special ed program was operating. . . . I don't think people like to see you come in with a halo of authority. I would always say we should sit and talk. First we had discussion time. I would say to them, 'I need to know what I'm doing when I'm in the room—so let's decide what your goals are and what you want to accomplish, and I'll talk about some of my goals and what I want to accomplish. Then let's figure out how we can do this together in the room at the same time.' Every person was different." One teacher and Joyce worked on flexible grouping, with students rolling in and out between them. For another teacher she modeled read alouds and having the children respond to stories. Joyce notes, "I had to give her something concrete, something predictable, something she could do every day by herself."

In the subsequent years Joyce's role has changed "because the teachers have gotten comfortable with literature-based instruction and teaching it themselves. I don't have to spend much time giving whole-class lessons. I'm spending more time with students, individualizing more. . . . I try to do a lot more things quickly—quicker than I used to. I make sure they read lots of books when I'm with them. I'm seeing the kids more often. The real secret has to be that the classroom teachers really know how to do instruction, and that we figure out a plan where some days I'm integrated in everything and other days maybe I'm not integrated. I'm working with my kids, but also I'm pulling out other kids that have that same problem." Joyce and the teachers she works with feel "that we are both responsible for all of the kids in that room," yet she works primarily with the kids that really need the additional instruction.

The remedial program has become very collaborative. Several times throughout the year substitutes come in, rotate, and relieve the classroom teachers to come down for roughly an hour-long conference with Joyce. Planning is done on the very specific needs of certain children and how they are going to address those needs. Joyce has changed from a complete push-in model to primarily a push-in model with two periods a day where she pulls out students for one-on-one tutoring. One positive outcome from all these changes is a large reduction in the number of children being labeled and placed in special education.

SO WHAT DO THESE CASES ILLUSTRATE?

What characterizes these exemplary early intervention efforts? In other words, what can we learn about creating exemplary early interventions? We think there are five themes that deserve particular attention.

Kids Read and Write a Lot

In both cases the design of the early intervention includes engaging children having difficulty in enormous quantities of actual reading and writing activity. Both efforts have these struggling first graders read multiple little books each and every day—in the classroom and in the special support programs. As with almost every human activity, becoming skilled at reading and writing requires lots of practice, and some kids need more practice than others to achieve the same level of proficiency.

Kids Have a Lot of Successful Literacy Experiences

One of the reasons, we believe, that the children involved in these interventions read and write a lot is that the teachers put just the right books in their hands—not too easy, not too hard, just right books. Early writing attempts are praised, responded to, and used to extend engagement with books, stories, characters, and topics. Lots of environmental supports (Word Walls, editing lists, etc.) are made available along with a large supply of just right books to read. In addition, both teachers skillfully introduce new books and both encourage—almost demand—rereading of familiar books (McGill-Franzen, 1993). This rereading builds fluency and fosters greater application of both skills and self-monitoring strategies.

Children Exhibit High Levels of Engagement in and Motivation for Reading and Writing

In these early intervention efforts, children do not need to be coerced into engaging in reading and writing—they just do it. In both cases we observed children continuing to read and write beyond the scheduled period and even into their scheduled recess time! These high levels of motivation and engagement are related, and both seem to stem from the following factors inherent in the design of the instruction. First, the continual opportunity to be successful is one key. This success comes from having the just right books at children's fingertips. However, children almost always have choices when selecting materials to read. That is, both teachers provide an array of just right books and children select those to be read and reread. Moreover, children are given opportunities to write about things that are of interest to them. In both reading and writing, the teachers provide carefully scaffolded instruction that fosters both success and independence. This instruction is personalized—just what the child needs to get beyond the problem that confronts him/her in the text he/she is reading or creating. The instruction, then, is also most often contextualized—designed to provide the specific skills or strategies needed to solve specific problems encountered while reading or writing today.

Fostering Independence and Self-Monitoring

There is another aspect of the instruction offered in these early interventions that must be recognized. That is the emphasis on developing independence and self-monitoring in participating children. As we observed both Georgia and Joyce teach we were struck by the number of times they asked their students, "What are you supposed to do when . . . ?" We were struck by the amount of praise they offered for successful strategy use ("Good job! You sounded that word out and then went back and reread to make sure it made sense."). We watched both teachers help children learn to select appropriate books and how to work through problems they encountered as they read and wrote. In both cases these teachers created interventions where children understood that they were to do most of the work. The students understood that a big part of being a reader or writer was figuring out how to solve the problems that are repeatedly encountered when one is reading or writing. In other words, these teachers worked hard to discourage the passivity and impulsivity that marks so many children who find learning to read and write difficult (Johnston & Winograd, 1985).

Close Coordination between the Classroom and Support Programs

Finally, the close coordination we observed in the lessons offered in the classroom and the special programs produced a useful integration of lesson content and emphasis into the larger set of daily and weekly instructional routines. In Georgia's room, the children who received extra instructional support received instruction that extended the classroom program—whether those additional lessons or practice opportunities were offered by Georgia, the reading/Reading Recovery teacher, or by the trained paraprofessional. When Joyce entered the first-grade classrooms in her school, it was with a clear understanding of what the first-grade teachers were working on and the difficulties that some children were having. In neither case did such coordination occur overnight. In both cases the classroom teachers and the specialist teachers worked together over a number of years to achieve the almost seamless intervention that we observed. But in both cases the coordination paid large benefits to the participating students.

CONCLUSION

Exemplary early literacy interventions begin with an emphasis on ensuring that all children have access to high-quality classroom instruction. But classroom teaching is complex and classroom teachers will likely never to be able to meet the substantial demands on time and expertise that some children pose. This suggests, then, two roles for special program personnel. The first involves working with classroom teachers to enhance the quality of literacy instruction offered as part of the general education experience. This might occur in any number of ways, but in the cases that we observed the specialists offered training, advice, information, and appropriate materials to classroom teachers in order to enhance classroom instruction. The second role was providing direct instruction to children who are finding learning to read difficult, but instruction that extended classroom lessons was offered in a more intensive and personalized manner. Delivering such instruction required working with classroom teachers over a period of time, but the benefits suggest that the effort paid substantial dividends.

ACKNOWLEDGMENTS

The development of the case studies reported in this chapter was supported in part under the Educational Research and Development Program (Grant Nos. R117G10015 and R305A60005) and the National Research Center on English Learning and Achievement, as administered by the Office of Educational Research and Improvement, U.S. Department of Education. However, the contents of this chapter do not necessarily represent the positions or policies of the sponsoring agency.

REFERENCES

Allington, R. L., & Cunningham, P. M. (1996). *Schools that work: Where all children read and write.* New York: HarperCollins.

Anderson, L. W., & Pellicier, L. O. (1990). Synthesis of research on compensatory and remedial education. *Educational Leadership, 48,* 10–16.

Bacon, R. (1993). *Scarecrow.* Crystal Lake, IL: Rigby.

Boyd-Zaharias, J., & Pate-Bain, H. (1998). *Teacher aides and student learning: Lessons from Project STAR.* Arlington, VA: Educational Research Service.

Cowley, J. (1990). *The bee.* Bothell, WA: Wright Group.

Cowley, J. (1990). *Dan the flying man.* Bothell, WA: Wright Group.

Cowley, J. (1990). *The ghost.* Bothell, WA: Wright Group.

Cowley, J. (1990). *Hairy bear.* Bothell, WA: Wright Group.

Cowley, J. (1990). *The monster's party.* Bothell, WA: Wright Group.

Cummins, P. (1995). *Going up?: The elevator counting book.* Glenview, IL: Celebration Press.

DeFelice, C. (1992). *The light on hogback hill.* New York: Scribner.

Frost, M. (1990). *Jack-o'-lantern.* Bothell, WA: Wright Group.

International Reading Association. (1994). Who is teaching our children? Implications of the use of aides in Chapter 1. *ERS Spectrum, 12,* 28–34.

Johnston, P., & Winograd, P. (1985). Passive failure in reading. *Reading Teacher, 17,* 279–301.

Keats, E. J. (1993). *Over in the meadow.* New York: Scholastic.

McGill-Franzen, A. (1993). "I could read the words!": Selecting good books for inexperienced readers. *Reading Teacher, 44,* 424–426.

Melser, J. (1990). *Sing a song.* Bothell, WA: Wright Group.

Mendro, R. L., Jordan, H., & Bembry, K. L. (1998, April, 16). *Longitudinal teacher effects on student achievement and their relation to school and project evaluation.* Paper presented at the annual meeting of the American Educational Research Association, San Diego, CA.

Pressley, M., Wharton-McDonald, R., Allington, R. L., Block, C. C., Morrow, L., Tracey, D., Baker, K., Brooks, G., Cronin, J., Nelson, E., & Woo, D. (1998). *The nature of effective grade 1 literacy instruction.* Technical Report, National Research Center on English Learning and Achievement, State University of New York at Albany.

Reber, J. (1991). *The eerie canal.* Unionville, NY: Trillium Press.

Rockwell, A. (1987). *The bear child's book of hours.* New York: Thomas Y. Crowell.

Ross, C. (1990). *In a dark, dark wood.* Bothell, WA: Wright Group.

Snow, C., Barnes, W., Chandler, J., Goodman, I. F., & Hemphill, L. (1991). *Unfulfilled expectations: Home and school influences on literacy.* Cambridge, MA: Harvard University Press.

Walmsley, S. A., & Allington, R. L. (1995). Redefining and reforming instructional support programs for at-risk students. In R. L. Allington & S. A. Walmsley (Eds.), *No quick fix: Rethinking literacy programs in America's elementary schools* (pp. 19–41). New York: Teachers College Press.

Ziefert, H. (1985). *Where's the Halloween treat?* New York: Viking Press.

Chapter 18

THE USE OF TECHNOLOGY IN LITERACY PROGRAMS

Linda D. Labbo
David Reinking
Michael C. McKenna

The three brief scenarios that follow provide insights into a classroom community of kindergarten children who are as comfortable with reading and writing on a computer screen as they are with reading and writing on paper. When the children work at the computer with another child or an adult, they have occasions for socially constructing concepts about print (e.g., directionality, matching speech and text), for gaining insights into functions and forms of literacy, for composing with a word processing program, and even enhancing their social status with their classmates. In part because the centrally located computer adjoins other areas of high activity, the computer is an integral part of the classroom culture (Haughland, 1992).

It is 9:20 A.M. on a cold October morning in Ms. Martin's kindergarten, and the room is filled with the sounds of children working at various centers. Patrick and Dartrell sit side by side in the computer center, which adjoins the sociodramatic play center and the classroom library. They are contemplating a color monitor that displays information about bats (see Figure 18.1). Earlier, during rug time when the children sat together on the floor to begin the day, the two boys had listened to their teacher introduce the unit for the week: "Creatures That Fly in the Night Sky." After listening to the text on the screen read aloud, the boys decide how to interact with the computer to receive additional information, in this in-

a b c d e f g h i j k l m n o p q r s t u v w x y z

bat

Other meaning

A bat is a small, furry animal with wings. Bats hang upside down to sleep during the day, and hunt for food at night.

Surprise me   Backtrack   Games   Quick search   Options   Quit
© 1995 Dorling Kindersley Multimedia

FIGURE 18.1. Patrick and Dartrell learn about bats.

stance an audio rereading of a definition, pronunciations of words that are highlighted in blue, digital drawings that will pop up in boxes over the text, or various sound effects. The boys confer briefly and click on an illustration that also provides the sound of a feeding bat. As Kelly, a classmate, walks by the computer, she stops, looks at the screen, and asks them a question:

KELLY: How did you do that? Get that up there [on screen]?

PATRICK: All you do is . . . Wait (*closes the application*). Like Ms. Martin did. All you do is . . . this (*demonstrates how to click the mouse and get access to the CD*).

KELLY: You're so smart, Patrick. You should be in college.

Word of Patrick's expertise quickly spreads throughout the classroom, and soon other children ask him for a demonstration of how this application works from the CD inserted in the CD–ROM drive of the computer. Patrick's computer ability seems to enhance his social standing with several of his peers, who seek him out for the first time as a reading partner during buddy reading.

A half hour later Ariel and Jasmine sit in the computer center and compare a story book version to an electronic book version of *Stella Luna* (Cannon, 1993). As a "page" of the text is highlighted and read aloud on the computer screen, Ariel points her finger to the corresponding text on a page in the book. Jasmine delights in using the mouse to click on a screen illustration of one of the main characters, a lost baby bat's mother. The girls watch the animation of the mother bat flying over trees, calling, and looking for her baby, who is lost but safely snuggled in a nest with baby birds. Later, when the two girls use a Stella Luna bat puppet and a bird puppet to retell the story in the sociodramatic play center, they are joined by three other children who serve as an audience. The story innovation they enact is filled with plot twists, melancholy dialogue, humorous events, and voices that sound a great deal like the characters from the electronic book.

During afternoon center time, JaMaris brings an informational book about bats and the Stella Luna puppet with him. He props the book on a small book-size easel that has been placed beside the computer monitor and holds the puppet on his lap. He has decided to contribute to a class book of collected stories on bats. His assignment is to draw and write something about bats using *Kid Pix 2* (Hickman, 1992). As he begins, he is joined for a few minutes by his teacher, who crouches by his side.

Ms. MARTIN: So, what's your story going to be about?

JaMaris: It's gonna be a story about a really cool bat named Spidey and his super powers.

Ms. MARTIN: OK. So, how do you want to begin . . . with "Once upon a time"?

JaMaris: No . . . my name first (*selects the keyboard function and types in the letters of his name using the hunt and peck method*) . . . and I want to draw Spidey.

Ms. MARTIN: That's not a bad idea. If you draw it, that bat, you might get some good story ideas. So, what does this old bat look like—like Stella Luna?

JaMaris: Sorta' like this one but with big green eyes (*pointing to the photograph of a bat on the book cover*). How do I get green?

Ms. MARTIN: Remember how I showed you the other day—during rug time? (*Before leaving the computer center Ms. Martin demonstrates how to access the color option from the program's menu.*)

JaMaris uses electronic artist tools to draw a bat with big green eyes, large fangs, and a crooked "B" on the chest (see Figure 18.2). He then writes a two-line story that consists of strings of letters and a word copied from the book cover. He makes two copies using the printer connected to the computer. One is placed in a folder of children's stories that will be bound into a class book, and the other goes into his backpack so he can show it to his mother.

FIGURE 18.2. JaMaris's bat story.

A classroom visitor, witnessing the children's computer work, might assume that they are all remarkably gifted or that they come from affluent homes where they have daily access to computers. However, quite the reverse is true. None of the six children mentioned in these vignettes has a computer at home, all qualify for free or reduced lunches, and all are of considered to be average or below average in their literacy development. The primary reason that the children are adept at using technology is because their teacher consistently plans inviting and enriching computer-related experiences. In Ms. Martin's classroom computer-related learning is meaningful and purposeful and is integrated fully into the daily instructional routine.

Although we still have much to learn about effective technology and literacy instruction in classrooms, research over the last decade (e.g., Fatorous, 1995; Labbo, 1996) provides insights into how to plan appropriate computer-related learning experiences that foster young children's literacy development. In this chapter we draw upon relevant research and underlying sociocognitive theory (Vygotsky, 1978) to offer suggestions for establishing a classroom environment that promotes demonstration, collaboration, and other forms of social interaction. We do so by describing how teachers can use technology to support children's conventional literacy development and the development of what has been called "electronic literacy" (Reinking, 1994).

Conventional literacy development refers to the language arts processes of listening, speaking, reading, and writing that are related to traditional typographic features of linear text, such as print, illustrations, and graphics. Electronic literacy expands conventional literacy to include digital and multimedia materials in these fundamental language arts processes. Others have referred to this expanded view of literacy in other ways. For example, Flood, Heath, and Lapp (1997) refer to the "visual and communicative arts," and the Vanderbilt Learning and Technology Group refers to "representational literacy," which includes a variety of new media that can be integrated with conventional texts to create meaning.

INTEGRATING TECHNOLOGY INTO THE SOCIAL ENVIRONMENT OF THE CLASSROOM

The social environment of the classroom will always play a central role in determining how a computer is used by children in schools. It is our belief that if computers are to adequately support both the conventional and electronic literacy development of children, then computer-related activities must be woven into the fabric of daily classroom routines through planned activities in areas such as (1) teacher interactive demonstration, (2) thematic integration and innovation, (3) diverse collaboration, and (4) addressing special needs.

Teacher Interactive Demonstration

Our research suggests (Labbo, Phillips, & Murray, 1995/1996) that integration of technology can be achieved when teachers demonstrate the use of a classroom computer during whole-group and small-group lessons; however, the makeup of the demonstrations should not consist only of the teacher explaining or modeling the use of a computer. Rather, demonstrations should combine teacher modeling with opportunities for children to become involved. For example, teachers can solicit children's input during demonstrations of how to use the computer to maintain a calendar of events, to compose and print out notes to parents, to write and print out individual copies of the morning message and daily news, to make lists of things to do, and to create signs for classroom events. By socially negotiating the form, content, and context of the demonstrations, teachers can help children create a rich schema for employing technology in ways that quite naturally involve many literacy-related activities. Thus, the perspective we advocate implies much more than perfunctory uses of technology that place computers outside the mainstream of literacy activities in classrooms.

For example, from a sociocognitive perspective, we posit that children who observe and interact with teachers during whole- and small-group technology demonstrations will internalize relevant vocabulary, develop approaches to problem solving, and encounter action schemes—all enabling them to use the computer as a tool for thinking, learning, and communicating. As Papert (1980) suggests, children will use a computer in ways that they see the adults in their lives make use of computers. Adult modeling of literacy activities is a major factor in children's acquisition of conventional literacy. It is no less so in the acquisition of electronic or digital literacy.

Other benefits of interactive demonstrations are evident when young children dictate personal news to add to the morning message, watch their words typed on the screen, and thereby have opportunities to become aware of graphophonemic aspects of print. Additionally, when each child receives an individual printout of the morning message and is invited to circle words, letters, or letter-sounds he/she recognizes, he/she has an opportunity to enrich or refine his/her conventional literacy knowledge.

Thematic Integration and Innovation

Creative teachers who put a classroom computer to its best use seem to consistently discover natural connections between curricular themes, learning objectives, and innovative uses of technology. The scenarios given at the onset of this chapter provide concrete instances of four guidelines that we have discovered to be instrumental in designing technology-related units such as the unit "Creatures That Fly in the Night Sky":

1. Collect, display, and demonstrate themed children's books and software related to the theme.
2. Design computer-based learning center activities connected to the theme.
3. Enhance sociodramatic play that connects the theme and computer-based activities.
4. Provide occasions for celebrating children's computer experiences and products.

First, collections of thematically related children's books and software are displayed, shared, and discussed. Just as books are selected to provide a variety of genres and perspectives on a theme, software can be selected to provide various types of literacy experiences related to the theme. Appropriate software for young children should be easy to open, easy to use, highly interactive, responsive to student choices, and ideally related to the other forms of classroom literacy experiences and skill instruction.

Some of the materials for Ms. Martin's unit consist of several fictional and informational books, two puppets with a puppet staging area, and three software programs that are displayed on a bookshelf close to the computer center. Her daily routine includes a shared reading of one of the books or a shared viewing of one of the software applications. On one day, she reads aloud the book *Stella Luna* (Cannon, 1993). Children discuss the story plot, the characters, and ways that the author of this fictional story helps us explore our feelings about bats.

On another day she conducts a shared viewing of the CD–ROM *My First Incredible Amazing Dictionary* (1995). Ms. Martin has a large monitor that allows her to display the computer output to all of her students. Much as a big book is recommended for sharing stories and concepts about print with a large group of children, a large monitor or some kind of projection equipment is recommended for shared viewing of software. Ms. Martin's shared viewing consists of the following steps:

• She begins by briefly introducing the title and general purpose of the software and then stating a specific purpose for interacting with the program. Her purpose is to find definitions and see illustrations related to unit topics. This activity helps her students understand that different software has different purposes and must be approached strategically depending on one's intentions. In other words, the decisions made before using the software will depend upon the intent. In this instance, the teacher shows how to access definitions through an alphabet index or a search and find function.

• Next, Ms. Martin reads or clicks on audio messages and animation that appear on the screen. While navigating through the program, the teacher briefly explains how selecting particular options helps to meet the previously stated goal of learning more about vocabulary related to the unit. While navigating through the program, children may be invited to take turns operating the software or offering opinions about the importance of various types of information included in the program. This activity allows children to develop strategies for making decisions while using the program on their own later.

• Last, after a shared viewing, Ms. Martin encourages the children to critically discuss the information, the presentation of the content, and the operation of the program itself. This activity helps students develop the ability to take a critical stance in using digital materials just as we hope they will in using conventional printed materials.

Second, center activities include computer-related activities aimed at accomplishing various literacy objectives. Ms. Martin's students all worked in the same computer center on the same day, yet they all selected different activities. By having a range of choices, the children learn how to select an activity that they find interesting and meaningful. They are also given occasions for making sense of topics across various classroom activities that include computer explorations. When children bring objects with them to the computer center, they may use the objects to inspire stories and illustrations, to focus them on the topic, and to help them acquire information from different sources. As Schwartz (1985) has pointed out, three-dimensional objects such as a stuffed animal or a book may help young children connect to a similar two-dimensional object on the computer screen.

For example, after hearing Ms. Martin read the story of *Stella Luna* (Cannon, 1993), Ariel and Jasmine interact in what we have called a "screen and book read along" (Labbo & Ash, 1998) in the computer center. That is, children connect the audio, text, and animation of the screen with the print and illustration of the book by turning the virtual pages on the screen and the real pages in the book simultaneously. They point to the words in the book as they are read on the screen. Whether children choose to listen to an electronic book, echo read, or chorally read, our research (McKenna, 1998) suggests that the listening version of an electronic story can help young children develop a sense of story, extend their vocabulary, increase knowledge of words, and enrich concepts about print. During repeated readings of electronic books, when beginning readers click on unfamiliar words and either hear the word or receive a phonic minilesson, they can make substantial gains in sight word acquisition. However, this effect seems limited to those who can name letters and have a rudimentary awareness of sound–symbol correspondences.

Third, sociodramatic or dramatic play is related to the unit theme and to the use of technology. In Ms. Martin's room, the sociodramatic play center was transformed into a puppet theater equipped with puppets related to the characters in the books and software. Reenacting and often extending the story through dramatic puppet play gives children additional occasions for trying out characterizations, reinforcing story structure, and reliving or innovating on story plots.

When sociodramatic play centers are enriched with literacy props, including a computer or even a cardboard model of a computer, children gain insights into the role of technology and literacy in various cultural and workplace settings (see Neuman & Roskos, 1992; Labbo & Ash, 1998). For example, if a unit theme focuses on various ways to travel, the socio-dramatic play center may be transformed into an imaginary travel agency. Children may make tickets, timetables, maps, travel posters, destination booklets, and passports to use in their play scenarios. The office may be set up with a cardboard model of a computer, available at local office supply stores, a play telephone, notepads, nameplates on desks, credit card facsimiles, and brochures. An interview with a travel agent or a field trip to a travel agency can help children understand how the office works, the role of literacy in the work that takes place there, what types of conversational discourse are appropriate in that setting, and how computers are an integral part of the environment. By playing in the center, children have opportunities to enrich their schema about workplace forms and functions of literacy.

Fourth, children's computer experiences and work are celebrated. When children learn how to use a computer to accomplish communicative tasks, teachers can invite them to demonstrate and explain their newfound knowledge to their classmates. Collections of students' theme-related work may be bound into a class book, exhibited as artwork, or displayed in a computer presentation such as an electronic slide show. As is the case with printed materials, celebrating accomplishments and finished products involving digital materials enhances motivation and engagement.

For example, in our work with students in the upper elementary grades we found that involving teachers and students in creating multimedia book reviews on the computer had far greater benefits for reading and writing than did conventional book reports. Students were much more engaged in creating the multimedia book reviews, and we found that their use of technology to respond to their reading involved them in a much richer socially interactive process. We found that these benefits were derived partly from the fact that, unlike conventional book reports, the multimedia book reviews were stored in a searchable database that was easily accessible to other students looking for books to read and to parents who visited the school at various times (including a school technology fair). Inevitably too, students' interactions about the books they were reading took place incidentally in the context of celebrating their accomplishments in mastering the technology. For example, when one student eagerly explained to another student, who was an equally avid listener, how he had added sound effects to his book review, the other student incidentally discovered an interest in the book that was the subject of the review. This example also illustrates how celebrating accomplishments in one medium can enhance involvement in another medium.

Our work (Reinking & Watkins, 1996) suggests that when teachers make children's multimedia book reports accessible through a networked framework that is authored and presented on hypertext, students electronically share book titles, exchange information about authors, and consider various responses to books. Additionally, a child can make intertextual links, or electronic connective paths, between information in their own book report and related information in the reports of their classmates. Having easy access and tools to make such links gives students a capability to manage the exchange of information that is unique to an electronic environment. Now teachers are increasingly aware that computers are becoming a central part of literacy instruction and learning in the classroom.

DIVERSE OPPORTUNITIES FOR COLLABORATION

Children who collaborate while working on the computer have opportunities to acquire conventional and electronic literacy knowledge. Traditional writing processes employing paper-and-pencil tools are enhanced by the electronic malleable screen, the keyboard, and the availability of tools for cutting and pasting elements of texts. Additionally, Internet and e-mail interactions can foster unique forms for students' socially constructed learning experiences.

For example, a process writing approach to composition, involving activities such as Writing Workshop may be enhanced by computer-based collaborations. When children brainstorm, write drafts, revise, edit, and publish with a word processing program, they can focus more on managing their ideas and less on tedious mechanical aspects of writing (Jones, 1994). When writing is supported by a word processing program, the computer may be viewed as an interactive partner in the writing process. Such a view is especially warranted when a child's communicative intentions involves multimedia, such as audio and video. Creating high-quality final drafts is also facilitated by desktop publishing capabilities such as formatting text, incorporating graphics, and selecting typefaces. Wild and Braid (1996) note that collaborative or cooperative computer-related word processing experiences foster children's cognitively oriented talk that is focused on the task of writing.

We believe that it is crucial for teachers to provide enough time for children to compose on the computer and not just type a handwritten draft in order to print out their work. To reap the benefits of technology, and indeed to prepare children to use the tools of contemporary writing, word processing must be integrated into all phases of the writing process. Students may keep an electronic file of their work, such as a reflective journal, topic ideas, responses to books, works in early draft progress, works to be edited or spell checked, or works to be read and responded to by a peer. In these instances, the computer is used as an organizer, a manager, and an electronic writing folder similar to a conventional portfolio. However, unlike a conventional portfolio, an electronic one reinforces the idea that electronic writing is never a final product. Each electronic file awaits future modification.

Paired keyboarding occurs when one child who has knowledge about computer operations and the Internet works together with another child who is less knowledgeable about accessing information from the Internet. Peters (1996) suggests that such interactions extend the less able partner's zone of proximal development, enabling the child to internalize strategies for successful explorations. Other effective collaborations can emerge from electronic pen pals. Garner and Gillingham (1998) explain how students use e-mail to communicate effectively with students in different geographic regions. Beach and Lundell (1998) report that shy students become more interactive and even develop unique on-line personalities when they exchange messages through electronic communication systems.

SPECIAL POPULATIONS

Technology can support the literacy learning of special populations of learners who may be mainstreamed into the classroom. Students in all grade levels who struggle with reading and writing may benefit from particular computer applications. Nonfluent readers, reluctant readers, or children who study English as a second language (ESL readers) may also benefit from features of software. We believe that teachers should approach the use of technology with special populations by following the guidelines we have outlined, namely, through teacher interactive demonstrations, thematic integration and innovation of software and books, and diverse collaboration.

Supporting Struggling Readers and Writers with Computers

Many children who struggle with learning to read and write in elementary schools can often benefit from the electronic text formats. Traditional instructional and tutorial approaches for readers experiencing difficulty learning to read have been based on a determination of a child's strengths and weaknesses. From this traditional perspective, a teacher or a tutor decides how to support the struggling reader by presenting materials, introducing skills, and managing reading practice at a slower pace than that of the regular classroom (Walmsley & Allington, 1995). Once struggling readers have become familiar with the unique features of hypertexts, they may be allowed to self-select the type of support they believe is the most beneficial, thereby allowing them to maintain a pace similar to that of the regular classroom.

How readers use supported text will vary with their developmental level. Emergent readers, for example, will gain more from accessing the full listening version of a text than from more advanced resources. Children who are functioning within the decoding stage, however, can be expected to rely heavily on digitized pronunciations. Those who are approaching fluency will have greater recourse to glossary entries, prose simplifications, digitized video clips, and the like as they endeavor to acquire content from expository text. At this stage, their comprehension will also benefit from accessing linked resources, such as graphic organizers, databases, or electronic encyclopedias. Since the efficacy of these resources is based on aligning software use with a child's stage of reading development, it is important that assessment be aimed at precisely determining that stage so that a teacher is able to guide the child toward the most appropriate use of such resources (McKenna, Reinking, Labbo, & Kieffer, in press).

A future abundance of supported text will bring both drawbacks and advantages for the struggling reader. Surely one of the challenges of electronic literacy is the need to develop the ability to strategically navigate through hypertext environments in order to achieve specific purposes. Even when the hypertextual elements are limited to a few helpful resources, the effect of so many choices can appear labyrinthine to a struggling reader. On the positive side, students will be able to read text independently that would have frustrated them without the built-in support of what McKenna (1998) has called "electronic scaffolds." Indeed, the very notion of the instructional reading level will have to be revised in electronic environments since many struggling readers will be able to read at or near their listening levels (McKenna, Reinking, & Labbo, 1997).

Supporting Nonfluent, Reluctant, or ESL Readers and Writers with Computers

Children who are nonfluent or reluctant readers may benefit from repeated or echo readings of text that is digitally read aloud. While reading to learn new information, a struggling reader may find it useful to compose and record summaries of passages on an electronic clipboard. Burns (1996) notes that multimedia technology can be used to facilitate the English language acquisition of non-native speakers. Multimedia resources accommodate the needs of ESL students as they progress in second language proficiency and gain specific content area knowledge. Many electronic, interactive books have the option of listening to the story in either Spanish or Japanese. More research about the effectiveness of such programs on children's acquisition of a second language and their understanding of specific reading passage content is needed.

Finally, speech synthesizer software offers some promising directions for supporting the spelling development of young, ESL, or nonfluent writers. Shilling (1997) introduced the use of a basic word processing program and an external speech synthesis unit that gave the children studied a choice of listening to a word they had attempted to spell on the screen, listening to the entire text that they had typed on the screen, or not using speech synthesis at all. Findings suggest that before children consistently benefit from synthesizer software they need to have acquired some basic concepts about print, phonemic awareness, and a notion of the alphabetic principle. As the capabilities of speech synthesizer software improves, continued research in this area is warranted.

A FINAL WORD

We hope it is clear in this chapter that digital forms of reading and writing not only can be but must be integrated into the mainstream of literacy instruction for children in the elementary school. Establishing a program of best practices in literacy instruction today means acknowledging that literacy is no longer a monolithic concept defined by print, pages, and books. Attention to conventional uses of written language centered in a world of print must be balanced by attention to how digital technologies are increasingly moving toward the center of what it means to be literate. Teachers, even those who teach young children at the earliest stages of literacy development, must begin to initiate their students into the use of digital forms of expression with a vigor equal to that they have dedicated to more traditional printed forms.

We would be the first to admit that this is no easy task. To integrate technology into their teaching, teachers must confront many challenges on multiple levels. Not the least of the challenges many teachers face is coming to terms with their own predisposition to favor printed materials, sometimes accompanied by a devaluation of digital reading and writing as inferior. It is hard for some teachers to consider, let alone accept, that emerging forms of electronic reading and writing may be as informative, pedagogically useful, and aesthetically pleasing as more familiar printed forms. To consider that electronic forms of text may in some instances even be superior is undoubtedly more difficult.

A reluctance to embrace technology is often sustained by insecurities in using computer technology. It is not trivial to note that today for the first time in the modern era teachers have an obligation to prepare children to become literate in ways that the teachers themselves might not be fully literate. This situation is created by the juggernaut of change that has occurred in the lifetimes of many teachers today who are witnessing the digital revolution but who themselves have to some degree been left in its wake. It is hard enough to think about preparing children for the fuzzy future of literacy in a posttypographic world. It is even harder to prepare children for a world in which our print-based literacy skills are less central, let alone for a world that may negate some of our most cherished assumptions about literacy.

Beyond these conceptual issues are a host of practical obstacles that teachers must often overcome. While the base of computer hardware in schools is generally seen as adequate, many schools do not have the physical or administrative infrastructure needed to use their computers effectively (Morra, 1995). For example, computers are of little use if there is not adequate wiring in places where teachers and students need to use them. Neither are they useful if there is no opportunity for teachers to learn how to use them and to become familiar with software and how it might be integrated into instruction. Neither are they useful when there are no established instructional niches in the curriculum and school day for computer use, especially in the language arts, at least beyond word processing. Moreover, there are logistical problems involved in bringing students and new technologies together in time and space. This challenge is often faced by teachers who have only one or two computers in their classrooms or who can only have access to a computer lab for an hour or two a week.

So, how are teachers to cope in achieving balance between a focus on conventional literacy and electronic literacy? We have found some commonalities among teachers who have successfully achieved this balance, especially among those who do not gravitate naturally to technology. Most teachers have been realistic about the obstacles they face in using technology and realistic about expectations given these obstacles. Often they have found a single computer-based activity or application that connects powerfully with their own teaching and with their personal conceptions of literacy. They may have found it at a conference, in a university course, or through a colleague; but it is something they find it hard to imagine teaching without, once they have discovered it. It may be a simple program addressing in some new way a problematic reading skill, or it may be a more open-ended and sophisticated application involving the internet. For many teachers finding such an application stimulates them to confront the challenges of using technology in their teaching. For them, it serves as a gateway to seeking more balance between conventional and digital literacies.

We recommend that teachers who wish to integrate technology into their literacy teaching consider several ideal criteria aimed at transcending perfunctory uses of computers. If technology is used to advance the goals of conventional print-based literacy, software applications should, at a minimum, be consistent with what the teacher knows and believes to be true about reading instruction (Miller & Burnett, 1987). Ideally use should be made of the unique capabilities of the computer to go beyond conventional materials, addressing some problematic area of literacy that would benefit from a new approach.

Different criteria are relevant if technology is used more to initiate students and teachers into the world of digital literacy. First, like other literacy activities, technology-related activities should ideally involve authentic and personally meaningful communication. Electronic worksheets are in the long run no more meaningful and useful to students' development than are printed ones. Using the computer to enable a kindergarten child to read more texts independently is more worthwhile, as is enabling third-grade children to use e-mail to correspond with other children and adults around the country. Another ideal criterion is that the activity will allow teachers and students to compare and contrast electronic and digital forms of reading and writing. For example, how is an electronic storybook different from a printed one? What are the advantages and limitations of a multimedia encyclopedia over a printed one? How is e-mail similar to or different from sending a letter mailed at the post office? Finally, computer-based activities that increase literacy in the digital domain should allow students to develop functional strategies for reading and writing electronic texts. For example, when might it be appropriate to seek out the pronunciation or definition of a word while reading? How are key words used efficiently to locate information in a computer database?

As Bruce and Hogan (1998) point out, technologies that are truly integrated into daily life are invisible. Fully integrated technologies blend into the environment by virtue of their repeated and natural use. No one views stairs leading from one floor to another as a complicated technology—except someone who is confined to a wheelchair. Integrating computer-based activities into literacy instruction in schools has a long way to go before new technologies are completely unremarkable. Nonetheless, teachers who choose *not* to wait until digital reading and writing are so widely used as to be scarcely noticed are laying the groundwork for the day when computer technology will be as fundamental to literacy as is print technology today.

REFERENCES

Beach, R., & Lundell, D. (1998). Early adolescents' use of computer-mediated communication in writing and reading. In D. R. Reinking, L. D. Labbo, M. McKenna, & R. Kieffer (Eds.), *Literacy for the 21st century: Technological transformations in a post-typographic world* (pp. 93–112). Mahwah, NJ: Erlbaum.

Bruce, B. C., & Hogan, M. P. (1998). The disappearance of technology: Toward an ecological model of literacy. In D. R. Reinking, L. D. Labbo, M. McKenna, & R. Kieffer (Eds.), *Literacy for the 21st century: Technological transformations in a post-typographic world* (pp. 269–281). Mahwah, NJ: Erlbaum.

Burns, D. (1996, March). Technology in the ESL classroom. *Technology and Learning,* pp. 50–52.

Cannon, J. (1993). *Stella Luna.* New York: Harcourt Brace.

Fatorous, C. (1995). Young children using computers: Planning appropriate learning experiences. *Australian Journal of Early Childhood, 29*(2), 1–6.

Flood, J., Heath, S., & Lapp, D. (Eds.). (1997). *Handbook of research on teaching literacy through the communicative and visual arts* (pp. 77–92). New York: Macmillan Library Reference USA.

Garner, R., & Gillingham, M. (1998). The internet in the classroom: Is it the end of transmission-oriented pedagogy? In D. Reinking, L. D. Labbo, M. McKenna, & R. Kieffer (Eds.), *Literacy for the 21st century: Technological transformations in a post-typographic world* (pp. 221–231). Mahwah, NJ: Erlbaum.

Haughland, S. W. (1992). The effect of computer software on preschool children's developmental gains. *Journal of Computing in Childhood Education, 3,* 15–29.

Hickman, C. (1994). *Kid Pix 2, Version 2.* Novato, CA: Broderbund Software.

Jones, I. (1994). The effect of a word processor on the written composition of second-grade pupils. *Computers in the Schools, 11*(2), 43–54.

Labbo, L. D. (1996). A semiotic analysis of young children's symbol making in a classroom computer center. *Reading Research Quarterly, 31*(4), 356–385.

Labbo, L. D., & Ash, G. E. (1998). Supporting young children's computer-related literacy development in classroom centers. In S. Neuman & K. Roskos (Eds.), *Children achieving: Instructional practices in early literacy* (pp. 180–197). Newark, DE: Inernational Reading Association.

Labbo, L. D., Phillips, M., & Murray, B. (1995/1996). "Writing to read": From inheritance to innovation and invitation. *The Reading Teacher, 49*(4), 314–321.

McKenna, M. C. (1998). Electronic texts and the transformations of beginning reader. In D. Reinking, M. C. McKenna, L. D. Labbo, & R. D. Kieffer (Eds.), *Handbook of literacy and technology: Transformations in a post-typographic world* (pp. 45–59). Mahwah, NJ: Erlbaum.

McKenna, M. C., Reinking, D., & Labbo, L. D. (1997). Using talking books with reading-disabled students. *Reading and Writing Quarterly, 13,* 185–190.

McKenna, M. C., Reinking, D., Labbo, L. D., & Kieffer, R. D. (in press). The electronic transformation of literacy and its implications for the struggling reader. *Reading and Writing Quarterly.*

Miller, L., & Burnett, J. D. (1987). Using computers as an integral aspect of elementary language arts instruction: Paradoxes, problems, and promise. In D. Reinking (Ed.), *Reading and computers: Issues for theory and practice* (pp. 178–191). New York: Teachers College Press.

Morra, L. G. (1995, April). *America's schools not designed or equipped for the 21st century.* Testimony before the Subcommittee on Labor, Health and Human Services, Education and Related Agencies Committee on Appropriations, U.S. Senate. Washington, DC: U.S. General Accounting Office, ERIC Document ED 381 153.

My first incredible amazing dictionary (CD–ROM). (1995). New York: Dorling Kindersley Multimedia.

Neuman, S. B., & Roskos, K. (1992). Literacy objects as cultural tools: Effects on children's literacy behaviors in play. *Reading Research Quarterly, 27,* 202–225.

Papert, S. (1980). *Mindstorms.* New York: Basic Books.

Peters, J. M. (1996). Paired keyboards as a tool of Internet exploration of 3rd grade students. *Journal of Educational Computing Research, 14*(3), 229–242.

Reinking, D. (1994). *Electronic literacy* (Perspectives in Reading Research No. 4, National Reading Research Center). Athens: University of Georgia.

Reinking, D., & Watkins, J. (1996). *A formative experiment investigating the use of multimedia book reviews to increase elementary students' independent reading* (Research Report No. 55, National Reading Research Center). Athens: University of Georgia.

Schwartz, S. (1985). Microcomputers and young children: An exploratory study. In *Issues for educators: A monograph series.* Flushing, NY: School of Education, Queens College, City College of New York.

Shilling, W. (1997). Young children using computers to make discoveries about written language. *Early Childhood Education Journal, 24*(4), 253–259.

Vygotsky, L. (1978). *Mind in society: The development of higher psychological processes.* Cambridge, MA: Harvard University Press.

Walmsley, S. A., & Allington, R. L. (1995). Redefining and reforming instructional support programs for at-risk students. In R. L. Allington & S. A. Walmsley (Eds.), *No quick fix: Rethinking literacy programs in America's elementary schools* (pp. 19–44). Newark, DE, and New York: International Reading Association and Teachers College Press.

Wild, M., & P. Braid (1996). Children's talk in cooperative groups. *Journal of Computer Assisted Learning, 12*(4), 216–321.

INDEX